# DREAM SONG

## The Life of John Berryman

PAUL MARIANI

PARAGON HOUSE

Paragon House paperback edition, 1992

Published in the United States by
Paragon House
90 Fifth Avenue
New York, N.Y. 10011



Library of Congress Cataloging-in-Publication Data

Mariani, Paul L.
Dreamsong : the life of John Berryman / Paul Mariani—1st pbk. ed.
p. cm.
Originally published: New York: W. Morrow. 1990.
ISBN 1-55778-454-X
1. Berryman, John, 1914–1972—Biography. 2. Poets, American—20th century—Biography... I. Title.
[PS3503.E744Z79 1992]
811' .54—dc20
[ B ] 92-763
CIP

10 9 8 7 6 5 4 3 2 1

# DREAM SONG

ALSO BY PAUL MARIANI

*Biography*
William Carlos Williams: A New World Naked (1981)

*Poetry*
Timing Devices (1979)
Crossing Cocytus (1982)
Prime Mover (1985)

*Criticism*
A Commentary on the Complete Poems
of Gerard Manley Hopkins (1970)
William Carlos Williams: The Poet
and His Critics (1975)
A Usable Past: Essays on Modern
and Contemporary Poetry (1984)

to the sacred memory of my mother,
Harriet Green Mariani (1923–1988)
*Monarchs' thunder from the delta floor . . .*

and for Terrence Des Pres (1939–1987)
*ave atque vale*

# Preface

The genesis for this book remains hidden in the dark underworld of the imagination. Some things I can chart in the way Poe said—after the fact—he was able to chart the makings of "The Raven." I do remember that the figure of Berryman attracted me years ago, even while I was at work on my biography of William Carlos Williams. And I can recall a schoolroom somewhere in West Springfield one winter's evening during a hypnosis session, when Berryman's dark projection assumed the figure of Baudelaire. Two years later I again mistook the figure I was after, this time for Robert Lowell.

But I had still not called the figure by its proper name, and it was only after spending two years working on Lowell's life that John Berryman walked out of the shadows with that now-familiar grin of his and told me whose life I was to do.

Part of indenturing myself to Berryman was the price I had to pay to exorcise the hold Williams had held over me for eleven years. Williams: that sun-drenched social democrat, the leech gatherer, Asclepius in Paterson with his brighter coign of vantage. Like one of Machiavelli's satellite nations seeking to escape the orbit of one power, I gave myself over to another force, one that—until late in his career—had little to do with Williams, and much of whose poetic development had run counter to Williams's own.

Every history is necessarily written from a point after the fact, and I am not unaware that the underlying historical reason for choosing Berryman may well be my sense of the rise of a new formalism and a new historicism in American poetry in the decade during which I wrote this book. I must add too that Berryman did not treat me half as well as Williams had. He has not been an easy master, Mr. Berryman, something I state merely for the record for any who may wish to follow after. Much of what Berryman wrote about himself in his various autobiographical guises was brilliant and highly original in its manner of saying. But it was also oblique, defeated, and—because of his long obsessions with alcohol, love, and fame—often, as he himself came to understand, delusory.

He worked hard—harder than most of us will *ever* have to work for anything—to become a first-rate poet, and to follow in the track of his life, through the mountains and valleys of manuscripts he left behind, has been—to say the least—as sobering as it has been electrifying. Those who lived in close proximity with him for even a few days and nights bear witness that they came away exhausted, giddy with an intellectual exhilaration perhaps only another working poet would care to understand. But some also came away in tears. Having lived day and night with Berryman now for the better part of six years, I can understand why people would feel that way. And lest I be misunderstood as privileging a difficult sort of excellence in poetry, I hasten to add that, except for the intense industry, the lifelong obsession, and the indescribable joy of getting words down on the page and getting them absolutely right, there is nothing out of the ordinary about what Berryman did.

As with that other suicide, Sylvia Plath, it is still too early to decide what Berryman's place in the pantheon of poets will be. But it is my bet—paid for up front with a sizeable slice of my own life—that the full impact of Berryman's poetry has yet to be felt. The reasons are many and even—this late in our Modernist century—commonplace, but they are there. Foremost among them is the excuse that—since Berryman was a drunk with a long history of alcoholic abuse—his vision and even his ability to write had to be profoundly and adversely affected. No doubt there is some truth there, but the issue is far more complex. For there also remains the body of extraordinary poems, including what Berryman, thinking of his own precursor, Yeats, came to see as his mysterious late excellence.

Sober, a contrite Berryman knew his faults as well as anyone. In fact, he was harder on himself than anyone else ever was. When, after twenty-five years, he finally realized he was suffering from the disease of alcoholism, he sought help, failed, sought help again, failed, and finally—thinking himself unable to change—in exhaustion took his own life, in part at least to spare his family and friends. He could be arrogant, dismissive, selfish, irritating, irascible, belligerent. But he could also be incredibly kind, especially to others like himself who seemed lost: writers down on their luck, students with personal problems, returning veterans of World War II, Korea, and Vietnam, drunks of all descriptions whom he found on the locked wards of hospitals with himself, almost everyone really but those deluded by their own self-complacency and supposed "sanity."

Still, Eileen Simpson and Saul Bellow are right to speak of Berryman's inability to "act" like most other human beings. Berryman's world was even more interior than Wallace Stevens's, and he had to struggle to do even the simplest things well, like cook a meal for himself, remember to do his laundry, comprehend his bank statement, or converse with other human beings. "Know that your facilities are perfectly inadequate," he dismissed one poor deskclerk in an upstate New York motel. He never learned to negotiate a car very well, nor, for that matter—if his record of broken arms, wrists, ankles, ribs, and legs is any indication—even a flight of stairs.

Something in him was clearly bent on self-destruction. His father was taken violently from him when Berryman was not yet twelve, and that original wound never properly healed over. Afterward, as an adolescent, Berryman—like the other members of his family—tried hard to forget what had happened. In time, however, he learned that to get past that first terrible loss, he would first have to face it in whatever way he could. To do that, he needed other fathers to guide him past his first father's ghost, and these fathers came in many guises, from a little Belgian priest in a mission church in Oklahoma, through a series of popular culture heroes, themselves transformed into teachers like Mark Van Doren, R. P. Blackmur, and Allen Tate, and finally into a pantheon of poet fathers: Keats, Auden, Hardy, Stevens, Ransom, Eliot, Pound, but especially Yeats, Shakespeare, and Hopkins. Toward the end he sought quite consciously to attain union with that Prime Mover, God the Father.

Women remained—always—more problematic and terrifying for Berryman in large part because of his attachment to and hatred of his mother, a woman every bit as complex, devious, and self-destructive as he himself was. He was engaged twice and married three times, yet he never seems to have learned to engage women as true partners. He either idolized them or savaged them, turning afterward to remorse and then to fear. He gloated over his conquests, though, as he grew older, he did try to see women rather as friends and sisters and himself less as their seducer and more as their quixotic, damaged protector. But this was a learned response, and he still dreamed even at the very end, when his creative powers were draining from him, of the old sexual power that had been his. He remained both magnetized and repulsed by women, fearing them as he always feared his mother. If he was Henry/Achilles, hero of his fabulous *Dream Songs,* the woman remained Penthesilea, big-breasted Amazonian *and* slayer of Achilles.

But in the *Dream Songs, Love & Fame,* and *Berryman's Delusions, Etc.,* as in the marvelous essays collected in *The Freedom of the Poet,* the Stephen Crane biography, the unfinished novel *Recovery,* the lectures, and the letters—in all of these, much of the old magic remains. Difficult as the poems are, they reward our scrutiny and attention, for Berryman is one of the few poets we have had with the courage and raging humor to say exactly what was on his mind, whether what he said was silly, outrageous, stunning, or—as it often was—sublime and terrifying, as Longinus and Kant understood those terms.

The poets who knew Berryman understood something of his difficult greatness, and just to list them is to call the honor role of poetry written in this country in the period from the forties through the early seventies: Delmore Schwartz, Allen Tate, Randall Jarrell, Robert Lowell, William Meredith, James Wright, Elizabeth Bishop, Philip Levine, Donald Justice, Howard Nemerov, Richard Wilbur, Adrienne Rich. Then too there were those others, critics like Mark Van Doren, R. P. Blackmur, Edmund Wilson, and novelists of the caliber of Ralph Ellison and Saul Bellow.

It was a bracing community, and he loved it. For he truly loved his friends and thought of himself as forming part of a larger literary community. Often his friends shored him up against his own ruins. For the most part, as he said of his namesake, Henry, he "saw with Tolstoyan clarity/ his muffled purpose," a purpose he had to work out for himself alone, daily performing operations of great delicacy on himself, as he complained, in complete darkness.

It took him thirty years of excruciating labor to strip his language naked and step out before his readers dressed only in his grotesque masks since, language and poetry in this century being what they are, there seems to be no other way for us to speak to one another about the mysteries of the heart. He took gigantic chances with himself, using his own blue-black skin on which to write our story. In the gift of poetry that he left behind, he invites us to find the precise configuration of a human being every bit as complex as Hamlet, every bit as driven by dizzying contrarieties as Macbeth. Even more, he invites us to find in the bizarre hall of mirrors of his Songs and poems the terrifying yet paradoxically comforting and comic truth about ourselves.

—PAUL MARIANI
Montague, Massachusetts

# Acknowledgments

Unlike Williams, whose manuscripts are scattered all over the United States, most of Berryman's are collected at the Manuscripts Division of the University Libraries of the University of Minnesota on Berry Street, just over the city line in St. Paul, near the trucking depots a mile from where Kate (Berryman) Donahue still lives with her younger daughter, and two miles from where Berryman taught and died. I owe a special thanks first to Kate, as literary executor for the Berryman estate, and then to Alan M. Lathrop, curator of the Berryman Collection, and his very capable staff assistant, Vivian Newbold. Across the Mississippi River, at the west-bank campus, near the once-notorious Five Corners section of the city whose bars Berryman often frequented and where he wrote so many of his early *Dream Songs,* is the library that houses special collections and rare books, and here is every letter Berryman ever wrote to his mother, along with Berryman's evaluations of teaching assistants and other documents, and I want to thank Austin McLean, curator, for his patience and help with this collection.

I also owe a very special debt of gratitude to Boyd and Maris Thomes for providing me with copies of Berryman's letters to them, for making available to me their collection of tapes in which Berryman reads his poetry, lectures at the university, or talks in his highly idiosyncratic manner on the telephone with a friend (Ellen Siegleman) about the beauties and hazards of traveling in India. Thanks too to Richard J. Kelly, editor of Berryman's letters to his mother, published as *We Dream of Honour;* to Charles Thornbury, editor of John Berryman's *Collected Poems: 1937–1971,* who was especially helpful to me during the early stages of my researches on Berryman's life; to Ernest Stefanik for his extremely useful bibliography of Berryman; to Joel Conarroe, for his splendid and high-spirited *John Berryman: An Introduction to the Poetry;* and to John Haffenden for his pioneer biography of Berryman.

Thanks too to the various library staffs at the Beinecke's American Literature Collection and the Sterling Libraries at Yale, the Widener and Houghton Libraries at Harvard, the Arthur and Elizabeth Schlesinger Library at Radcliffe, the Butler Library at Columbia, Princeton University Library, the Joseph Regenstein Library of the University of Chicago, the Henry W. and Albert A. Berg Collection of the New York Public Library, Astor, Lenox, and Tilden Foundations, all of which provided me with manuscripts from their various collections, and to the University of Massachusetts at Amherst.

I owe a special word of thanks to E. Milton Halliday, author of *John Berryman and the Thirties: A Memoir,* for making available to me Berryman's letters to him as well as for long talks about Berryman at Columbia and later, and (once again) special thanks to James Laughlin, for inviting me to his home in Norfolk, Connecticut, to read through Berryman's often cantankerous letters to him when Laughlin was his editor. Thanks too to Ralph Ellison (the "invisible man" behind the interlocutor who keeps Henry honest in *The Dream Songs*), Robert Giroux, Valerie Trueblood, Sally Fitzgerald, Eileen Simpson, C. F. Powers, Sister Agnes Fleck, Penelope Laurans Fitzgerald, Sidney Monas, H. Wendell Howard, Richard Kostelanetz, Joel Connaroe, William Pritchard, George Ford, Kate Daniels, Charlie Miller, Frederick Turner, as well as Dulcie Scott, Paul Cubeta, and the late Reginald "Doc" Cook. Special thanks to all those nameless men and women in Alcoholics Anonymous who shared their stories and their agonies with me, especially Ed, who has been my poor man's Virgil on this journey. I apologize if I have overlooked anyone.

A special note of gratitude to Lois Tyson and Midge Eisele, faithful research assistants who saved me months by collecting so many of the thousands of books, documents, and manuscripts that had to be read and gone through before I could even begin writing my biography. Also, though he may not remember this, it was Jonathan Galassi who suggested to me back in 1981 that I should do Berryman's life before Lowell's. That suggestion has now become reality.

Over the years of researching this life, I found that one of the most gratifying sources of information for understanding Berryman was through talks with Berryman's fellow poets, most of whom knew Berryman personally, and it is a pleasure to acknowledge their help and support here: Michael Anania, Marvin Bell, Bruce Berlind, Robert Creeley, Michael Collier, Jorie Graham, Michael Harper, Richard Harteis, William Heyen, Ed Hirsch, Garrett Hongo, Mark Jarman, Donald Justice, Allen Mandelbaum, William Matthews, John Matthias, William Meredith, John Montague, Howard Nemerov, Robert Pack, Wyatt Prunty, Adrienne Rich, William Stafford, Charles Simic, James Tate, Richard Wilbur, Nancy Willard, Ellen Bryant Voigt, and especially Philip Levine, whose sense of Berryman Levine rendered so vividly and compassionately for me on many occasions, down to his imitating Berryman's voice with uncanny precision, an ability that once unnerved Berryman himself.

I also want to thank those closer to home for their help and encouragement. First to my department, and especially to my chairmen, old and new, Vincent DiMarco and Robert Bagg, then to a group of enlightened administrators who materially made this book possible: Deans Murray Schwartz and Samuel Conti, Provosts Loren Barritz and Richard O'Brien, and finally Chancellor Joseph Duffey, who have all made the University of Massachusetts at Amherst an exciting place where serious work could be encouraged. I also want to thank my students—colleagues, really—who listened to me while I carried on like one possessed (or dispossessed) about Berryman, especially those in my three Berryman seminars, including one funded by the

National Endowment of the Humanities for Secondary School Teachers.

I want to thank too the National Endowment for the Arts, the National Endowment for the Humanities, the Guggenheim Foundation, and my university for generous grants during which much of the actual writing of this book was done. Early versions of two chapters appeared in *The Prairie Schooner* (chapter 4) and *The Kenyon Review* (chapter 24), for which hospitality I thank their editors now. Thanks too to the Bread Loaf School of English and the Writers' Conference, where some of these chapters were first read and where I found so much of the necessary support to go on with the project. A very special word of thanks to my editor at William Morrow, Maria Guarnaschelli, who supported me throughout, and who helped me cut the manuscript, step by step, rewrite by rewrite, from an obsessive 1,250 pages to half that length, until the blurred outline of Berryman's face loomed before me with its distinctive, quizzical, and tragic profile.

A very special word of thanks to my wife, Eileen, and our three sons for years of putting up with this dark intruder's life, and for supporting me every troubled, giddy step of the way. In truth, my wife turns out to have been there to overhear my daily conversations with Berryman's ghost, to question, to guide, to encourage, to deflect. Finally there are two people I would especially like to thank. One is Terrence Des Pres, for helping me look at the terrible darkness without flinching. The other is my mother, for the courage of her example till the very end in staying faithful to her covenant to remain sober, and for keeping her sense of humor even as cancer shut down her lungs. Since these two dear people have now crossed over to the other side of the great divide, I have dedicated this book to their sacred memories.

# Notes on Sources

After John Berryman's death, the bulk of his manuscripts were given by his widow, Kate Donahue, to the University of Minnesota, and deposited at the annex on Berry Street in St. Paul's where the Architectural and Immigrant collections are housed. The Berryman Collection is huge—about forty linear feet now—and includes nearly all of the manuscripts and typescripts of Berryman's poetry, fiction, essays, journals, and criticism, as well as thousands of letters written to him over a forty-year span, including those from Beryl Eeman. Any biographer or researcher, as John Haffenden found, must continuously refer to this collection, and so individual footnotes for this volume—of which there would be thousands—would have to refer continually back to this single collection. Three people especially made this collection accessible to me: Kate Donahue (Mrs. John Berryman), Alan Lathrop, curator, and his assistant, Vivian K. Newbold. Berryman's letters to his mother are located in the Special Collections of the University Library under the curatorship of Austin MacLean, who generously made these letters available to me. Berryman's own library is housed in a separate room of the main University library.

John Haffenden queried many people about their memories of Berryman in the decade after the poet's death, and the responses to these queries are now housed at the Butler Library at Columbia University. These I have read and studied with interest, and all Berryman biographers and researchers owe a debt of thanks to Haffenden for the immense labor involved in undertaking to interview by letter so many individuals who were either centrally or peripherally involved in some aspect of Berryman's life. The documents are there, though often the reading I have chosen to give to the "facts" embedded in those responses differs from Haffenden's.

Berryman's letters to E. M. Halliday, so central to the poet's years at Columbia and Cambridge (England), were generously made available to me by Halliday himself, before this collection was sold to the University of Minnesota and placed in the Berryman archives. Halliday's *John Berryman and the Thirties: A Memoir,* published by the University of Massachusetts (1988), for which I provided an afterword, places many of these early letters in their particular context, though, again, I have reinterpreted some of these letters to Halliday within a larger context.

Berryman's early letters to Eileen (Berryman) Simpson are in the Berryman collection at the University of Minnesota. Early in my researches Mrs. Simpson graciously granted me an interview, but remained silent when I asked to see—either in full or in part—Berryman's diaries and journals for the years 1942 to 1956. Originally these materials formed part of the Berryman archives at the University of Minnesota, but when Mrs. Simpson learned of their existence—during the period Haffenden was engaged in writing his life of Berryman—she asked that they be turned over to her, a request to which Kate Donahue complied. It is hoped that these materials will eventually be returned to the collection to which they belong. Although other documents exist for this crucial period in Berryman's development, for this biography the inaccessibility of the journals proved to be a biographer's black hole.

Berryman's letters to James Laughlin, founder of New Directions and Berryman's early publisher, are still housed at Mr. Laughlin's offices in Norfolk, Connecticut. Of what was once a flourishing correspondence with Delmore Schwartz, only four of Berryman's letters and a postcard survived Schwartz's moves from one seedy hotel to an even seedier, and these are to be found in the Schwartz Collection now at the Beinecke Rare Book and Manuscript Library at Yale. Also in this collection are Berryman's letters to Ezra Pound, Edmund Wilson, and Robert Fitzgerald, as well as his correspondence with Robert Penn Warren and Cleanth Brooks, during their editorship of *The Southern Review*. Berryman's letters to Dwight Macdonald are at Yale's Sterling Library.

Berryman's letters to William Meredith are in the Henry W. and Albert A. Berg Collection of the York Public Library, copies of which were graciously provided me by Richard Harteis. Berryman's letters to Jarrell are also in the Berg Collection. Letters to Adrienne Rich are at the Schlesinger Library at Radcliffe College; those to Allen Tate at Princeton University Library; to Saul Bellow and to *Poetry* magazine at the Joseph Regenstein Library of the University of Chicago. Several Berryman letters may be found among Haffenden's papers at the Butler Library at Columbia. Among the letters still in the possession of their original recipients that I have seen are those to Bruce Berlind, William Heyen, Donald Justice, Valerie Trueblood, Sister Agnes Fleck, and Boyd and Maris Thomes. William Heyen graciously provided me with the full typescript of his interview with Berryman in October 1970, as well as with copies of the comments Berryman made during his reading at Brockport.

# Contents

# PART I

## *1914–40*

# chapter 1

# Death of a Father

## 1914–26

From his twelfth year John Berryman was made to understand that the Fates had title to his life. It had not always been so, for his beginnings had been different—safer somehow—when he still had his first name and his first identity, when he was not John Berryman but John Allyn Smith, Jr. But that first world ended abruptly for him when John Allyn Smith, Sr., walked out into a Florida dawn and—allegedly—shot himself. By that one act Smith senior left the way open for his rival, a man named John Berryman, to step in, take Smith's wife, and give Smith's sons a new name and a different identity. As for John Allyn Smith, Jr., now renamed John Berryman, his strategy for surviving would be to try to erase the trauma of that compound theft for as long as he could. Later, when he could no longer run from his father's ghost, he would reverse himself in an attempt to enter the black hole opened by the loss of his father. Yet, in spite of extensive therapy and the delicate operations he performed on his psyche in what he described as a world of complete darkness, in spite of extensive dream analysis and his poems—his Dream Songs—in spite of liquor, drugs, and the intimacy of fifty women, he never managed to get beyond the mystery of that early expulsion from the garden.

He was born in rural Oklahoma, in what is still called the Territory, in the fall of 1914, with winter already in the air and a war raging five thousand miles away. He was the older of two sons of a schoolteacher named Martha ("Peggy") Little, whose family hailed from Arkansas, and John Allyn Smith, a small-town banker whose family came from Minnesota and before that from the Green Mountains of Vermont, a family who claimed Ethan Allen (reworked as Allyn) for their ancestor. In the years following the Civil War and the opening of the West, the Smiths did their part in the making of the great western coral reef of settlers that formed along the Minnesota and Nebraska territories.

John Allyn Smith, Sr.'s own father, Leonard Jefferson Smith, had been a Maine Volunteer and had had his leg shattered by a minié ball in the Battle of the Wilderness. Flint-hard, he insisted on re-upping after his army discharge so he could finish out the war. Leonard was a brooder, a stoic, tall and broad-shouldered, like his sons and grandsons. He tried farming in western Minnesota, but the Indians, already there and unwilling to give up their ancestral lands, forced him back to the edge of "civilization," where Smith worked in the lumberyards of the St. Croix Lumber Company in South Stillwater, east of St. Paul/Minneapolis, for the next forty years.

On October 30, 1869, in Minneapolis, Leonard Smith married Mary Kenna, twenty-two, an Irish Catholic from Indian Town, New Brunswick, whose family had earlier emigrated from County Cork. She was parochial, puritanical, sharp-tongued, and as hard as her husband. Over the next eighteen years she gave birth to six boys and four girls, the last the "spoiled" baby, John Allyn, born at the spring equinox, March 21, 1887.

John Allyn attended school in Stillwater, and at eighteen enrolled in a business course at Globe College in St. Paul. Afterward he moved back to Stillwater, and for several years worked at the Inter-State Lumber Company at a job his father helped him get. In 1911, at the age of twenty-four, he went down to Oklahoma to join his brother Tom in working for their older brother Will, forty, in his bank in Holdenville. Will had already made a small success of himself in the frontier banking business, but soon after John's arrival, he caught pneumonia and died. After Will's brothers buried him in Holdenville, Tom got caught up in a bank scandal and absconded from Oklahoma without leaving a forwarding address. John Allyn in the meantime went to work at Will's branch bank in "a godforsaken little hole" called Sasakwa in the Oklahoma hill country. It was at a boarding house there that he met and courted seventeen-year-old Martha Little.

Martha's maternal ancestors, the Shavers, for their part had been diehard Confederates from Arkansas, and it was only by accident that Martha herself was born up North, in Du Quoin, Illinois, where her mother had been visiting at the time. Martha was the only child of the shaky union of Martha May Shaver and Alvin B. Little, and when she was five, Alvin deserted the family. Much as her own sons would do years afterward when they tried to imagine their father, Martha "Peggy" Little came to see her father solely through her mother's unforgiving portrait of him.

In contrast to Smith's Puritan Yankee ancestors, Alvin Little's star would have had little chance of shining against the brilliant light cast by his father-in-law, General Robert Glenn Shaver of the late Confederate States of America. Early in the Civil War Shaver commanded the 7th Arkansas Infantry—"The Bloody Seventh"—in the fighting around Shiloh, where, though he had two horses shot out from under him, he kept fighting until an exploding shell tore open his left side. The following year, 1863, at the head of the 38th Arkansas Infantry, he covered the evacuation of his troops south from Little Rock. His was the last organized army to surrender to the Yankees.

After the war General Shaver became commander of the Ku Klux Klan in Arkansas until a federal warrant for his arrest was issued on charges of murder, arson, robbery, and treason. Rather than face arrest, he fled with his family to British Honduras, where he remained for four years, until the charges against him were dropped. On his return home he became sheriff of Howard County and practiced law. Until his death in 1915, Shaver suffered in his flesh and mind from what Shiloh had cost him. But what a figure he remained in the younger John Berryman's imagination! For, though Berryman came to despise the South, especially for its treatment of blacks, half a century after General Shaver's death Berryman could still attend a Halloween costume party dressed as his grandfather, replete with Confederate gray and a wild, flowing gray-brown beard.

Abandoned by Alvin Little, Martha May came in time to regard all men with contempt. Husbandless, she and her fatherless daughter became suspect outsiders, the daughter little better than a bastard (as she herself would remember). Even in a place like the Oklahoma Territory people kept their distance. But the young Martha was bright and determined, and at fifteen she matriculated at Christian College in Columbia, Missouri, graduating two years later as valedictorian of her class.

Young Martha had hoped to continue her studies—in philology—at the University of Oklahoma, but her mother needed her to work and found her a job as a schoolteacher in Sasakwa, sixty miles west of McAlester. In September 1911, she began teaching the fourth, fifth, and sixth grades. She did well, but the work proved too much for her, and at Christmas she returned to the boarding house in McAlester where her mother was staying. It was there that the younger Martha met John Allyn Smith. Seven years her senior, he began courting her and, according to what she told her son years later, made her marry him after he'd first forced himself upon her.

What really happened is now beyond recovery, and Martha's testimony would prove to be extremely unreliable. Soon after John Allyn's death, she turned her husband into an archvillain, then later amended the stories by blaming her mother instead. In years to come Berryman grew to hate John Allyn for deserting his family, then, growing, pondered over what he thought his father had done and tried to forgive him. As he himself came to better understand the vicissitudes of the human condition, Berryman would ask his mother pointed questions about his father, hoping to recover something of the truth about him. Each time the story came back altered.

Documents show that on July 25, 1912, there was a wedding at All Saints Catholic Church in McAlester, with Mrs. Little and a relative—Dorothy Shaver—as witnesses. Immediately afterward John Allyn took his bride by train to Minnesota to meet his family. The reception in Stillwater was icy, Martha would remember, warmed only by an awkward show of affection from her father-in-law as she was preparing to return to Oklahoma. From the beginning the marriage seemed doomed, lacking as it did passion and mutual respect, at least according to the bride, and her attention was soon transferred to her sons.

The Smiths' first child was born by Caesarian section on October 25, 1914, in McAlester and the doctor, who had never done a C-section before, performed it incompetently. Five weeks later, on November 29, the baby was christened John Allyn Smith, Jr., at St. John the Evangelist, the local Catholic Church. Two years later the family moved to Lamar, where John Smith, Sr., once more found work in the local bank. In 1918, Smith moved his family to Wagoner, Oklahoma so that he could work at the bank there. In Wagoner, Martha found herself pregnant once again. She would later swear to her older son that she had fought to keep this baby against her husband's—and her mother's—attempts to persuade her to have an abortion. The older Martha's health and John Allyn's fears that his salary as a provincial bank manager was not enough to support a second son were among the reasons given for this advice. But Martha defied these pressures, and on September 1, 1919, gave birth to her second—and last—child, Robert Jefferson Smith.

In the winter of 1921, at the beginning of the Harding administration, the Smiths moved with their two small sons—John, six years old, and Robert, fifteen months—to Anadarko (population: five thousand) into a five-room white house at 516 West Kentucky. There Smith, thirty-three, began his duties as acting vice-president and loan officer at the First State Bank. Oil had been discovered in Oklahoma sixteen years earlier, and now Anadarko had oil rigs and the feel of new wealth everywhere. The all-white West Grade School, which John, Jr., attended, was only a block away. (There were two other grade schools in Anadarko, the East Grade School, also white, and a "Negro school"). The Smiths attended the Catholic mission church of the Holy Family, staffed by Benedictine fathers, and it was here that John, Jr., made his first communion in 1923 and became an altar boy. Two years later he was confirmed in the same church. Till the end of his life Berryman would remember with fondness the "squat . . . good, stern, friendly" Belgian priest, Father Boniface Beri, who soon became a second father to him. Mornings the boy served in his black robe and white chasuble, his Latin answering the priest's in the mostly empty church. "I believed in God and my guardian angel to the hilt," Berryman would later remember with a mixture of pride and disbelief that he and that boy had ever been the same person.

At that young age John Allyn Smith, Jr., was only dimly aware of the tensions between his parents. But when he was a man himself, his mother would tell him that, once, in Anadarko, she'd fallen "desperately, instantly, totally, forever in love" with another man—later to become governor of Oklahoma—a man who, she insisted, had wanted to marry her. So the affairs had begun, at least on her side, early on. Perhaps it was in retaliation that John Allyn—according to his wife—himself took up with a friend of Martha's, taking the woman with him when he went to Chicago on bank business.

But there were happy memories as well. In Berryman's letters and journals we glimpse images of his father at the bank or fishing, or on summer maneuvers in his Oklahoma National Guard captain's uniform, replete with flat-brimmed hat and puttees, commanding Battery E, 160th Field Artillery, at Fort Sill, amid the fierce explosions of field cannon. He would remember his father playing baseball and handling a sidearm. Two photographs taken in the summer of 1915 capture father and son. In one, the father holds baby John in the crook of his right arm, his other arm stiffly at his side. He smiles, but the baby looks serious, tentative, as if he were afraid he might fall from that enormous height. In the second, the baby stands facing the camera, his tiny hands grabbing his father's for support as he leans into his first, awkward steps, barefooted. In another photo young John smiles and waves, while his mother, youthful despite her steel-rimmed glasses and headband, also smiles. In another, a five-year-old John sits on a sofa in navy blouse, shorts, and leggings, his short hair cut straight across his forehead. His smile reveals a missing front tooth. His right arm supports his baby brother.

In March 1924, a little over three years after beginning his management of the First State Bank, John Smith resigned. One version of the story has it that he was replaced by a rival. But in Martha's version, Smith insisted on going fishing in Colorado when he was needed at the bank and was afterward dismissed. In any event, his management of the First State Bank could hardly be called a great success. When he became vice-president and chief loan officer, the bank had assets of $500,000. When he left, in spite of its being a boom period in Oklahoma, those assets had dropped to $300,000. And yet there is also evidence that Smith did his work well and was considered "honest, sober and industrious and strictly reliable." In any event, two weeks after leaving First Bank, he was appointed assistant game and fish warden for the State of Oklahoma, and in July he was on National Guard duty at Fort Sill. There is a photo of the Smiths from this summer, husband and wife looking fit and smiling, standing together outside a huge army tent.

Then, in September 1925, the Smiths sold the house in Anadarko, stored their furniture in a local warehouse, and drove with Martha's mother down to Florida. It was the period of the Florida land boom, and Martha Little had property in Tampa. Fortunes were being made, so it seemed, overnight. The boys were placed in St. Joseph's Academy, a Catholic boarding school in Chickasha, twenty miles east of Anadarko, while the parents made the move to Tampa. But within weeks, the boys were finding it very hard being separated from their mother.

John, Jr., made friends and counted hungrily the postcards his mother sent him. He played "rook, pitch, dominoes and checkers." He earned good grades, knowing they would make his mother happy. He tried to sound cheerful in his letters. Mrs. Dutcher—a neighbor whom the boys affectionately called "Grandma"—came over from Anadarko in early October and promised to return for John, Jr.'s eleventh birthday and take the boys back to Anadarko for the weekend. When the nuns refused to let him take books from the library, he wrote his mother asking for old copies of *Adventure, Cosmopolitan,* and *Hearst's International* to help him pass the time.

By mid-October he was writing his parents about how cold the weather had become. He wanted to come to Florida, where at least it was warm. By then, too, his grades had begun to suffer. What he did not tell his mother was that he and his brother had already been beaten up by the older boys. There was one in particular, he later recalled, a bowlegged kid, who had organized half the dormitory into a gang. Angered by the bully's taunts, John had lashed out and hurt the bully. But the victory was short-lived, for the bully bided his time, then beat him senseless to show him he was still in charge. Nor did John tell his mother about the afternoons spent in a deserted gray classroom, listening to his classmates playing football outside as he wrote over and over and over, "I must not throw chalk in geography," or "I must bring my missal to Sacred Studies." What helped him was learning how to write with four pencils held in his right hand at the same time.

But Mrs. Dutcher knew how desperately unhappy the Smith boys were. When she wrote their mother in November, suggesting they stay with her until Martha could come for them, Martha took the train to Oklahoma. She found the boys early that December looking miserable and waiting for her in the principal's office. They were clutching paper bags full of their belongings and ran to her when they saw her. She lost little time getting her boys down to Tampa.

With the money realized by the sale of half the land Martha's mother had bought years before, the Smiths had opened a family restaurant in Tampa called the Orange Blossom. Smith kept the books, did the purchasing, and made extra money selling real estate and insurance out of their apartment at 725 South Boulevard. His mother-in-law did the cooking for the restaurant, while Martha worked the soda fountain and handled the cash register. Christmas came and went. The boys attended public school and played in the sun. Then, in the spring of '26, the Florida bust followed the boom, and huge fortunes suddenly evaporated. Every day now, Berryman would remember, somebody went out and shot himself.

The Orange Blossom became another casualty of the bust, and the Smiths sold it for a third of what they had paid seven months earlier. In June they took a cheaper apartment at the Kipling Arms on Clearwater Island, across Tampa Bay. The building, facing onto the bay, was owned by a couple in their late forties named Ethyl and John Angus Berryman. Soon Martha and John Angus, a dapper Georgian twenty years Martha's senior, began having an affair. Each day Berryman lunched with Martha at the Smiths' apartment while Smith tried to figure out how to put his shattered world back together. John Angus himself had pulled out of the real estate business just in time to save his money. Now, John Angus's wife told him it was time for them to move to New York. Instead, he sold his holdings, split the profits with her, gave her the car, and told her to take off. So Martha would recall for her son many years later, failing to mention that she had been the main reason the first Mrs. Berryman had left Tampa.

As for John Smith, like many who had families to support and who had lost everything in the bust, he now became unstrung. He began chain-smoking and drinking heavily. He could see what was happening between his wife and Berryman, and in retaliation told his wife he'd fallen in love with a Cuban woman. There were accusations back and forth and the talk turned to divorce, of letting Smith have his Cuban woman as long as Martha got the children and half the money. As Smith's drinking increased, he began walking the beaches distractedly, at times dangling a .32 caliber automatic from his right hand. Often he swam out into the gulf as his older boy anxiously watched him disappear. Once Smith took six-year-old Robert for a swim so far out toward the western horizon that Martha and her mother became hysterical. When John Angus swam out after him, he found him with Robert tied to a rope in front of him. Only then did Smith seem to come out of his daze and swim back to shore. Martha later recalled that her mother had screamed at him, swearing he'd meant to drown his boy. But just as likely it was Martha who was screaming. Smith shrugged it off and walked away.

The boys must have sensed what was happening. As Smith saw himself replaced in his wife's eyes by an older, more successful man, he vacillated between fits of anger and hopeless withdrawal. Nor did it help that John Angus was called in to act as mediator in the Smiths' domestic crises. Martha would later insist she had done everything possible to help her husband. She'd taken him to a psychiatrist and had unloaded five of the six bullets from his gun, burying them in the sand along the beach. But she never explained why she didn't empty the sixth chamber or hide the gun itself.

Within weeks Smith's mistress deserted him, taking whatever money he had, and returned to Cuba. In the meantime divorce proceedings progressed, Smith feeling more and more alone. On Friday night, June 25, he went to the Kipling Arms to see his wife. He was confused, frustrated, defeated, afraid. He wanted the divorce, but now he felt unsure. Maybe he and Martha could go away together and try again somewhere else. The talk went on and on between Smith and Berryman until finally Martha fell asleep in the living room.

About one in the morning—as she later recounted—Martha awoke to find that Smith and Berryman had left the room, Smith going to the bedroom, and Berryman going back to his apartment. Martha dozed off again, then awoke in darkness. She got up and went to the bedroom, opened the door, and saw her husband sleeping there. Then she went back to the couch and fell asleep again. When she woke it was just after 6:00 A.M. She went back to the bedroom, but this time her husband was not there. Thinking he was sitting out in his car, she went downstairs and looked, but the car was empty.

A few minutes later, as she walked to the rear of the building, she found him. He was lying by the steps, face up, his arms and legs spread-eagled. The .32 lay near his head, and there was a bullet hole in his chest. She ran inside to John Angus's apartment and woke him. He put on something, then ran out to look at the body. The muzzle of the gun was still warm. Martha got a bedsheet and covered her husband while John Angus called the police. The coroner pronounced Smith dead, and the body was taken away. The police asked Martha some questions, and then she went to her sons' room to tell them that Daddy had gone away forever.

With the land bust, suicide had become a common occurrence, and to the Tampa police, Smith's death merely added one more victim to the grisly statistics. The pistol used in the shooting had belonged to Martha Smith and had been given to her by her husband four years earlier and the coroner judged that John Smith, age thirty-nine, had died of a self-inflicted wound from that gun. Irregularities in the reports were passed over. So, for example, while there were bloodstains on Smith's shirt, there were no powder burns, impossible in the case of a self-inflicted gunshot wound. When the police questioned her, Martha told them she'd looked out the window that Saturday morning on waking and thought she'd seen her husband sitting in their car, but when she'd gone downstairs he was no longer there. She had gone back upstairs to get her car keys and had then found a note on her husband's dresser "weighted down by pocket articles." It read: "Dear Peggy: Again I am not able to sleep—three nights now and the terrible headaches." The note had been left unsigned.

Alarmed, she said, she had run back downstairs, and there, at the back of the apartment, she had discovered her husband's body. Much was made at the hearing of Smith's insomnia and depression, but nothing of his marital problems or the impending divorce or the absence of powder burns. For the police, it was an open-and-shut case: one more casualty of the Florida land bust and the failure of the American Dream. The body was waked in Tampa, then shipped by train to Holdenville, accompanied by Martha and her sons, and laid to rest alongside the body of Will Smith, John Allyn's older brother.

After the burial Martha took her boys to Stillwater to visit her husband's family, whom she had not seen since her wedding fourteen years before. The visit turned out to be even worse than the earlier visit, for Leonard Smith, the one person who had shown Martha any kindness, had since died. The family had accepted John Smith's death as a suicide because one of Smith's sisters, two years older than himself, had already committed suicide. Only Cora, (Aunt Code), the oldest sister, believed Martha had killed her husband. No wonder that, as soon as she could get away, Martha took her sons and left for New York. There, on September 8, just ten weeks after her husband's death, "unwilling to have her children remain fatherless," as she explained to her older son long afterward, Martha married John Angus. The family spent several weeks in Gloucester, Massachusetts and then moved to Jackson Heights, Queens.

What the death of the father meant for the sons would become clearer only with the passing of time. One thing it surely did for the older son, who now took his stepfather's name, was to erase his youth. With time young Berryman came to understand what had happened through his mother's eyes. Of his father he retained very few vivid images: a tall man with dark, close-cropped hair who smoked Camels, a summer soldier. If his father seemed to him even-tempered, distant, and self-centered, it was because his mother reinforced that image of John Smith, and something in the son refused to peer down into the past to see for himself just how his father might be doing in his tormented grave.

*chapter 2*

# Growing Up and Other Agonies

## 1926–32

In the 1920s Jackson Heights, Queens, served as a middle-class commuter suburb of Manhattan, a good place to call home for a bond salesman who traveled to Wall Street each morning. The Berrymans moved first to an apartment on Bedford Street and then to a better apartment at 78 Twenty-sixth Street. Young Berryman sailed through junior high at P.S. 69. He had two girlfriends: Charlotte Coquet, whose house he skated past, hoping his devotion would not go unnoticed, and Helen Justice, taller than him by a head, the amanuensis who wrote out in longhand in two brown-wrappered volumes his unfinished science fiction novel "about a trip to Neptune & Ee-loro-a'ala."

Schoolwork came easily to him, and he spent most of his free time reading pulp magazines. When he graduated from the eighth grade in June 1928, his classmates voted him "most studious boy," and he looked every bit the part. Though he was acquiring his father's broad shouders and wiry physique, he was too uncoordinated to be an athlete. He was still under five feet, weighed ninety pounds, and at thirteen already wore glasses.

Photographs of him taken at graduation show an awkward boy in dark jacket and light pants, hair parted on the left and plastered down, wearing the thick horn-rimmed glasses that would soon earn him the nickname "Blears."

With the death of their father, the boys had joined the Episcopalian Church, Martha's church before she'd married Smith. Berryman was accepted to South Kent School in South Kent, Connecticut, for the fall, a small all-boys school run by Episcopalian priests. The school had been incorporated five years earlier and had an enrollment of seventy-five in forms two through six, there being no first form. The forms were equivalent to the eighth through twelfth grades. South Kent was the offshoot of its successful parent, the Kent School, and like Kent was run by the Fathers of the Holy Cross. The School throve on a form of Emersonian self-help—"unfancy living with a job-system of self-help," which included "dish-washing, shovelling snow, freezing the rink on a nearby lake, and leading a rugged and pretty much monastic life." The school was not a good choice for someone as unathletic and as emotionally dependent as Berryman, and its promise of making young men out of its boys made it a cross between purgatory and hell for him.

From the start, there was only a superficial interaction between young John and the man he called "Uncle Jack." They discussed men's fashions, stocks and bonds, smoking, and drinking. But the truth was that Uncle Jack accepted the boys because they had come with Martha. Moreover, both parents were now working full time, Martha rapidly becoming the more aggressive of the two as she worked her way up from part-time secretary to management in various business firms and advertising agencies in Manhattan. For these reasons she had found it more expedient to send her older son away to boarding school.

South Kent consisted mostly of a cluster of converted farm buildings along a country dirt road, the nearest general store and gas pump being several miles away. The New Haven Railroad ran two trains each day through Kent and served as Berryman's tentative link with New York City and freedom. He arrived by train late Monday evening, September 17, and began classes the following Saturday. When his teachers gave him two hours of homework that first day, he knew he was in for it. His room was on the third floor of the "Old Building," a large barracks dorm that he shared with nineteen other second formers.

From the beginning he was given a taste of the caste system imposed by the sons of the affluent on those beneath them. Most of the boys' parents were like Berryman's parents, only more so. The fathers bought and sold stocks and bonds, ran banks, belonged to country clubs in privileged enclaves like Old Saybrook and Darien. The boys were expected to dress appropriately for classes, which meant knickers, tie, and jacket. As young Christian gentlemen, they were also expected to attend daily prayer, to ask politely for the potatoes at lunch and dinner rather than simply grabbing for the bowl, and, as their fathers had before them, to subdue their competitors on the muddy playing fields and iron-hard ice rinks. There was a strict hierarchy, beginning with the "Brats" of the lowly second form and rising through the imperial sixth. Berryman began as a Brat.

The school reflected the spirit of its headmaster, Sam Bartlett. Still only in his late twenties, Bartlett was a staunch New England Episcopalian layman, possessed of a strong sense of right and wrong (his right, his wrong). He was aloof, opinionated, intelligent, yet fatherly and compassionate. He had graduated from Kent, an outstanding athlete remembered for his skill on the football field, and in his last year at Kent his team had gone undefeated. The message he radiated was one of muscular Christianity. Sports made the man, and studies followed as they could. He wanted healthy minds, and he wanted them in healthy bodies. He stressed self-reliance, rugged individualism, and what passed for conduct befitting young Christian gentlemen preparing to hold the reins of power in tomorrow's world. In effect, he became for young Berryman a strong, stern father substitute. Winter came early and settled in with a vengeance, and for the class scholar of P.S. 69, South Kent very soon became a farm prison.

Quickly he earned the nickname "Blears" on account of his poor eyesight and "Burrs" from his habit of rumbling into his initiatory comments with a deep *ahhhhhhr*. He had the habit too of forcing out his last name as "Burrman," as though it were still foreign to him. He made an easy target for the bullies, a scapegoat for whatever was troubling boys older and bigger than himself. To make matters worse, his face broke out with a terrible case of acne, which left him psychologically scarred for years. He tried for popularity by studying the magazine images of the popular young man of his day. He kept up with current fashions in men's clothes, tried smoking, holding the cigarette between the third and fourth fingers of his left hand, and sang snatches of the popular tunes of the day whenever an occasion arose. He learned how to play (though wretchedly) tennis and Ping-Pong, the game craze of the thirties. He became first a storyteller and then a raconteur. He quickly learned how to turn his tongue into an instrument of wit and humor, by turns affecting a world-weariness or honing a savage edge to his retorts against the bigger and more slow-witted athletes.

Soon after their arrival, the Brats were assembled and instructed by the Old Man on how to conduct themselves. The gist of the message (and veiled threat) was that, until they proved themselves otherwise, Bartlett would consider them "thoughtful, polite, courteous, sportsmanlike gentlemen." Berryman took English, math, ancient history, Latin, and French. He read *A Tale of Two Cities,* and liked the colored maps of ancient lands in his history book. He was glad too for the few women at South Kent, especially his housemother, Miss Dulon, who served him South Kent brew, a mixture of tea and milk, together with homemade cookies.

The regimen began at half past six (quarter past for those boys who wished to go to morning chapel). Breakfast was at seven o'clock, followed by a round of "man-building" chores, such as making beds and sweeping stairs. There followed a morning of classes, then lunch at one, with a mandatory study hour afterward. From three until five most of the boys played sports, but because he was the smallest boy in the lowest form, Berryman signed up instead for gardening rather than play on the Kids' football team. After sports, the boys performed their evening chores, then marched into dinner at six. Study hall followed until lights out at nine.

Soon Berryman was discussing questions about the nature and origin of the universe. He wrote his mother, asking about the origins of the human race and, while he was on the subject, about the problem of evil. Had Adam and Eve ever lived? "And if so, to what race did they belong? And from what race did we develop? The Neanderthal? The Cro-magon [sic] man?" Did she think the earth had been thrown off from the sun? And how did "God make the land, waters, etc., as it says in the Bible?" He was asking her because nobody at South Kent seemed to have the answers.

In October, Berryman's family moved from Jackson Heights to 6 Burbury Lane in Great Neck, a longer commute to Manhattan and a sign of their new prosperity. It was going to feel strange, Berryman told his mother, to come home to a house of their own in the suburbs. In the November elections Martha and John Angus, staunch Democrats, voted for Al Smith, and Berryman wrote to cheer them up when Herbert Hoover won. After all, he commented, the new president had carried forty of the forty-eight states, and that proved he was going to make a good president.

If he couldn't yet play football, Berryman quickly learned how to write up the game, first in letters home and then for the school newspaper, *The Pigtail*. Rummaging through a barrel in the trunk barn in November, he found an old Bible. It was the first he'd ever owned, he reminded his mother, and he'd begun poring over the stories in Genesis until he'd worked up to Abraham's sacrifice of his son. At Thanksgiving his mother and stepfather drove up to spend the day with him. Then it was winter, and Berryman tried to learn to skate on his weak ankles. If he practiced hard, he wrote his mother plaintively, he might just make the Kids' team in another year.

In mid-January 1929 he wrote his mother about a nightmare in which she had died before he could get back from South Kent to see her. He was undoubtedly feeling guilty about being separated from her, at the same time aware of how she played on his guilt. In the dream he saw her laid out on her bed, and as he approached, she opened her eyes, stood up, and began chasing him around the room. At last she stopped and told him she was sorry she had died and that it was too bad he'd come too late. Her eyes, he remembered with terror, "were glassy and pitiful" and she had been "pale and stiff." He had awakened crying, his skin clammy and cold.

The trouble was that not even his mother had remained the same. She was no longer Martha now, but—at Uncle Jack's urging—had changed her name to Jill Angel. Berryman called her that as well as "de Bebe Dirl." If Bebe Dirl ever really thought of dying and leaving him alone, he warned her now, he would kill himself.

That winter word spread that Berryman was at least good for telling a good yarn, and the boys on his floor began asking him to tell them ghost stories after lights out. One story he came up with even involved an old house with a black pit beneath it. "There were murders and at last an octopus [was] discovered in it." So successful was his story-telling that he had to repeat it to another group of boys the following day. It was good to get the attention, he told his mother, but he could not see how anyone with any intelligence could enjoy such trash. A few days later he wrote a long story with a first-person narrator who was on a trader ship on his way from San Francisco to Australia in search of his lost brother. It contained all sorts of "weird adventures among fantastic peoples," culled from his reading of Edgar Rice Burroughs's *Tanar of Pellucidar*.

One night that January the headmaster suddenly materialized in Berryman's dorm just before lights out and insisted on a complete reorganization of the room. Berryman and the other Brats had to shift their beds and belongings around while three senior prefects stood by like drill sergeants. No reason was ever given for the change. Two weeks later the Old Man summoned the Brats to his study and berated them, singling out Berryman for writing so often to his mother. When *he'd* been at Kent, he told Berryman, he'd "trained" his parents to expect one letter a week and no more. From now on Berryman would be limited to just that: one letter home a week. It was time for him to grow up.

One cold, dark morning in February, Berryman went to chapel to pray for his father. Something about the silence and the altar, some residual memories of those mornings in Anadarko when he had served with Father Boniface, could still draw him to the altar. For a long time after his father's death, he had not gone to church, he confessed to his mother, but now he felt compelled to go. He had stayed away, he explained, because he'd been angry with God for taking Daddy away. Now even that hurt seemed at last to be scarring over.

He was still the butt of bigger boys. There was one Brat named Brown (Brown II, Berryman called him, to distinguish him from Brown I), who simply did not like him. One morning Brown taunted Berryman and Berryman hurt his hand wrestling with him so that he could not dress in time for assembly. For punishment he had to clean up the schoolroom in addition to his regular chores. But because he had only the one hand to work with, the cleaning failed to pass inspection and he was reported a second time. Two weeks later his hockey skates and stick were stolen from his locker. When they were discovered out by the lake, one of the Sixth Former prefects bawled him out for saying they'd been stolen. Outraged by these injustices, Berryman complained directly to the Old Man, who seemed to listen but then later had a good laugh with the Sixth Formers over Berryman's mishaps. Thus was Berryman being prepared to take his place in a man's world.

By late March he had become a regular contributor to *The Pigtail*. He was given work as a "heeler," one of the lower-formers who wrote without official recognition. He also tried writing for the pulp westerns he loved to read, sending one magazine a story called "The Law Goes Pistol-Whipping." That spring he was beaned trying to catch a baseball. Then he managed to fall down a flight of stairs and knock himself unconscious. So prone was he to such mishaps that he began to expect them as his due. And though he easily led his form academically (in fact, he was second in the school), the honor carried little weight at Kent. So, when Brown II's father donated fifty thousand dollars to build the school a new infirmary, Berryman understood what realities actually powered South Kent.

In his second fall at South Kent, Berryman tried out for the Kids' football team. He had hoped to work the backfield to avoid the worst bruisings, but he could neither catch nor pass. In fact, he sprained his hand so badly trying to catch a pass that he could not type for a week. Finally the coach made him a guard and put him on the line. He played as well as his scrawny body would allow, but mostly he suffered. In one scrimmage against the Heavy Kids team, he blocked an extra-point kick with his face. He remembered seeing the punter's foot coming and the ball hitting him "hard as a thunderbolt square in the face" and nearly knocking him unconscious. After a few minutes he managed to hobble off the field. His coach patted him on the back for that effort.

Early in the term he had a frantic note from his mother that his ten-year-old brother had found Uncle Jack's automatic pistol while rummaging through his mother's bureau drawer. Jill had written Berryman at once, demanding to know what he knew about the gun. Berryman wrote back, terrified and guilt-stricken. One day that past summer, he confessed, he'd been putting socks away in her bureau and had found the gun. Bob had been in the room with him, and he'd called his brother over to show it to him. Now Bob had taken the gun out and had brandished it about the house, and for that he would have to be punished, especially in light of what a gun had already done to the family.

By the end of September, Wall Street investors were watching the steady declines in the market. Jill wrote Berryman not to expect too much for his birthday that year, and he wrote back that he'd been slow at first to understand "the money situation," but now that she'd explained it to him, he wouldn't "feel bad or anything" if he didn't get a present. Besides, he added plaintively, already learning how to induce guilt for his own ends, his birthday wasn't really all that important. For a moment the market trembled and tried to right itself. But on October 29, the entire economic edifice collapsed. Within three weeks, $30 billion—twice the national debt—simply vanished. Yet now that this second Crash had come, Berryman turned his attention elsewhere, unwilling to face any more of the dark than he had to.

That January the entire world seemed covered by ice for Berryman. He hurt his hand again, this time trying to play hockey. When the Old Man assured him the hand would be fine, Berryman grumbled to his mother that he would "give a great deal to have the same thing happen" to Bartlett. It was hard having to wear glasses and play hockey at the same time, so why couldn't God, who went around creating people in His image, give them "a little better eyesight!" In late February the Old Man invited Berryman up to his house. "I told him about Florida and Oklahoma and Michigan"—he meant Minnesota, but one state was as indistinct in his mind as the other—"and my life, etc," he wrote his mother afterward, "but nothing personal of course (like how Daddy died or anything)." About "Daddy"—his real father—very few knew, or would for years to come. His only connection with his paternal relatives now came from his Aunt Code, his father's oldest sister, the one who was sure Martha had killed John Allyn. Aunt Code would keep a trickle of letters coming over the next ten years. Otherwise, Daddy's world was as silent now as Daddy himself.

Berryman worked harder than ever to make for himself an

image acceptable to his peers. He smoked Lucky Strikes and collected pictures of movie stars, including Nancy Carroll and Joan Crawford, then shifted his interests to learning the words to popular tunes like "Ten Cents a Dance," "St. James Infirmary," and "The Stein Song," as crooned by Rudy Vallee. When spring came, Berryman helped prepare the tennis courts, since tennis, he had decided, was the only sport where he stood a chance of not humiliating himself.

In September he entered the fourth form. In his two years at Kent he'd grown eight inches and put on thirty-seven pounds, but there were several in his form who were at least six feet tall and outweighed him by forty pounds. He covered sports for *The Pigtail* and continued to excel in all his classes except Latin, where Caesar's *Gallic Wars* almost defeated him. That fall he read mostly short stories: Edgar Wallace's "The Crimson Circle," "Beau Geste," "The Lone Wolf Returns." Most important to him, however, was his growing record collection of top hits.

On the morning of his sixteenth birthday—October 25, 1930—he put his hand through a window fooling around and was ordered by the Old Man to replace the window at once, birthday or no birthday. Afterward he was driven in an open touring car in freezing weather to a rival school's football field and was knocked around some more. By then he had come to loathe the private-school system, the Old Man, the prefects, even his roommate. Because of a snowstorm, he did not get to see his parents that Thanksgiving. Then he learned that Uncle Jack was ill and his bond business in even worse shape.

Still, the Depression's worst ravages had till then bypassed his family, and Jill Berryman made sure her son dressed the part of the successful young man. For Christmas she bought him his first tuxedo, which he wore to two New Year's parties. On New Year's Day he listened with interest through the broadcast static as Benito Mussolini addressed the American people by radio. He took in two Broadway shows and all the movies he could, including one that sobered him: *All Quiet on the Western Front*.

During the winter of 1931 he played a wobbly right wing for the Kids' hockey team and began writing to several new girlfriends. At table he listened while his French teacher spoke of "clubs, Yale, dancing, femmes, college life," until he was awed by so much worldliness. If no one else did, at least Berryman considered himself quite hip and a cut above his classmates. He worked to stay on the cutting edge of fashion with his mother's encouragement, and this meant seeing the latest movies and memorizing the lyrics to the hits of the week and playing them on his new Chromonica. By late January he knew, by his own count, the lyrics of 154 songs by heart.

He also learned that it was possible to lock a weak teacher out of his classroom and get away with it. And he saw what happened in South Kent's world of sports to those at the top who fell into disfavor, as happened to the captain of the hockey team when he was disgraced and dropped to second-string defense for being, in the coach's words, "yellow." To avoid being called yellow himself, Berryman found himself getting into new fights. One was with a boy named Bayley. A few blows were exchanged, enough to make Berryman realize that Bayley and the entire school gave him "a pain." A week later it was another fight with someone else. Half-blind with tears, his glasses slapped off his face, Berryman flailed wildly until he smashed his knuckles against the wall. For fighting that badly he knew he would take "a razzing . . . for a month." But, as much as he wanted to go home, he was powerless to do so. Kids, he was learning, were nothing but "a cruel, selfish, dishonorable bunch."

But there were also moments of incredible beauty. One morning that winter he watched from his study-hall window as dray horses pulled plows through a foot of fresh snow to clear the rink for hockey. But the following day he slipped on that same ice, hurting his leg seriously enough to be sent to the new infirmary, where Mrs. Lyons could mother him. There he could take tea, chat, be cared for, and even read in bed. Getting hurt in order to be mothered became another behavior pattern Berryman would carry into adult life.

At last his studies became more interesting. He read the nineteenth-century masters Scott and Dickens, and George Eliot's *The Mill on the Floss*. Such works made "a much deeper impression than any other reading" he'd so far done, because, he believed, they portrayed "life more accurately." His letters home now began to manifest a new sophistication, even a certain pompousness, a style culled in part from the smart magazines of the day to which his parents subscribed. "I hope that Uncle Jack's cold is much improved or entirely vanished," he offered in one letter, "and that his business and yours are disporting themselves well, but not well enough to overwork you."

He brought some of this new sophistication to his other writing as well, as in his movie review of *The Bonanza Buckaroo* for *The Pigtail. Buckaroo* was a poor movie, he decided, because Buffalo Bill had failed to play up "the traditions of the Old West." So, instead of saving the girl from a runaway horse, the hero had merely rescued the girl's mother from a runaway car. This sort of updating of the old Saturday matinee rescue lacked for Berryman—and the other kids he interviewed—the melodrama they had all come to expect.

As the roads began to clear in late February and watery afternoons returned, Berryman began running to get in shape for tennis. The railroad tracks, half a mile away and uphill, made a good loop out and back. He alternated long runs with hard sprints, knowing there was stiff competition for a place on the team. Running toward the icehouse on the afternoon of March 7, he spotted three upper-formers horsing around. One was his friend Forester, from Great Neck. Robbins, with whom he'd already had two fights, was the second. The third was Brown I, one of the jocks. There were words and snickers, then Brown pitched a snowball at him. It missed and Berryman kept running, but, when at last he circled back around the icehouse, the three of them were waiting for him.

Brown threw another snowball and missed again. Angered, he hoisted a chunk of snow and ice, ran after Berryman, who was winded now, and brought it crashing down on his neck and back. Berryman turned and swung wildly, trying to defend himself. That was fine with Brown, who hit Berryman in the face and knocked him down. Then, for good measure, he pinned Berryman's arms with his knees and began pummeling him. The others watched while Berryman struggled to get up, crying at the stupid injustice of it all.

Then, in the distance, Berryman heard the afternoon train. Brown, finished now with Berryman, let him up. But by then Berryman was hysterical. Which train was coming? he demanded, and when one of the boys told him, he dashed for the tracks and threw himself into the path of the train. Frightened at this unexpected turn of events, the others ran after him and managed to pull him off the tracks moments before the train sped past.

After supper, Forester and Robbins sought out Berryman and had a long talk with him about what had happened. It ended with their apologizing and promising to leave him alone. They had hurt him, he knew, but they had also come to his rescue. And now they were sorry for their part in the affair. It was a lesson worth remembering.

A few days later Berryman was back in Great Neck for spring vacation. He danced and necked with a new girl named Marie and noted in his diary that she had seemed willing "to do more." Most of his vacation, however, he spent as he had the others, seeing the latest movies in Manhattan, often at the rate of two double features a day. One evening he went with his mother and grandmother to hear Rudy Vallee and the Connecticut Yankees. On the new electric radio his mother gave him he listened to the National indoor tennis finals. He got himself a "good haircut" from Uncle Jack's barber on Wall Street and visited both Uncle Jack's and his mother's offices. He smoked openly with his parents and played bridge with them until the early morning hours.

It was the life for a sixteen-year-old. To bed at 3:00 A.M., then up at noon to go into the city. On March 24, he met his parents at the Hunt Club on West Forty-fifth Street, a fashionable speakeasy that—his mother told him—had eighteen thousand drinking members. His parents sipped martinis while he drank ginger ale, listened to a "swell negro" play the piano, and then watched a burlesque show afterward. Later he and his parents went to the Palace to hear Vincent Lopez and watch George Burns and Gracie Allen do their comedy routine.

Back at school he read Tennyson's *Idylls of the King* and short stories by Galsworthy, Willa Cather, D. H. Lawrence, Katherine Mansfield, and Ernest Hemingway, as well as Robert Graves's memoir *Goodbye to All That*. He tried selling jokes to *Life* and *Judge* magazines. He took a nature walk with another classmate and brought back some frogs' eggs from the pond: "queer black specks in [a] transparent jelly substance." When the boys returned to the pond to get some more frog jelly, they wound up spending the afternoon talking "smut." It may have been on this occasion that, as he confessed years later, he experimented with sex by "sucking off" his classmate.

A few weeks later one of his teachers read an English translation of M. Arlen's "The Gentleman from America." It was this story, Berryman would later recall, that awakened in him a sense of the power of literature. But that spring his grades slipped, and even his tennis game—like his acne—went from bad to worse. For his poor backhand he had no one to blame, but as for his complexion, he confided to his diary, that was surely his mother's fault. At least she might have had a specialist look at him. How much, after all, did she and Uncle Jack really care about him?

When Uncle Jack came up to South Kent in early May for Fathers' Weekend, he brought Bob with him to take the school's admissions exam. The three of them watched the sports events together, took tea in the Old Man's living room, then had supper. Afterward, Uncle Jack drifted off while the two brothers talked. On Sunday, stiff and tired from sleeping in the barn (having given up his room to Uncle Jack and Bob), Berryman got up, showered, and attended Sunday services with his family. Then, in the middle of chapel, to Berryman's embarrassment, Uncle Jack suddenly walked out. As soon after as he could manage it, Uncle Jack left South Kent, explaining that he had to meet Berryman's mother to look over some real estate. "Uncle Jack had a certainly good time and I know he gave me one," Berryman wrote his mother that evening. The truth was too painful to face.

A few weeks later Berryman had a surprise visit from a cousin of his on his father's side. He'd met Hal Kelly on his trip to Minnesota five years earlier, and he described him now to his mother as "a big smoothy in brown wing-tips" who wore "weird golf hose, white knickers" and a "blue golf sweater," and whom he found leaning against a coupe with a friend and two girls. Kelly, he learned, was working in Bridgeport, Connecticut, for General Electric. So this was his father's family. How far away they all seemed now.

By mid-June, Berryman was back home. He spent this vacation following the same monotonous routine as the others, going to the movies, talking sex, smoking, dancing, and seeing his girlfriends, Lillian, Jean, Imogene, and Pidge. He played poker, blackjack, Ping-Pong. He saw Fred Astaire perform on Broadway in *The Band Wagon*. He passed his driver's test, spent afternoons knocking a tennis ball "against the clubhouse with Daddy's old racquet," browsed through magazines, and read haphazardly everything from Dashiell Hammett and Agatha Christie to *Volpone* and Lawrence's *The Man Who Died*.

In September, Berryman returned to South Kent. He was now in the Fifth Form. Bob, who had just turned twelve, went with him to begin school there. Ironically Bob throve at South Kent from the beginning, and Berryman had to marvel at how "fiercely" his little brother played football. Jill took the train up to see her sons for Berryman's seventeenth birthday. Thanksgiving came and went. After exams ended in mid-December, Berryman headed for New York, with a detour at his classmate Jim Leonard's home in South Norwalk, where he had a man-to-man talk with Leonard's father on topics ranging on everything from pop psychology to the wisdom of investing in Oklahoma oil.

Earlier that year the Berrymans had sold their Great Neck house and moved into an apartment at the Gilfort in Manhattan. Now Berryman met them there, after dropping his bags off at his room at the Shelton that he was sharing with Bob for the holidays. Most days the boys lounged in bed until early afternoon, then window-shopped along Fifth Avenue. Berryman saw his old girlfriend Marie on East Fifty-second Street, then went with his mother to take in a balalaika orchestra and a floor show with six chorus girls. He noted one "very cute hussy with rolling eyes, a huge ass and plump breasts" and wanted very much to dance with her. Instead, he danced with his mother to the strains of "Good-Night, Sweetheart."

Christmas morning the brothers walked over to their parents' apartment and exchanged gifts. Then the family went to a deserted Loew's Theatre to see *Rich Man's Folly*. Berryman listened, embarrassed, while his mother sobbed her way through the picture. Afterward Uncle Jack showed his stepson how to smoke a pipe. Berryman's friend Leonard came into the city, and the two of them took dates to the Paramount to hear Bing Crosby sing "Sleepy Time Down South" and "Too Late" and Cab Calloway do "Minnie the Moocher" and "Sweet Georgia Brown."

After the boys dropped off their dates, they took in a burlesque show at Minsky's. There were some "swell" strippers there, Berryman had to admit, and it was all "very suggestive and filthy.'' Around midnight they went to a dance hall at Fiftieth and Broadway called Honeymoon Lane and found some ''buxom hostesses in nothing but gowns'' with their ''breasts hanging out.'' Then he and Leonard walked to Forty-second Street to see *Palmy Days* with Eddie Cantor. After that they played Ping-Pong in the nearly deserted lounge before calling it a night. As they walked back to the hotel at half past three in the morning, a man stepped out of the shadows and offered to show them both a good time. Shaken, they half walked, half ran back to their hotel.

Next day they made some recordings in a local music shop, Berryman belting out the choruses to ''Good-Night Sweetheart,'' ''Faded Summer Love,'' and ''Without That Gal.'' Then he saw Leonard off at Grand Central. He'd had a grand two days, but when he got back to the hotel, there was hell waiting for him in the shape of his mother, who lectured at him for staying out till all hours of the morning and worrying her half to death. She could see that he was becoming more and more like his father. Chastened, Berryman promised once more to reform.

Through the dreary winter months of 1932, Berryman kept close to the radio. Mostly it was music he was after. But there were also rumors of war in the Far East, and he feared he might have to fight like that fellow in *All Quiet on the Western Front*. He read some good literature that term, which he was sure would help him when he majored in English in college as he now planned to do. Among the books he read were *Main Street, My Ántonia, The Dubliners,* and a number of one-act plays by Tarkington, Dowson, Milne, Lady Gregory, and Synge. He tried Eugene O'Neill, but found him ''too mature.'' He listened to an Anglican priest lecture on the hundredth anniversary of the founding of the Oxford Movement. He was the first real Englishman Berryman could ever remember seeing, and they talked for hours on everything from life in London and New York to tennis. Someday, Berryman promised himself, he would see England for himself.

In mid-March he told his mother about his interest in English. He knew now it was the only subject for him. His English teacher had been giving his students short daily themes, and Berryman had noticed that one fellow was particularly interesting because he knew how to write in a personal vein. His own papers, by contrast, were still too "cold and calculating," too detached, in the manner of Francis Bacon. Then he'd tried an essay on slang and had received high marks for it. He was determined now to write more of what he actually thought and felt and less like a machine. He did not yet know what he would do after majoring in English in college, though he thought he might try working on Wall Street for a while.

Spring vacation came and went. Uncle Jack's job became virtually nonexistent, and he spent more and more time at home, while Berryman's mother, at thirty-seven, took over the primary financial responsibilities for the household. She began meeting men at her job, men younger, more vibrant, more successful than her husband. For his part, young Berryman ignored these new turns in their domestic affairs as much as he could. Money became tighter, and it was clear that neither Berryman nor his brother was going to be able to return to South Kent in the fall. Anticipating this, Berryman applied to Columbia University and won a partial scholarship and his earlier dream of attending Princeton was forgotten. Once again the family moved into another apartment, closer to whatever work Jill could find.

In June Berryman took his final exams and scholastic aptitude tests for college and then left South Kent. Now that he would not be returning, he felt a pang of loss for the school and even for its headmaster, who had actually begun treating him decently these last months at school, perhaps because of the final collapse of Uncle Jack's bond business, perhaps because Berryman had approached the threshold of the Sixth Form, only to have it taken from him.

Suddenly his prep school years were behind him, though he would return the following June to "graduate" with the Sixth Formers. For the next thirty years he would keep in touch with his alma mater, even visiting it a quarter-century later. He would become particularly anxious to keep the Old Man aware of honors as they came to him, for he had suffered too much at South Kent to let the record close with 1932. If he'd had an undistinguished career there (except for his grades, which seemed to matter precious little), the ugly duckling would one day demand attention as the swan-bright alumnus he could dream he was destined to become.

# chapter 3

## Fair Columbia

## 1932–36

Except for the loss of Uncle Jack's income, his mother's growing disenchantment with her domestic arrangements, and the deepening Depression, it was a peach of a time for Berryman. From his apartment on East Sixtieth Street, he listened on his electric radio to the Wimbledon matches, played tennis on the city courts, browsed through the second-hand record shops and the stacks of the Cathedral branch of the New York Public Library, and invited his soul to loaf. He pored over Amy Lowell's biography of John Keats, a Russian primer, a book of modern plays, a German novel in translation called *Sheba Visits Solomon,* Oscar Wilde's *Lady Windermere's Fan,* and the plays of Sheridan and Yeats. He dreamed now of becoming a famous playwright. He took to stopping by his mother's office for chats, and joined the YMCA to play Ping-Pong and swim. For his part, Uncle Jack became mostly a fixture around the apartment, making meals for the boys and reading the want ads in search of work.

There were still the occasional flamboyant gestures, like Uncle Jack's treating the boys to a real haircut from his old

Wall Street barber. The three bachelors did their daily chores around the apartment; otherwise the time was Berryman's to waste as he wished. He wrote an occasional letter to a girlfriend and took in the midnight burlesque shows. He cheered as Elsworth Vines crushed Austin to win the Wimbledon. He saw Paul Robeson perform in *Showboat* and listened to the Mills Brothers, Bing Crosby, and Burns and Allen on the radio. In early July the family celebrated Jill's thirty-eighth birthday at an Automat. At the YMCA, Berryman was soundly beaten at Ping-Pong by "a cheating Jew," the easy, vicious phrase picked up at home and from the boys at South Kent.

In early August he visited Grandmother Little in Roxbury, a small town in the Catskills, where she now ran a small restaurant. He found the locals there churchy and dull, and passed his days reading in the local library, playing tennis on a "moth-eaten court," going to the movies, or listening to his radio. Again the family moved, this time to a cheaper apartment on East Eighty-fourth Street. Bored with his inactivity and the growing strain of living at home, what with his mother's star in the ascendency and her scarcely veiled flirting with other men, he waited for the blessed fall and the start of college life.

At Columbia, Berryman was determined *not* to repeat his dismal South Kent experience. From the beginning he tried to make himself popular. He memorized the names of every freshman who entered with him in the class of 1936—"the Perfect '36," the class came to call itself. He went out of his way to meet as many co-eds as he could from Barnard—Columbia's counterpart across the way—at the weekly tea dances. He ran track (the 440) and rowed crew. He gladhanded in an aloof sort of way and went in for college politics, though he refused to try out for a fraternity, remembering the power plays of the boys at South Kent. With two classmates, Tom McGovern and Paul MacCutched, he formed the Interclass Independent party for the spring 1933 elections. "Vote Early and Vote Independent" was their less-than-catchy motto. He ran for vice-president and lost by a very narrow margin to a fraternity man he summed up as a "void." He cut as many classes as he could. No one, either at home or at South Kent, had yet convinced him of the value of the life of the mind. He was eighteen and still skating on the surface of things.

At the beginning of his second semester he met E. Milton Halliday, a graduate of Andover living with his family in Brooklyn Heights, who would become Berryman's closest friend over the next four years. They met that February in the lobby of Brooks Hall at Barnard College while pursuing the same girl, a freshman named Flora. Halliday, 6′ 3″, with dark good looks, was immediately struck not only by Berryman's handsome face (the acne having by then cleared up) but by the cut of his clothes and his newly acquired sophistication and courtly manners as well. The son of a Congregationalist minister, Halliday was now anxious to put that life behind him in his hot pursuit of women. The only trouble was, he told Berryman over coffee in a local drugstore that first day, that he wasn't quite sure how to go about meeting them. Columbia freshmen met girls at tea dances, and he could not dance. Berryman assured him he might be able to teach him a thing or two. The young men took to each other at once.

Berryman began by showing Halliday, till then a teetotaler, how to drink. He started by offering Halliday beer from Uncle Jack's bootleg supply. Then, with his parents out of town, Berryman offered his friend something stronger: a martini. One night Uncle Jack took them to visit his own speakeasy, anxious to do so before the Volstead Act and Repeal made speakeasies a thing of the past. Halliday was also impressed with Jill, so different from his own mother. Here was a real dresser, a raconteur who could tell a peach of a joke, like the one about the guy who told his wife he was late because (it's delightful, it's delovely, as the song had it) and he'd been "delaid." Uncle Jack countered by showing Halliday how to make scrambled eggs.

Berryman continued Halliday's sentimental education by taking him to a tea dance and showing him how to dance with girls. Hold tight and don't pull back, he counseled, even with an erection. He took Halliday to Minsky's and the Apollo for the slapstick routines of Phil Silvers and Bert Lahr, and ogled, along with the other Columbia students, the all-white striptease "tit shows." Best was the Savoy in Harlem, where they listened to Chick Webb, Duke Ellington, Jimmy Lunceford, Ella Fitzgerald, and Billie Holiday, while young black couples did the new dance craze called the jitterbug.

To learn more about the mysteries of women, Berryman

tried translating Ovid's *Ars Amatoria*. Together he and Halliday studied medical diagrams in search of the clitoris. They even found themselves attracted to the same girls. But the girls, themselves mostly products of all-girl prep schools, really knew little more than their male counterparts. It was the generation of heavy petting and necking in the back of steamy coupes. But saving one's virginity for one's husband, considering the social and economic stigma attached to unwed pregnancy, remained the bedrock rule.

In mid-June 1933, Berryman went to South Kent for his graduation with the Sixth Formers. Afterward, he stayed on with two other boys, working around the school in the mornings and swimming and playing tennis in the afternoons. He felt the need to spend time there, but since the nearest movie house was ten miles away and the local beer "perfectly awful," he soon found himself bored. Halliday, spending the summer with relatives in Michigan, wrote him long, erotic letters about the women he'd met, and Berryman wrote back, lamenting the fact that he himself was so "womanless" he'd been reduced to making passes at a friend of the family. What had given him pause was the realization that the woman in question was nearly thirty.

That September, Berryman moved into a campus dorm room in John Jay Hall. He and Halliday enrolled in an advanced composition course taught by Mark Van Doren, and Berryman was struck at once by Van Doren's discipline and dedication. It was the force of this man's example, Berryman always insisted, that first made him seriously think about becoming a poet himself. Here was someone to emulate: a sane, intelligent individual who had not only published studies of Dryden and Shakespeare, but fiction and poetry as well. Moreover, Van Doren was accessible, as ready to listen to a student's personal problems as to talk about Shakespeare's plays. It did not take Berryman long to become one of Van Doren's disciples.

Women, of course, still remained the driving force for Berryman, and that, together with his newly found freedom in being on his own, led to some strange new behavior. To save time for more important things, he began going without a shower or a shave for days at a time. He cut classes—all but Van Doren's—and waited till the last possible moment to catch up on his reading. Except in Van Doren's class, his grades for the fall semester were mediocre.

On December 5, Utah became the thirty-sixth state to ratify the Repeal Amendment. Roosevelt signed the bill, and suddenly Prohibition was over. All over Manhattan, as around the country, crowds gathered to celebrate and drink openly for the first time in fourteen years. Naturally, Berryman and Halliday were there. One night soon after, Berryman and his friend Dana Crandall were returning to John Jay after a drunken binge when Berryman, opening the door to his sixth-floor room, was hit in the face and knocked cold. An ambulance was called, and he was rushed to the hospital. When the dean investigated the incident, he found an empty whiskey bottle on the floor under Berryman's bed. Apparently a drunken student in the courtyard below had hurled the empty bottle and it had sailed through Berryman's open window just as Berryman walked into his room. If something *could* happen, it seemed always to happen to him.

Berryman celebrated New Year's Eve with an attractive Barnard freshman from South Carolina named Garnette Snedecker. That week he read Will Durant's *Story of Philosophy,* O'Neill's *All God's Chillun Got Wings,* and Milton's *Paradise Lost.* He had a "swell theological discussion" in Van Doren's class on Milton, his agnostic soul delighted when the students cornered Van Doren into admitting that there were inconsistencies in Milton's theology. But when Berryman read Milton's "Lycidas," he was so struck by the poem that he read it through three times. It was, he wrote, "magnificent," and it remained a literary touchstone for him for the rest of his life. He was coming to value literature more, even as he grew increasingly dissatisfied with himself for spending so much time chasing women when there was so much work to be done.

He wrote on love for his Milton course, calling on his own limited experience and what he could remember from his talks with his friends. He also wrote essays on *Samson Agonistes* and the *Areopagitica,* both of which essays Van Doren thought good enough to read aloud to his class. Berryman visited the Cathedral of St. John the Divine with his fine-arts class and, floundering for modifiers, found the edifice "marvellous" and "amazing." So impressed was he with its splendor that he took Garnette Snedecker there to listen to "the wonderful organ in a little chapel'' where the two of them, he sighed to his diary, ''loved each other hugely.'' Yet despite his love for Garnette, he took another young woman to a dance and spent the following night necking with her. ''Picture of me at midnight, disorderly, unstudied, thinking abt women,'' he wrote, bemused with what he thought of as his herculean capacity for love.

In late January finals began and Berryman found himself cramming to get a semester's work read in three sleepless days. Not unexpectedly, his exam in French poetry turned out to be ''a bastard.'' He managed to see Garnette and ''talk sex'' with another woman before returning to his room for an all-nighter in preparation for his English exam. He slept two hours, then rushed to take his test, which turned out to be ''horrible.'' To make matters worse, he learned that Halliday had called Garnette for the Dean's Drag, but was relieved to hear that his ''angel'' had turned Halliday down. He crammed for his Contemporary Civilization and Geology exams, again going without sleep, so that he did not notice the last page of his contemporary civilization exam until it was too late. Afterward he walked out into falling snow covering the walks and lawns of Columbia and once more the world seemed beautiful. Exams over, he took the train up to his grandmother's in the Catskills for a few days' rest.

He spent his spring term going to tea dances and worrying about the vicissitudes of love. He continued dating Garnette and an assortment of other women. In May he turned in an essay to Van Doren on Marcel Proust's *Swann's Way,* including a ''Foreword'' in which he expressed his fascination in ''recording an experience unparalleled in my previous literary walks'' (he was nineteen) and only regretted he'd ''not allowed myself sufficient time to do justice, in my finished essay, to the abundant material that I have collected in the reading of this volume.'' While he had had to leave his essay unfinished, he did have ''some seven or eight thousand words in short discussions of various aspects of the novel—these are in more or less complete form—and about fifty pages of very detailed notes.'' He regretted that his ''indolence'' had made it necessary to write his exam after having read the first volume only of Proust.

After another two pages of special pleading, Berryman ended by noting regretfully that his writing would seem ''loose and poorly phrased,'' and asked Van Doren to consider ''the thought and disregard . . . the expression.'' Such excuses had worked with his mother; they might work now. ''As far as it goes, fine,'' an exasperated Van Doren wrote across the title page of Berryman's returned essay. ''The writing is mature, skilful, and interesting, and you have really penetrated the book. But I must take account of 1) your brevity 2) your rage for apologizing. *Some* time do try to finish something and to present it without preamble. B-.''

Berryman had also enrolled in Van Doren's Eighteenth Century Literature course, and was hopelessly behind in it as well. He wrote what he thought was an excellent final, but, out of loyalty to Van Doren, noted on the exam itself that, of the forty-two books required for the course, he had read only seventeen. In effect, he challenged Van Doren to come to his rescue. The answer came a few days later when he was called before Dean Hawkes and told to take the fall term off while he reconsidered his future. Suddenly Berryman found himself suspended and his scholarship rescinded.

Jill's manner of dealing with her son in such situations was to first berate him and then freeze him out of her life, as though he no longer existed. It was a strategy against which he had not yet found a defense. Uncle Jack, no longer any match for his wife's sharp tongue and strident monologues, stayed out of the argument. Berryman promised to change his ways; he would get a job and go back to school, and this time he would excel. To make amends, he began writing a series of poems that he dedicated to his mother. These came to four stilted Shakespearean sonnets in honor of her fortieth birthday that July 8. The form he chose to begin his career as a poet with was also meant to honor the man he'd ''betrayed'' that term: Van Doren the Shakespearean scholar, who had already published several accomplished sonnet sequences himself.

Though outwardly conventional, Berryman's sonnets veiled a wish to be allowed to find his own direction in life. Choking from his mother's smothering, he begged her not to let him ''grow too closely dear,'' for if he could hold himself apart, he stood his best chance of gaining ''in strength under/His own will, on his own life-path.'' That said, the poems continued as love songs to the woman who had not had an easy life of it but who had maintained her dignity and her wit, a woman whose very words were poetry to him. If he was the struggling poet, he wrote to her, she was his poem. With a growing sense of nausea, he had managed for the moment to placate his mother and pay his dues.

He found work typing and editing rough drafts of pulp stories—westerns, crime stories, detective novels, mysteries, love stories—for a woman (a southerner, from Savannah) who lived on Staten Island and who wrote endless reams of drivel under the pen name Clinton Dangerfield. It was straightforward enough work. She would narrate her stories into a dictaphone, and Berryman would listen to the records back home. He was paid fifty cents per thousand words and a dollar an hour for editing. He hated the work, hated writing for money. "God knows," he told Halliday, "I'll probably be a famous fifth-rate Western writer shining from the pages of Argosy and Range Romances, and every Goddam thing I believe and hope for will be ground to the proverbial dust under the economic treadmill."

With Halliday now at the University of Michigan, and Berryman's relationship with Garnette Snedecker cooled, he sought out other friends. One night he went up to Columbia with Dana Crandall and Tom McGovern and got so drunk he passed out, the following day feeling as "dead as several volumes of the Anatomy of Melancholy," with "a brown taste you could practically wrap around your arm." But his poetry was not forgotten. On July 31, he wrote a villanelle in a diction fifty years out of date: "Silent as death and sere as bone/ Along a waste unvisited/ I thread ethereal paths alone." At nineteen that was how the sad, sad poet composed himself.

In mid-September 1934 the Berrymans moved to a seven-room fifth-floor brownstone on 115th Street. The apartment was awful, Berryman told Halliday, but it was close to Columbia and was, besides, "dirt-cheap," which was why, with both his parents out of work at the moment, they'd taken it. Garnette was still as "unkind as ever" and he was brokenhearted that things had worked out as they had. But he had decided to remake himself once more and had grown a mustache that was "the sensation of the campus." He was delighted that it made him look years older, and he was going out to "find the best ten honeys" among the entering freshman class of Barnard and lay as many of them as he could. He had not been out with a girl since May, and was afraid he was going "to shrivel up and die."

By then he was collaborating with Dangerfield, revising her rough narratives, giving them shape, and splitting the money fifty-fifty. But his family was "broke as hell" at the moment and he was turning everything over to his mother. Still, he kept enough for periodic drunks with Steve Aylward and Dana Crandall that fall at places like the Gold Rail, where on one occasion the three of them composed questionable limericks far into the night, insulting "everyone from the Dean up and down, particularly down."

In October he turned twenty and felt, he confessed in a sober moment to Halliday, less self-important than ever and more "bewildered by the futility and insignificance" of the little he'd actually done. Yet in the same letter he could crow that he'd become "the goddamest woman-thief on the campus." He'd gone to every dance he'd heard about and was furiously necking "with anyone worthy." He and Crandall had crashed the Junior Formal and he'd managed to "play" with four women while being "charged with two others," though he was so drunk that night that afterward he could remember nothing.

But he also kept up with his reading, including Mencken's *Prejudices,* the Eighteenth Century Literature syllabus that had been his downfall, and *Moby Dick*. Melville he found a new experience altogether; here was a writer capable of "a splendid casual prose" laced with a realism so much better than anything a John O'Hara could produce. In Melville, in fact, he'd found "a mystic of the first water."

Berryman's verse had also improved over "the morass of adolescent love-verse" that had "cluttered" his summer. He tried forms like the double quatrain and a "mystic phrasing with Shakespearean theme." He also tried "couplets of uneven length" (eye/cold and dry/as an old drab/on a slab) and a short sequence of "narrative sonnets" on the final thoughts of men about to die. He had even begun using poetry as a way of finally laying his father's ghost to rest, even as he realized the impossibility of such a task:

> No man retains his malice toward a shade.
> He stood erect and free, and set to work,
> Regretting the need to touch again remains—

An hour, the face was covered, the grave was filled.
He shrugged a dismissal, strode away . . . the murk
Concealed a shapeless horde of little fiends
That rose and stalked his footsteps. . . .

In one sequence he even experimented with the voice of a doomed atheist, he wrote Halliday, because his own beliefs were crumbling and he no longer knew anymore what to believe. He even began to doubt whether he actually could write poetry. Only Van Doren continued to show any interest in what he wrote. But if he ever gained any "real power over poetic expression and diction," he added, it might well be with the "narrative sonnet form."

With the approach of Christmas, Berryman grew anxious once more to see Halliday. He and his buddies would be waiting for ol' Milt at the train station "with phallic symbols in our hats, bitches under each arm and liquor on the beastly hip" in their flasks. True to his word, when Halliday returned, Berryman had a reunion for him at the Gold Rail and another with Winanne, an old friend from Columbia. It was at Winanne's apartment that they met two Smith women: a buxom blonde named Dorothy Rockwell (whom Halliday began to pursue), and a brunette, Jane Atherton, whom Berryman immediately fell for. On New Year's Eve he and Halliday donned their tuxedos, split the cost of a half-pint of Four Roses, downed it in Berryman's apartment, and then tried to crash the Columbia faculty dance. When the doorman refused to let them in, they snuck around the back of the building, climbed through a window, and went out onto the crowded dance floor. When the security guards spotted them, they ran out, sliding down the main hall banister past the startled doorman, shouting "Happy New Year" as they left.

Since the evening was still early, they took the subway to the Village and walked to E. B. White's apartment to wish Van Doren a happy New Year. By the time they got there, however, the Van Dorens had left, and Berryman and Halliday found themselves in a room full of intensely sober people discussing literature, among them the critics Kenneth Burke, Horace Gregory, and Eda Lou Walton. As soon as they could, the young men excused themselves and walked to the Fourteenth Street

Station, Halliday to return to Brooklyn while Berryman went uptown to another party.

A few days later Berryman learned, to his immense relief, that he'd been readmitted to Columbia for the spring term. He continued to drink and write poems on such grand immensities as death and fame, including a three hundred-line prose poem inspired by Van Doren's just-published novel. One night Berryman went for a joyride down West Side Drive and rolled in to his parents' empty apartment at half past four. For several nights he necked with a girl who lived in the same building, getting back to his own apartment at 3:00 A.M., until one night he was surprised to find his parents home from their trip earlier than he'd expected. In what he called a "long, furious talk," his mother threatened once again to wash her hands of him. It was what he feared more than anything, for it was that rejection, he was convinced, that had caused his father's death.

To get back into his mother's good graces, he promised once more to reorder his life. He cleaned his room, revised and ordered four of his poems, and wrote a solemn sonnet after Stephen Spender on the problem of Time. When Spender proved too oblique for him, he turned to Auden, then to Rilke and Robinson Jeffers. He even got up early to do the dishes. Then, having performed enough in the way of filial devotion, he spent the evening talking frank sex with two young men he'd recently met. The following evening one of them telephoned to invite him to a formal. Berryman noted that something about himself had no doubt fascinated the boy, but when he went to the formal, he became frightened when the young man told him he was in love with him. The friendship ended at once.

On February 6, spring semester began. Berryman worked on his "cursed and triplecursed" eighteenth-century list day and night. It was something, he told himself, that he had to do to square things with Van Doren. He was still hoping to graduate with his class, and he would have to work like hell if he was going to make it. He had taken light loads in his freshman year, had dropped one course and flunked another as a second-semester sophomore, and had been out of school now for half a year. But he could still graduate on time if he went to summer school and took "a perfect bastard of a curriculum" his senior year.

Again his brain teemed with poems. He sent *The Atlantic Monthly* five and *The New Yorker* six. When *The New Yorker* rejected all six by return mail, he swore never again to send them anything. A few days later his poems came back from *The Atlantic Monthly* as well. Disconsolate, he sent Halliday a grim sonnet that looked ahead, reluctantly, to the time when he and Halliday would both be dust.

He registered now for Van Doren's Eighteenth Century English Literature course, Clifford Odell's Modern Drama (a "peach of an old fellow"), Dean Hawkes's Solid Geometry, a "bewildering course in Sociology with Casey," and a required course in geology. When classes began, so too did the beginning of what he promised himself and his mother would be his "ordered existence." He finished the eighteenth-century syllabus, taking careful and lengthy notes of each book he read: *Moll Flanders, Clarissa, Joseph Andrews, Tristram Shandy,* Gibbon, Paine and "marvellous" Blake. He read the eighteenth-century poets from nine one evening until five the next morning, slept three hours, then read them again all that Saturday until four the next morning. He was exhausted, but felt a "marvellous satisfaction in the inevitability of industry once one is set." He slept for a few hours until Sunday morning, necked with one of his girlfriends, then went back to the eighteenth century. He grabbed a few more hours' sleep, attended classes, then read Paine and Gibbon far into the night. He would prove to Van Doren that this time he meant business.

The last book on his list was Hume's *An Enquiry Concerning Human Understanding,* and when he finished that at four in the morning, he realized he'd read sixteen books in five days, as well as filling an entire notebook. "A tremendous load gone," he noted in his diary, "and I feel older, stronger—a phase is past." At noon that day he turned in his notebooks to Van Doren who was so pleased that he had Berryman's "F" changed to a "B." Soon the entire English faculty had heard about the young hero's achievement.

"Van Doren knows it was done mainly as a mark of esteem for him and to show *him* I wasn't as worthless as he may have supposed," Berryman wrote Halliday afterward. *There* was a model to emulate, he added, there was a man who never wavered "from the line he has set for himself, and it's the best line in America today." By sheer industry, the little tragedy he had brought on himself eight months before had been transformed at last into a comedy. It was another lesson worth remembering.

The day he turned in his notebooks, Berryman had a talk with the editor of *The Columbia Review* and showed him some of his poems. Impressed, the editor asked if he might publish a few. At first Berryman demurred, but then offered him a lyric beginning "Delinquency has been my portion," and another called "Essential." "It was no pose, my refusing," Berryman explained to Halliday, since the magazine printed "so much shit, and since I've never had anything published." But both poems were as finished as he could make them and—more importantly—"sufficiently impersonal" to allow them to see print.

The following noon he dropped in at the Review's office and met some of the staff, among them Robert Lax, another young poet, and Robert Giroux. Berryman's initial and unearned impression was that, except for the editor, who had sought him out, the staff was composed of drips. He went to his first meeting of the Columbia literary society, *The Philolexian,* with Lax and a fellow named Thomas Merton, later to become renowned as a Trappist monk and author of *The Seven Storey Mountain.* Berryman read them three poems he was sure they'd been impressed with, but which, it turned out, they'd merely endured. A few days later he spoke with his parents about publishing a book of poems. *Junior Year* was a good title for a belated junior, his mother suggested, playing as it did with the idea of a young man's first book. Uncle Jack suggested he close the book with a preface.

He went to the Barnard Sophomore Formal with a girl named Roselle, hoping to find Garnette and a new love interest there, another co-ed from Barnard, Elspeth Davies. He congratulated himself on how well he danced that evening, noting that Garnette had had a hard time holding herself aloof from his charms. A week later he crashed the Barnard Junior Prom and got into an argument with a woman he put down as distinctly his "mental inferior." He promised not to let himself get into another situation like that again.

Rehearsals for the all-male Varsity Show Chorus began in late February. Berryman was outfitted as both a nursemaid and as a belle, which allowed him to wear a "gorgeous & full-breasted" gown. Since rehearsals at the Astor Hotel began at six and lasted until two in the morning, he was soon cutting classes again. The show opened on March 12, and his parents found it "very funny" and "very dirty." But when the show played the following night to a rowdy all-male Columbia audience, he was annoyed at the barrage of sexist remarks hurled his way as he sang and danced in his evening gown. On the fifteenth he picked up a copy of *The Columbia Review* and found his poem there. It was his first time in print, but he was too exhausted to feel very much. Instead, he went home to get some sleep. The next thing he knew, his parents were waking him up. It was after ten and he had missed his performance.

He now began pursuing Elspeth in earnest and composed a long poem and several sonnets in her honor. But while his heart soared with love and fame, he noticed a rash on his scrotum and wondered what could have caused it. It turned out, his doctor informed him, to be scabies, and he was advised to wash himself and change his clothes more often. Going without showers, it had turned out, was not the best labor-saving device he had come up with. At the Fencing Ball, which he attended with Elspeth, he bruised his leg badly doing his banister slide. When he hobbled over to see her the following afternoon, he found her with another man and wrote her a sonnet—this one imitating E. A. Robinson—complaining of her heartless indifference.

Midterms began. He listened with rapt attention to Van Doren read his new poems in *Winter Diary* at the Casa Italiana. He crammed for Van Doren's American Literature course, reading Melville, Whitman, Twain, and Henry James, and dreaming that someday he too would be published in the Random House series along with Blake, Coleridge, Swift, and Donne. He had a serious talk with his mother about his literary ambitions, then wrote a poem in her honor that he titled "Genius." He submitted a sheaf of fifteen poems to the Boar's Head contest for Columbia undergraduates.

That spring business picked up briefly for Uncle Jack, and in early April he left for Buffalo on a two-week business trip. Two days later, Jill Berryman left with a gentleman business associate for a weekend in the country. Berryman understood, but did not dare talk to her about the matter. If his mother said she was going away on business, it was business. Uncle Jack had long ago given up trying to stop his wife from doing whatever she set her heart on doing. After all, Jill looked and dressed like someone a generation younger than her husband, and she knew how to keep him in his place. By then everyone knew who ran things in the Berryman household. If it came to that, she knew how to dress her boys down as well.

During spring break Halliday showed up at Berryman's place. He was still "a heller & superb friend," Berryman wrote in his diary, and for a week the two of them had long talks and took in the movies. On April 12, in rain, Berryman and Crandall attended an antiwar strike held in the Columbia gym. Berryman had gone because Elspeth was the lead-off speaker in the effort to keep America out of Europe's affairs. He watched her, microphone in hand, speaking from a platform constructed of raised tables, surrounded by a mass of Columbia men in homburgs and raincoats and posters reading LIFE IS SHORT ENOUGH. Afterward he took her to lunch and then back to her apartment. When a photograph of "Else Davees" appeared in the New York papers the following day, Berryman made sure he saved one.

He sent another batch of poems to *The Columbia Review* and reworked the manuscript for his book of poems for the Yale Younger Poets series. Intensely dissatisfied with what he had written but with a deadline upon him, he mailed it off and went on to other things. He took second prize for a group of poems in *The Columbia Review,* the same issue that carried his review of Van Doren's *Winter Diary,* where he praised the poems for their realism, reticence, and "good breeding." Van Doren was the only teacher he cared about impressing anymore, and the only one, in fact, he did impress that semester. For while Van Doren gave him an "A-" in American Literature, he received a low "B" in sociology and mathematics, and a "C+" in Modern Drama and geology. On the other hand, he managed to win the annual Van Renssalaer prize for the best lyric by a Columbia student: a poem in praise of the late Edwin Arlington Robinson. Bennett Cerf and William Saroyan, he noted with mixed feelings, were among those in the audience at the Faculty Club when he gave his "bad, short speech."

The city was intensely hot that June, and Berryman longed to escape to the country. But he had three courses to take over the summer if he was to graduate on time. He sent a sheaf of poems off to *Poetry* magazine and had them returned with a comment from Harriet Monroe that he was straining too hard for his effects. Hard as it was to swallow such criticism, he knew she was right. Van Doren, however, was kinder. "Go on and strain," he told him. "Naturalness will come later." Youth was the time for strain, the time for Berryman to pull at himself until he could find "the shape which is to be yours uniquely and permanently." And not even "Delphic Harriet" could know what that shape would be.

That summer Berryman read Maxwell Bodenheim and the "amazing" Hart Crane, whose last poem, "The Tower," inspired him to compose an "Elegy to Hart Crane." On July 10, *The Nation* published the Robinson poem that had earlier won him the Van Renssalaer prize. It was his first publication in a national magazine, a six-line gem marred only by the awkward final line. The poem managed to catch not only Robinson, but Berryman as well,

> forever walking
> A little north
> To watch the bare words stalking
> Stiffly forth,
> Frozen as they went
> And flawless of heart within without comment.

Berryman's parents were away on one trip or another for most of the summer, and since Halliday could not find a job, he found himself drifting over to Berryman's apartment, waiting for Berryman to finish classes and take a break from his reading so they could play tennis or go for a swim. Berryman resumed his friendship with Jane Atherton, home from Smith for the summer, and the three of them spent a good part of the summer together. Several times Mrs. Atherton drove them out to Jones Beach in her coupe, the Athertons and Berryman up front, Halliday in the rumble seat. On one such excursion Berryman tried to finish one of his term papers by shouting his dictation out the open window to Halliday, who transferred it to a portable typewriter on his lap. Soon the situation degenerated into pure comedy, Berryman beginning every paragraph either with "Obviously," or "It is now clear," the pet phrases of his Dryasdust professor of Egyptian culture.

Sometimes the three went to the Claremont Inn on Riverside Drive to dance and watch the lights flickering off the George Washington Bridge onto the oil-black waters of the Hudson. Once they went to Radio City Music Hall to see the silver images of Ginger Rogers and Fred Astaire in *Top Hat,* and sat through the entire show twice. Another time it was Brooklyn Heights to swim in the saltwater indoor pool at the St. George Hotel, staying afterward at Halliday's apartment, "chaperoned" by Halliday's older sister. That night Berryman borrowed a pair of Mr. Halliday's pajamas and went in to say good night to Atherton. Halliday heard shrieks of protest, and soon Berryman emerged from the room frustrated and muttering to himself.

For his two English courses that summer—Continental Literature and The Development of the English Novel—Berryman received "A"s. To show his Egyptologist professor in The History of the Ancient Orient what really mattered in life, Berryman wrote him a long poem on Egyptian religion for his final and received a "B" for the course. After classes ended in late August, Berryman worked again on Miss Dangerfield's "tripe," browsed through the city bookstores, and continued to write and revise his poems. One afternoon he and Atherton went up to her roof to take snapshots of each other, and Berryman wrote a bad *carpe diem* poem called "The Photograph," modeled on Hart Crane's "At Melville's Tomb":

> And this the hour: what will be said of you
> Later is rumorless, content to give
> All eye to the now as progress, and will throw
> No question to the toneless hush of the grave.

He spent five hours with Atherton one evening and finally managed to undress her, though she resolutely refused to sleep with him. He repeated his performance the following night, and then the experiments stopped. On September 23, sure by then he was in love with her, he drove up to Smith College with Atherton and her mother in the coupe to help Atherton settle in.

Three days later his last year at Columbia began. He would have to take six courses and get "A"s in five if he was to graduate the following June. He took Van Doren's Shakespeare course, Weaver for Renaissance, Edman for Metaphysics, and retook Odell's Modern Drama. He was surprised and pleased to hear shortly afterward that Edman had told George Santayana, the onetime teacher of Wallace Stevens and a poet himself, that Berryman was a real poet. Berryman also took the yearlong required sequence in the Romantics and Victorians with Emory Neff. From the first day, however, when Neff dryly intoned Wordsworth's verse, Berryman knew it was going to be a long year. Neff quickly ruined Wordsworth for him, and soon Berryman was writing Halliday that the poet's full name must have been "Words worth Shit." If Neff made life difficult for him, however, Berryman repaid him in full. He was sarcastic, ironic, aloof, haughty, and tripped Neff up whenever he could. Worse, he got his friends to do the same. And just in case Neff tried anything funny, Berryman decided to keep a complete journal of his reading for the class.

Edman's seminar on Plato, on the other hand, was heaven. The small, intimate seminar met weekly at Edman's West Side apartment, with Brahms, cigarettes, and wine, while the class discussed the *Charmides, Taches,* and *Meno*. Berryman also loved Van Doren's lectures on Shakespeare, and wished Halliday could hear "VD be VD day after day." He worked on a long autobiographical poem called "Prospect," another imitation of Hart Crane. By then he was so enamored of Crane that he thought of writing a biography of the poet who had killed himself just two years before by jumping from a ship. "Anonymous memorial," he wrote,

> to those
> Who flowered in the noon and in the evening
> Held colloquy with the ending sun and sank
> To their great peace and were inscribed.

He read Dante's *Vita Nuova* in the Rossetti translation, F. R. Leavis, Archibald MacLeish, Henry Roth's *Call It Sleep,* T. S. Eliot, Yeats, Pound, and William Carlos Williams, whose style he saw as lying at the antipodes of what he himself was after. He wrote poetic tributes to Shakespeare and several that sounded like a mixture of Eliot and Auden ("Your roads are trampled by desires/ Mixing mud with conflict. . . ."). He reviewed Auden and Isherwood's *The Dog Beneath the Skin* for

*The Columbia Review* and began reviewing for Joseph Wood Krutch at *The Nation*.

By the time he was two weeks into the semester, however, Berryman was going on four hours of sleep a night in order to keep up with his courses. He was so tired, he told Halliday, that he was meeting himself "coming and going." Moreover, he was now definitely in love. The only girl he cared for, he confided to Halliday, was Atherton, and now he wanted to marry her. Every day he wrote to her, but heard little for his effort. He saw Elspeth again, and then berated himself for his unfaithfulness. But a few days later, his resolve gone, he necked with Elspeth in her apartment (the first time ever) only to be forbidden by Elspeth's aunt from seeing her again. Then several "sweet" letters arrived from Atherton.

On October 25, he turned twenty-one and his mother threw him a champagne party in their apartment. Three of his teachers were there: Edman, Weaver, and Van Doren, as well as many friends: Winanne, Elspeth, Aylward, Giroux, Crandall, Rockwell and, most important, Atherton. He wanted her desperately, and it crazed him that she remained so elusive, aloof. He hoped somehow that his birthday would make the difference. But the birthday turned out to be a disaster. Many years later he would recall bitterly the night Steve Aylward took his Atherton "up to the roof of my apartment building . . . and kept her there hours." Unable to make it back East for Berryman's birthday, Halliday had sent him a telegram, timing it to arrive at the height of the party. The celebration, however, had ended early, and the telegram arrived when only Rockwell, Aylward, Atherton, and Berryman were still there. Hearing there was a messenger downstairs, Aylward rushed past Berryman, ran down the stairs, grabbed the telegram, and read it aloud while Berryman was still signing for it. Then Berryman grabbed it away from him and walked back into his apartment with Rockwell, while Aylward sat out in the hall, a broken Berryman wrote Halliday two days later, "with the girl I love at my party on my birthday." A friend just wasn't *made* "of stuff like that," he added, forgetting how often he'd played the same game himself.

For Berryman, however, the real betrayal occurred the following night, when he took Atherton to a formal at John Jay Hall. He danced only two numbers with her before Aylward cut in and disappeared with her. "You can do a lot of looking and dying in three hours," he wrote Halliday. Finally, at 2:00 A.M., the two showed up, Atherton looking drunk and Aylward looking "sneaking and dishevelled." Berryman's first impulse had been to smash Aylward's face, but he could not bring himself even to look at him. He and Atherton had been over to Alpha Delt house, Aylward explained. But since Alpha Delt included some of Berryman's worst enemies, the news did not soothe him. The upshot, Berryman explained to Halliday, was that he was abandoning a long autobiographical poem he had been working on. Too much in his life had changed for him to go on with it.

"How did we break it off," Berryman would write thirty-five years later, the sad music of that evening still audible to him:

> Did she date somebody else
> & I warred with that & she snapped 'You don't own me'
> or did the flare just little by little fall?
>
> so that I cut in & was cut in on,
> the travelling spotlights coloured, the orchestra gay,
> without emphasis finally,
> pressing each other's hand as he took over.

Only afterward did the others understand how deeply Berryman had been hurt. Atherton wrote explaining that she'd simply had too much to drink and had passed out. Aylward, she insisted, was completely loyal to him. Besides, he would have to understand that he did not own her and that she was not in love with him. For his part, Berryman vowed never to utter Aylward's name again, and even thought of taking his own life. Aylward, sick at what had happened between him and Berryman, tried to apologize, but Berryman froze him out. Berryman stopped shaving, lost sleep and weight, and soon it was clear even to his teachers that he was in very bad shape. He managed to avoid Neff, afraid of what he might say to his teacher in his present mood.

Again it was Van Doren who helped Berryman through his crisis. When he saw Berryman in his Shakespeare class, Van Doren knew something had gone terribly wrong. He took Giroux aside afterward and told him he was ready to talk with Berryman if he could be of any help. That afternoon Berryman spent three hours with Van Doren, in what turned out to be "the best talk I've ever had with anyone except for three or four of our classic conversations," he wrote Halliday afterward. "Somehow he managed to send me out of his office feeling absolutely straight and right with myself and outside, beyond it all. That sounds like incredible shit, but it's true."

Atherton herself came down to New York the following weekend to talk with Berryman and tell him she was not in love with him, though she hoped they might still be friends. The trouble with Atherton, he grumbled to Halliday afterward, was that she had "no conception of the social contract." Now that he had been hurt himself, he told Halliday, he was sorry for his own insensitivity and promised always to remain loyal to his friends. "Van Doren and I agreed . . . that loyalty (trust, faith, fidelity, call it anything) is the most important thing there is."

Quickly now Berryman recovered his equilibrium and returned to his work. He took his mother to see Eisenstein's *Ten Days That Shook the World* and Clair's *À Nous La Liberté*. He became more and more amazed at Shakespeare's genius. Here indeed was writing that could not "be learned and can't be written" except by a handful of the great, writing that "swells and transcends sound and was deathless when it began." Hopkins had something of this rare, powerful music, as in the opening stanzas of "The Wreck of the *Deutschland,*" as did Donne, in his sonnet "At the round earth's imagined corners." It was Mark who had opened this world for Berryman, and Berryman had responded by offering Mark his friendship. He felt now that he could talk about anything with his teacher, "without awkwardness or constraint," and that counted for more with Berryman than any relationship, he consoled himself, he might have had with a woman.

In November he reviewed Auden and Isherwood's *The Dog Beneath the Skin* for *The Columbia Review,* describing its satire as "mature and relevant . . . witty, bawdy, unexpected, mordant, weird and immediate." The play was the best thing these "young English Communist writers" had so far written. In December the magazine carried Berryman's "Notes on Poetry: E. A. Robinson and Others," a review of Robinson's posthumously published *King Jasper,* in which Berryman particularly praised Frost's introduction. Robinson Jeffers, on the other hand, he accused of being a fascistic misanthrope.

But most of his comments he reserved for the twenty-one-year-old winner of the Yale Younger Poets Award, Muriel Rukeyser, for her *Theory of Flight*. Her book, he wrote generously, while uneven, was "the most effective and diverse [new] poetic talent" to be "displayed . . . by an American in some time." And though she was his exact contemporary, "her passions, political and personal" were based on a "wide experience" he knew he himself did not possess. If no "single poem here [was] uniformly good," he added, the blame was to be laid to Hart Crane, who had proven to be "both a good and an unfortunate influence" on Rukeyser's work. For while Crane's "deft, liquid phrasing never obscures the component words," still, "the successive logical disintegration in his poetry" was partly responsible for Rukeyser's failure to achieve an "effective unity" in hers. Consciously or not, Berryman had defined his own practice as well. It was "reassuring," he closed, again pointing obliquely to himself, to know that England did not have a monopoly on "the eloquent young."

Just before Thanksgiving he drove to Northampton with Mrs. Atherton to see Jane, angry with himself to find, in spite of his resolve, that he was still in love with her. But when Atherton gave a cocktail party in New York for the millionaire Bobby Winslow, to whom, it turned out, she was now engaged, Berryman finally understood. "There's no help for us," he wrote Halliday, "we're going to fall in love with bitches, and we're going to be hurt, to the last syllable of recorded time." Better to be free and open with one's love, to be cynical and just plain promiscuous. In fact, he told Halliday, he'd just gone to a tea dance at Barnard and had run into a young woman named Jean Bennett, who had confessed to him that she'd had "a *burning passion*" for him since June. Well, he added, not willing to be burned again so soon, time would tell what would come of that.

On New Year's Eve, 1935, Berryman, dressed in white tie and tails, went with Atherton (this was an old obligation) and Halliday down to the Van Dorens' Bleecker Street apartment to help ring in the New Year. Just before midnight the critic Clifton Fadiman arrived with his gorgeous new wife and several bottles of champagne, calling for highball glasses all around, which he filled. There were the traditional strains of "Auld Lang Syne" and the too-sudden downing of large amounts of champagne, and soon Halliday was following the wife of one of the guests up the stairs and into the bathroom and then carrying her into the bedroom with all the coats stacked upon the bed as if it were some royal divan. In a few moments he was stalled over her as he heard her murmur to him, "Please do, please do."

Suddenly there were sounds in the hallway, and Halliday sobered up enough to picture his head being staved in with a magnum of champagne. He managed to stumble upstairs into Van Doren's study, where he found a volume of Spender and read it until he passed out. When he woke up, it was 3:00 A.M. He went downstairs to find the party over and Atherton and Van Doren talking quietly before a fire in the living room. Berryman too had passed out and was sleeping it off in the guest room, so Mark made Halliday and Atherton breakfast before Halliday escorted Atherton home in a taxi and then took a subway back to Brooklyn. Later that day, still hung over, Berryman left the Van Dorens to continue his New Year's visits in his rumpled tuxedo.

Yet despite this wild and irresponsible streak in Berryman, there was his earnestness as well. On January 10, a bemused Van Doren, writing to his old friend Allen Tate, mentioned that Berryman had been studying Tate's poems and had come into his office earlier that day "with the most serious look on his face—as if there were a tripod in the room," and had said, "Mr. Van Doren, you know Tate is one of the very best poets we have!" Van Doren knew that that meant Berryman would soon be after him to borrow Tate's new book of poems.

Two weeks later the Columbia faculty awarded Berryman the Euretta J. Kellett Fellowship to study at Clare College, Cambridge. He would have two years in England to read, on a generous stipend of two thousand dollars a year. Now, in spite of illness and severe insomnia, Berryman began cramming for his finals. This time he was rewarded with "A"s in all his papers and exams. The first half of his hell year was over, and he was still on track. After exams he went up to South Kent to tell the news to Old Man Bartlett, who was, Berryman reported to Halliday, "properly ecstatic."

He was even beginning to feel educated. "As you know,"

he wrote proudly to Halliday in the same letter, "I have been accustomed for some time to compensate for a huge classical ignorance with an inordinate emphasis on the contemporary scene in so-called literature." But his reading over the past half year had come as a revelation; Shakespeare continued to grow for him, and he was beginning to understand Plato. Even Neff had taught him the historical bases of criticism and comparative analysis. He did miss time to do his own work, for he'd written no poems for the past two months. But, his mother had reminded him, "everything in its time."

By comparison, Atherton and her "omnipresent Bobby" Winslow dwindled for him into insignificance. He even argued with her about Maxwell Anderson's *Winterset,* over which she had raved. The play, he informed her, was simply miserable, and as poetic drama "unspeakable." If it was popular, that was because Americans left their minds at home when they went to the theater. "They read and see nothing but shit," he complained to Halliday, "so they have no standards of comparison." With Jean Bennett he remained aloof, until he was sure she was "desperately" in love with him. He knew it was a mean, "stupid and selfish" way to act, he confessed to Halliday, "because she's young and must not be seduced," but he was only doing to her what Atherton had done to him. He enjoyed his new freedom from emotional attachment and preferred seeing himself rather as the campus "rake and genius." The pose was pure "shit," he knew, but it seemed to work well enough.

Pushing himself as he had for weeks at a time without sleep, however, finally took its toll. Even as he began his last semester, he was down with grippe, bronchitis, eye trouble, and an abscessed ear that had to be lanced. He was so sick, in fact, that he once more contemplated suicide. Better to go out that way, he told Halliday, since he seemed "incapable of giving happiness either to myself or to anyone else."

As soon as his head stopped spinning, he wrote Richard Blackmur on behalf of the Boar's Head Poetry Society. Each year, he explained, there was an undergraduate contest for the best poem, decided by three judges. This year the judges would be Mark Van Doren (presiding), Eda Lou Walton, and Ben Belitt, and the society wanted to honor Backmur for having written *The Double Agent*. For personal reasons too, he was anxious to meet Blackmur. Blackmur not only agreed to attend, but promised to contribute a review of Allen Tate's *Reactionary Essays* to *The Columbia Review*. Berryman was delighted with the essay and wrote Blackmur afterward that it was "absolutely firstrate." He noted too that Blackmur and Tate had taken "distinct but analogous" critical approaches to the problem of "form," Tate through "insight," Blackmur through "craft." He enclosed copies of the poems and reviews he'd printed in the *Review* and apologized for not making them better. Blackmur read the poems and offered one change only. Might not Berryman employ the word "raven" as a verb in his poem, "Notation"? It was such a good word, and so little used since Shakespeare. Berryman, honored, complied. The reading itself took place on April 30, when Berryman dined at the Faculty Club with Blackmur and Van Doren, and later that evening received first prize for his poem "Trophy."

In his autobiographical work, *The Seven Storey Mountain,* Thomas Merton would remember Berryman as "the most earnest-looking man" he'd ever met at Columbia. Van Doren too, looking back years later, would remember Berryman as "a literary youth" whose every "thought sank into poetry, which he studied and wrote as if there were no other exercise for the human brain. Slender, abstracted, courteous, he lived one life alone, and walked with verse as in a trance." Merton too, Van Doren recalled, was writing poems then, but unlike Berryman, "they appeared to be by-products of some rich life he kept a secret." Berryman, on the other hand, was even then too willing to sacrifice even his health to his art.

"When a writer," Berryman wrote that May for Edman in Philosophy, "has given us satisfactory work—King Lear, say, or Moll Flanders or Ode on a Grecian Urn—we need nothing, properly, outside the work, and interest in circumstances or in the author as individual becomes recognizably what it in fact always is, vulgar and unwarranted curiosity." Blackmur and the New Criticism had done its work on him. He struggled to draw a mask over his poems and render them as opaque as he could. It would cost him years, it would cost him his friendship with Blackmur, it would even cost him his health, before he changed his mind and made poems out of the stuff of his life. By then he would also come to believe that all that mattered, finally, was the work itself, even if it cost the life.

* * *

Berryman's final semester continued the courses he had begun in the fall, with the addition of a seventh on the Philosophy of Art, since he still needed twenty-one credits to graduate. But Neff, that "great ass," as Berryman had now taken to calling him, nearly succeeded in wrecking Berryman's chances of graduating, which would have cost him his fellowship as well. All year he'd made Neff's life hell, gambling that he would pull straight "A"s in all his other courses, which would give him the credits he needed to graduate. If he got "A"s in everything else, he would only need a "B" from Neff. But Neff had come up with a plan of his own. He would hold his grades until he'd sailed for Europe, and then have his assistant post them. He planned to sink Mr. Berryman with a "C."

Again it was Mark and Dean Hawkes who came to Berryman's rescue. Clearly something was wrong. Berryman had taken top grades in eleven of his twelve courses for his senior year, had won the coveted Kellett, been elected to Phi Beta Kappa, and here was this anomaly of a "C." Neff, of course, was on the high seas, and so could not be reached. Now Berryman produced his notebooks for the course, and Mark and the others decided to give him a second examination. He "killed" it, Berryman crowed, and a committee, which included Van Doren, voted to give him a "B-," the lowest grade necessary to allow him to graduate with honors. But for the rest of his life, Berryman could hardly bring himself to utter Neff's name.

Berryman spent the summer of 1936 recuperating and writing poetry. By then he was in love ("as it were," he added when he told Halliday) with Jean Bennett, her persistence and good nature having won him over at last. He had the friendship of Mark Van Doren, had met Blackmur, had made some small mark at Columbia as a poet, and had even published in *The Nation*. Now he was ready for T. S. Eliot and the world. Soon after graduation he sent five poems to Eliot at the *Criterion*. A month later Eliot returned them all, rejected.

Berryman spent several weeks with his grandmother in Roxbury, playing tennis and resting, trying to coax his exhausted body back to health after what he'd put it through for the past year. He had "nothing to do with the assorted spread legs of the town," he wrote his mother, except talk. He managed a few poems, including one on the train up from New York, which he "modestly" hoped was a "masterpiece in the Yeats manner." He had had what Blackmur called the moment of "insight," had borrowed a pencil from a passenger, and applied Blackmurian " 'craft' to the end-leaf in my Yeats on the train." He read Whitman, Shakespeare, and *Pride and Prejudice* ("definitely one of the best—It's so big and strong that the palpable defects don't matter"). He also read with new intensity Allen Tate's "Ode for the Confederate Dead," for on July 2, amid his grandmother's memories of Great-grandfather Shaver, he began an elegy for the Civil War dead. The particular incentive for writing now was *The Southern Review*'s contest for the best long poem, the judges for which were Tate and Van Doren. Once more Berryman found himself working furiously to meet a deadline.

At first the poem refused to yield itself. Then, after two weeks of false starts, Berryman left for Uncle Jack's sister's farm in Reisterstown, Maryland. From there he went down to visit Arlington National Cemetery. By the following night he had thirty-six pages of preliminary notes, including two hundred lines of verse. Then he scrapped it and began all over again. He called his poem "Ritual at Arlington," and over the next three days he wrote 360 lines, sending them off on the last day of July, just under the deadline.

"Ritual" was his most overtly autobiographical poem to date, and a tribute to Allen Tate. In it he recalled his great-grandfather Shaver's devotion to the lost cause of the Confederacy. He evoked Lee's Mansion at Arlington and the graves of those killed at Bull Run and along the Rappahannock. Then he recalled the ten years since his father's death, marked now only by "a distant grave/At Holdenville," where only the wind blowing through the lonely cottonwoods kept vigil.

Again he rested, spending his afternoons on his aunt's porch drinking Maryland-style mint juleps, watching the tenant farmers file by, and feeling "quite decadent." He wrote Mark that the writing of "Ritual" had been for him an "achievement." A few days later he was back in New York, sitting in on Allen Tate's lectures on modern poetry at Columbia. These were mostly close analyses of poems by John Crowe Ransom, Hart Crane, and Yeats. Soon he was having long talks with Tate, whom he quickly came to like. It was Tate who introduced him to the poetry of the Southern Fugitives: John Crowe Ransom, John Peale Bishop, and George Marion O'Donnell, whom he also met and found "an appallingly able chap and very nice." It was the Fugitives' charm and brilliance, he complimented Tate, that had attracted him to them. For the first time in his life, Berryman seemed proud of his southern heritage.

Ten days after *The Southern Review* contest closed, Berryman sent a new draft of "Ritual" to Van Doren, who wrote back reminding Berryman that the revisions had arrived too late. Better, he told Berryman, to forget about the contest altogether and wait to see what happened. Six days later, when he had not heard from Berryman and thinking he might have hurt him, Van Doren sent a second letter, softening what he'd written earlier and asking his difficult student to try to understand his position. After all, Berryman was "a good guy and a good poet" and Tate thought so too. And without Berryman's presence, Columbia was going to be "barren bricks" come winter. Berryman had to know that even if he didn't win the prize, he would still be loved.

Berryman wrote Van Doren to tell him he was leaving for Canada on August 25 for health reasons: "general breakdown, nerves, blood pressure." He was going to Williamsburg, Ontario, to consult with a Dr. Locke before leaving for England. Part of the reason for the nervous disorder was the nearly inhuman pressure he'd put himself under to graduate on time, followed by the work on "Ritual." But though he could not bring himself to tell even his friend and mentor, the real reason he was going away was to get away from his mother. She was smothering him with her obsessive monologues and her inability to listen to anyone else.

Williamsburg was a spa with a reputation for treating nervous disorders, and Berryman found elderly invalids everywhere, a few of them famous, all rambling on about one disease or another. The place, he thought, looked like something out of Thomas Mann's *The Magic Mountain*. The morning after his arrival he had his first treatment "by the Ontario myth, Herr Locke," who each day saw several hundred patients. The procedure took half a minute, with Locke simply cracking Berryman's feet "without saying a word or looking at me." Soon he was having second thoughts about this restorative pilgrimage.

He stayed in Williamsburg a week, reading Yeats "systematically book by book" and hoping for some relief from his headaches. But when he felt no relief after a week with Dr. Locke, he left and went up to Quebec to the shrine of Saint Anne de Beaupré, hoping to find relief there.

Finally, he returned to New York. He had hoped to see Halliday before leaving for England, but Halliday had already left for the University of Michigan to begin graduate work in English. Back home Berryman found a letter from Van Doren, anxious to let his former student know that he and Tate had enjoyed "Ritual" and had placed it fifth out of the forty-five entries. Unfortunately the poem had proven too ornate for their tastes. He hoped Berryman might someday soon try "the bonier music of monosyllables."

Before he set sail, Berryman went to see a doctor in downtown Manhattan to have some blood work done. He had apparently visited a prostitute in the city to see if she could help his nerves and was now afraid he had contacted gonorrhea. He gave as his name "A. Ward" and his home address, and told his mother as little as he could about what had happened. Apparently his long bout with chastity had come to an end. The test results, fortunately, proved negative. On September 16, he wrote Mark to say good-bye and to thank him for the trouble he'd taken to read "Ritual." He himself now considered the poem merely "a large smear," though writing it had marked "an important personal stage" for him. Three days later, at noon on Saturday, September 19, he sailed out of New York aboard the Cunard liner *Britannic,* bound at last for England.

# chapter 4

# Mr. Berryman Goes to Cambridge

## 1936–37

As the *Britannic* churned through rough seas, Berryman spent most of his time with a thirty-two-year-old Basque journalist and political caricaturist named Pedro—or, as of the moment—Pierre Donga. Donga was returning to France after covering the 1936 elections in the States. He spoke English but preferred French, and Berryman tried to oblige him. Each day the two men talked, as they circled the ship, sat in deck chairs, or drank at the ship's bar, as Berryman felt America recede, along with its "numerous tangible and intangible claims." Day and night they worried the war in Spain and the Depression and argued "anatomy, psychology, sociology, painting [and] metaphysics" until the trip was suddenly over and Donga was disembarking at Le Havre. By then Berryman had promised to spend Christmas with Donga in Paris.

The following morning, September 28, the *Britannic* sailed up the Thames. Berryman disembarked at Tillbury, took the train to London, and spent the afternoon touring Westminster Abbey and the Poet's Corner. He walked the city streets and learned "how to use the excellent Underground and the still confusing omnibusses," then found a cheap room at the Seymour Hotel, ate dinner, and took in a variety show. London, he was discovering, was more "like a group of villages" than the huge, undifferentiated mass that made up New York. From the start England proved itself a "boon" to his creativity, for in his first few days there he wrote two poems. He was very proud of himself. On the thirtieth he walked to Tavistock Square to see if Virginia and Leonard Woolf might be willing to print "Ritual." Miss Woolf, he learned, was in the country, and he decided instead to contact her after he got to Cambridge. He began writing long letters home to his mother and the friends who mattered most to him: Halliday, Giroux, Van Doren, Jean Bennett. The letters, he decided, would form the diary of his time in England.

When he arrived in Cambridge on October 1, he found it even better than he'd dreamed. "Magnificent" modern rooms awaited him at M4 Memorial Court. Neaves (not Mr. Neaves, just "Neaves" ), the head porter, was there to carry Mr. Berryman's suitcases to his rooms, where there was a fire in the grate and everything was "clean and straight, bed made, drawers open." It was all "very welcome." What luxury, in this year of the Depression, 1936, with a civil war in Spain, and Hitler and Mussolini on the rise. What peace, in this short interim before lectures began, to sit before a fire reading Keats, while a gyp served one strong, hot tea.

Berryman's tutor would be George Rylands, M.A. of King's College, a Shakespearean and the author of *Words and Poetry,* and at once Berryman set about building himself a library, buying books mostly on credit. Where in America could one get such finds . . . and so cheaply! In London he had already found a 1925 copy of Yeats's *A Vision* (privately printed and withdrawn), and now, in Cambridge, he bought a dictionary, Empson's *Seven Types of Ambiguity,* the poems of Dryden, Arnold, Tennyson, and Louis MacNeice, Blake's prophetic works, Yeats's *A Full Moon in March,* the letters of Keats, Auden and Isherwood's new play, *The Ascent of F6,* Dr. Johnson's *Lives of the Poets,* I. A. Richards's *Practical Criticism,* and *The Oxford Book of Seventeenth Century Verse.*

"Perfection is perfection and its given name is Cambridge," he wrote Mark on the eighth. The place was "staggering" in its beauty, "austere, magnificently calm" and he was happy "beyond expression," "enchanted" with Keats's letters and as "thick with Yeats as ever, the rich true colour of the man's line, his organization and massed splendour." He liked Rylands, though he was astonished to learn his tutor had never even heard of Hart Crane and hadn't known that Van Doren wrote poetry. How he wanted to be able to write just one poem, he wrote Blackmur that same day, one poem "with all the uncanny shock of Yeats' 'Fisherman' or Crane's 'Paraphrase' and at the same time ordered strength, as Ransom or Stevens." He owed Blackmur a great debt for his essays on Yeats, having found in them "complexities and vastness" he had not known existed in the poet. But how little the English seemed to know about American poetry, even of Frost and Dickinson, who were "essential" to any understanding of the subject. By then he'd heard from Allen Tate, who explained to Berryman that he'd found "Ritual" too much like his own "Ode to the Confederate Dead." The Kenyon prize had finally gone to Tate's protégé, Randall Jarrell, for his "Orestes." Berryman magnanimously wrote Tate back that he was glad Jarrell had won, because Jarrell, after all, wrote "damn good poems." But to his mother he still insisted that he'd said "something damn important" in "Ritual," whether Tate and Van Doren saw it or not.

Soon Berryman was making new friends among his fellow students: Andrew Chiappe, Ramsay, Langley, and Gordon and Kay Fraser, owners of "a splendid bookstore" in Portugal Place in Cambridge. He reread *Lear* and "wept blindly" for "the first time in my intellectual life, over Lear's last lines." He went to the Cosmopolitan in Cambridge to see *The Immortal Swan* and began to see just how little he knew about music and dance. At a meeting with the Renaissance scholar E.M.W. Tillyard, he discussed Blake and the problem of philosophical form in poetry, and realized too just how thin and tortured his "Ritual" actually was.

The problem for the serious poet, Berryman was beginning to see, was to find the *right* system on which to hang one's poems. With this in mind, he began rethinking Yeats's symbology and Hart Crane's "dynamic materialism." His greatest struggle, though, was with the idea of God, whom he and his family had taken to calling "Beetle." The problem was particularly vexing to him because in every logocentric system he had encountered, God took center stage. The trouble with such a formulation, he noted wryly, was that he'd saved that place for himself.

On his twenty-second birthday Berryman wrote an ecstatic letter to Halliday. "Yesterday and today have been beautiful beyond any days I have ever seen," he wrote. "Full Autumn, but green, green lawns and parks, undiminished glory of gardens, and the complex splendor of the leaves falling and fallen." He had spent the weekend on the River Cam in both a punt and a canoe and it had been "like a dream, drifting . . . . under ancient bridges and the shadows of stone and wood, into the clear sunlight bordered with green." But he did not enjoy his enforced chastity. Even to talk "to a presentable girl," he sighed, "would joy me hugely." To know, really *know,* the English literary tradition, he understood now, one had to know England itself firsthand. So, he believed, Rylands could know Wordsworth as no American could. On the other hand, for twenty-five years American poetry had been "more resourceful, more interesting, more excellent" than its English counterpart. It was the English who lost out by ignoring that work.

Berryman wanted a strong and distinctive voice for himself in his poems, and to do that he meant to imitate the one poet who had summoned out of the living English tradition just such a voice: William Butler Yeats. Whenever he looked up from his desk now, Berryman looked into Yeats's stern, impassioned face, all "strength and rigorous attention." Like Yeats he would write plays, dramatic things, he explained to Van Doren, as a "mask for my life, a discipline, a stylized order." He knew he was under the influence of the Romantics, especially the questionable influence of Hart Crane, a man without "moral integrity" or "intelligence" or "discipline." But he meant to free himself of Crane by making his own poetry more objective and disciplined, more like Baudelaire's, more like Yeats's.

Armistice Day came with its commemoration of the end of the Great War and marked another sort of ceremony in England, with its stately rituals for the dead. Ceremony here was less noisy, he wrote his mother, less thumping and fascistic than parades in the States. But now there was troubled news from home to spoil his idyll. Jill Berryman, he learned, had relocated to Philadelphia by herself to begin a new job, had failed, and had returned to New York. Uncle Jack was still unemployed. So now, it seemed, Berryman's parents were living virtually separate lives. Berryman countered now by dwelling on his own growing sense of loneliness. As winter came on, he complained, the English, with few exceptions, seemed more and more "a smug and passionless people of ugly women and remote men." Alone, he took long walks with his camera, snapping photos of Cambridge and the river and sending them home.

He wrote a poem for Yeats and, after some hesitation, sent it to him, stunned when Yeats wrote back thanking him. Even T. S. Eliot's visit to Cambridge four days later paled by comparison with that polite note from Yeats. Eliot, Berryman noted, was merely an "ordinary looking" fellow whose lecture, "The Idiom of Modern Verse," he'd found "monotonous," "humorless," "shy," even "neurotic." Eliot had spoken of the "necessity of poetry to observe prose values, the values of the spoken speech of one's time," of the need to "escape blank verse in . . . verse drama." But after Eliot "gratuitously" insulted two of Berryman's favorites, Hopkins and Housman, Berryman was ready for combat in the question period that followed. Why, he asked Eliot, was it necessary to "escape" blank verse, since no one spoke blank verse anyway? Wasn't the real problem the fact that English verse drama had never escaped the overwhelming shadow of Shakespeare? Eliot agreed, but added that it was useful to rotate one's crops from time to time, and it was time now to return to a reinvigorated verse line different from Shakespeare's. Berryman apparently missed the point of Eliot's metaphor, in part because he was determined not to be awed by Eliot's "slow mind."

Though Eliot had raised one of the central issues of modern poetry—the relation of "verse to the spoken idiom of one's own time"—Berryman failed to see its practicality. Who had ever solved the problem of the spoken idiom in verse? he wondered. On the other hand, in Yeats's most recent poems, he'd detected a recognizable idiom together with a "complete avoidance of rhetoric," something he also found true of Eliot's own poetry. Even if "Gerontion" seemed closer to prose than the poem on which it had been modeled, Wordsworth's "Resolution and Independence," Berryman wondered, did that make

Eliot's the better poem? And of what use was it to write poetry that sounded like prose anyway? Whether he knew it or not, Berryman was still in the shadow of Hart Crane's orphic poetry.

The following Sunday Berryman met W. H. Auden, who, though only seven years Berryman's senior, was already recognized as the foremost English poet of his generation. Auden had come up to Cambridge to address a meeting of the Spenser Society, and afterward talked with Berryman at a party in Rylands's rooms. The two hit it off at once, and that night covered a host of subjects, including Ransom, the London production of Auden and Isherwood's *Ascent of F6,* the "damned neglect of American letters" by the English, and Tom Eliot's penchant for practical jokes, including the slipping of exploding sugar into the tea of friends, Virginia Woolf among them. When Berryman brought up the question of Yeats, he was surprised to learn that Auden's generation had read him "almost not at all." He was no Auden fiend, he confessed to his mother afterward, since Auden had written too few intelligible poems. But Auden had mastered a technique, and that had been enough to get him where he was.

But Berryman was also coming to realize that being published wasn't everything. The touchstone by which he would measure Auden, Eliot, and even Yeats would be by the example of the Great Dead: the blessed circle of poets who had gone before him. In the long run, the moderns would have to be measured against such touchstones as Crashaw's "Hymn in Adoration of the Blessed Sacrament," a poem of amazing honesty and craft without the disfiguring rhetoric that blighted so much modern poetry. Here was language that sang in its own sphere apart. What matter if it served no practical necessity? Such music was its own reason for being. If only one could be content to write in secret as Crashaw had, avoiding the "self-deception and pretension" that fame brought with it.

No poet, he understood, no matter how good, was without his imperfections. Even Yeats had made egregious errors of taste in assembling *The Oxford Book of Modern Verse*. In his introduction, for example, had not Yeats extolled such nonentities as Herbert Read and Oliver St. John Gogarty over the worthier Moderns? The problem was, as Berryman saw it, that even Yeats had not read deeply enough in the poetry of his time, so that he had—"most staggering defect of all"—excluded Wilfred Owen from the canon. Nor did it help matters to find that, except for Pound and Eliot, Yeats had also excluded the Americans.

On November 26, Berryman took his American friend Kay Fraser to Trinity Hall for a traditional Thanksgiving dinner. Some one hundred Americans, all studying at Cambridge, were invited, and it turned out to be a warm and convivial time. The occasion was all the sweeter because it came in the midst of the terrible war news out of Spain. With Germany, Italy, and Russia now all involved in Spain's civil war, Berryman was afraid there would be a general war in Europe by the beginning of the new year. If war did come, he realized, both he and his brother would probably have to fight. But, he told his mother, before he did that, he would take Bob and Halliday and go off to "shoot mongeese in remotest Canada."

By then Berryman had ceased attending lectures altogether, calling them a waste of time. Instead, he read Henry James: *The American, The Aspern Papers, The Turn of the Screw,* and *Portrait of a Lady,* "one of the finest novels in the language." James's late style in *The Ambassadors,* with its near absence of statement and its endless qualifications and ambiguities, also intrigued him. In addition, he read Mencken on *The American Language,* listening for the subtle and extensive differences between English and American speech rhythms. He knew he was here to study Chaucer and seventeenth-century literature, but what was the point of being here if all one did was "follow American graduate school grind-teeth curricula?" All he really wanted to do anyway was write just "one decent poem" to justify his two years abroad.

By then he was suffering again from nerves and wild mood shifts. He wrote Halliday he was afraid something was seriously wrong with him, and characterized his condition as a form of manic depression: "mental instability, fits of terrific gloom and loneliness and artistic despair alternating with irresponsible exultation." One moment he was frivolous, and serious the next. He missed Jean but was still not sure he was in love with her. He hated his enforced chastity and complained that the girls at Cambridge's two women's colleges—Newnham and Girton—

would have nothing to do with him. He was sure the fault lay with them, and in any event Englishwomen were "horrible, dull . . . and graceless."

Mark wrote to cheer him up. He'd heard Dean Hawkes telling an alumni committee about what happened to Kellet fellows like Berryman. They seemed to "go through definite stages." First: they were all lonely and bewildered. Then, after several months, they became busy and enthusiastic. Eventually they turned serenely mature, and by the end of their second year they were happy to come home again, though they also seemed to find English girls to marry.

In the meantime Berryman pondered "by the fire for hours over the question of time and life and God . . . reading Revelations and Job and the New Testament" and wondering whether he would ever accept Christianity, as he "passionately" wished he could. There was no justice anywhere, he grumbled to his mother, "no compensation here and nothing beyond." All was "greed, starvation, darkness without memory." People were like bats striking walls blindly as they waited for the end to come, "some generously . . . some without ear or tongue or sight," some "in anguish unspeakable."

On December 12, while spending the holidays with the Frazers in Cambridge, he met a young woman at a local tavern named Christine or, more familiarly, Bunny. He invited her back to his room (separated from the Frazers) and there ended his long sexual abstinence. Years later he would joke about his unseemly haste as due to "a prepotent erection brought overseas/ needing to be buried in you/ C B, my delicious amateur/mistress of a young interne in London"). On the twenty-second he finally wrote his mother that he'd been living "in a fog of ease," sleeping late, having breakfast in bed, and reading Elizabethan drama. But he was more direct with Halliday. He'd had a very good time these past ten days lolling about with a "young & gorgeous artist . . . with quite the best body (& the most accomplished) in the Empire." It was nothing serious, but "mutually admiring & fun." Bunny was engaged, though her fiancé, "a nice chap who went down from St. John's last year," didn't seem to mind his presence.

Then he was off to spend the holidays in Paris with Pierre Donga. On the three-hour Channel crossing he started up a conversation with an Irish medical student and his female companion, and soon the talk turned to a young Welsh poet named Dylan Thomas, whom the woman seemed to know quite well. Berryman had read Thomas's poems and found them "fairly good." But it was strange to him that this Welshman, a man exactly his own age who spent his time alternately contemplating the flights of seagulls and drinking "madly" until he went "blind for weeks at a time," should already have begun to turn into the stuff of legends while he himself had nothing to show for his own efforts.

Berryman arrived at the St. Lazare station at six that evening and waited an hour; when Donga did not show, he went to Boulevard Haussmann, the address at which he'd been writing his friend. When he got there, however, it turned out to be only Donga's mail address. By then it was getting late, and Berryman decided to get off the *métro* at the next stop and find a place to stay. He found a cheap room on the sixth floor of a hotel at 4 Rue Cadet, just off the Faubourg Montmartre, settled in, then went to the Paris-Folies and saw *Le Gangster de Cannebière*. Afterward he went to a bar and drank.

When he woke on the morning of the twenty-fourth, he was suffering from a terrible hangover. He went for a walk to clear his head, collected his mail at the American Express office, then went back to his hotel. At three-thirty that afternoon Donga finally showed up. Since he'd last seen Berryman, Donga had married and was already separated. He was writing for a number of Paris newspapers, including *Le Rappel*. He apologized for not being able to offer Berryman better hospitality, and was glad Berryman had found a room. In the three months since they'd seen each other, it was clear Donga's enthusiasms had found other outlets. After Donga left, Berryman went to the movies and watched the world news and two feature-length films. During intermission in the nearly empty theater a baritone boomed out Christmas cheer.

Christmas Day, alone and miserable, Berryman ate fried bread and butter, drank a "marvellous" French hot chocolate, smoked a package of Celtiques, and spent the afternoon writing to his mother. In the evening he felt a vague urge to pray, and wondered cynically to whom he might pray. Instead, he ate, went for a long walk around the district, then returned to his room at half past ten and wrote Van Doren. Paris was "light, bright, delightful" after England. He understood better now just how far he had yet to go if he was ever to become a poet. Unlike Auden, however, he was not interested in writing political poems, which he dismissed as mere hysterical venting. Instead, he preferred "the engraved perfection" of a Vaughan and "the inevitable mountain of Shakespeare": an older, tragic literature, which he hoped one day to restore to its proper place. Alone in a strange country at Christmas, he also wished he could share in the glow of Mark's familial happiness.

But the following day a play began forming in Berryman's head. He called it *The Architect,* and listed the names for his characters: Blake and Sandra Puritan, Prescott North, Zelma Van Riper, Jane Bishop. He modeled one female character on Jean Bennett and chose the name Hugh Severance for the character most like himself. He was anxious to follow the classical unities, but by the time he had plotted the first act and written several blank-verse speeches, he'd already increased the list of characters from five to seven. He decided to set the play in a New York bar called the Random. At one in the morning he tried to get some sleep, but his mind would not stop racing. Instead, he got up and went back to work.

All next day—the twenty-seventh—he stayed in bed writing. Not since he'd worked at "Ritual," he wrote his mother, had his brain been at "such valuable heat." He tried threading three separate dictions together: the "inanities" of cocktail talk, the nondramatic verse he had employed in "Ritual," and the "free, large general rhetoric" of the Elizabethan and Jacobean dramatists. He knew the play had autobiographical elements, especially as "certain persons & incidents remarkably resemble things in my biography." But he was not, he insisted, Hugh Severance.

The play ground to a halt the following day when, after "raising hell" at the Paris branch of the Chase Manhattan Bank, he finally got his money transferred and was able to make a withdrawal. Flush, he took a taxi to meet Donga for lunch at La Maxeville on the Boulevard des Italiens. He saw construction work going on for the '37 Paris Exposition and walls covered with Anti-Franco propaganda; he explored the Seine and some of its thirty bridges, then the Champs-Élysées. New Year's Day he strolled along the Left Bank, in the evening going to the Champs de Mars to study the outline of the Eiffel Tower. The following day he visited the Tomb of Napoleon and saw Louis Jouvet in Molière's *L'École des Femmes* at the *Athénée,* counting thirty curtain calls for Jouvet before a full house. It was "the finest dramatic performance" he'd ever seen. Over the next week he and Donga and a young reporter named Marguérite Desseigue met each morning for breakfast and talk at the Dome—"the celebrated postwar Hemingway place" near his hotel.

He felt "magnificently filled" with poetry, he wrote Halliday on the second, now that his "days of starvation" were over. For the four days he'd been penniless, he'd had to go without food and cigarettes, and since then it had been "impossible to get enough to eat." He had come in that very evening, discovered he was still hungry, and gone out again to eat, enjoy a cigar, and drink a bottle of Haut-Barac. Half-drunk now, he was determined to "outrage Anglosaxon convention" by telling Halliday how much he loved him.

Berryman left Paris by rail, took the Channel steamer *Brighton* across to Newhaven, and then the train to London. He was glad to find so many letters and packages waiting for him when he finally made it back to Memorial Court, including two portraits of Jean Bennett, several Rembrandt reproductions, and Stevens's *Ideas of Order.* There was even money to buy the two-volume edition of Vaughan he wanted.

He was invited to address the Clare Literary Society on the topic of Yeats's development and welcomed the invitation, since he was sure he knew "as much about Yeats as anyone but a dozen critics here and in America." On January 14 he went to London to see Laurence Olivier act in *Hamlet,* but found it "unbelievably bad." Compared to Jouvet, Olivier was "meagre," having "wept a great deal" and mouthed his lines "poetically and wretchedly, without vigor or conviction."

He talked with Rylands about American critics, chiefly Van Doren, Blackmur, and Tate, all of whom Rylands merely dismissed as "desperately and unwarrantedly *earnest,*" and soon convinced Berryman of his way of seeing things. For all their "eager fanaticism and prodigal energy," Berryman now saw, Blackmur and the others had yet to arrive at a balanced judgment about literature, Blackmur himself being a man who had "spent too much of his prodigious energy dealing with the minor details of minor poets." The British, on the other hand, read more deeply. Eliot's critical habits, in truth, were British rather than American, demonstrated by his uncanny ability to stroll through an idea and then strike "to the core of the matter." That was how one should read a book, Berryman now saw: "so slowly and thoroughly that you . . . made contact with the whole creative mind and its product" by the time you finished. After all, it was England that had produced poets in such numbers that his head sang just to think of their names. Struggle as he might with Ryland's dismissal of the Americans to the point that he actually became hysterical and lost his temper with his tutor, he still had to concede that Rylands was right.

Having changed that much, Berryman went even further and dismissed the idea that there *was* a viable American verse tradition. It was not easy to have to admit to himself that the work of Crane and Tate and Blackmur was in the long view merely inconsequential, and for two nights afterward he dreamed Blackmur was dead. As he continued to read American poetry with Rylands, he came to disregard more and more of E. A. Robinson, MacLeish, and Jeffers. Even Van Doren's poems began to seem "clouded and . . . odd." The only Americans, in fact, who survived his scrutiny were Dickinson, Whitman, Ransom, and Stevens, as well as a few poems by John Peale Bishop, Tate, and Crane. He understood now that the standards for good poetry were "very high, English, very old and almost absolute." Rylands was right. America had "damn little tradition, and no myth," and the American sensibility was altogether far too "raw." The upshot for Berryman was to freeze his own creativity, for nothing he had as yet written now seemed good enough to publish.

Soon afterward Jean Bennett wrote to say that Jane Atherton was about to marry Bobby Winslow. What a "bitch" Atherton was to do that, he wrote bitterly to Halliday, still harboring deep and unresolved feelings for his old flame. At the end of January he wrote a verse epistle to Atherton, urging her not to marry such a "mild insipid man." The poem was pure Swift and Yeats, aloof and disdainful. "I am, probably, unreasonably distressed about Atherton and her imminent marriage," he wrote Halliday, enclosing a copy of his poem with the explanation that it had "naturally" lent itself to verse.

Too much energy went into women and copulation anyway, he added. Better to be like the cat he'd seen in a tea shop in Magdalen Street, unmoved by it all. How "wretched" really were a nude woman's proportions . . . and "how monotonous" the sameness of every woman once undressed: the "ineffectual skin, two nipples more or less brown, a mat of hair, and two legs that coyly open on an odorous and impatient portal." By then it was clear he had become bored with Bunny, whom he'd hardly seen since his return to Cambridge except for an occasional "orgy." His prolonged reading in Swift, that "gigantic, uncanny man, riddled with mortal pride and terrible rage," and "one of the central glories of English literature," had clearly helped shape his own misogyny.

At the beginning of February, Berryman began preparing in earnest for his talk on Yeats, scheduled for the evening of the sixth. There was so much he wanted to say, far more than he would be able to cover in an hour: Yeats's autobiographies, his translations from the *Upanishads,* his politics; he was also dismayed at how little good Yeats criticism there was. Even Edmund Wilson's much-touted essay on the poet in *Axel's Castle* he found "contemptible." Perhaps he himself was the man to do Yeats's biography.

So intense had his preoccupation with Yeats become that the night before his talk he had what he called a waking vision of the poet. He'd been reading in his rooms when his attention began to wander. "I shut my eyes and an image rose before them, not clear but strong: I saw that it was the figure of Yeats, white-haired and tall, struggling laboriously to lift something dark which was on his right side." It turned out to be "a great piece of coal, irregular, black," which Yeats raised "high above his head, hair flying and with a set expression, brilliant eyes, and dashed it to the ground at his feet, a polished ground that might have been a floor: the pieces rolled away silver." The Blakean poet, then, transforming the coal of experience into the silver of art. You could not summon such an "aesthetic emotion," he explained to his mother, but when it came, as it had come violently to him several times that week, you saw at last how each word and metaphor in the poem of a master like Yeats worked to create a "beautiful and dynamic" balance of forces.

In mid-February he saw the Abbey Players perform Synge's *Playboy of the Western World* (he judged it "the best play the twentieth century" had so far produced) and O'Casey's *Juno and the Paycock,* but was disappointed by the way the Irish players resorted to stage Irish for their Cambridge audience. O'Casey he dismissed as "a poor confused hysterical man without learning or ability" whose dramatic characters, unlike Synge's, were without "dimension or nobility."

Two weeks later Berryman met a group of "mad poets" in Cambridge, chief among them Dylan Thomas. For a week they all drank and recited poems to each other day and night. Till then, Berryman had thought Thomas's work overrated, but meeting the Welsh poet, he revised his estimation upward. Thomas reciprocated by inviting his American friend to visit him in Wales during the spring vacation. But when Berryman began staying out after curfew, he was summoned by the dean and told that his behavior was "unprecedented and heinous." It looked as if he would be sent down for breaking university rules, but then his "little escapade" was "blinked at," probably because, he told his mother, for each of the last three or four terms some undergraduate had hanged himself, "and they think me a queer one anyway and so don't want to provoke me."

The need to write one solid, genuine poem became so intense for Berryman now that he was able to write nothing. The crisis, initiated by his discussions with Rylands, was brought to a head now by his attempt to put together a sheaf of twenty-five of his best poems for Robert Penn Warren and *The Southern Review*. The blockage was not helped by seeing Dylan Thomas writing good poems even when he was drunk and sleepless. On March 15, Berryman burned "several hundred" of his poems, feeding his fireplace with one crumpled poem after another. In spite of his efforts, he believed, everything he'd written had dissolved into "mere pieces, without form or context." Reading through his early poems before destroying them, he had at least caught intimations of a style. But in what he'd written since coming to England, even that was missing.

When the crisis passed, he started again, writing, revising, reshaping his poems. Like Thomas, he began drinking more and more heavily and again going without sleep. Finally he collapsed, and the doctor had to insist that he stop drinking and rest or risk a nervous breakdown. Berryman, however, ignored the advice and continued drinking, believing that was the only way he could recover his creativity. In his creative impotence he became more and more obsessed with the idea of possessing a woman. So bad did the situation become that he wrote Halliday he'd "nearly raped the wife" of his best friend, Gordon, though, he added, no harm had actually been done. When Halliday upbraided him for the nasty poem he'd sent Atherton, Berryman excused himself by explaining that he was going "mad" in Cambridge, experiencing constant bouts of hysteria between intense periods of work. He had drunk too much with Thomas and his crew, and he was still drinking too much. He had even gone so far as to write a drunken letter to his mother, and was in fact drunk as he wrote Halliday.

He had been out of his sickbed one day when he went down to London for spring holiday. It was imperative now to get to Ireland to see the seventy-one-year-old Yeats while there was still time. He had hoped his friend Patrick Barton would go with him and show him about, but that plan soon fell through. Meanwhile, he stayed with Fitz and Arthur Vogel at 44 Cartwright Gardens in the Bloomsbury section of London while he considered what to do. He saw Jouvet in the film *La Kermesse Heroïque,* and Jessica Tandy in *Twelfth Night* at the Old Vic, and resolved to do nothing but Shakespeare when he returned to Cambridge.

He spent eight days in London, intending each day to go to Dublin but unwilling to travel alone, a prospect, he told his mother, which he found about as exciting as trudging through the bottom of Dante's hell. Finally, he took the train to Liverpool and spent "a most uncomfortable and entirely sleepless night" on the night boat, arriving in Dublin in a dark rain at six in the morning. He took a room at the Phoenix Park Hotel in Kingsbridge, ordered breakfast, then wrote his mother before he slept. Later he walked about Dublin, visiting the sites made holy by Swift and Yeats, including St. Patrick's Cathedral, where Swift had been dean and where he now lay buried. Once Parnell and Yeats had stood where he stood now, and he trembled with the realization. He found Yeats's address from the note Yeats had written him, only to learn that the Master was in London preparing one of his plays for the stage. Berryman went to the Cuala Press, where he spoke with Yeats's sister. He decided to wait for Yeats to return.

He found a cheap bed-and-breakfast place at 25 Harcourt Street, and over the next few days browsed in the shops along Nassau Street and visited the lunatic asylum at Grange Gorman, a sight he was sure he would not forget. On the evening of the sixth he attended the Peacock, an experimental Irish theater, but came away disappointed. He had gone there in hopes of finding Yeats's eighteen-year-old daughter, Anne, who had designed the costumes for the play, having a "passionate desire" to see her and a fantasy of perhaps marrying her, so in love was he with the lines her father had written for her in "Prayer for My Daughter." When he spoke with Anne after the play, however, he was surprised to find her not only mortal but rather plain.

He wrote one poem during his stay, on April 9, after visiting the National Gallery. It was titled "On a Portrait of Swift by Buidon" after the painting that hung there. That same night, when the weather showed no signs of improving and Anne was still not sure when her father would return, Berryman took the boat and train back to London to see if he could arrange to meet Yeats there.

When Yeats learned that Berryman had been looking for him in Dublin, he sent a note to him at the Vogels asking what it was Berryman wanted, implying at the same time that he was too busy to see him anyway. But two days later, on the fifteenth, Yeats had a change of heart. "Are you still free tomorrow afternoon?" he wrote. "Could you have tea with me at 4. At a little after 5 I must lie down as I am dining with a friend & I do not want to go to him tired. I look forward very much to meeting you. I thought I was returning to Sussex this morning, but my Sussex friend is ill." Berryman could hardly believe his good fortune.

But Dylan Thomas, also in London at the moment, had other plans for his friend. He found it funny how solemn Berryman could get with his talk of sipping tea with Yeats. So, a few hours before Berryman was to see Yeats, Thomas took him to a pub and fed him drinks. As the hour for the meeting with Yeats approached, realizing what Thomas was doing, Berryman rushed home to take a cold shower and straighten himself up as best he could. For the rest of his life he would remember his hour with the Master, when he had actually been permitted to light the Great Man's cigarette. In that time Yeats touched on many subjects: Swift, Indian philosophy, "artistic pessimism," Spengler, the dance plays, the play he was working on. He never revised anymore, he confided to Berryman, "except in the interests of a more passionate syntax, a more natural."

Yeats had turned out to be an even larger presence than Berryman had imagined, though "very weak now with the heart asthma from which he nearly died a year ago." The next night Berryman was back in Cambridge, the meeting with Yeats already working deeply on him. If the last six weeks had been a period of "vicious inactivity," especially the time he'd spent with Dylan Thomas and his crew, Berryman vowed from now on to work as the Master had, "without cease." From this point on, Berryman promised himself, everything was going to be different.

# chapter 5

# The Real Thing

## 1937–38

Back in February, Berryman had noticed a beautiful young woman playing—ironically—the role of the mother in *The Revenger's Tragedy*. Her name, he'd learned, was Beryl Eeman. He saw her again shortly before he left for London on holiday, this time at a luncheon at Magdalen College, and had been so taken with her that he found himself unable either to eat or speak. She was twenty years old, a former ballet dancer, a student of modern languages at Newnham, and—as he informed his mother—"the most passionate & versatile actress in Cambridge."

A week after returning to Cambridge, wheeling his bicycle into Portugal Place, Berryman saw her again. She recognized him, they spoke, and before long he was asking her to tea at his rooms the following day. He could hardly believe his ears when she accepted. "O! I had my gyp *prepare* that tea," he would sing years later. She had never met an American before, much less an American poet, she told him over tea. They talked of ancestries, of Shakespeare and Racine and her father's pioneering studies in sleep. They got along well, and then better than well. By quarter past six that evening, Berryman would remember with joy and wonder, she "had promised to stop seeing the other man."

There was of course the problem of Jean, who had recently written to say how much she missed him. It was "heartbreaking" to read her note, Berryman told his mother, and he would kiss his fiancée "senseless" when he got back to New York. For the present, however, he was busy reading "the authorities"—the Roman historians and five modern texts—preparing himself to write a "short, stylized play about Cleopatra, from a most unfamiliar and historically accurate angle," in order to write an un-Shakespearean Cleopatra. The play, he failed to mention, was for Beryl Eeman.

At the beginning of May he wrote Van Doren that he had an outline for his play, including two songs and "a hundred odd lines" completed, and was going to see about getting a local theater group to do it in the fall. He thanked Van Doren for having taken him through all of Shakespeare in chronological order, because now he had a structure by which to study the critical texts themselves. He was finding patterns in Shakespeare—"formula lines" he called them—which he thought might provide clues to Shakespeare's later development.

On the fourth he wrote his mother that he would not be coming home for the summer. It was cheaper to go to Europe, perhaps southern France, where he could study Shakespeare in preparation for taking the Charles Oldham examinations in October. In addition to receiving the most prestigious honor bestowed by an English University, the winner of the Oldham would be awarded a stipend of some seventy pounds ($350), and winning it would not only "justify" his existence in England but get him through the following year, which looked to be "most complex financially" otherwise. In the meantime there were the Mays—the first year final exams—and *Cleopatra* to finish. He wanted "frightfully" to see his family and Jean, but he had to rid himself of "this mania of spiritual absolute dependence" on them all. A summer in Europe, he thought, might do the trick. The real reason, of course, was that by then he'd fallen in love with Beryl and meant to spend the summer with her.

On May 7, he celebrated Beryl's twenty-first birthday at the Garden House Hotel in Cambridge, where he partook of strawberries and hock. They spoke of their summer together and decided on spending it in Heidelberg. For appearances' sake, Berryman would go there to see Arthur Vogel and Beryl to study German, but they would live together until Beryl's parents arrived to visit their daughter. At the end of May, Berryman vacated his rooms at Memorial Court and moved to cheaper lodgings at 34 Bridge Street, where he worked without sleep on his essay on Shakespeare's heroines for the Harness competition, handing his essay in just before the deadline at 5:00 P.M. on the thirtieth.

On the eve of his departure for Germany he finally broke the news to his mother that he was "definitely and deeply and very happily in love" with Beryl. How could he not be in love with someone so "beautiful and vigorous and graceful, with a strong, direct, skeptical intelligence, no sentimentality, but a powerful emotional nature held rigidly by will and self-examination"? For her part, Beryl had come "slowly and profoundly" to love him, and he felt as if they were already married. He had not written Jean because he had wanted to be sure of his "own mind." Now that he was sure, however, he would write. He also warned his mother not to mention politics when she wrote him in Heidelberg, and asked her to pray for their "safety among the Nazis." The following day he wrote Halliday that he was "deeply & joyously in love with the most remarkable girl" he'd ever known and asked to be forgiven for his "foolishness" over the Atherton business. By then all that seemed very far away.

A few days later, while he and Beryl were at the American Express offices in the Haymarket, Berryman was surprised to see Jane Atherton sitting in a car, waiting for her husband. They spoke, and soon Bobby Winslow himself appeared, dressed in what Berryman described as his best "gay-American-tourist-college-sports clothes," and the four of them went off to a café to talk. There was "no strain" in the meeting, Berryman noted, and Atherton seemed "to be making a good job of it," though he was convinced that life with Winslow would have to be "hell-boring."

In Heidelberg, Berryman found rooms for Beryl and himself at the Hotel Wagner. A week later he sent Halliday a postcard of the castled city. "You cannot believe a place can be so lovely," he wrote, with its "heavenly hills & woods & river & shops & people & food & coffee & beer & the Schloss & plays & Beryl & Shakespeare." Never in his life had he been so happy. He brought with him only the Shakespeare "Folio & a few odd volumes of modern text," enough to allow him to study *The Winter's Tale, The Tempest, Lear,* and *Hamlet*. He and Beryl hiked up the Heiligenberg, sunbathed at the base of the ruins of the basilica, and toured the new Nazi stadium. They acted out scenes and plays for each other, including *The White Devil,* which Beryl would perform in Norway and Sweden that September. On June 21—the solstice—they saw *Romeo and Juliet* in the courtyard of Heidelberg Castle as part of the *Reichsfestspiele* that Goebbels had assembled, and Berryman was awed by the sight of "several hundred actors storming in from four angles, brilliant lighting, fireworks at the banquet . . . drums & swords & dances & a 20-minute wordless procession to lay Juliet in the tomb." After the performance they had lunch with Carl Kuhlmann, the German actor who'd played Capulet.

But Berryman understood the dark side of these Wagnerian celebrations as well, though he was careful not to mention it in his correspondence. Nor was it a topic of conversation between him and Beryl, herself part Jewish, when they were in public. Everywhere they went in that "Hitler stronghold," they saw red flags with black swastikas flying and the clusters of uniformed soldiers, including "boys of 14 on bicycles with bayonets & guns." Berryman wrote several poems in Heidelberg, including one inspired by the ascent up the Heiligenberg, when he saw "the river's lilt" mourning "the ambitious and hysterical dust" of Hitler's regime, and another poem toward the end of their stay dedicated to Beryl, whom he called now his very "heart."

On August 4, Beryl left for Munich, and Berryman drove with her parents north along the Rhine Valley. He and the Eemans stopped in Frankfurt for a few hours and wandered through the Kaiser Dom, "the Imperial Cathedral where German Emperors were crowned for 800 years." But he was relieved to finally get through the border check and into Belgium, having witnessed the "vast network of new huge two-track highways" the Germans were building to expedite troop movements "behind the front," as well as "the immense fortification & underground defense[s] just inside the Belgian border." War would come when Hitler was ready, Berryman wrote his mother, and it would come within two years.

In the week following his return to Cambridge, Berryman wrote four poems, including a lengthy "Meditation in Rain" that he thought a "masterpiece." He wrote his mother, counseling her to do what she needed to in her failing relationship with Uncle Jack. As for himself, he told her, Beryl had become his "one chance for a full and rich and permanent (if, necessarily, desperately partial) human happiness." He spent ten days at Stratford-on-Avon seeing Shakespeare and studying the Shakespeare folios and, he told Van Doren, "such Quartos as I have, the Cambridge 1863–6, some Furness volumes, some Arden, the erratic New Sh[akespeare] as far as it goes . . . Johnson, Richardson, Hazlitt (hell take him), Coleridge, Bradley, Greg." Now he was reading *Henry VI, Richard III,* "& the first 4 comedies (in my order, Errors, Shrew, Two Gentlemen, Love's Labour's Lost), Hamlet & Lear, Measure for Measure, and the Romances." He had already read Webster, Middleton, Tourneur, *The Witch of Edmonton, The Revenger's Tragedy, Every Man in His Honour,* and *The White Devil,* "in which my fiancee has been playing Vittoria in the Scandanavian Countries (she did Gratiana in the Tourneur play)." What a world Van Doren had opened for him!

On Saturday, October 2, Berryman sat for the first part of the Oldham, writing what he called "a full and considered account" of "The disintegration of Shakespeare." In the afternoon, he wrote another essay, this one a "general paper" on "The Soliloquy." The following morning he was up early, going over *Othello, The Tempest, Henry VIII,* and *Hamlet* a final time. The second half of the test began Monday morning, when he annotated passages from the tragedies and poems, then did the same for the comedies and histories in the afternoon. He wrote essays on Shakespeare's satire, on the chronology of the histories from the evidence of the texts themselves, and another essay on *The Tempest*. Afterward he celebrated the end of the exam with his friends Chiappe and Boydell at the Corner House.

The critic F. R. Leavis was to have been Berryman's supervisor during his second year, but he declined when he sensed

Berryman's hostility toward him after one of his lectures. (By then he had no doubt heard something about this "difficult" American from Rylands as well.) The dean, either convinced that Berryman could work on his own (as Berryman thought), or—more likely—finding it increasingly difficult to find someone to work with Berryman, eventually secured the mild-mannered Elvin of Trinity to supervise him informally. Every two weeks Berryman was to meet with Elvin to discuss readings in the history of criticism from Aristotle up through Dryden. In the meantime, Berryman worked on *Cleopatra,* his Nohlike play for Beryl, concentrating on the dialogue. It would be a short play, he decided, with three characters only: a Narrator, Cleopatra, and Caesar, the action taking place in Cleopatra's "villa in Rome in 45 B.C., at Caesar's return from the Spanish war in which . . . Pompey, her first lover, was killed." The dialogue, he hoped, would be stylized and passionate like Yeats's.

Berryman awoke on the morning of his twenty-third birthday obsessed with thoughts of Hamlet and his own death. Beryl gave him a "great glass ash-tray" for his cigarettes and a knife he hoped "never to use." That fall he took Beryl to London to see *Measure for Measure*. He spent hour after hour listening to classical music, especially the Brandenburg Fifth, until he could follow its major themes. He also learned that the Harness, for which he'd sat in May, would not be awarded this time around.

The more he read, the stricter his critical standards became. When he read *All God's Chillun Got Wings* by Eugene O'Neill—the same man who a few years before he'd found so deep—he dismissed it as "erratic & fragmentary." He read Allen Tate's new *Selected Poems* and judged them to be "minor and finical as Stevens [but] with more moral pretension." But now he was hard on the English as well. When he took Beryl to hear Stephen Spender speak on "Modern Poetry," what he saw was a "tall, thin, very attractive" and very young-looking man who had delivered a "foolish talk very badly." Worse, the man had "no mind at all."

He read I. A. Richards's *Practical Criticism* and became so enraged with those of Richards's students who had preferred Edna St. Vincent Millay to Donne and Hopkins that he was convinced there was "something to be said" for a literary "dictatorship.'' Yeats and Swift were right: someone had to shepherd. He went to hear Christopher Isherwood ''set up a programme for poetic drama'' and was still angry with the man when he got back to his rooms. ''He's not the fool Spender is,'' he wrote his mother, ''but all this rant about politics and expressionism and symbols exasperates me.'' A few days later, however, when he read Auden's *Paid on Both Sides* and *The Orators,* he had to concede that Auden was ''the best British poet alive,'' even if he did too much ''damned psychologizing.'' Berryman even began reevaluating Beryl. He'd seen her at least once every day since the beginning of term, and after a month of that decided it might be better to see her less often.

Alone in his rooms reading the Great Dead or listening to his record collection, however, his spirits could revive. Here he was, he wrote his mother in mid-November, sitting before his gas fire, listening to music on the secondhand ''3-feet-high Cowey gramophone (wind-up)'' he'd bought for himself several months earlier. He might re-read Dryden or Villon or *The Ambassadors* or listen to Beethoven's Fifth or Bach or Franck or Berlioz's *Symphonie Fantastique,* as he emerged from his ''profound'' ignorance of music. How wonderful to spend one's life among such brilliant minds who asked so little of one and proffered so much.

He was pleased to hear from Robert Penn Warren that *The Southern Review* was taking five of his poems. But the best news came on the afternoon of November twenty-third, when Beryl rushed to his rooms to tell him he'd just won the Oldham and eighty-three pounds (about $425). Excited as he was, he remained outwardly cool, explaining to his mother the following day (when *The New York Times* announced the award) that he hadn't expected that much perspicacity from the examiners, whom he had earlier dismissed as two ''nonentities.''

Then, a few nights later, Beryl broke the news to him that she thought she might be pregnant. ''I hope it is not so,'' he confided to his diary. The following day Beryl returned to London, leaving a note for Berryman that, if she were pregnant, she would like to have the baby. Berryman himself was far less sanguine. Soon after, Beryl returned to Cambridge, still worried, then went back home on December 6. By then Berryman was at wit's end. ''I hope her father can advise her,'' he wrote in his diary on the evening of the fifth. "I am ignorant and penniless." But on the seventh, there was a reprieve. That day Beryl wired him two words: ILIYITCHINA POSTPONED.

By then, however, everything seemed dark to Berryman. "I am quite calm this evening," he wrote his mother as term ended, "but I can say with Baudelaire that my habitual condition is rage." And what good was such rage, he wondered, rage at "all literary fashion, all parasites, all the spurious and the touted, all vague, all worthless thought"? He was horrified by the prospect of returning to America, a "land teeming with clever people, all capable of competent and almost instantaneous extroversion." Not that England was any better, for it had turned out to be a "well-fed" and "disagreeable corpse, arrogant in its senility, fantastic in the ruined house." To make matters worse, the English borrowed American technology and cursed the givers even as they imitated them. Neither country, it seemed, really understood the other nor even cared to.

Silence seemed to be the only answer; one had to learn to live life as "a single moral act of vision" in which one worked for oneself, for the few who would understand, and finally "for the recognition and establishment of a relationship with God." So many, he saw, had sacrificed themselves for art without even their names surviving. On the other hand, what mattered was that all who had given themselves to their work had their real reward in having actualized themselves. Moreover, Berryman had come to see, there could be no real competition among the communion of artists. One did what one could:

> in the single sky
> Crashaw and Shakespeare go together by,
> Neither being foremost, both having won
> The difficult altitudes of the sun.

For the Christmas holidays Berryman stayed with Beryl's family in London. He and Beryl attended several parties, saw new films, took in the National Gallery and "rummaged in" the Keats Museum until Berryman felt "a ghoul and fled." They saw John Gielgud in *The School for Scandal,* a "decent" production of O'Neill's *Mourning Becomes Electra,* and a "damn bad" one of *Macbeth*—again with Laurence Olivier—on New Year's Eve. The night before, Berryman wrote a New Year's

Eve poem entitled "At the Year's End." All things vanished, he reminded himself once again, except for the "copper songs" one wrote.

Four days before term began, Berryman returned to Cambridge to work on a new play as well as on an essay on "Shakespeare and the Metaphysical Style." He wrote his mother, trying to assuage her feelings of guilt for not having let Bob finish at South Kent so he could follow her brilliant older son at Columbia. What was he, after all, Berryman told her now, but "a disagreeable compound of arrogance, selfishness and impatience scarcely relieved by some dashes of courtesy and honesty and a certain amount of industry." He knew how "thoroughly disliked" he was by almost everyone who knew him, and, what was even worse, nothing he'd ever published meant the slightest thing to anyone.

In mid-February, Berryman took Beryl down to London by train to see *Volpone* at Westminster. But because he'd forgotten to bring his cap and gown, they could not return to Cambridge together afterward without Beryl's getting in trouble. It was just one more example of Berryman's growing indifference, and when she got back to Cambridge Beryl wrote him a twenty-page letter telling him that she was going to leave him if he didn't change. By then he had reverted to his worst undergraduate habits, going to bed at five or six in the morning and getting up as he pleased. He broke engagements on the slightest pretext, he let his beard go, and his clothes looked as if he slept in them, which in fact he did. He ate poorly and he mismanaged finances terribly. He had four hundred pounds ($2,000) a year to live on, which was more than adequate, and still he had nothing, even with the additional funds from the Oldham. He had been rude to Beryl's parents, to her friends, to his own friends. He resented not being more highly thought of at Cambridge, but—she reminded him—who, after all, was he? If he treated her like this now, how would he treat her when they were married?

Once again Berryman tried to reform. He planned a trip to Paris with Beryl for spring vacation, followed by an invigorating walking tour of the Lake District with his young friend John Bateman. He trimmed his beard and had a new suit made for himself by Frazer's tailor. He gave a reading of John Crowe

Ransom and Wallace Stevens for the Poetry Society. He wrote new poems: "Professor of Psychology," "The Possessed," "The Sense of Guilt." But because Beryl had dared to remind him of his shortcomings, their relationship began to cool. He wrote Halliday now that his plans as far as Beryl were concerned were becoming vaguer than ever. He also told his mother that he desperately needed the kind of "moral supervision" that only she, Van Doren, and Rylands had provided. About Beryl he was silent.

Shortly before spring vacation in mid-March, he had to vacate his Bridge Street rooms when his landlady gave up the house. Fortunately, he found new lodgings at 32 Thompson's Lane. Two days later he and Beryl crossed the Channel by way of Newhaven and landed at Dieppe. He could hardly afford a vacation at that point, but he had to get out of England for a while. He stayed with Ben Brown on the Left Bank at the Hôtel de l'Univers, while Beryl stayed with friends near the Place Victor Hugo. He and Beryl took in a production of Aristophanes' *Plutus* as well as "an intolerable performance of *Polyeucte* at the Odeon." They saw Jouvet perform opposite von Stroheim in *L'Alibi*. Beyond that, Berryman spent hours along the quais buying books: Laforgue, Valéry, Stendhal, Racine, Kierkegaard, Verlaine, Torneille, Rimbaud. His French steadily improved, and he fled the "detestable" Americans in the city whenever he ran into them. He felt good in Paris, better than he had on his first trip fifteen months earlier. But he could not help noting the growing signs of war everywhere. Paris, he sensed, was quickly becoming "a city of death." He wrote only one poem during this trip, "De la Rotonde," later renamed "Paris Letter," composed at a restaurant on the Boulevard du Montparnasse. It was, he said, a poem "of absolute despair."

Back in London at the beginning of April, Berryman wrote his mother from Beryl's home in Hampstead that, because he had spent his money and did not yet have a job, he would return home without Beryl and reorient himself to America. In the meantime, Beryl would go to Italy that summer and come to America in the fall, *if* it was something they both wanted. He no longer cared how he did in his final exams, for, having won the Oldham, the exams signified nothing. Besides, he felt no debt to Columbia, for the university had refused to hire him for the fall. He'd been reading Hardy—"the poems and *Jude* and the *Mayor of Casterbridge*"—and found his own sense of fate very close to Hardy's.

When he returned to Cambridge on the 5th, he learned that his poems had been rejected by Eliot at *The Criterion*. But there was good news as well: a letter from Van Doren suggesting the possibility of a teaching position at St. John's College, Annapolis. Van Doren had written his friend Scott Buchanan, dean at St. John's, to see if he could hire Berryman for the fall. Berryman had been the best student he'd ever had, Van Doren had written Buchanan; his "appetite for knowledge and wisdom" was "enormous" and he was already "a fine poet." Buchanan wrote Van Doren to say he would see Berryman, though there were serious questions at the moment about the school's solvency.

Mark passed the news on to Berryman, explaining why he thought St. John's would be the ideal place for Berryman to begin his teaching career. First of all, he could continue his own education, for everybody there learned "Greek, Latin, French, and German" and read "Euclid and Newton as well as Homer, Dante, and Shakespeare." With that knowledge, Berryman might well become not just "a good poet" but a great and wise one as well. The emphasis at St. John's was on the tradition, in Mark's opinion "the best emphasis . . . for a living poet." Berryman wrote back at once. He had great respect for Buchanan for having begun the Great Books program, and he was willing to learn Greek and Mathematics and sharpen his philosophy. Annapolis was ideal too because Mark would be nearby in New York.

On the train, returning from his walking tour through the Lake Country, Berryman wrote a poem called "On the London Train," about the double-edged fate of those who married. Then, back in Cambridge, he found a letter from Halliday. "Halliday, I love you," Berryman wrote back. "The letter I found here this afternoon is one of the old, marvellous letters." He blessed his friend for his wit, especially since the world news was all "insolence and disorder." Bach might momentarily restore him (he was playing that composer on his gramophone as he wrote Halliday), but he was in need of some stronger discipline and order. How he wished he had more of Halliday's blessed, unthinking "enthusiastic animalism." Bob, now eighteen, had just pawned his possessions and was wandering around the country, and Berryman was worried. He worried too about money, about not having a job, about his inability to take care of a wife. For her part, Beryl remained optimistic. She had made a commitment to Berryman, but she could not help wondering if Berryman really did want to marry. He seemed to be getting more and more depressed, until, as the time for departure neared, he stopped writing to everyone.

In May he heard from Dylan Thomas. Thomas and Caitlin were settled "in a fisherman's cottage" in Wales, and his stories were due out any day now. James Laughlin, the young editor of New Directions who was publishing Pound and Williams and would soon be publishing Thomas, was coming to stay with Thomas for a few days and wanted to see Berryman. Laughlin and Berryman did meet in Cambridge shortly before Berryman's departure for the States, and Berryman gave Laughlin three Audenesque poems for his New Directions annual. A few days before the Tripos—the final exams—Berryman finally "woke up" and began to study. Suddenly, doing well on his exams and getting his Cambridge M.A. mattered very much.

Then, except for the "packing, bills, farewells, confusion," Berryman's two years at Cambridge were over. But, while all about him people celebrated the end of school term with parties, Berryman worried instead about his "acute financial strain." Unable to pay his bills, he was forced to leave behind most of his newly acquired library as collateral. It would be years before he was able to retrieve it.

On June 7, he heard from Buchanan, asking Berryman to set up an interview with him when he got back to the States. That same day Berryman wrote his mother his last letter from England. He warned her that he'd changed a great deal since she'd seen him, though the changes, he assured her, were all for the better. But he would only "begin to live again," he added, "when I get off the boat and kiss you." He needed her so that they could "reinforce each other." As his ship neared America, he would search for the New York skyline until he found it, and then everything would "be sane again." The following day he had a note from Beryl. She was so unhappy about his departure she could hardly bring herself to think about it.

* * *

On June 21, when the *Île-de-France* docked in New York, Jill Berryman and Halliday were there to greet Berryman. Crowds milled about the summer docks as the passengers streamed down the gangplanks to the New World, but Berryman was not among them. Finally, after the crowds had thinned out, they spotted someone walking slowly toward them, an umbrella under one arm, as Halliday would remember, a book in the other. It was Berryman, his head characteristically tilted to one side, sporting a reddish beard and wearing British tweeds. In a clipped British accent Halliday heard this half-stranger inquiring if indeed they had been waiting "vewy long."

## *chapter 6*

# New York & Other Betrayals

## 1938–39

As soon as he was settled into the apartment on West 115th Street, Berryman was on the telephone talking with Buchanan in Annapolis about the fall. He would be in New York after July 4, Buchanan told him, and they could talk then. Meanwhile Berryman searched for a job in New York and came up with nothing. "L'Etat (de pauvreté), c'est moi"— "I am the State (of poverty)—he wrote to Mark on June 25, in a humorous paraphrase of the Sun King's famous quip. Returning to New York had been "the most painful" thing he'd ever had to do, and Berryman was still "unsettled" about his future. The interview with Buchanan took place on July 9, and Berryman put the best face on things he could when he wrote Mark two days later that Buchanan had all but promised him a job for the fall.

Living at home likewise turned out to be different from anything he'd imagined. Bob was gone, and Uncle Jack was living with his sister in Reisterstown. Moreover, his mother had changed even more than he had. At forty-four she was lively and attractive and youthful; she was dating and was busy making a professional life for herself. She even insisted that when she and Berryman went out together he introduce her to his friends not as his mother but as his older sister. After all, with his beard and conservative dress and manner, they did seem more of an age. There was no arguing with her. If he tried, she barraged him with an incessant stream of small talk until he became ill. In the two years since he'd been with her, her non-stop talking had become more neurotic than ever.

Three weeks after he'd returned home, the heat in the apartment, together with the "strain, anxiety," and "loneliness," had become so claustrophobic that he wrote Mark asking if he could visit him at his home in Falls Village, Connecticut. He had just had an "hysterical fit" in his mother's apartment, and was afraid he might be going mad. What had caused the fit he did not say, but in fact he had discovered that the only way to stop Jill's monologues was to faint. As her verbal barrages intensified, Berryman would suddenly stop arguing, his eyelids would begin to flutter, his eyes would dilate, and he would collapse. His mother, forced to stop talking, would begin to take care of him, chafing his wrists and trying to move him to the couch or bed to make him comfortable. After a few minutes, pale and drawn, he would regain consciousness and retreat to his room.

Berryman reached Falls Village on a Saturday afternoon in mid-July and spent the next few days with the Van Dorens enjoying himself. Clifton Fadiman was there as well, and they all went to see Allen Tate and Caroline Gordon, who had rented a place nearby for the summer. The Tates took some snapshots of their visitors, including—as Mark emphasized—Berryman's beard, which he wished Berryman would get rid of. In fact, Mark was so put off by Berryman's British affectations that he avoided seeing him again for several months. He did, however, offer some much-needed praise of Berryman's new poems, and before Berryman left to return to New York, he slipped him some much-needed money.

Back in New York, Berryman sent Van Doren a new poem called "Plumage," filled with sexual disgust and despair. He sent several poems to *The New Yorker,* and again had them rejected. He applied for teaching positions at Queens College and at Princeton and was rejected at both places. He revised upward once more his assessment of American poetry, this time without considering "patriotism at all." America's "first-rate verse in the present century" was after all "far greater in bulk" than England's, as indeed he believed "it should be." If he ever put together an anthology of modern poetry, he decided, it would include "fifteen or twenty American poets" and only "six or seven" English.

At the end of July a friend of Halliday's from Ann Arbor, Jean Curtis, stopped in Manhattan for the night before sailing for Europe, and Halliday invited Berryman to join them for drinks at the Savoy. Afterward, Berryman and Halliday escorted Curtis back to the Wellington, where she was staying. The following morning, however, Curtis was surprised to find Berryman standing at the door of her hotel room. She let him in and offered him a drink while she continued packing, wondering what he was doing there. But when he made his advance, she understood at once. It took some doing, but finally she got him out the door. Halliday might never have learned about the incident except that Berryman, crestfallen, later "confessed" to him that Curtis had set up a rendezvous with him back at the hotel just before the two men had left her to go home. He'd been sorely tempted, he told Halliday, but their friendship had forbidden his going back.

Only later did Halliday learn from Curtis what had really happened. When Halliday confronted him, Berryman pleaded long separation from Beryl, compounded with aggravated sexual deprivation. In his journal the day after his confrontation with Halliday, Berryman noted that he had quarreled bitterly with Halliday over "J.C. and the Savoy." They had settled the matter—"told, accounted for, compromised, defined" it. But there had followed such an emptiness and "haggard silence" that Berryman had left Halliday without saying another word. It was a pattern, this attempt to steal women from his friends, which would repeat itself many times, each time followed by explanations, awkwardness, and mutual pain.

Beryl, meanwhile, had left London for Cortina and summer employment with the family of an Italian count. There were horror stories in Europe about the treatment of Jews in Vienna, and one about a man who had died in an internment camp called Dachau. Then things soured for her at Cortina, when the count began paying too much attention to her and the countess had to let her go. When Berryman got this news from Beryl in early

August, he went into a depression. Jill decided it was time now to take matters into her own hands and wrote Beryl's parents, pleading with them to let their daughter come to New York to stay with her and her son, at least until Berryman was on his feet again. Alarmed, Beryl promised to come as soon as she could get away.

That July, Berryman met the Campbells. Robert Bhain Campbell had been Halliday's roommate at the University of Michigan and Campbell and his wife, Florence, had come East for the summer so that he could pursue graduate work in English at Columbia. Three years older than Berryman, Campbell was a Marxist who had tried unsuccessfully to join the Abraham Lincoln Brigade fighting in Spain. He had traveled through Europe, "weeping in every capital," as he told Halliday, "especially Moscow." Later, working in Detroit, he had watched with hatred as goon squads broke up leftist and communist demonstrations and strikes against Ford and the other moguls there. Campbell was open and handsome, with piercing blue eyes and a trim mustache. A poet, his first passion was Shelley, the Romantic revolutionary. What the Campbells, for their part, first saw in Berryman was someone trying to act more English than the English. "The Tewwible Bewwyman" they called him that summer, a man, as Florence would remember, by turns "witty and sulky, entertaining and repelling, brilliantly gifted and more than a bit ridiculous." In spite of these differences, the two men formed a deep attachment and saw each other often that summer.

At the beginning of August, Berryman wrote Laughlin at New Directions about the poems he'd given him when they'd met in Cambridge two months before. They had been "early" versions of work in progress, he explained, and now he was sending finished copy. When Laughlin answered that the poems were already in press, Berryman called him at once, protesting that the drafts were "full of errors." But it was too late. "I've no readers," Berryman complained to Van Doren, "but I feel as if I'd betrayed them all."

With still no word from St. John's, Berryman began thinking of working with Orson Welles. He knew it sounded silly, he told Van Doren, but he wondered if Krutch might not introduce him to Welles. In the meantime Berryman worked on a radio version of his *Cleopatra*. Then, in mid-August, Allen Tate invited him for a visit to West Cornwall. The invitation had come, Berryman noted, in "the nature of divine grace." He spent the days driving the Tates' car over country roads, enjoying the country air and the restfulness of northern Connecticut in late summer. He read Tate's novel, *The Fathers,* and Van Doren's book of essays on Shakespeare. He visited the Van Dorens, though Mark was still a bit standoffish. He wrote poems, including a good one based on Herodotus. Then, on the twenty-fifth, there was a "most kind letter" from Buchanan telling him that there was no job at St. John's after all.

In late August, Jill moved into a larger and more modern apartment at 41 Park Avenue. She had the money now and would need a larger place if she was going to have room for her son and Beryl. The apartment, with its large back room and separate entry, would allow them all privacy. But Berryman was in no hurry to return home, and extended his visit with the Tates into September. His writing flourished there; he worked on a long poem called "Meditation" and put the finishing touches on another, called "The Trial." He wrote a verse letter to Bob for his nineteenth birthday, closing the poem with a series of wishes addressed as much to himself as to his brother. Like Bob, he too had had to escape from their mother in whatever way he could, but now he urged his younger brother to act responsibly. He wished him peace and whatever other good could be got

> From the violent world our fathers bought,
> For which we pay with fantasy at dawn,
> Dismay at noon, fatigue, horror by night.
> May love, or an image in work,
> Bring you the brazen luck to sleep with dark
> And so to get responsible delight.

He showed his verse letter to Van Doren and Tate, then sent it to Ransom. "I wished the poem had turned out more cheerful," he told his mother, "but I couldn't falsify the evidence." The more he separated himself from her, he explained, the more he was coming to trust instead on his own "inner authority."

Although he was without a job, he did have a group of new poems, besides four old ones that had just been published in *The Southern Review.* On the train down to New York from the Tates that Labor Day, he wrote an elegy for Plummer Bird, one of Uncle Jack's Maryland relatives whose death he had just learned of. But it was the true aristocrat in himself that he acknowledged in the passing of Plummer.

That Berryman had not managed to find a job by then was due as much to himself as to the Depression, his British accent and British ways and disdain for things American continuing to alienate him everywhere he went. When he interviewed for a position at *Time* magazine in October, he made it clear that, while journalistic work was beneath him, he might—*might*—consider such a job should one be offered. But, it was, he added, an "incredible" exercise, this being asked impertinent questions by strangers.

At the end of September, "looking toward Madison and Fifth" and "thinking of England," he wrote a verse "Letter to B." He had written Beryl early in August, hinting at his nervous condition and telling her that it was now imperative that she come to America as soon as possible to help him recover. Three days later, on the thirtieth, he wrote another poem to her, more urgent than the last, and called it "The Summons." On October 1 Beryl wrote from Brussels that she would sail on the nineteenth and would arrive in New York for his twenty-fourth birthday. She was concerned about his illness, but she had been in Switzerland trying to help some people whose lives were in danger. She had returned to Brussels via Basel, Strasbourg, and Luxembourg along the Maginot Line and had witnessed blackouts in Switzerland. Even the tracks over which she had traveled had been laid with mines against the possibility of a German invasion. Her parents had been fitted with gas masks, and defense trenches had been dug near their home in Hampstead. Since war was expected momentarily, moreover, she had promised her parents to return home by Christmas.

To signal the change in his fortunes heralded by Beryl's coming, Berryman shaved off his English beard. He had clung to his English experiences because England had brought about great changes in him that no one but he understood. Personally, he cared nothing for what Americans thought of him. "The men I have been talking with during these days of looking for employment are stupid," he noted, though they did have "a kind of practical shrewdness and self-absorption hideous to see."

He hated the bourgeoisie with their "sly, brutal faces," and he hated the poor, the "obvious victims" staring into showcase windows as he walked the streets of Manhattan looking for employment. By then the interviews had become for him "a sickening affair" that left him wanting to "clean out [his] mind afterwards." This was not his world. *His* world lay in the towers of Cambridge reading Vaughan and Crashaw and Shakespeare, or writing poems in his study at 41 Park.

He read in the papers of a window washer who had fallen from a skyscraper to his death and wrote a poem called "Accident." Two days later he wrote another called "Father and Son," its lines recalling his duty to write his father's memory large. If he did not attend to that memory, who would?

> The man taken this morning from the water
> Has had his turn, and he is written down
> In all the dusty offices of failure
> But one. Surviving him there is a son
> Who yet may patch the name and memory
> For annalists in the great times to be.

On October 19, Berryman wrote Mark a cheerful letter. He had decided, just that afternoon, "not to try any more at present to get a commercial position" since he was getting nowhere and was in any event preoccupied with writing poems. Instead, he would work on his "Cambridge Journal" and send it to *The Atlantic Monthly*. There were also plays and reviewing to attend to. Surely he could "average the pitiful $25 a week some bloody agency or store" would pay him. In another year he was sure to be teaching somewhere. In the meantime he had to get out of his depression or he was going to "land in a nice premature grave." The only good he'd had out of his black moods were his poems. Mark wrote back encouragingly. The important thing was to write and be ready "to take anything real that comes along in the way of a job." He cheered Berryman's new "courage" and expected it "to continue."

On the morning of October 25—his twenty-fourth birthday—Berryman began working again on "The Architect," the play he'd begun in Paris nearly two years before. That evening Beryl arrived aboard the *Île-de-France,* carrying with her his record collection. Settled into their room that night, she brought

Berryman up to date on Europe and her rescue work in Switzerland. Then, in tears, she confessed to an affair she'd had that summer, and that she'd only hinted at in her letters. Now, however, she told him about the young Italian ski instructor she'd met in Cortina.

Suddenly Berryman went into a sullen, catatonic rage. He got out of bed and sat on the floor, rocking back and forth for what seemed like hours, impervious to Beryl's beseechments. He would remember that night for the rest of his life, especially the betrayal and the wound to his own ego as he played over again the scene he had created in his imagination of some "dago" thrashing above her. Finally they reached a reconciliation. For his part, he did not think it opportune just then to mention Jean Curtis and the Savoy incident.

He saw Giroux over Thanksgiving, and they discussed Berryman's progress on "The Architect." The American number of *Twentieth Century Verse* with "The Trial" in it arrived, filled with errors. Enraged, Berryman wrote Julian Symons, the magazine's editor, quoting from Walter Savage Landor that God alone had preserved him from cutting his throat after what his editor had done to his poem. Shortly afterward, Samuel French Morse wrote asking him what he thought was distinctly American about American poetry, and Berryman answered that the American issue was in fact a non-issue.

Beryl and Berryman saw several plays that fall, including *Tobacco Road* and *Our Town,* and attended a performance of *Siegfried* at the Met. They also saw the Van Dorens at their home in the Village. To make a few dollars, Berryman tried teaching French to a young girl, but soon gave up. He reviewed Laura Riding's *Collected Poems* for the *New York Herald Tribune Books,* those five hundred pages being "the most exhausting reading" he'd ever done. A week before Christmas he began a new play called *The Dictator*. Beryl and his mother and brother were enthusiastic, Halliday less so.

One cold Saturday that December, Halliday arrived at 41 Park around noon and found Beryl, "pale and bleak, huddled on a couch," while Berryman paced "back and forth like a tiger in the middle of the big room, looking distraught and clutching a copy of Wordsworth's collected poems." He told Halliday to listen, then read out the ending of "Resolution and

Independence,'' about the leech-gatherer who refused to be discouraged:

My former thoughts returned: the fear that kills;
And hope that is unwilling to be fed;
Cold, pain, and labour, and all fleshly ills;
And mighty Poets in their misery dead.
—Perplexed, and longing to be comforted,
My question eagerly did I renew,
'How is it that you live, and what is it you do?'

He with a smile did then his words repeat;
And said that, gathering leeches, far and wide
He travelled; stirring thus about his feet
The waters of the pools where they abide.
'Once I could meet with them on every side;
But they have dwindled long by slow decay;
Yet still I persevere, and find them where I may.'

The leech-gatherer symbolized the poet, gathering his poems by dint of long labor where he could in a time of diminishment. ''That's the way I must be!'' Berryman shouted. ''That's the way I *will* be.''

When he wrote Mark in early January, 1939, thanking him for sending along his essay on the Metaphysical poets, Berryman added that he hoped the best poetry of the next decade would come to ''rely less on Donne, Inc.'' and more on the plain style of Wordsworth's ''Resolution and Independence'' and on Yeats. He too had once admired the ironic and oblique poems of those writing in the Metaphysical tradition, like John Peale Bishop, but now he thought that direction ''monstrously cramped.'' On the other hand, there was the poetry of the left to contend with, itself a far cry from Wordsworth's plain vision of things.

It was Bhain Campbell who now articulated the left's position for Berryman. No wonder *The New Masses* crowd was dissatisfied with the older visions of American poetry, Campbell wrote him, whether it was Hart Crane's apocalyptic rhetoric or Eliot's retreat to the Church. Not that Campbell blamed

Eliot. Nor did he blame those on the left "who write naively of capitalists as if they were Mystery satans, and of workers as if they were itinerant saints." But what poet, Campbell wondered, could possibly face up to the horror of Nazi Germany? Poets would have to learn to "capture the turbulence of the time with sociology and psychology," answering violence for violence. Indeed, they had a moral imperative to make things happen. In Berryman he believed he had found the beginnings of just such a style. But Berryman knew Campbell had given him too much credit, for at least *he* knew he had yet to find his voice.

Still, Berryman was closer than he realized to finding, if not a voice, then at least the beginnings of a distinctive syntax. In early January he wrote a poem titled "Nineteen Thirty-eight" and, a few weeks later, an apocalyptic piece called "Cloud & Flame." But the technical breakthrough came on the twenty-eighth, when he wrote "Winter Landscape." From the beginning Berryman understood that here he had finally done something new. He and Halliday had been rummaging through the Marlboro bookstore, looking for bargains, and had come on a remaindered book on the work of Pieter Brueghel the Elder with an introduction by Aldous Huxley. The reproductions were of poor quality, but the book cost only forty-nine cents, and Berryman bought one. It was Brueghel's "Winter" that caught his imagination, though the poem, he would later insist—correctly—was not about the painting at all but about himself and a world in danger of being crucified by the terror gathering then in Europe:

> The three men coming down the winter hill
> In brown, with tall poles and a pack of hounds . . .
> Are not aware that in the sandy time
> To come, the evil waste of history
> Outstretched, they will be seen upon the brow
> Of that same hill: when all their company
> Will have been irrevocably lost,
>
> These men, this particular three in brown
> Witnessed by birds will keep the scene. . . .

The following day he learned from Halliday that Yeats had died in southern France. An age was over. That evening and the next day he worked on a poem he called "On the Death of Yeats":

> There passed away from eye, from hand,
> The greatest among us. Let the bells toll.
> He alone saw to the core, and having seen
> Terror on all sides, was compassionate.

He wrote an unsigned memorial piece on Yeats that appeared in *The Nation* on February 4, calling Yeats the "latest, perhaps the last, master of English poetry." The piece proved to be a "most difficult labour," for he had been allowed only three hundred words and had paced up and down in his room "like a madman" trying to find the exact words to say what had to be said. For him nothing less than a major symbol had been permanently altered.

By Christmas, Berryman had the first act of *The Dictator* down on paper. The second act he finished on January 7. He planned to complete the third and final act by mid-January and spend a week revising, but twice sickness intervened, followed by Yeats's death, so that a draft of the play was not ready until February 7. By the twenty-fifth he had revised it. Satisfied, he sent it to the Brandt & Brandt agency under the pseudonym "Jonathan Grant," hoping to make some much-needed money on it quickly. But nothing came of the project.

"Remarkable verse-activity," he noted to himself at the end of February. In a few weeks, besides reworking his play, he had revised several poems, including "Prospect," "Conversation," and "The Councillors." He considered writing a pamphlet on the events of 1938 called *The Dangerous Year*. He also hoped to edit a memorial volume for Yeats and broached the subject with an editor at Macmillan, Yeats's American publisher, then began writing several critics asking for contributions. He wrote Blackmur, asking if he might reprint his essay on Yeats's late poems. He wrote Cleanth Brooks, asking to reprint his essay "The Vision of WB Yeats." He also considered writing Tate, Warren, Ransom, John Peale Bishop, Theodore Spencer, Eliot, Delmore Schwartz, Pound, and Auden.

Before he heard Auden read in New York, Berryman called ahead and asked him to read his elegy for Yeats. "I had intended to ask you for prose," he wrote him the day after the reading, and "was astonished and delighted to hear last night the poems." He wondered if he could include the elegy in his memorial volume. In mid-April he met with his editor at Macmillan. He planned three sections: elegies, essays, and analyses of Yeats's poems. The last section would also include brief tributes and an essay on Yeats and music by his Irish friend Brian Boydell. The answer came by mail eleven days later: Macmillan was not interested after all in publishing the book, and the Yeats project went the way of the others.

As the time for Beryl's departure neared, Berryman still procrastinated about their future. Living with Berryman *and* his mother while being in large part supported by Jill had not been easy for Beryl. Moreover, Berryman's nervous collapses did not disappear with her arrival. Halliday and Beryl were both treated that winter to one of these during a violent quarrel between Berryman and his mother. When it was over and Berryman had recovered, he and his mother carried on as if there had never been an argument. Finally, Beryl confided to Halliday how distressed she was that Berryman had not changed after all. When she was not with him, Halliday could not help noting, she seemed lighter and freer. How gravely beautiful she was, and how beautiful her speech. No wonder Berryman had changed his American English in an attempt to imitate her English. She was witty, sensitive, and intelligent, and she moved with all the grace of a dancer. Yet all this Berryman was about to let slip from him forever while he continued to worry over his future.

On April 2, Berryman saw Beryl off on the *Normandie*. She wore a bouquet of white iris, a bon-voyage gift from the Van Dorens. The day before she left, Berryman had written a poem about the anxiety he was feeling as she returned home. It was called "Departure & Storm." When she wrote Berryman, twice, on the return trip, she tried to sound cheerful, but in truth she was heartbroken. On the tenth, toward midnight, she wrote from Hampstead. Amid the chaos at home and abroad, her play, which had seemed so important to her, now seemed like so much "tripe." Mussolini had just taken Albania. Could war be far behind? She pictured Berryman, indecisive as ever, standing there on the dock on tiptoe "waving little love-signs" to her.

On the sixth Berryman went to Columbia to hear Auden

read with Louis MacNeice and Christopher Isherwood. Auden, Berryman noted, appeared unaffected and at ease in a "most dilapidated suit" and read "extremely well" from the poems of Rimbaud, Rilke, Kipling, Yeats, and Spender. Again he read his elegy for Yeats. MacNeice seemed "dark, vain" and "nervous" and "read miserably" from Housman, Graves, Lawrence, and then himself. Isherwood, "bright [and] undistinguished," read "at tedious length from a China diary." Before the reading Berryman had called Auden, asking him to read "Our Hunting Fathers," and Auden had complied, saying that "someone" had requested the poem. When Berryman went up to him afterward, Auden apologized for not recalling his name.

That night Berryman dreamed he was in a train on his way to Dublin. He saw an old woman trying to look younger than she was. He had found some money, and people began pointing at him, accusing him of stealing it. Suddenly he was back at South Kent School, except that the place had become a morgue. He was watching silent films with the other kids as he used to do on Saturday nights. Then, just as suddenly, he was at the end of the whip on the skating pond. The whip picked up momentum. Soon he knew he would be pulled from the rest of the boys and would "fall and be killed." He screamed that he was all alone, pleading with the others to help him, but no one seemed to hear. Then he was lying awake in the darkness of his bedroom, sweating and terrified.

With Beryl gone, he worked hard to lose himself in his work, writing and sending out poems to the quarterlies. Columbia offered him a teaching assistantship for the coming year. It paid only a thousand dollars for the year but he accepted, meanwhile hoping a better position might materialize elsewhere. On April 25, he had another piece of luck. Delmore Schwartz, author of *In Dreams Begin Responsibilities* and a rising star at *The Partisan Review,* stopped by 41 Park. As poetry editor of the magazine, Schwartz told him, he was interested in printing some of Berryman's poems. Berryman was immediately impressed by the man's intelligence and vividness. One thing they spoke of that afternoon was the violence Schwartz found running through Berryman's poems. Yes, Berryman wrote Schwartz the following day, it was no accident that his poems were violent, since violence was the mark of the times. Were not the newspapers and the radio reports continually forecasting violence? How then could poets avoid the issue, particularly on the eve of another world war?

When he wrote to Van Doren a few days later about his meeting with Schwartz, Berryman told him he'd never liked "anyone better at first sight." He enclosed three new poems, noting that two were about the very "principle of violence which occupies so much of my book," but that the third, "Disciple," which he'd written only the day before, consciously sought to avoid that violence. But the new poem, which was about Christ's crucifixion seen from the perspective of one of the disciples, did not, after all, really avoid violence. Like all of Berryman's poems, it too contained a barely suppressed rage and terror.

On Sunday, May 7, sitting on a bench at the southern entrance to Central Park before the statue of the nineteenth-century figure of Humboldt, Berryman composed "The Statue," a poem about the elusiveness of fame and the failed poet. In fact, the poem was about himself, a man whose name, he feared, would be lost to the future, so that he too would one day simply

> close his eyes
> Mercifully on the expensive drama
> Wherein he wasted so much skill, such faith,
> And salvaged less than the intolerable statue.

Four days later he composed another poem, this one based on random items caught in the insane mesh of the news of the day. He called the piece "World-Telegram," which had found juxtaposed in the columns of the daily paper the following items: the opening of the 1939 World's Fair in Flushing Meadows, a Ceylonese man with a tail brought to the fair "in the interests of science" to be gawked at by the mob; difficulties with the Rome–Berlin military pact; machine guns being set up in Harlan County, Kentucky, by the local militia against a mine strike in which several miners had already died; a six-year-old Indian girl in Lima who had just given birth to a boy by Caesarian section; a father and son crushed against a loading platform by a truck while the rest of the family looked on. Each day people read such things, Berryman wrote, but did they understand what they read and what the papers told people of themselves? And if they really did understand what they read, might not such nightmares "Curry disorders in the strongest brain,/ . . . Stop trains, break up the city's food supply," and "demoralize the nation"?

In the next few days he wrote a poem addressed to Delmore Schwartz, another called "Revivalist," then another about his illustrious great-grandfather and his lost dream of the Confederacy. On May 21, he left New York to stay with his uncle Jack's family at Fountain Valley. Mostly he spent his time lolling on the verandah with a drink or reading his aunt's lovely bound sets of Dickens and Thackeray and catching up on a year's correspondence. But shortly his idyllic regimen was shattered by a violent argument at breakfast, and Berryman let it be known that he would no longer put up with the family's "blind fable and superstition." By then he had had enough talk about the "niggers and Jews" and the superiority of southern manners, and he had stormed out of the dining room, feeling, as he confessed to Halliday, "extremely sour." Living with Uncle Jack—he called him John Angus now—and his family was like living "in a world of reminiscence, peopled by the ill and the dead," where the same old stories made their daily rounds. From then on he stayed close to his study, where he knew the others dared not disturb him.

On the thirtieth he wrote "World's Fair," a poem about his father. While in New York, he had gone with Halliday out to Flushing Meadows on several occasions to see the international exhibits and enjoy the rides. One evening they split up, each forgetting where they were to rejoin. While he waited by the roller coaster for Halliday, Berryman became aware once more of his father and thought he saw him, the man "loved once, long lost" now "in torn images," whose fate could still rob him of his peace. What the poem also veiled was his anger at his mother for betraying his father, a betrayal he saw now in terms of some ancient tragedy of doomed beginnings, ignominious endings, and sexual theft, all ending in an untended and forgotten grave:

> The Chast Mayd only to the thriving Swan
> Looks back and back with lecherous intent,
> Being the one nail known, an excrement;
> Middleton's grave in a forgotten place.

He pictured himself in the poem standing angry, exhausted, and alone, while couples mounted the roller coaster of life for the "complex drug of catapult and fall," seeking to "blot out" what they could not "understand/And never [would] forgive."

On June 9, Berryman attended a high school dance with Ingreet Butler, age seventeen, a neighbor of his aunt's in Reisterstown. He had become friends with the Butlers and needed some diversion from his regimen. And though he had not done much dancing since his college days, he found himself dancing with Ingreet Butler through the night. Afterward he was startled to see that what he was doing was not so different from what his mother had been doing in dating someone so much younger than himself. The "horrible coquetry of aging women" matched exactly his own inappropriate "lust."

But he could not get Ingreet out of his mind. In a poem called "At Chinese Checkers" he wrote of Ingreet's haunting, musical voice as they played Chinese checkers one night. He tried to sound fatherly in his concerns for her, but what he really felt was something else:

> The shy head and the delicate throat conceal
> A voice that even undisciplined can stir
> The country blood over a Southern hill.
> Will Ingreet's voice bring her renown, bring her
> That spontaneous acclaim an artist needs
> Unless he works in that solitary dark?

On the twenty-second he wrote a poem called "For Ingreet Butler," another Yeatsian imitation employing the *ottava rima*. This time he came closer to writing a prayer for the young woman's protection and tried as best he could to see her as a sister. It was another of his night poems in which he could see nothing of what lay in store for him. After he left Fountain Valley, Ingreet wrote him and once or twice he answered her letters, and that was that. But even thirty years later, when a critic, eager to understand the allusions in "At Chinese Checkers," asked him who Ingreet was, Berryman snapped that it was none of his damned business.

At the beginning of June Berryman had written "an extremely stiff letter" to Margaret Marshall at *The Nation* about the quality of poetry they were publishing, and was surprised when she wrote back "as to a long-lost son," suggesting he take over as poetry editor. It paid almost nothing, but it would be an "admirable thing" to do, he thought, and he accepted. When Delmore Schwartz learned that he had taken the editorship, he wrote suggesting Berryman go for broke and ask Wallace Stevens for a poem. Berryman did, and Stevens sent him the poem, "On an Old Horn." He liked the poem very much, Berryman wrote Stevens, though the meaning of the last lines escaped him. Stevens wrote again, explaining that if one arrived "at a state of chaos," and no longer had "a belief on which to rely," there still remained "the fundamental animal." What Stevens had gone to the trouble to explicate were the lines, "Pipperoo, pippera, pipperum . . . The rest is rot."

Berryman also wrote Ransom, Warren, Auden, Tate, and others requesting poems. By the end of June he had poems from John Peale Bishop and Auden. Auden had written him on Thomas Mann's stationery, and for a moment Berryman felt as if he'd entered Valhalla. He himself sent ten poems, mostly early work and all unpublished, to Laughlin for Laughlin's 1939 New Directions annual. "For God's sake," he pleaded, "don't refuse RITUAL, whatever you do." It had already suffered "a distinguished career of rejection," in part because it had been "a bit hot to handle." A week later Laughlin wrote back accepting seven poems and returning three. Among the poems he had rejected was "Ritual."

For the first time since his return to America, Berryman was actually making money. On the twenty-fifth he sent ten dollars to his mother and gave his Aunt Ethel twenty dollars to pay for his meals. By then he had written eighty letters and rejected in one day thirty groups of poems for *The Nation,* "all with notes." Now he heard from Halliday saying that he'd lost his woman to a man named Dow. On July 1, Berryman sent a verse letter to console his friend:

> If after all your conjuration, pleas,
> Fraudulent calm and walking on your knees,
> Still she will not be had, won, yours—move out,
> Ease from that tangle your exhausted heart,
> And to the steady, the unspeakable Dow
> Let her go, let her go.

Bhain Campbell, visiting his in-laws in New York that summer, wrote to say how disappointed he was to hear that Berryman was in Maryland. Come fall, he would begin teaching English Composition at Wayne University. He had been offered $1,700 the first year, with an increase to $2,000 for the second and $2,400 for the third, more than double what the University of Michigan would have paid him for the same period. It was also, Berryman realized, far more than Columbia had offered him. Hoping there might be something for him as well at Wayne, Berryman went up to New York on July 5 to talk to Campbell.

A few days later he wrote Beryl, explaining that he had at last diagnosed his fainting spells. They had been caused, he told her, by the strain of prolonged sexual abstinence. For the sake of his health, then, he had decided to have an affair with a woman named Harriet, a close friend of the Campbells. Beryl was to understand that this was being done strictly for his physical well-being and that his heart was still hers. Actually "Harriet" was Florence Campbell's younger sister, Annette. In mid-July he drove to Grand Marais with the Campbells and Annette for the summer, stopping first in Detroit for an interview with Dr. Hillberry, the English department chairman at Wayne University. Berryman was told that he could have the job if enrollments warranted it.

By then, however, the relationship between Berryman and Annette had dissolved into a farce. Halliday ran into the Campbells at the Michigan League cafeteria in Ann Arbor on July 19 and was surprised to learn that Berryman, who—he thought—was still in Fountain Valley, was sitting outside in the Campbells' Oldsmobile with Florence's sister. The following night the five of them had dinner together and before long Annette was asking Halliday if she could stay with him. Halliday took her back to his apartment, then called to tell Berryman that Annette was staying with him. Outraged, Berryman lied that the woman had syphilis.

The following day there was a conference with everyone present except Berryman about Annette's fate, when it was decided that Annette would stay with Berryman and the Campbells. Berryman and Halliday shook hands stiffly, and the two couples drove off for the blue waters and sandy dunes of Grand Marais. In Ann Arbor, Berryman had managed to write a poem

The young John (Smith) Berryman and his mother, Martha (Jill), Oklahoma, 1916

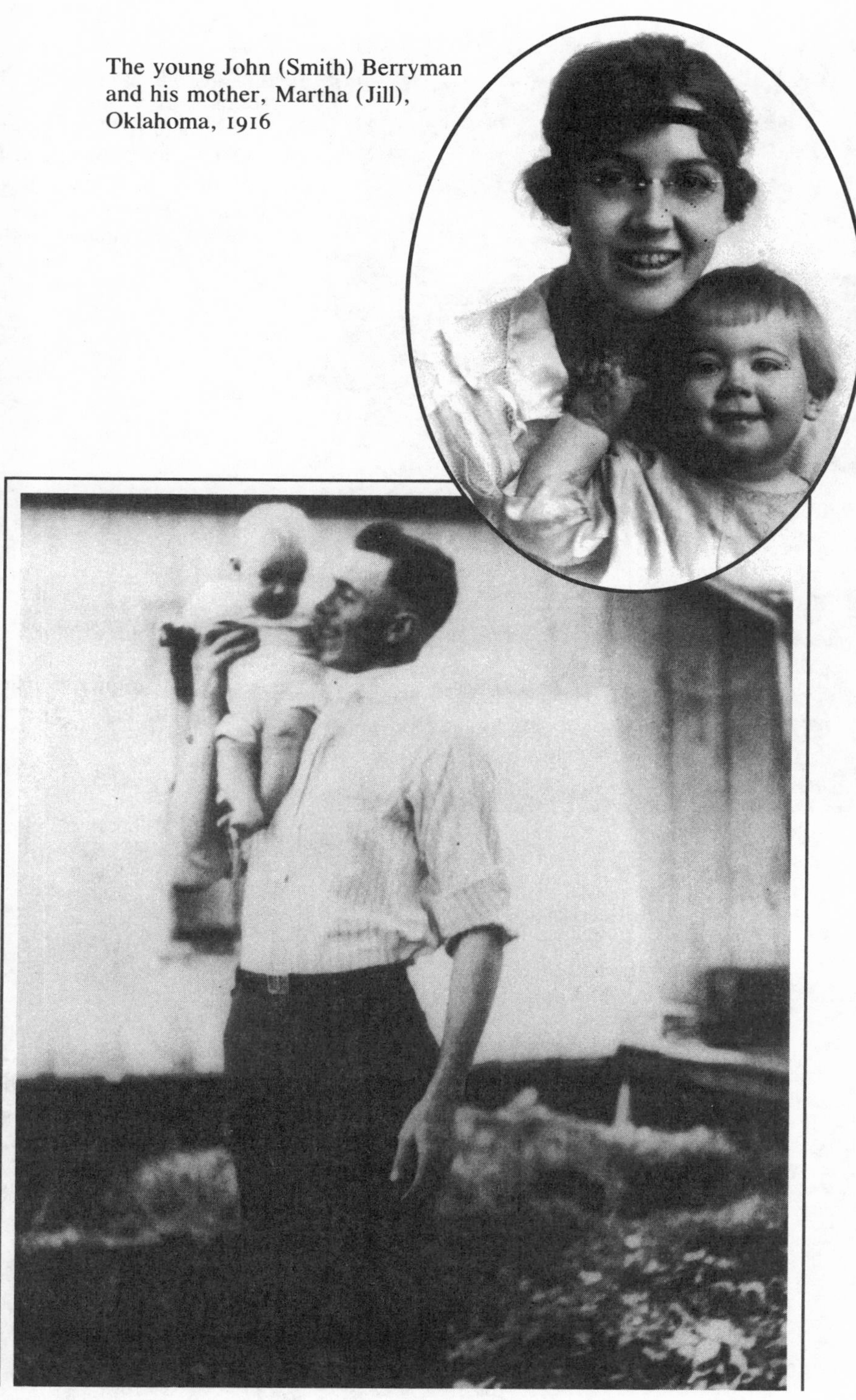

John Berryman and his shadowy father, John Allyn Smith, Oklahoma, 1915

Jill and Captain John Allyn Smith in command of Battery E, 160t Field Artillery, Fort Sil Oklahoma, about 1924. Lon afterward Berryman woul remember his dead father as tha "summer soldier."

Five-year-old John (Smith) Berryman in boy's military uniform. Photograph taken at Corpus Christi, Texas, March 9, 1918.

John Berryman with his brother, Robert Jefferson, 1920, in Oklahoma

An awkward, geekish John Berryman, 13, graduating from the eighth grade at P.S. 69 in Jackson Heights, Queens, June 1928. His seven-year-old brother, Robert Jefferson, stands next to him.

Berryman with his brother and their "Uncle Jack" Berryman in front of their apartment in Jackson Heights on the day of Berryman's graduation, June 1928

John Berryman, aged 17, photographed with the Fifth Form at South Kent School, Connecticut, in the fall of 1931. Berryman is in the first row, far left.

E. Milton "Milt" Halliday, Berryman's closest friend at Columbia and afterward, until betrayals on both sides ended their friendship

Mark Van Doren, Berryman's mentor at Columbia, the man, Berryman acknowledged with deep gratitude, who turned him to the study of Shakespeare and, even more significantly, to the writing of poetry

Jane Atherton on the roof of Berryman's apartment, with Grant's Tomb in the background, 1935. Berryman himself took the picture. "How did we break off, now I come to it," he would write at the end of his life. "Did she date somebody else/ & I warred with that & she snapped 'You don't own me'/ or did the flare just little by little fall?"

Berryman's first fiancée, Jean Bennett, 1936. His "little Jean." She burned all his letters after they broke up, then later offered her apartment for the wedding reception following Berryman's marriage to her friend Eileen Mulligan.

Berryman and Pedro (Pierre)
nga on board H.M.S. *Britannic*
ing the heady Atlantic crossing
September 1936, with England
d two years of Cambridge on a
Kellett Fellowship beckoning

Berryman reading in his spacious rooms at M4, Cambridge, England, December 1936, just before he took up with "the most accomplished body" in all of England

about the divided self called "The Animal Trainer," arguing there with his heart, which he threatened to leave and live instead in the "steady and exalted light of the sun." But heart had insisted on having the last word. Even if his heart made life hell for him, Berryman knew, he could not live without it. He dedicated the poem to Van Doren, the one man he knew who had managed, he thought, to marry head and heart.

On July 24, Berryman reached Grand Marais. Awaiting him were a pair of shoes he'd ordered, some books, including a copy of Yeats's *Last Poems,* letters from Halliday, Bob, Aunt Ethel, some literary correspondence, and three letters from Beryl. She was heartbroken by the news of Berryman's affair, though she tried to be philosophical. She hoped he would keep the thing as quiet as possible and asked him to be honest with "Harriet" and care for her and not get her pregnant. She also asked him to send back her play.

A week later Berryman was writing his mother that Annette had "turned out to be neurotic," causing all of them "no end of difficulty and elaboration." They'd located "an admirable house cheaply" and were settled on "Blue Superior, [with] a bay, a spit, dunes, Northern winds and sun." What a place this was, he told her, "where granite resists the lake and our type of thinking ends." Bhain's friend Kimon Friar came up from Chicago with his family and rented a house nearby, and over the next two months they all picnicked, swam, danced, and drank at the local fisherman's bar.

Meanwhile, Berryman continued writing new poems: "Caves at Dieppe," "River Rouge," "Wind and the House," and a long one called "Wave & Dune." That poem remembered a walk at sunset across the dunes, when Bhain had shown him how to let himself go and fall backward toward the water below:

> Halfway the height we hang, on the dune's face
> Digging our heels in, leaning back

as through nothingness, until the warm sands rushed to embrace him. He loved Bhain's animal trust and instinct, traits that did not come easily to himself. Years later, Berryman would remember this walk in the best short story he ever wrote, "Wash Far Away."

He was glad he'd come to the Upper Peninsula, he wrote Van Doren on August 20. The "burst of energy" he'd had in Maryland had continued, and his book of poems was "half again as large" as when Van Doren had seen it "and far far better." The northern landscape was spectacular. "Miles of dune and wood, deer, Northern sun and Northern fog and last week the most remarkable electrical storm I've ever seen." The town —what was left of it—was "directly on Superior, once a lumbering centre" which had "collapsed decades ago," leaving nothing now but five taverns. He and Campbell swam "and curse[d] the mails," but mainly they wrote. He had even taken up the study of Greek. Schwartz had lent him an old text, and he was at last "getting into the Iliad." It was "a most brilliant language" and he spent hours walking up and down the dunes "chanting and feeling Homeric." He told Van Doren about Wayne University. He would be making seventeen hundred dollars, he explained, and would be able now to send for Beryl.

A few days later Berryman heard from his brother, who had been hitchhiking cross-country. Bob was wondering if he might come to Grand Marais for a few days and Berryman wrote back "enthusiastically." For the next few days the two brothers walked along the dunes and had long talks together. Then, on the morning of the twenty-ninth, Bob left to hitchhike his way back to New York for a job interview. The following day Berryman received a Western Union telegram. AM IN CHEBOYGAN GENERAL HOSPITAL, the message read. NOTHING SERIOUS BUT WOULD BE GLAD IF YOU COULD COME. Berryman was sick with worry as the Campbells drove him south all next day. Mostly they drove in silence, with a red moon hanging above the pines, as Berryman recalled in a poem he wrote afterward called "Travelling South."

That night they reached the tiny hospital in Cheboygan. There was his brother, his face swollen and purple-black, a hole where his front teeth had been. All day and into the night Bob had hitchhiked until, exhausted, he had fallen asleep along U.S. 27. At half past one in the morning, a '35 Ford driven by a man named Gordon Babcock had struck him as he slept, knocking out four of his upper teeth. Gordon's brother, Archie, thought at first that maybe they'd hit an animal. But when they turned the car around, they found a hunched figure rocking in pain, blood pouring from his mouth. Then they packed Bob into their car and took him to the police barracks and the hospital. It was a week before Bob could be released in his brother's care.

Berryman made three trips that week to see Bob. He even tried locating the Babcocks through the Michigan State Police and drove to Wolverine looking for them, hoping to make them pay for his brother's bridgework and hospital bills. He found another Babcock brother and an aunt, but they "knew nothing of any insurance or the accident or where Gordon might be." They were "close-mouthed, like hill people," Berryman wrote his mother in disgust. Finally he had to let the matter go.

Afterward Bhain, Florence, Annette, and the Berryman brothers drove to Bhain's parents' place on Union Lake. Then Berryman and his brother took the train to New York. "Trouble," Berryman had written in his poem, "Travelling South," "but trouble that would soon be past." He knew the Headsman had once again come close to taking someone he loved away from him forever. For the time being, however, Berryman had been made to understand, the Headsman had merely brushed against his brother and then moved on, indifferently looking for someone else.

## *chapter 7*

# Alone in a Tormented City

## 1939–40

The day after the German invasion of Poland, Berryman wrote a poetic meditation on his fears for Beryl's welfare. He set the image of wartime England against the primal vastness of Lake Superior as the nights continued to grow longer and colder:

> Children were sent from London in the morning
> But not the sound of children reached his ear.
> He found a mangled feather by the lake,
> Lost in the destructive sand this year
> Like feathery independence, hope. His shadow
> Lay on the sand before him, under the lake. . . .

He was back in New York at his mother's apartment on East Ninth Street two weeks when Bhain wired that Berryman had the job at Wayne. He would have three classes at ten, eleven, and six in the evening on Mondays, Wednesdays, and Fridays, besides an evening class from seven to nine that met on Tuesdays and Thursdays. That came to thirteen classroom hours a week. Frightened by the prospect, Berryman went to see Van Doren, who advised him to work hard, keep steady, and not let himself get depressed. It would be tough going at first, Van Doren warned him, but things would improve in time. Then Berryman took the train to Michigan to begin teaching.

When he wrote his mother from Union Lake the following Sunday, Berryman told her he was finding teaching "absorbing" and much to his liking. But elsewhere he would remember the terror of his first day of classes and how the kindness of one of the older professors who had taken the time to introduce him to his students had helped steady him. Since he would not receive his first check until mid-October, he borrowed five hundred dollars from a local bank to help pay for his mother's move to a new apartment, get Beryl through a rough stretch, and repay Columbia some of the tuition he owed them. He also enrolled in two graduate courses at the University of Michigan at Ann Arbor.

At the beginning of October he and the Campbells moved into a third-story walkup at 5421 Third Avenue in the heart of Detroit. The apartment was pleasant and cheap and only four blocks from the university. But after the first few days, he began to feel the burden of teaching and class preparation, which now became "exhausting and continuous." What bothered him most was that his 131 students kept him so busy that he had no time for poetry. He managed one poem called "Communist," but had to abandon an elegy for Freud, who had recently died in London. Nor did he get on with the other faculty members, most of whom he considered idiots. He began to lose weight and withdrew more and more into himself. Unable to sleep, he walked the streets until the early hours of morning, drank alone, then slept a few hours until his classes began once more.

At first Berryman and the Campbells got along fairly well. The men played handball and were often joined by Florence for chess in the evenings. But eventually Berryman's mood swings got to them, and his enforced chastity made him irritable and wolfish. On one occasion he turned to them and snapped that, in his opinion, a man was "nothing but an ambulatory penis." He treated Florence either with an "almost archaic delicacy" or simply dismissed her. To help alleviate tensions in the fragile household, Bhain introduced Berryman to Mary Jane Christenson, one of his students. She joined them for dinner each week, after which Berryman, according to Campbell, would maneuver her into his bedroom with the door shut for several hours.

Still, as the pressures of teaching mounted, Berryman's seizures returned more and more frequently. After each attack, he would retreat to his bedroom for several days. Once, Florence sat with him through the night, holding his hand, to help him cope with his tormenting anxiety. "I am more and more lonely and more and more tired," he wrote Delmore Schwartz. "My University work has increased, I'm not very well, and there is no one here to talk with except Campbell, who is nearly as busy as I am." The only pleasure he still had was knowing that he had turned out, after all, to be a good teacher. But he was about to turn twenty-five and had been bitterly mulling over what Eliot had said about that age separating the poetasters from the poets, knowing he had little enough to show for himself. Delmore wrote back from Yaddo to remind Berryman that he was indeed a member of the sacred priesthood of the imagination and that he should do everything he could to survive the coming war for the sake of his art. At that point, Berryman hardly felt like a priest of any sort.

But bad as things were for him, they were far worse for Beryl. In mid-October he heard from her that she was about to become an air-raids-precaution warden in Hampstead. She described the balloon defense barrage over London and the constant presence of British aircraft overhead. She had been working on her German and Italian in case she was needed as an interpreter. Gordon Fraser was a staff officer for the medical corps in Cambridge, and others whom Berryman had known in Cambridge were now in the British Army.

Months earlier, James Laughlin had had the idea of putting together an anthology called *Five Young American Poets* that would include five promising poets—four men and a woman—none of whom had yet published a book of their own. Berryman held off, hoping to publish his own book with Allen Tate's help, but when that project fell through, Laughlin nudged Berryman again. The other poets would be Elizabeth Bishop, Randall Jarrell, W. R. Moses, and George Marion O'Donnell. But Berryman continued to hold off, telling Laughlin that he was in no hurry to publish a book. When Tate got wind of this, he assured Berryman that he and Jarrell were the best poets of their generation and urged him to get into print as soon as possible. Even Auden, Tate reminded him, had first been published as part of a group with Isherwood and Spender.

Meanwhile Berryman continued to write poetry with the little spare time he had. Ironically, even Bhain's communism and his communist friends finally had their effect on this most antisocial and private of poets. At first Berryman had managed to hold Bhain off with irony, but in late November he began writing several communist pieces. On Thanksgiving eve, sitting in a local bar called the Morocco Club with the Campbells, he wrote a piece on labor unrest in Detroit called "Lockout." "Shall Labour/Rejoice?" he wrote,

> Or curse? Shall Labour spit that turkey?
> In an elaborate spot on Six Mile Road
> The men at the bar and the women on the couches
> Are dancing, drinking, singing vainly.

Then, in early December, Berryman collapsed. Feverish and unable to sleep, he awoke at 3:00 A.M. on December 6, and began writing "A Night Piece for Delmore Schwartz." "From my bed, stupid with pain, I see a light," he wrote, invoking the apocalyptic image of goon squads busting up the unions in the city. There was no way he could evade any longer the angry crowds gathering outside his window:

> My muscles are uneasy, from side to side
> Exhaustion takes me on the tedious bed.
> The sedatives have had no effect on me.
> Roar and retreat of traffic in the street—
> My head is spinning . . .
> The goon squads roam and strike.

He decided to go in with Laughlin on the condition that he would not have to write an introduction to his poems. Hearing this, Delmore offered to write an introduction for him. A few days later Berryman in turn wrote Laughlin that, though he was so ill he wanted to "scream and smash things," he was in if Delmore did the introduction. He'd heard that Elizabeth Bishop had refused to join the group, and he urged Laughlin to persuade her to change her mind. She was too good a poet to lose.

For ten days Berryman retreated under his covers while

Campbell took over as many of his classes as he could while also teaching his own. On December 16, too weak to take the train, Berryman decided to fly to New York. He had never flown before, and Campbell, who drove him to the airport, seemed far more excited by the prospect of flying than Berryman did himself. Campbell watched as Berryman's twin-propeller transport taxied to the runway, the ground trembling as the engines roared for takeoff. After the plane had lifted off and disappeared into the night sky, Campbell began a poem, "A Letter from the Airport." He recalled his and Berryman's six months together, unified by images of the rivers and lakes they'd seen together: a Greek restaurant above the Hudson looking toward Manhattan; swimmers at dusk at Grand Marais, the glacial rock, the Arctic lights, the "chill gale hissing at our stumbling feet" as they climbed to the top of the dune and saw Lake Superior vast and blue stretched out before them; the view from the twentieth floor looking down on the Rouge and Detroit rivers at the Ford assembly plant where seven years earlier men desperate for work had been cut down by machine-gun fire. As a poet, Bhain reminded him, Berryman had a moral responsibility to come down from his lofty, melancholy heights and join the fight for social justice:

> The plane is in the air. Your intellect
> Ascends, above the dark wing and the engines.
> Man's movement is political. Look down
> On cities starving toward their time. Look down,
> As long as you can see, look down, look down:
> This shape is red, and like a beating heart.

For his part, Berryman stared out the window as he hurtled along at the rate of two hundred miles an hour, seeing the pulsing outline of Detroit, then Buffalo, and finally New York, "beautiful clusters of fairy lights hanging in space, winking, laid out in ordered lines like a Marxist heaven." But when he reached his mother's apartment on East Thirtieth Street, he collapsed. He did, however, manage to get up from his sickbed to meet Delmore at the Museum of Modern Art to see the Picasso exhibit. Earlier that day, Delmore had gone out to Brooklyn to visit Auden, and Berryman had to wait two hours with Delmore's new wife, Gertrude, for Delmore to show up. By the time Delmore arrived, Berryman was so weak he fainted. Delmore, who had a habit of attributing Machiavellian motives even to those closest to him, told his friends that Berryman had fainted because he—Delmore—had been invited to Auden's.

Otherwise, Berryman spent the holidays in bed. On Christmas night he fell and hurt himself so badly that his mother called in a doctor to examine and sedate him. Since mid-September, Berryman had put off writing to Beryl. Now, the day after Christmas, he wrote to tell her of his "general nervous collapse." Both Campbell and his mother had called in doctors, but no one seemed to be able to find anything the matter with him. Yet he knew he was "restless and nervous in the extreme, half the time unable to sleep, uncontrollably irritable," and sedatives merely left him feeling stupid. He put the letter aside. On the twenty-ninth Tate drove to New York, bundled Berryman up, and brought him back to Princeton with him to see the year end. On January 2, Berryman flew back to Detroit, the city he had taken to calling hell.

Late in January, 1940, Berryman had a letter from Beryl, chiding him for having worked himself too hard. She was now an understudy for a production of *Desire Under the Elms* and was studying first aid with a surgeon. England was preparing for the German offensive in the spring, and she was worried about her relatives in Brussels. Had he received the Yeats volume she'd sent him for Christmas? She thanked him for sending the Picasso catalog. But still he held off writing her, retreating more and more deeply into himself. He loved her, or believed he did, but—like his father—she had gone away. The Campbells heard nothing more of the woman Berryman had so often spoken of as his "wife."

Studying a map of Africa, he noted in his journal that "every square foot" of the continent was "owned or 'protected' by some European Power." If he ever got a study of his own, he promised, he would hang a map of Africa there to remind him constantly of "human oppression, human intolerance, human greed." On February 7, he began a long poem that would intermittently occupy him for the next two months. It was called "A Point of Age" and, heeding Eliot, it looked back over his wasted life. How was it that at twenty-five he had wound up in Detroit, he wondered, alone in a tormented city filled with strikes and police corruption? At last he was ready to confess to his father's ghost that even his name was a mockery and betrayal of his true origins. He summoned his warrior ancestors, Ethan Allen and General Shaver, and then the crucified Christ, as his witnesses. As paralyzed as he was, he promised to get on with his life once more. He asked only to be allowed to exhaust himself in doing something "honorable" before he joined his father in death.

When she did not hear from her son for six weeks, Jill flew out to Detroit on the pretext that she was in the area on business. What she saw shocked her. Berryman was pale, emaciated, feverish, and depressed, and several specialists had already been brought in to examine him. A few days later, on February 16, Dr. Gene Shafarman (a friend of Bhain's and a fellow communist who had been treating Berryman free of charge) told Berryman that he had been diagnosed as having a mild form of epilepsy called *petit mal*.

Strangely the news comforted Berryman. At least his illness had been real and had a name. "I learnt yesterday what it is," he began another letter to Beryl. "I think I kept quite calm, but small things all day sent my spirits to ebb. Epilepsy—it is nothing but a word, and the condition seems slight. . . . Today the knowledge has somehow brought me back to life: I read with absorption for the first time in weeks." He was resolved now to forget about fame and get on with his poetry while there was still time. Then he put aside that letter as well. If the "brainwave machine" was right, he wrote his mother, what he had could be treated easily enough and he would still be able to teach. The real annoyances were insomnia and a general sense of fatigue.

Then Berryman learned that the Campbells were about to vacate the apartment—filthy as it was, he noted—in effect deserting him. Let them go, he shrugged. He would move into better quarters as soon as he could find them. But the reason the Campbells were moving out was because Berryman's behavior had begun to frighten them to the point where they'd taken to sleeping with a chair wedged against their bedroom door. After they'd gone, Berryman busied himself reading in the large, empty apartment while snow descended over the city. "A page of good prose is a beautiful thing," he noted as he read Hawthorne again. "I wish I thought I could write one.

Perhaps I one day will—prose is not a young man's art. The massing of effect, the order, the justice, come with age if at all. Shakespeare, even, matured into his prose.'' Professional photographs of himself arrived by mail, including one—mustached, pale, inward-gazing, the *poète maudit,* the very thing itself—which he sent Laughlin for his proposed anthology. ''How unpleasant, imperfect and fascinating one's appearance is,'' he wrote. ''I would like to be reconciled to mine, but I think it is not possible.''

Now too the nightmares returned, and he awoke nightly ''retching with grief.'' He spoke to no one but his students, with whom he was ''all right'' as long as the conventions and proper distances were observed. He suspected he did not really exist for them as a person anyway, but merely as a facilitator, a grader. He taught, held office hours, then returned to the cold loneliness of his apartment.

At the end of February, Bhain wrote Halliday that Berryman was still at odds with the world and doubted that ''the contest'' would ever be settled. At least the world didn't seem ''likely to cry uncle, and no other possibility offers itself.'' Poor Berryman, ''alone in that vast damned stripped apartment, paying forty a month for five rooms and living in one.'' As for that mysterious illness, ''after five hundred bucks of medical attention'' for which he would never have to pay Gene Shafarman a penny, all Berryman really needed was two teaspoons a day of calcium lactate for his diarrhea: ''the milk of the mother, I take it, who has set him at war with the world.'' Bhain, at least, sensed the real source of Berryman's troubles.

Though he and Berryman were not talking, Bhain took it on himself to write Laughlin on his friend's behalf. Laughlin should know, Bhain wrote, that if he did not hear from Berryman, it was because of his ''curious illness.'' He would not have written, knowing Berryman would think him disloyal, but he was afraid that Berryman's unwillingness to speak or write to anyone, even his refusal to read his mail, might be taken as a sign by Laughlin that he no longer cared about the New Directions project. The truth was that Berryman did care, and once Berryman shook off his despondency and inertia, Campbell was convinced Berryman would be grateful for those who had stuck by him. He knew Berryman needed ''human affection desperately,'' even if all he seemed to know were ''methods of loss and separation." He knew that he and Florence were Berryman's only friends in Detroit, but he'd done what he could until he'd "wearied beyond patience." Someone else would have to help Berryman now.

Besides, it was Bhain who was going to need help. In early March he learned that the small growth that Shafarman had discovered on his left testicle the year before was cancerous and would have to be removed at once. A week later he wrote Halliday from Grace Hospital in Detroit to say that he had "suffered an orchidectomy, which is to say the removal of my great and tumorous left ball." So intense was Berryman's isolation by then that he did not hear of Campbell's operation for several months. Moreover, by mid-March he had moved into another apartment on Second Avenue.

Despite his depression, Berryman continued to teach conscientiously, often giving his students the attention of a private tutor. Even the dean told him he was the best instructor he'd ever had. He even managed an occasional review and a few poems that spring. Easter came early that year, and he ate his dinner that day alone at a local restaurant. Waiting for his waitress, he grew exasperated and began a poem called "Easter, 1940." The Resurrection, was it? And his father moldering in Holdenville?

Man outward watches: on the table-top
Reflections, accidents in the hot air,
The incorrigible fat woman, the delay,
The restaurant men are aging day by day,
Contorted faces turn as a cup and saucer drop. . . .
The Resurrection, as the waitress calls,
Teases the late disordered skeptical man
Back to the garden where his pain began
To curse the parents and fall and try to pray.
The garden is cold; no one is there.

During spring break he tried to catch up with the poems that had piled up for *The Nation*. On March 31, he wrote a poem "To Dylan Thomas," congratulating him on his "brilliant book." He submitted two manuscripts to the Hopwood competition at the University of Michigan: a sheaf of twenty-five poems and his play "The Dictator." When he heard that John

Malcolm Brinnin had also applied for the Hopwood in poetry, he went to Ann Arbor to talk with him, suggesting that one or the other drop from the contest. As it turned out, Brinnin won an award for seven hundred dollars and Berryman won nothing. At the end of April Berryman at last wrote his mother. He had not written earlier, he explained, because he was "under continual and paralyzing treatment" by a Dr. Salutsky for his *petit mal* and had been in a "savage humour" for weeks. He'd also just had another molar removed and the gas he'd been given had been like "a kind of death." He had sixty research papers to correct, each ranging in length from two thousand to five thousand words. On top of everything else, the news out of England was so bad he could not bear to write Beryl.

Though his manuscript had grown by then to seventy poems, he was less eager than ever to publish a book. Since January he'd sent nothing out and had not even looked at his five Cambridge vintage poems in the current issue of *The Southern Review*. By then those poems merely bored him, and, worse, they were surrounded by "contemptible company." He had no plans for the future, but he knew he did not want to return to Wayne. Kenyon was a possibility, and Delmore, teaching at Harvard, had intimated that there might be something for him there in another year.

On May 5, he wrote Delmore, congratulating him on winning a Guggenheim. He was still suffering from "violent headaches, insomnia and fatigue," and was glad there were only four weeks left in the term. He had finished the revisions of "At Chinese Checkers," a poem he would refer to years later as a "compost heap," but a poem that nonetheless had caused him endless hours trying to get right. Was there, he wondered, any way he could begin teaching at Harvard that coming fall? Delmore wrote back, telling him to write to Theodore Morrison, in charge of freshman English A sections. Berryman jumped at the chance, giving as his references Van Doren, Tate, Dean Hawkes at Columbia, his chairman at Wayne, and Delmore. Then he waited.

A few days later Delmore wrote to say that he'd heard from Morrison that several English A instructors had withdrawn at the last moment and that Morrison might be able to use Berryman after all. Then Morrison himself wrote Berryman, inviting him to come to Cambridge by June 10. Meanwhile, Berryman grew frantic over the news of the German invasion of Belgium and the Netherlands. On May 22, a week after the Germans invaded France, he cabled Beryl, pleading with her to come to America while there was still time. On the twenty-eighth, the night Berryman learned of the Belgian surrender, he wrote a chilling poem reminiscent of Auden's elegy to Yeats, which he called "The Moon and the Night and the Men." In it two men played chess while the German and Allied Armies made their moves and a moon rose

> Late, a delayed moon, and a violent moon
> For the English or the American beholder;
> The French beholder. It was a cold night,
> People put on their wraps, the troops were cold
> No doubt, despite the calendar, no doubt
> Numbers of refugees coughed, and the sight
> Or sound of some killed others. A cold night.

On May 30 Beryl finally answered Berryman's cable. Now more than ever she belonged in England. DARLING, she wrote, I THANK YOU BUT FEEL I CANNOT LEAVE NOW HAVE TRAINED CIVIL DEFENSE AND FIRST AID AND WOULD HAVE NO PEACE OF MIND OUT OF ENGLAND HAVE WRITTEN YOU BUT LETTERS UNANSWERED WRITING NOW VIA MARK AT COLUMBIA BLESS YOU LOVE.

Through all of this, Berryman looked for any chance to get out of Detroit. Columbia, he knew, was probably closed to him forever, and early in June he wrote Van Doren not to intercede on his behalf with the chairman there, who had undoubtedly already written Berryman off as hysterical. Besides, except for Van Doren and Weaver, Columbia was "a cemetery." An exasperated Van Doren responded with some fatherly advice. Better, he said, not to confide to men in positions of power (like departmental chairmen) the inner workings of one's mind while one was trying to find a job. By chairmen, he explained, he meant "the world." Since Berryman needed the world, it would be better for him to act according to its dictates until he was free to do otherwise.

Berryman returned to New York, then went to Cambridge to be interviewed by Morrison on June 8. Three days later, back in New York, he heard from Morrison that he had a job at Harvard, though all Morrison could offer him at the moment was a two-thirds position at a salary of $1,333.32. That was four hundred less than he'd made at Wayne, but at least he would be out of Detroit. He wrote back accepting, asking Morrison to see if he could find him a third section for the fall. Eventually, Morrison did.

With the Harvard position secured, Berryman rethought his summer plans. Until the invasion of Belgium and France, he had vaguely hoped to spend the summer in England with Beryl. He might still get to England if only he could get enough money together to fly across, since the shipping lanes were patrolled by German U-boats. He asked *The Nation* and Giroux at Harcourt-Brace for an advance against a series of letters he planned to write in England that would be a record "of the death of our kind of life." He also wrote Laughlin asking for an advance against royalties on the anthology. But in the midst of these bizarre efforts, there was more bad news. The Germans were poised to take Paris. France would fall, and then the Germans would turn their attention to England. It made no sense after all to go to England if he and Beryl stood no chance of getting out, and slowly Berryman gave up his hopes of seeing her. "God help the French & the English," he wrote his mother from Detroit. "This is the low water mark of human history or it is to come."

Laughlin came through with a small advance and another small check for Berryman's poems in the 1939 New Directions Annual. Giroux, Berryman needed to believe, had been interested in publishing his poems, and he worked furiously now to get a manuscript to him. If Berryman got his poems out now, he could still drop out of Laughlin's scheme. So, at the end of June he spent twenty hours nonstop arranging, revising, and typing his manuscript, then sent it airmail to Giroux. It contained fifty poems: nine from 1937, twelve from 1938, twenty-three from 1939, six from 1940. It began with a revised version of "The Animal Trainer" and ended with "A Point of Age."

Giroux wrote back at once, saying he would do what he could to get the book published, but when they'd spoken, he reminded Berryman, they had talked about "a book of notes from England." Instead, a book of poems had arrived. What could Berryman have been thinking of? To save face, Berryman wrote back that he had sent the poems because he needed "detailed criticism," since Detroit was for him a vacuum. The English journal was a separate issue altogether, and he understood now that, until he wrote that book first, the poems stood little chance of being published.

At the same time a letter from Beryl arrived. Until the wire had come asking if she was safe, she explained, she'd heard nothing from Berryman since Christmas. She knew how precarious everything was, knew very well she might be killed at any time. If she could not see him, she at least wanted a photograph. Soon, a second letter arrived. The casualty list had grown steadily. With the fall of France there would be hundreds of thousands of new casualties, and she had lost all contact with her friends on the Continent. The news from England was as terrible as Berryman had feared.

But there was worse to come. After months of estrangement, he learned now about Bhain's cancer. He made peace with Bhain at once and tried to do what he could to help him. On June 28, he joined the Campbells at Union Lake. Two days later he wrote "A Poem for Bhain":

Although the relatives in the summer house
Gossip and grumble, do what relatives do,
Demand, demand our eyes and ears, demand us,

You and I are not precisely there
As they require: heretics, we converse
Alert and alone, as over a lake of fire

Two white birds following their profession
Of flight, together fly, loom, fall and rise,
Certain of the nature and station of their mission. . . .

On July 2, he wrote his mother that he would be staying in Detroit for most of the summer, revising his poems and writing the dreaded introduction for Laughlin. It was better not to return to New York now, given the mood he was in. Besides, he had a "duty to be as useful to Campbell" as he could be, even if he could see him "for only a few hours each week." On the ninth he wrote Bhain how unpleasant it was to hear that his condition had worsened. Couldn't the X-ray treatments begin at once? He wished he'd studied medicine so that he could help his friend. "Have you tried fixing the growth with a baleful glare?" he asked, trying to make light of the worsening situation. He chided Bhain for wasting his time listening to the gramophone when he might be reading Henry James or Henry Adams or T. S. Eliot.

Bhain wrote back. The pain had spread to his right side, and there was a new growth on his neck. He did not think he had six months left. Again Berryman wrote, pleading with him to do all he could to resist the cancer. "Remember that you talked about exerting will in the hospital." That was helpful, but rather "like holding northern France after the Nazis have the Channel." Bhain had to understand that his body was at war with him and that he would have to change his "form of government," resisting the enemy by eating "everything possible." And though he himself was now as "poor as a Dutch Jew," Berryman would stay on in Detroit as long as he could to help him.

"Set your mind on death as little as you can," he wrote again. "I believe we have been too inclined to despair." How insane it was "to prepare for death if it may be the preparation that will let the cancer kill you." He continued to urge Bhain on in letters every few days. Bhain had a duty to live to speak for the voiceless. But Bhain's condition only continued to worsen. He dropped to 125 pounds and could not keep food down. It was not simply a matter of willing away the cancer, he tried to explain to Berryman. Ultramicroscopic forms were eating away his body. Instead, he tried to console Berryman for the trouble he was having writing his preface for Laughlin.

In the meantime Laughlin cajoled, threatened, and pleaded with Berryman to send him the preface. "You are holding up everything and jeopardizing the commercial success of the volume by delaying its appearance," he wrote Berryman on July 25. "Unless I hear from you shortly I shall be forced, unwillingly, to drop you from the project." The ultimatum lodged the preface loose. By then Berryman had written seven prefaces in all, he complained to Laughlin when, on the morning of the twenty-seventh, he sent the preface off with the excuse that it had been delayed because of his health. In any event what he was sending was not very good, since it was "difficult to write when one had "nothing to say."

In his preface, entitled "A Note on Poetry," Berryman remained as aloof and objective as he could, choosing to focus on an explication of his poem "On the London Train." He concentrated on versification, rhyme, stanzaic pattern, and trope. But though he did not mention her by name, the poem he chose to talk about concerned loneliness and separation from Beryl. On July 29 he wrote her. He was sick again, sick with the "same weakness I had last winter, difficult to describe in a letter," though he did not want her worrying about him. Still, he blamed her; had she been with him, "it would have never occurred."

He returned to New York, then went up to the Catskills for a short vacation. The trip back out to Detroit at the end of August turned out to be a nightmare. Shafarman looked Berryman over and found that he was suffering from malnutrition, in large part a sympathetic response to Bhain's terrible loss of weight. He'd be able to teach that fall, Shafarman told Berryman, if he just took care of himself and ate well. By then Bhain was in Detroit's Women's Hospital, and Berryman visited him there every day. Then, on September 14, Berryman went back to New York. Two days later, with his brother at the wheel, he drove to Cambridge to begin teaching.

"Don't anticipate too much evil at Harvard," Van Doren had counseled him, trying to get him to be more accepting and not see enemies where there were none. "There may be less than you think, or, d[eo] v[olente], none at all." The Berryman brothers stayed at Peabody House at 1581 Massachusetts Avenue while Berryman went in search of an apartment. Bob had hoped to begin classes at Harvard, but was advised instead to take a preparatory year at Boston University. Within a few days Berryman found an apartment at 10½ Appian Way, close to Harvard Square. It was a ramshackle apartment built off the main house, which Bob remembered as being so poorly constructed that, if you pulled the blinds shut during the day, "you could look out through the walls."

On September 28, Berryman wrote to Van Doren. On the one hand, Widener Library was the best library he had ever used; on the other hand, his students displayed "a form of illiterate urbanity" that would soon become "very depressing." Moreover, with air raids daily over London now, there was also Beryl's danger to worry about. And there was Bhain. Berryman tried to bear up as best he could. "Dearest," he opened his letter to Bhain on the night of September 23, following the advice of Chekhov that one's truest emotions be expressed openly. He hoped Bhain was breathing more easily now, and that the spots on his chest were gone. Hard as it had been, Berryman had at last come to accept the fact "that everyone suffers and a time comes when no one can do another one good." He was glad to have Bhain's new poem, "Of the People and their Parks," which he'd shared with Delmore. Harvard, he was finding, was "a haven for the boring and the foolish."

Shortly afterward he heard from Florence. Bhain had been released from the hospital and they were settled now on the eighth floor of a new high rise that overlooked the tall trees on Palmer East. Bhain loved the apartment and appreciated the bookcases and furniture Berryman had given him from his old apartment. He was busy writing his autobiography and reading the biography of Lincoln Berryman had also given him. For the intense pain, Florence was keeping Bhain sedated with codeine.

Meanwhile an exasperated Laughlin waited for Berryman to send him a revised preface he could use. He knew Berryman was now "in excellent health and spirits . . . and quite capable of writing it." Berryman tried again, first showing the revised preface to Delmore before sending it to Laughlin on October 14. He hoped Laughlin liked it, he told him, because it was the last one he was going to do. Tersely Laughlin wrote back, thanking him for the preface, which he thought "most adequate." For the interminable delays he did *not* thank him.

Each night Berryman prepared his three classes and graded freshman themes. Mornings he taught, and afternoons he held student conferences. His head colds returned, and he became so tired he could hardly speak. It did not take him long to see that it was going to be another "wasted year." On the afternoon of October 16, he went to Widener Library and registered for the draft as required by the Selective Service Act, reminding himself that he'd "never felt less patriotic." America's "passion" for defense made him uncomfortable, he noted to himself, as if there were something "dirty" at the heart of all this protestation of one's loyalty.

But he knew that the young men he taught were facing far worse than he would have to when the United States finally declared war. On October 31, administering his midterm exam in the New Lecture Hall, he tore a page from an exam booklet and wrote a Yeatsian meditation:

> Hundreds of heads bend to the black & white
> November horrors of the examination,
> Read, try to remember, to conquer fright,
> Sigh, settle back, write: What will be their end?
> Who in the dark prepares their destination,
> Inscrutable as question three? In the Yard
> Who will inform them, who will be their friend
> And tell them how they must go & go hard
> Into the degeneration of the night?

Twelve days earlier, in a "hasty ceremony" at the city clerk's office in Cambridge, Bob, now twenty-one, married Barbara Suter, whom he'd met while living up in Roxbury, New York, with his grandmother. It had all happened so quickly that Berryman found himself becoming disoriented and ill after the ceremony. He hoped they would be happy, at least happier than he and Beryl had been for the past two years. Once, in another time and place, he and Beryl had met and fallen in love. Now they were separated by an ocean and a war and were further from marriage than ever. His birthday that year was as dark as any he'd ever experienced. "Twenty-six years ago I was born," he wrote to himself, "at what cost of distress and hope, and how little glad I am. . . . I work and work and postpone my disappointments." If it were not for Beryl, he told himself, he would just as soon be dead.

For a while that fall it seemed as if Bhain might rally. Florence wrote to say that Bhain was eating at the table now and was still working on his autobiography. He had already finished the sections on his childhood and high school years. But by the end of October Bhain could no longer get out of bed, and he was no longer capable of writing. What richness and variety there was in the portion of the autobiography that Bhain had managed, Berryman wrote him in early November. Soon he would be out to see him again and they would talk about themselves and "about poetry and history and people and in short we will have us a conversation." By then Bhain could barely even comprehend Berryman's letter.

"Westward a thousand miles Campbell is dying," Berryman wrote to himself on the eve of his return to Detroit:

His breath less, pain more, and he cannot write;
This is the man to whom I fastened hope
And my complete affection. In the east,
An ocean eastward, at dawn, my darling lies
Alone in a tormented city. Patches and rust,
Pain and fatigue. . . .

Florence wrote to say that, strangely, the weaker Bhain got, the stronger became his determination to live. It was the last delusion. Halliday had visited Campbell earlier that fall and had been shocked by the sight of Campbell lying there, yellow, sunken, twisted with pain, raving that he was going to beat the cancer. Now Berryman too was about to see for himself how things actually stood. He left Cambridge after his last class on the twentieth (Thanksgiving break) and took the night train to Detroit. Florence had tried to prepare him, but nothing could equal the horror of what he saw when he entered Bhain's room. Seventeen years later he would tell James Dickey what had greeted him that day: "He was saffron-coloured, his eyes danced, his teeth shot from retreating gums like a madman's, and dying he was full of the senseless hopes (encouraged by his mother who sought quack remedies) that tubercular patients have at the end. . . . I thought life wd bring me nothing like this again."

There was little he could do for Bhain except be there, and on the twenty-fourth Berryman returned to Cambridge. A week later he sent Robert Penn Warren at *The Southern Review* a copy of Bhain's "Of the People and Their Parks," with a note. "Mr. Campbell is very ill," he wrote. "Indeed he is dying; and I beg you to decide with Mr [Cleanth] Brooks on the poem more rapidly than ever you decided on a poem before. I do not exaggerate: if you want to print the poem, the knowledge may be important to Campbell, and every day of delay will decrease his chance of hearing it. After two weeks, that chance, if it still exists, will be very slight." If they could print it, he begged them to write Campbell and tell him at once. Campbell was not to know of his intercession.

Late on the afternoon of December 3, the telegram Berryman most dreaded arrived. It read simply, BHAIN DIED THIS

AFTERNOON. Berryman carried the telegram with him as he crossed Harvard Yard, dully trying to comprehend what had happened. That night he wrote Mary Jane Christenson, anxious to know how she and Florence were holding up. Two days later he heard from Florence. On the day he had died, she wrote, Bhain had awakened her in the predawn dark, thrashing about in "delirium and derangement." She had called in Shafarman, who had diagnosed "cerebral anaemia." The end was near, he'd told her. Then Bhain had lapsed into a coma. By noon he was dead.

Berryman could not bring himself to go to Detroit for the funeral. Instead, he did his mourning in Cambridge. On December 9, he wrote Laughlin, thanking him for inviting Bhain at the last to send something to New Directions, though by then it had been too late. On November 19, in the midst of Bhain's final agony, Laughlin had finally published Berryman's poems, but in Berryman's distress, his first book publication went unnoticed.

A few days before Christmas, Berryman returned to his mother's apartment and spent the holiday in a mindless frenzy, hopping from party to party, trying not to think of Bhain's death. After driving with Florence from Detroit and taking her to her parents' apartment in New York, Halliday looked up Berryman, and the two of them went in search of their old Columbia crowd. On the first day of winter they took the subway to Morningside Heights, but their gang had long ago dispersed.

As they rode back downtown, Berryman remained quiet. To lighten things up, Halliday began talking about their old times with women, and Berryman remarked that Mary Jane Christenson had had the best breasts of any woman he'd ever seen. Since the fall Halliday too had been seeing Christenson, though he'd carefully kept that information away from Berryman. Now, he wondered if Berryman had heard about the affair and was trying to trap him. Better to play it straight, Halliday thought. Yes, he answered, those breasts certainly were. Berryman looked at him. Oh, then he'd seen them? Halliday nodded just as the train pulled into Times Square Station. Abruptly, Berryman pushed past him onto the platform, turned, and waved goodbye, wishing Halliday a Happy New Year as the doors shut closed between them.

# PART II

---

*1941–53*

## chapter 8

# The Terrifying Bride

## 1941–42

On New Year's Day, 1941, Berryman began another unsent letter to Beryl. "For two weeks," he wrote, "I did nothing whatever except drink and wander from party to party—not for pleasure, I promise you, but desperately, to avoid thought." One of the parties was at 109 West Twelfth Street, the brownstone apartment of auburn-haired Eileen Mulligan (Rusty to her friends), an attractive Hunter graduate and a close friend of Berryman's first fiancée, Jean Bennett. In her memoir, *Poets in Their Youth,* Eileen would remember Berryman coming through the door into the crowded room that afternoon, "a black-and-yellow muffler, as long as he was tall, wrapped around his throat, eyeglasses, high cheekbones, the slim build of a runner—obviously ill at ease among strangers." Clare College, Cambridge, for the muffler, he told her, and a "jaunty bow tie" beneath. He was there only a short while, but in that time his discomfort dissolved long enough for him to steer Eileen under the mistletoe and, insisting on his respect for tradition, kiss her.

A few days later, back in Cambridge, he had a letter from

Beryl. He tried once more to answer her, talking to her as if she were there in his room. "I can see no fate for Europe but prolonged suffering and terror—and America moves nearer [war] every day. We picked, you and I, in history, a poor scene for our love; that it continues at all is a miracle. I begin to feel the wear and change of time as you do, as I thought I never would. . . . We are living out our youth apart, my darling. . . . Two years! . . . Mere pieces of time together, and other people, and dependence, and my horrible immaturity and temper." How could he have been blessed with a woman like her and have acted as he had? It was "insane,—horrible, senseless." He put the letter aside, unable to go on.

In mid-January fall term ended, followed by three days of conferences and the grading of papers. He had ten days to read and write before spring term began, and from the seventeenth to the nineteenth he worked on an eighty-line poem called "Night Club: Boston" (He would later change the title to "The Enemies of the Angels"). On the twenty-second he wrote Van Doren that his poem was "so exceedingly & complexly ironic" he was sure it would "have a great success" when they found it after his death, *if,* from what he'd seen of his Harvard freshmen, there was anyone left who could read. The poem was set in a local nightclub filled with a noisy bunch of Boston Irish and Italians. Nightclubs had become the new focal point for the modern masses, he wrote, with their chorus dancing, master of ceremonies, female impersonators, and alcoholic maze. The other modern gathering place for the masses was the movie house, with its modern democratic hero Charlie Chaplin. Both, he sighed heavily, were ways of losing oneself for a few hours, of forgetting the boredom and the insults until the last image faded and the lights blacked out for good.

At the end of January he began once more keeping a journal. But it was so introspective and so depressing that he soon forgot about it. One thing of interest he did note, however, was how much the modern sensibility resembled Hamlet's, with its tendency to freeze rather than take strong, decisive action. Delmore told him a poet could do worse than return to the classic texts of Aquinas and Augustine. Was that true? Berryman wondered. It was probably truer for Delmore than for himself, he concluded, since he believed he was more interested in people than Delmore was. But a few days later, with his mother visiting, Berryman noted just how "far out of touch" he had become even "with those who have been closest to me." He found himself avoiding her to maintain his sanity. Still, that did not assuage either the guilt or the suppressed rage he felt toward her. In short, the visit turned out to be a disaster, since from the start Jill had chided him for his lack of regard for his brother. For though Bob and Barbara were living with him, he virtually ignored them as he had earlier ignored the Campbells.

In early February, Mark wrote to congratulate him on "Night Club," but warned him that the social satire of the poem was not all that subtle. Berryman might do well to learn to take the world a bit more as it was and try to sound less hysterical. But by then Berryman was feeling every bit as exploited at Harvard as he'd felt at Wayne earlier. How was it, he wondered, that Delmore found time to write nearly every day? That night he got drunk at a local bar and was soon arguing with a stranger over the state of poetry. When he sobered up, he once again resolved never to let that happen again.

He began work on a long poem he at first called his Saint-Gaudens piece, and which he later titled "Boston Common." It was the most formidable and complex lyric he'd yet undertaken. He read William James and Aristotle and Donne by day and waited for night, the only time he found he could work on his poem. He struggled to approach what he called its "unsayable centre," yet each session left the poem more unsatisfactory than ever. When Eileen Mulligan came to visit him in early March, he pushed the opening of the poem on her, then realized he'd made a mistake. He had expected her to see at once the poem's every nuance, and was upset by the puzzled looks she gave him even as she tried to sound encouraging. He was glad to see her, though—still engaged himself—he questioned his own motives. "Of E & me together," he noted to himself, "it is a nice question which is the more insincere. Not that we have not each an object!—although," he added coyly, "what mine is I scarcely know."

A few days later he and Delmore walked out to the Mount Auburn Cemetery to pay homage at the grave of Henry James in imitation of Auden's recent poem, though, at the grave, Berryman was surprised to find he felt nothing. He and Delmore both winced at the engraving on James's stone—"Novelist-Citizen of two countries—Interpreter of his generation on both sides of the sea." It might have been worse, Delmore quipped. "They might have said, 'The Greatest American Writer.' " So this, Berryman realized, was where even great writers ended. A few days later he wrote a poem about "the epistemology of loss." He called it "The Ball Poem," and it would turn out to be his best early lyric. For the first time in his work, he employed a double vision: the child's first realization of loss—a ball floating out into the ocean—and the sudden realization from the adult's perspective—looking forward and simultaneously looking back—that life was inevitably made up of many such losses:

> Soon part of me will explore the deep and the dark
> Floor of the harbour . . I am everywhere,
> I suffer and move, my mind and my heart move
> With all that move me, under the water
> Or whistling, I am not a little boy.

That month he became an uncle when Bob and Barbara had a baby girl whom they named Shelby, though Berryman had to confess that he felt "no avuncular sensations." For the most part, his life passed between periods of "intense activity" in the classroom and periods of "intense gloom" in his corner of the apartment. He thought constantly of Campbell, and in early April he wrote some lines about the epistemology of that loss as well:

> I told a lie once in a verse. I said,
> I said, I said, I said "The heart will mend,
> Body will break & mend, the foam replace
> For even the unconsolable his taken friend."
> This is a lie. I had not been here then.

"Many times this spring I have wished for death," he wrote Beryl in mid-May. Only she and Bhain had it in their power to make him "lie still, rest, not hurt." And now one had gone away and the other was gone forever.

When copies of Oscar Williams's anthology with Berryman's poems included arrived later that month, Berryman wrote Williams explaining why he had not attended the publication party in New York. After all, he asked, what was "more depressing than twenty writers and forty hangers-on gathered together?" As for the photograph Williams had printed—the one of a pale, angular mustached Berryman with eyes looking down and inward, which had been taken in Detroit—he was "sorry to see it" and hoped to hell Williams would write and explain how he had come to use a copyrighted photo without first getting permission.

He reviewed Laughlin's New Directions annual for *The Kenyon Review,* singling out for special praise James Agee's "sensitive, strenuous, exact" prose, and George Orwell's "impressive essay" on Henry Miller. The poetry selection, however, he found indifferent, except for the Surrealists, all of whom were excruciatingly bad. Why, he wondered, didn't Laughlin have the sense to ask him whom to print? At the end of May he heard directly from Laughlin, inviting him to be one of his "Poets of the Month" for 1942. It would be a small book, Laughlin explained, but at least it would be all Berryman's. "In spite of Allen Tate," Laughlin joked, "I think you are a very satisfying poet." At once Berryman began assembling the poems for the twenty-five-page pamphlet. This, he decided, would be Bhain's book, the poems bracketed by the time they'd spent together, and it would end with these lines:

> He died in December. He must descend
> Somewhere, vague and cold, the spirit and seal,
> The gift descend, and all that insight fail
> Somewhere. Imagination one's one friend
> Cannot see there. Both of us at the end.
> Nouns, verbs do not exist for what I feel.

He returned to New York for the summer and began seeing more of Eileen, and soon her good spirits helped him recover his interest for life. One night they went dancing on the rooftop of the Hotel New Yorker; Tommy Dorsey's band was playing, and as Berryman negotiated Eileen through a series of his old "demon dips and dervish whirls" across the dance floor, he sang in her ear his French translation of "Night and Day." Soon they were lovers, and Berryman moved out of his mother's apartment into "a low dark long damp room" below ground at Lexington Avenue and Thirty-sixth Street. Eileen was working on lower Broadway at the time, and after work they would meet for a drink at the Jumble Shop on Eighth Street or at the Brevoort Café on lower Fifth Avenue. Sometimes they went to see films like *Potemkin* and *Alexander Nevsky* on the Lower East Side or Louis Jouvet at the Forty-second Street Apollo.

Or they took long walks across the city from the Hudson to the East River or from the Battery to Fort Tryon, often talking until three in the morning, when Eileen would try to catch a few hours' sleep before going to work. Often Berryman steered the conversation toward poetry with an intensity that demanded all of Eileen's attention. He loved teaching her, and she seemed willing to learn. It disturbed him, he confessed to her, when he thought of how little he had done with his life. He was the age now when Keats had died, and all he had to show for it was a *fifth* of one book.

One night, after saying good night to her and heading back to his apartment, Berryman was attracted by a crowd gathered in Union Square. People were arguing with a haranguer over whether or not America should become involved in the war, and soon Berryman, disturbed by the haranguer's rabid, half-formed arguments, began arguing with him. Suddenly the man pointed at him and called him a Jew. Confused, Berryman began to protest. There had to be some mistake. He was not Jewish. The haranguer stared hard. "You look like a Jew, you talk like a Jew, you are a Jew!" he shouted. If Berryman wasn't a Jew, let him prove it by reciting the Apostle's Creed.

Suddenly all eyes were on Berryman. Before he realized what he was doing, he was trying to remember the prayer he had memorized fifteen years before in Latin, reciting it in the shadows of the mission church in Anadarko with Father Boniface: *Credo in unum Deum . . . Patrem omnipotentum. . . . unam, sanctum, catholicam . . .* His memory failed him. Here was proof, he could hear the bigot saying, if proof were needed, that this Jew *was* a Jew. The crowd moved on while Berryman stood there paralyzed. What in God's name had happened? Then it dawned on him that he had, after all, swallowed the man's bait. For the rest of the night he walked the city's streets, trembling with rage and terror.

On September 1, he typed out some lines for his brother's twenty-second birthday. He and Bob had spent an evening in New York with Barbara and Eileen, drifting uptown to a concert, which they'd missed, then downtown again to Times Square. He thought of Bob's life and then of his own and found himself sorely wanting:

> I would say that you are farther on than I,
> I would say you came more carefully and more
> Kindly, kindly, from the human island. . . .

At least Bob had a family, while he, nearing his twenty-seventh birthday, was still alone. "Out of a full heart" for his brother, he wished him past his "threshold quietly" into a new year and a new beginning.

Back in Cambridge he moved into a new apartment, this one across the Charles in Boston, far enough away from Harvard to give him some privacy, yet within walking distance of the subway and Harvard Square. His new, upstairs apartment was in a converted townhouse at 49 Grove Street on Beacon Hill. Eileen spent a weekend with him, then Jill came up to help her son put the apartment in order. As he arranged his books, Berryman listened to Roosevelt's "fireside phillippic" on the radio and was dismayed to hear how provocative the president sounded. He was convinced that, if Roosevelt didn't declare war on Germany soon, Hitler would save him the trouble.

On September 19, after lunch in Cambridge with Delmore and Philip Horton, Hart Crane's biographer, Berryman met with Ted Morrison and the English A staff. He spent the weekend reading *Don Quixote* and Joseph Conrad and tried writing Beryl once more, his remorse for his silence so palpable it was like a devil stalking his room. He promised once more to order his life. He would get out more and leave himself more time to write. He would not engage in departmental politics or waste his time discussing "the various neuroses of his colleagues" with his students. He promised to answer (and did) all requests for poems: from *Accent, Furioso,* the New Directions annual (which Delmore was editing), and Oscar Williams ("our most famous literary buffoon") for another of his anthologies. He would start the new school year "in a healthy, ambitious state."

Meanwhile he barraged Eileen with letters, telling her how anxious he was to hear from her, that he was like a little boy running down the stairs whenever he heard the mailman. But he also warned her he might revert at any time to his "ancient tyranny of demanding letters but not writing them." He recommended the Jooss Ballet in New York, "The Green Table" and "their masterpiece, "The Big City." He advised her to read T. S. Eliot and David Garnett's "War in the Air," about the Royal Air Force's struggle against the Luftwaffe over England. He sent her his telephone number, but warned her that he hated talking on the phone. His letters grew more intimate.

Eileen went up to Boston Columbus Day weekend, lugging nine records Berryman had ordered when he was in New York, her presence providing a tiny oasis before Berryman was pulled under by work again. On October 21, he got a note off to Mark. " 'Mi ritrovai per una selva oscura,' " he lamented, quoting Dante. Once more Berryman had found himself in a dark wood, though he could see that he was happier than he'd been in a long time. That Saturday he received an RCA radiogram from London. HAPPY BIRTHDAY ANGEL, it read. It was from Beryl. He was twenty-seven.

"The completely happy man," he wrote Beryl that evening, would "never act, never speak, never think—least of all, measure or confess his happiness." For years he had believed he would die young, but he wanted to live to be with her and to write. In spite of his depressions, he knew he had it in him to be happy. As a boy he'd been happy, but had lost that happiness when he'd lost his father. Then, at twenty, finding her, he'd found happiness once more. He was determined now to find it yet again. But the monotonous repetition of teaching was paralyzing him. Here he was, "qualified as few men in the country are to lecture on Shakespeare, on 17th C verse, on modern verse," unable to advance at Harvard because he was without a doctorate. So it would be freshmen, freshmen, freshmen, "until they fire me or I cut my throat." He put the letter aside.

In spite of his promise to become more social, except for Eileen and the Schwartzes he saw no one. Instead, he thought continuously of Beryl. On November 16, he wrote her an angry, worried letter, protesting that, in spite of having written her five or six letters, he'd heard nothing from her in two months. Either they lived alone and apart or they really "participated in each other's lives." What he failed to tell Beryl was that he'd mailed none of these letters. Nor did he mail this one. Instead, he wrote Eileen, who, in spite of himself, was becoming more and more his new center.

On Sunday, December 7, along with millions of other Americans, Berryman heard the news of the Japanese surprise attack on Pearl Harbor. The following day came Roosevelt's announcement that the United States was at war with Japan and Germany. On the eleventh Berryman wrote to Eileen. He was actually relieved, he told her, that after the intolerable strain of waiting for so long, the inevitable had finally come. As for himself, he wrote, "The poverty of my mind is really indescribable. I would like to write some angry poems but I have forgotten how. . . . I postpone, I postpone my life." He knew he was miserable company, and if she wanted to end the relationship, she was free to do so. But a few days later he wrote again, telling her that her loss would be "a kind of suicide" for him.

"We have at last blundered our way into the War, where we should have been last year," he wrote Mark. "Nevertheless I had some bad hours over it & will have more." He had heard from Beryl: a letter she'd posted three months before, telling him about her part in the war effort and asking after him. But all he could bear to do since war had been declared was "brood & listen to music." He'd been in touch with Mark's friend Bernard Haggin, the popular music critic, whose book on how to collect records Berryman had consulted for several years now as if it were Sacred Scripture. Now Haggin had sent him "(unsolicited) his phone number" and he felt suddenly as if he were "in touch with the immortals."

On January 19, 1942, he read a UP report about an Australian officer named Jack Leslie Perry, who, recuperating in Sydney after having lost an eye in combat, was handed a white feather by a woman on the street, her way of calling Perry a coward. In a gesture Berryman delighted in for its irony, Perry had reciprocated by plucking his glass eye from its socket and handing it to the woman. Not all wounds, Berryman understood, were visible. The dispatch intrigued him enough to sit down and write, "in two minutes," a short poem called "White Feather." By January, in fact, his imagination was "in a state of frenzied activity." He read *Crime and Punishment* as if he "were driving a pack of hounds through a wood, feverishly." Everything about the book he found so "unbearably interesting,'' he told his mother, that he wanted ''to stop and examine it for a long time,'' except that ''the hounds are off ahead and won't let me stop.'' Even his ''unhappiness,'' he added, seemed ''acute, sharp, engaging.''

On the evening of February 3, sick with another cold in his frigid apartment, he wrote Halliday. What, he wondered, were they to say to each other after all this time and at this juncture in history? It had been over a year since he'd seen or heard from his old friend, married now and serving in the army. So far Berryman had been rejected for military service. And in spite of Eileen and his music, he found himself mostly depressed. Harvard he hated more each day and there were family problems as well. Bob had left Barbara and the baby and gone west in search of work at Pearl Harbor, but without luck. His mother too had lost her job.

At the end of the month Berryman picked up ''the finest poem'' he'd ever planned, ''Boston Common,'' afraid that if he didn't get at it, he would lose it for good. He stopped writing to everyone but Eileen and narrowed in on the poem. But within two weeks the poem ground to a halt once more. Then his gramophone broke down and he began to think continually of the wonderful gramophone he'd heard one evening in Bernard Haggin's apartment over Christmas. Before that evening had finished, Haggin had hinted that he was looking for a new machine. Now, in spite of the fact that he was living from paycheck to paycheck, Berryman convinced himself that he had to have Haggin's gramophone. Within days he was writing Haggin, asking him how much he wanted for his marvelous machine.

Berryman blamed the fact that he hadn't heard from Beryl now for nearly half a year on the ''murderous complacency, inefficiency and greed of the governments of America and England,'' which had forced Americans into the war. He hated Churchill for his skillful and inflammatory rhetoric; Russia was little better. It was a strange moment Western civilization was passing through, he wrote Beryl; in fact, the last five years seemed to him ''sordid and unreal.'' He wanted to teach at Harvard that summer, but Morrison could not even promise him that he'd be teaching in the fall. ''After two years at Harvard,'' he complained, ''I know exactly three men, all of them useless to me elsewhere. I have taught at times brilliantly, at times well, at times badly, and no one has given a damn except my students.'' Delmore advised him that the best thing that could happen to him would be for him to lose his job so that he could get back to his writing. That was fine, Berryman complained, until it came time to eat.

Delmore also had his own opinions about Berryman's poor state of health. The only thing wrong with Berryman, he wrote Van Doren, was ''some kind of hysteria. The fainting fits he has occur when he is spoken to sternly or contradicted.'' If Beryl would only come to America and marry him, it would do Berryman a world of good. ''Living alone as he does, in Boston not Cambridge, and seeing no one at all for days at a time, he is really not well off; and being improvident, he sometimes spends all his money and then tries to feed himself on chocolate bars, until the first of the month.''

Berryman spent Easter alone in his apartment, struggling to come up with a draft of ''Boston Common.'' But by the following Wednesday he'd had enough, and he wired Eileen at the Canadian Aviation Bureau where she was working that he would arrive in Grand Central that night and that she was to meet him. When he returned to Boston a few days later, he learned that he had a teaching job for the summer that would earn him five hundred dollars. For him that meant he could buy Haggin's gramophone, and he went back down to New York the following weekend and lugged it back up to Boston. It was an intense effort, for he had to carry the machine several blocks when his cab broke down, but it was all worth it, he decided, when the music from it flooded his apartment. That machine was the very embodiment—''beautiful and diabolical''—of modern civilization.

At the end of April he tried his hand at a preface to the *Poems* Laughlin was publishing. To hell with the critics, he wrote. He wasn't writing for them anyway, but to pay a debt to his family as well as to Van Doren, Schwartz, and Campbell. Publishing these poems would be, for him, a moral gesture against the ''unspeakable men'' who had destroyed so much of his world. His closest friend was dead, his fiancée separated from him for the past three years, and his whole generation ''shredded by war.'' These poems would be his testament. But the preface was too angry, personal, and theatric, and he left it unpublished.

* * *

When classes ended on May 20, he tried once more to write about his encounter with the bigot in Union Square the year before. "Once more," he wrote now,

> I am ashamed tonight—deep in
> The columns of my body and about my heart
> The blood rises. . . . I would be a Jew
> And suffer indeed what I imagine now.
>
> Walking one summer night, O very late,
> In Union Square, I came on argument
> Ignorant and intolerant, and spoke
> Fact to assist one man against the rest. . . .

But he had yet to find the form that would reveal the hard truth about himself that he had learned that night.

His mother and grandmother wrote him from Mexico City to say they were going to visit friends in Oklahoma. "How strangely I have come from those years," he wrote his mother, "from the fat and affectioned child of your photographs and my blocked-out memory." How little his old neighbors would understand of what he had done with his life. He still felt the loss of that world keenly, he admitted, and yet he knew he had to go on with what he was doing. "Advance would be impossible else," he resigned himself with a tiny flourish, "but one gives up much, gives up the home of the human heart."

He cabled Beryl for her birthday, but no word came back. Nor had there been any word now for seven months. On June 6, he wrote her about the war news, mentioning the Greek diplomats who had reported on the numbers of Greeks being starved to death by the Nazis. His ex-fiancée, Jean Bennett, had recently married a multimillionaire and there had been a reception for the couple in Boston shortly after the New Year, which he'd attended. What he'd seen there was a glimpse of "an enormously powerful, indifferent, vanishing class," so at odds with the suffering occurring worldwide. To comfort himself, he had taken to drink: Scotch and ice and water. "The new Trinity," he called them. Less consoling "perhaps than the first, and with no such magnificent corollaries as the Virgin," but at least they were "more available, more real, able to exist in the twentieth century world, in short the survivor." He asked Beryl to come to America. Not permanently, he added, "but for as long as you shall like." Here at least she would be safe "from the last desperate bombings which Hitler" might throw against London. But his letter became more insensitive and more unreal the more he wrote. He did "not know what the losses at sea" were "in the various kinds of travel possible," he ended, but he was sure Beryl could find out.

In early July he went to New York to stay with his mother at 121 Madison Avenue and help her celebrate her forty-eighth birthday. But he was back in Boston on July 29, when Beryl's letter reached him. It was dated the eleventh and it was an answer to his letter of June 6. Beryl apologized for not having written sooner, but she'd been on leave from her work with British Intelligence when his letter had arrived. The reason he'd not heard from her for so long, she explained, was that she had not written. The war had taken an enormous toll on her, and she had had to avoid all strain if she was to come through. Since February she had wanted to tell him that she had decided not to marry. Looking back, she could see that doubts had begun to cloud their future together as far back as their first year together. New York had made their differences even clearer, and she no longer believed they could help each other. She was not in love with anyone else, perhaps not even with herself, for she had been through too much. Indeed, she did not think she would ever marry or ever fall in love again.

What Berryman had most feared and yet hoped for had happened. At last he was free, without having had to call off the engagement himself. Ten days later, in a restaurant in Connecticut, he asked Eileen to marry him. They sat there, "in a town where neither of [them] had ever been before," and, in spite of misgivings on both sides, Eileen said yes to his proposal. The following afternoon, back in Boston, Berryman wrote to Beryl. His hands were still trembling, he told her, he was in a stupor "of grief & desperation," and he had not slept since getting her letter. "I dare not intrude on the passivity & bitterness which are so powerful & strange in your letter," he wrote. He loved her and knew he would always love her. But he too saw that they could not marry. Now he had asked his other friend to marry him. He was sure Beryl would like her, for Eileen was "good, sensitive, intelligent, kind, and beautiful."

At half past four the next morning, still unable to sleep, he wrote to Van Doren to explain what had happened. "So I have a chance, a chance at health & work, life even so far as the War will permit it." Van Doren wrote back to say he thought that for Berryman to marry Eileen would probably be best for everyone. He wished the couple happiness, adding pointedly that "the amount of this commodity" would depend largely on Berryman himself.

On August 29, passing a bookstore in Cambridge, Berryman spotted a copy of a slim pamphlet in a green cover. It was, he was surprised to see, his new book of poems, with the simple title *Poems*. He had told Laughlin the book was to be titled *Poems, 1939–1940,* to commemorate the year he had spent with Bhain, for *Poems* was to be the title he was saving for his first full book of poems. He was angry too that the pamphlet had been published before the October date agreed upon, for Ransom was to have published "A Point of Age" in the fall number of *The Kenyon Review*. Upset, he wrote Laughlin, demanding payment for the poem Ransom would not be able to use. He was "sorrier and angrier" than he could say that Laughlin had taken it on himself to change the book's title.

In the meantime Jill decided to take her future daughter-in-law under her wing. She had already counseled Eileen not to take to heart Berryman's reading and rereading of Beryl's letter breaking the engagement between them. Her son had always had a tendency to idealize the past, she explained, and to want the impossible. On August 20, over lunch at the Claremont Hotel in Manhattan, she gave Eileen a ring to wear as a sign of the engagement. Berryman himself was too busy, apparently, to protest his mother's intrusions into his affairs.

For his part, what he feared most now was that he and Eileen would quarrel and that the wedding would be called off. He even wished they *would* quarrel and get it over with. He also hated the idea of a Catholic wedding, for, he confided to his diary, there was "not a shred of reason for believing Anything or Anyone" was out there. He even wrote out an anti-prayer: "Comfort now, and relieve, Master of lies and hatred and sorrow and death, Your faithful daughter Eileen Mulligan, Your good daughter who believes in You. Bring her happiness and peace, Who have tortured and destroyed since the beginning of time the best of men and the worst of men and all men, according to Your Will.'' For Eileen's peace of mind, he told the priest that he was a "fallen away" Catholic instead of the out-and-out atheist he felt he was.

Eileen's grand-uncle, Charles Tully, arranged for them to be married in St. Patrick's Cathedral on Saturday afternoon, October 24, but when Eileen lost her job and had to take on a menial day job, the cost of the ceremony—thirty-five dollars—seemed almost prohibitive. But Eileen had a strong will of her own, and the wedding went as planned. In the meantime Berryman did what he could to plan for the future. He would become a Shakespearean specialist and edit the corrupted text of *King Lear*. He also pursued the issue of lost revenue with Laughlin until Laughlin sent him a check.

On October 10, Berryman wrote his mother from Boston. "All the arrangements for the wedding disgust me," he confessed. "I grind my teeth in the morning, I clash them at night, I sleep badly, I haven't swallowed properly in ten days, my head aches, I breathe with difficulty, ugh, contempt and hatred." Eight days before his wedding, he gave orders at Tiffany for a ring to be engraved. The inscription read, J.B. TO E.M.—NOW AND THEN ONE—24 OCTOBER 1942. That could read: "Now and then, present and past, we are one." Or: "At moments only have we been one." The irony masked the terror and resentment he felt as his wedding neared.

Unfortunately, Halliday had not been able to get leave from the army to attend. Nor could Bob Giroux, his best man, get leave from the navy. So it was left to Van Doren, gallant as ever, to stand in for Giroux. When Uncle Charles gave Eileen away (Eileen's parents both being dead for many years), Berryman could not help noticing how frightened and even faint she seemed under her veil. But it was he who was actually terrified and Eileen had to steady him as they moved toward the altar to be married by Father Michael Deacy. Afterward he would note, "God was not there. I watched for him."

Jean Bennett Webster held a reception for the couple at her home at River House on East Fifty-second Street. Eileen's sister, Marie, and her husband, Jim Mabry, were there, as well as Eileen's aunt and Florence Campbell and Mark and Jill. In the evening Berryman and Eileen attended the ballet, where they saw *Billy the Kid, Pillar of Fire,* and *Coppelia* at the Metropolitan Opera House, then spent their wedding night at the

Murray Hill Hotel. Next day, after a champagne party to celebrate Berryman's twenty-eighth birthday, the newlyweds took the train to Boston.

On the day he had given instructions for the engraving of his wedding ring, Berryman wrote out some lines entitled "For His Marriage." The wedding ceremony, he was afraid, prefigured the time when that other bride, Death, would come to lock him in her grasp forever. It was not Eileen he was afraid of, he understood, for he loved her insofar as he was capable of loving anyone. It was, rather, the enormity of what he was committing himself to. His father too had married once, and where was he now?

Lilies of the valley
And the face of the priest.
The pushing eyes
Upon my back of guest and guest.
Music, and crush of fear
I never felt before.

. . .

Resist, resist, pressed Heart,
In the breast be still.
If you can still and stay
Perhaps I will
Until comes lover to my side
The terrifying Bride.

## chapter 9

# Down and Out in Boston & New York

## 1942–43

At the Grove Street apartment, anxious to follow ancient ceremony and custom in such things, Berryman carried Eileen across the threshold. For the first few weeks they saw virtually no one, talking for hours, as Berryman phrased it, "about all the numberless violent calm remarkable familiar absorbing things" they were used to talking about. The weeks leading up to their marriage, Berryman saw in retrospect, had been "the most racking" in his life. He had upset Eileen badly and knew she had "grave reason for uneasiness" in marrying a suffering artist, one of the company, as he saw it, of Peter Warlock, Bix Beiderbecke, and Hart Crane, all of whom had killed themselves.

Eileen soon found employment in Boston in the legal department of Liberty Mutual Insurance Company. The work was dull, but Berryman took care of the household chores and they managed to entertain occasionally, including several colleagues whom Berryman particularly liked—Mark Schorer among them—as well as several students like Tony Clark, a young artist and illustrator, and Claude Fredericks, who was a printer of fine books and would eventually produce some of Berryman's own work. And of course they saw the Schwartzes. In December, Berryman helped Delmore with the page proofs for his long poem, "Genesis," while Delmore commented on Berryman's recent work. At Christmas, Eileen returned to New York, while Berryman stayed in Boston. The season, he wrote in his journal, stood in his mind "like other holidays for unsatisfied hopes, vanished chances, the frenzy of expectation & the fall of unfulfillment." For the past dozen or so years, he had been able to think of Christmas in the modern world only with irony. "Ah, do You look down," he wrote on Christmas Day, addressing his absent God in a poem he called "Kyrie Eleison":

> I almost think
> Today, today you do—
> Where tattered men upon torn knees sink
> Hopeful & hopeless O that You
> Pierce the floor of cloud to where
> The world shudders in war?

For the New Year he resolved to keep his temper, remain calm, and use his gift for irony only on those occasions when he was sure it would be appreciated and understood. He also promised himself to be a better husband and friend, and, strangely for an atheist, "To learn to know Christ."

On January 5, 1943, he wrote Halliday. "My thoughts just now would amuse nobody but Satan who has a taste I am told bizarre bizarre." Here he was, going on thirty and still a mere instructor making next to nothing in an inflationary wartime economy. The trouble was that early in his life he had acquired certain tastes for such amenities as food and clothing, which he found "it difficult to rid" himself of. Most nights that winter he and Eileen sat up listening to Mozart on Haggin's powerful gramophone, burning newspapers (and once even some of Berryman's early poems) in the grate and drinking hot chocolate—when they could get it—to keep warm against a particularly bitter winter. If only he could get chocolate, cooking chocolate, hot, at night, Berryman sighed to Halliday, for it was his and Eileen's "only resource against the bloody housewives who have stocked up on all the meat & butter & everything in the country." It was ten years to the month since he and Halliday had met, he reminded his friend, and if Halliday could find him "ten worse years in human history" he would present him with "an ounce of butter (my last)."

In February, Eileen's uncle Charles, the man who had given her away, died. Then Delmore began to go into a decline, unable to teach, unsure of the worth of his poetry, until the strain created by his depression led to a separation between him and Gertrude. As for himself, Berryman needed to believe that he and Eileen were as happy as they'd ever been. She was, he noted, the very "top of Wife." His mother married again—a business associate—and he wished her all happiness, though he was afraid she had married without first bothering to obtain a divorce from Uncle Jack.

With Delmore's help, Berryman put together a book of poems that Delmore promised to show Harcourt Brace. Berryman had been feeling nearly invisible at Harvard, but now, in his last year of teaching there, he was invited by Theodore Spencer to give one of the Morris Gray Poetry Readings. With Uncle Jack now completely out of the picture and living in Reisterstown, Berryman became more openly interested in his past and asked his mother to send him a list of his ancestors. He also asked to borrow the letters he'd written to her while he was in England, ostensibly to search them for poetic topics for a series of poems that he had begun the previous summer and that he had taken to calling his "Nervous Songs."

These poems were based in part on his reading of Rilke, a poet he believed could teach him something about pace and limpidity of phrase. For years he'd known he himself was a huddle of nerves, and in the section of Rilke's *Book of Pictures* called "Songs" he had found a form and a voice he could use to express his wired intensities. From Rilke's "The Blindman's Song," "The Dwarf's Song," "The Drunkard's Song," and especially "The Idiot's Song," with their deracinated and altered states of perception and sudden and unexpected shifts of voice, he moved to his own "Song of the Bridegroom" and then to other Songs. These consisted of three 6-line stanzas, variations played on the iambic pentameter, partly rhymed and partly unrhymed, a form equivalent in timing and linguistic and emotional weight to the traditional Italian sonnet. It became a favorite of Berryman's, a form he would play with and refine over the years until he could make it do anything he wanted. But in 1943 the tortured syntax jerked and stuttered:

> Do not approach me! If I am on show
> Compassion waves you past, you hoverers.
> Forms brutal, beating eyes upon my window,
> Because if I am desolate I have—
> Have emanations, and it is not safe.
> Rising and falling fire, ceremonial fire.

He sent Mark a revision of "Animal Trainer" and Mark wrote back encouragingly. "I had forgotten, outside Delmore's loyalty, what praise could taste like," Berryman told Mark. "My palate is odd to it, but then I had the taste once." He sent Oscar Williams "Boston Common" and, a week later, a note urging him to publish Bhain's "Of the People and Their Parks." Then he wrote Florence Campbell. It was time now, he urged her, to see to the publication of Bhain's poems. She had been reading John Pick's *Gerard Manley Hopkins: Priest and Poet,* and now Berryman took the time to note some of the book's shortcomings. Hopkins had come to stand for Berryman as the model of the poet as artist and as human being. But to understand Hopkins, Berryman explained, one had to understand the literary canon, for no "account of Hopkins' literary thought which ignores his elaborate & profound comment upon Shakespeare, upon Milton, upon Keats" was worth attention. What he himself had especially noted in reading Hopkins were the contrarieties, the particular mixture of "vigour & fatigue, confidence & despair, the elegant & the blunt, the bright & the dry." What he did not say was that he was now trying to get those same complex levels of diction into his own poems.

Late in March, Berryman wrote Mark again, hoping Mark might be able to help him find work once again, now that Harvard was definitely letting him go. Since his lease at Grove Street would keep him tied to Boston until September, he would need a summer job nearby and then another job beginning in September in New York. After June he would have no salary coming in, and Eileen's salary came to only one hundred dollars a month. It was all Harvard's fault, he complained, the place being "disagreeable & hypocritical as usual." He would be happy to go, *if* he could only "find somewhere to go *to*." As for Boston itself, Henry Adams had been right to consign it "to the sea-slime from which in fact I am unable to distinguish it."

As usual when he was under pressure, Berryman came down with something and had to stay in bed. Only the necessity of giving his poetry reading at Harvard roused him, and he spent nine hours the day before preparing for the event. The reading was held in the Poetry Room at the top of Widener Library on the afternoon of April 7, with Eileen and Delmore and Gertrude Schwartz present to lend him moral support. Afterward he wrote his mother a full account of the proceedings. Theodore Spencer had been there: "big, bland, self-absorbed, wanting-desperately-to-resemble-Yeats," and Robert Hillyer, "a poetaster of Eliot's generation . . . a constant alcoholic, Boylston Professor at Harvard, smug politic & powerful." And then there was Morrison himself, "undoubtedly the most ear-shocking poet the language has yet had, a very mild handsome disappointed man of forty, a Master bore." He had resolved before the reading to curb his irony and say nothing savage because Eileen and Delmore, "who much exaggerate anyway my conversational ferocity, were very nervous lest casually I turn in some remark and decapitate someone present." But he had not expected the committee to actually like his reading, as indeed they had. Morrison, in fact, had flattered him, and Spencer had afterward hosted a cocktail party in his honor.

At the end of the month, Berryman went to New York searching for work at one of the city colleges, but without luck. He hated having to grub for work like this, and he was worried Eileen might not be able to take the strain that this uncertainty was causing. Yet, he noted with surprise, "under galling conditions of debt & work & war, she says we have done very well together & I think we have." But if his finances were in disarray, they were models of order compared to his mother's. One morning in May he was shaken to find two Internal Revenue Service agents knocking on his apartment door asking where they might find Jill. He knew she was living in Washington with her new husband, but he tried stalling the agents by giving them her old New York address. Still, he was terrified. What was the situation with regard to perjury? he wrote her at once. He was afraid, he told her, she might involve him now in some scheme to avoid the IRS, and swore that if she tried, he would develop a "very serious illness." There was no need to elaborate. His mother knew very well what that meant.

At the end of May his book of poems was rejected by Harcourt. He had written only one poem in months, a short piece that he'd dedicated and then sent to Alfred North Whitehead, and he was still so dissatisfied with "Boston Common" that he slashed the galleys and rewrote it for a seventh time, trying to get it right. As if that wasn't bad enough, he was still without a job when classes ended. He wrote Robert Kerr, the governor of Oklahoma and an old intimate of his mother's, on the chance that he might know of some teaching position in that state, but there was nothing. He tried the State Department. Again nothing. He wrote inquiries to fifty colleges. Again he came up with nothing. "This whore this Harvard," he wrote exasperatedly to his mother on June 13. He had tried all over Boston and "the neighboring slums" and found exactly nothing. He even tried the Folger, asking about a research grant for the editorial work on *Lear* he'd recently begun, and Delmore wrote Allen Tate as curator of American Poetry on Berryman's behalf. That day alone, he told his mother, he had written nineteen letters and had seven more to go before he slept. He was already "*dead sick* of trying to sell" his "bloody services."

A few days later he went back to New York to see what he could find. He stayed at Eileen's sister's apartment until Eileen could join him. But as the days dragged on and nothing came of his search, he grew more desperate and his gallows humor sharper. Finally, on July 11, he placed a personal ad in the pages of *The New York Times*. It read:

> POET, 28, married, 4F, educated here and abroad, critic, editor, and experienced and competent university instructor, would like to continue living and writing if possible.

But even irony got him nothing. In desperation he took the only job he could find: selling encyclopedias door-to-door in Harlem. By the end of the second day of canvassing, however, he could see how "thoroughly dishonest" the outfit he was working for was and, without having placed a single order, "trembling & half-mad," he quit in disgust. In mid-July he and

Eileen moved to Eileen's aunt's apartment on 163rd Street in the Bronx. Then he went down to his mother's apartment in Washington to see what he could find there.

On July 18, he wrote Mark from the capital that he'd "hunted, all right. In Boston and Washington and Princeton and New York. Universities and colleges and schools and pseudo-schools and Government and newspapers and agencies." But all the jobs were somewhere else. When Berryman learned from his mother that Halliday was at Officer Candidate School in nearby Fort Washington, Maryland, he went out to visit him. Unfortunately, Halliday could get away for only half an hour, and the two of them stood by the guardhouse in the intense heat and talked, mostly about Berryman's failed job search. In all the years he'd known him, Halliday would recall, never had he seen Berryman look so underweight, pale, and miserable.

Berryman had also been to see James Agee at his office at *Time* magazine several times in early July and been given a runaround. Finally, at the beginning of August, he was granted an interview there with Whittaker Chambers. But he knew the interview was not going well when Chambers asked him offhandedly if he'd ever blown up a bridge. At last Berryman was told to come back after he'd written a review in the *Time* style. Four days later Berryman returned, only to have Chambers tear his review to shreds and tell him the magazine couldn't use him. Desperate, Berryman offered to rewrite the thing for Chambers and then left. But once outside, he became angry at the treatment he'd been given and stormed back into Chambers's office. It was unreasonable for Chambers to expect him to keep writing these reviews for nothing, he told Chambers. Chambers agreed. It would be better for Berryman to simply stop trying.

So here it was, "the middle of the greatest employment boom of our time," Berryman wrote afterward, and he without a job. He had nothing but contempt for the interviewers who had turned him away with equal contempt. The worst of it was watching Eileen suffer from loss of weight, headaches, fatigue, colds. What kind of man was he, he asked himself, that he couldn't make money, write, or "care for Eileen's health or prevent her unhappiness"?

What troubled him even more, however, was that she believed, as had Tate and his mother, that he could control his nervous seizures if he wanted to. To him, his epileptic seizures were things of "undifferentiated terror, inadequacy, weakness," which took hold of him when they wanted. So afraid of the seizures had he become by then that he several times considered taking his life until he had to promise Eileen not to dwell on such thoughts. Still, there were times when he longed for oblivion. Alcohol helped, but that was one of the things he could no longer afford. The only thought that comforted him was knowing nothing—not even life—lasted forever.

By mid-August the only possibility that had offered itself was a job teaching Latin and English at Iona Prep, a Catholic boy's high school in New Rochelle: six classes a day for twenty-four hundred dollars a year. At the end of August, he and Eileen took the train to Boston to store their furniture and books, then traveled to Brattleboro, Vermont, to see Bob, now working in a tannery there, Barbara, their niece, and infant nephew. On September 8, Berryman went to Iona Prep and formally accepted the position. Classes began on the twelfth. "This is not a subject for congratulation," he wrote his mother, "but presumably we will be able to live through the year." Eileen was trying to find a teaching position, and they might be able to make it on two salaries. Then he locked himself away, studying Latin grammar for twelve hours a day. For the next five weeks he commuted daily from Manhattan to New Rochelle to teach two hundred students he was convinced hated not only him but the school itself. He found it difficult to believe how uneducated the boys were, especially after he had taught at Wayne and Harvard. Exhausted, he kept hoping against hope for another job to offer itself.

Finally, on October 8, rescue came in the form of an offer from Blackmur to teach at Princeton for the four-month term beginning November 1. Fortune had "suddenly smiled" on him, Berryman wrote his mother two days later, and he was "being offered a job . . . teaching civilian and Navy" personnel. He was resigning at once from "Hell-in-New Rochelle" and taking it. True, the job carried no tenure and no assurance beyond those four months, and he would earn only $225 a month, less even than Iona was paying him. But at least Princeton was human. He felt no compunction about resigning from Iona, "having been the victim there of what I am afraid I cannot describe as conscientious treatment, and what I must call inhuman conditions." He begged her never to tell anyone he had ever taught in such a place.

On October 24, he and Eileen celebrated their first anniversary. Though they had very little money, they managed to have a wonderful day, sharing part of it with Bob at Sullivan's bar on Ninth Avenue before Bob took the train back to Brattleboro. Afterward the Berrymans went down to Bleecker Street to see Van Doren for the first time since their wedding. Then they went to the Metropolitan to see *Pillar of Fire,* as they had on the evening of their wedding. The following evening, his twenty-ninth birthday, Berryman took the train to Boston to sell what he could of his furniture. Then he went down to Princeton to settle into the temporary quarters the university had found for him. He managed to bring his old red leather chair and a few other possessions down with him to Princeton, but everything else, including his library, had to be put in storage.

As luck would have it, just after he accepted the job at Princeton, several other university positions opened up, including one at Duke. Well, it was too late now to worry about that, he knew. Eileen, flush with new hope, took him to a fashionable clothier's to get him a new suit and overcoat. After she and Berryman had spent the year worrying daily about their future, Blackmur had played Prospero, and a bright new world was suddenly beckoning to them.

# chapter 10

# Rescue Work at Princeton

## 1943–46

After four years of teaching, Berryman found himself an underpaid instructor at Princeton, teaching 110 navy personnel in the wartime Armed Services Training Program. The schedule was unrelenting: classes Monday through Saturday from eight in the morning until six at night. But even at this level, Princeton seemed to him a "demi-Paradise." The navy program had been badly put together, but he did what he could, blundering forward like everyone else under spartan conditions, tired but "hopeful." What troubled him most deeply was knowing that some of these men would soon leave Princeton and their 4-F instructor for the islands of the Pacific or for Europe to meet early deaths.

On the other hand, Berryman had senior colleagues he could converse with, including several connected with the Institute for Advanced Studies. One of those he was closest to was, of course, the man directly responsible for bringing him here, R. P. Blackmur: dapper, mustached Blackmur, the once-poor boy who now shopped only at the best clothiers and vintners in

Princeton. Seven years earlier Blackmur had inspired Berryman to think about the high calling of the critic by a passage published in *Poetry* magazine, which for its complexity and authority Berryman would remember for the rest of his life. That passage read that the art of poetry was "amply distinguished from the manufacture of verse by the animating presence in the poetry of a fresh idiom: language so twisted and posed in a form that it not only expresses the matter at hand but adds to the stock of available reality." Now Blackmur became for him the model of the educated man, and Berryman was "astonished" at just how intelligent, moderate, wise, and charming a conversationalist the man was. Blackmur, that complex, divided individual, cerebral and Dionysian, whom Berryman would remember sitting in a chair at a cocktail party, quite drunk and holding out his thumb for the women to bite down hard on.

There was also Erich Kahler, the historian; Herman Broch, then at work on his *Death of Virgil;* Carlos Baker in English; the historian Cy Black; and Dean Christian Gauss, a formidable yet warm intelligence. There was also a good bookstore in town, the *Parnassus,* where Berryman spent endless hours browsing and talking. He stayed in temporary quarters at 36 Vandeventer Avenue until Thanksgiving, when he and Eileen moved into their tiny ground-floor apartment at 120 Prospect Avenue. At least it was within easy walking distance of the campus and the library, and it was affordable. Soon Eileen secured a job at the Institute for Advanced Studies, working six days a week for thirty-five dollars in the economics section of the League of Nations where, as Berryman put it, she met "Einstein at precisely 10:30 every morning."

Five weeks into his stay, Berryman wrote Mark. He knew well enough that Princeton might not renew his appointment when his four months were up, and that he and Eileen would once more be on their way. But from the larger historical perspective, at least, he was better off than the Germans, for, come March, he still expected New York and Boston to be standing (unlike, say, Dresden) and he was sure he would find work somewhere. How bizarre the war made everything seem, and more bizarre still how quickly the human mind got used to anything. Strange that he should just then be reading Mark's *Liberal Education,* which he found eloquent as Rilke on the angels, but which troubled him because of its faith in science, which in the last hundred years had done so much to make the world uninhabitable.

For the new year Berryman made a series of resolutions. He would endure things patiently; he would desire the best and try to stop playacting. He would no longer defer to anyone or conform to others' patterns of behavior, though he saw the inherent irony of keeping that resolution at the same time he was resolving to be patient. He would try to fulfill his duties and keep his true end—his work, his art—"always in full view." He also meant to work harder at being a good husband. Soon, however, his resolves were tested when his brother landed a job at *Time,* writing the "Milestones" section for the magazine each week. With mixed feelings, Berryman wrote his mother that it looked as if Bob was going to prove the more successful son, while he himself merely cropped "the grass and stamp[ed] the ground at the edge."

He and Eileen maintained their spartan existence in order to pay off the debts he had accumulated over the years. For his part, he bought only three books in his first three months at Princeton: an Aquinas, a Kierkegaard, and *Creve-Coêur,* Louis Aragon's recent book of war poems. On the other hand, in spite of a heavy teaching schedule, he read everything he could get his hands on: Arnold Toynbee, Werner Jaeger, Brooks and Henry Adams, Dante, "Egyptian history, Bulgarian history, poems, plays, novels, biographies, philosophy, logic, anthropology, neurology, God knows what, hundreds actually of books." He read James Agee's *Let Us Now Praise Famous Men* and found its prose standards so exact that the book made him feel as if everything he'd ever written were a fraud. That was unfortunate, since he had begun this voracious program in reading in hopes of getting back to his poems.

On March 1, 1944, he found himself once more without a job. All through February, he told Mark, he'd despaired once more for his future, on top of which his eyes had begun to give him so much trouble that he could not "read at all after dark . . . without chaotic effects." Feeling frustrated and useless, he had turned with an ironic eye to the Bible to support his sense of fatalism and found in Saint Matthew's Gospel a passage he could use: "Take therefore no thought for the morrow: for the morrow shall take thought for the things of itself. Sufficient unto the day is the evil thereof." The voice that could utter such words was surely one worth attending to: a voice, as Berryman saw it, with the ring of authority. He thought back to the previous summer and asked himself what had been gained for all his frantic efforts to find a job. After five months he had at last taken a job at Iona Prep that had nearly destroyed him. And then, suddenly, without lifting a finger himself, he had been invited to Princeton. In those five months he had written nothing and earned nothing beyond "a crude unsatisfying sense of . . . 'doing my best' while I violated my responsibility to write, my profession, my sensibility, my friendships and every instinct of humanity."

This time, then, he would sit tight and wait. He applied for fellowships from the Guggenheim Foundation, the League for American Authors, the Rockefeller Foundation. He considered working with Julian Boyd on the Thomas Jefferson papers Princeton was editing and read as much of Jefferson's work as he could. He thought he might still get a job teaching seventeen-year-old army reservists once the allotments were publicized at the end of March. He had a talk with the president of Georgia's Oglethorpe University and learned there might be a position opening there that would pay four thousand dollars a year. Then there were the women's colleges, Smith and Bennington and Greensboro, less seriously affected by the war than places like Princeton or Harvard. Moreover, Allen Tate was leaving the Library of Congress to edit the *Sewanee Review* and had expressed some interest in getting him to come down to Sewanee to help edit the magazine.

Berryman's best chance for employment, however, seemed to turn on the Rockefeller Foundation. Someone there had seen his essay-review, "Shakespeare's Text," which had appeared in *The Nation* the previous August, and the foundation was seriously considering financing Berryman's proposed edition of *King Lear*. Berryman, reviewing a book by the Shakespearean scholar W. W. Greg, had taken the occasion to summarize the textual scholarship done since the great Cambridge edition of Shakespeare of eighty years before. In doing so, he had mentioned the need for a new edition of *King Lear,* implying at the same time that he was the person to do the job. He decided now to wait until he heard one way or the other from the foundation.

But three weeks into his new unemployment he received two pieces of bad news in the same mail: a letter informing him that he had not received a Guggenheim, and another from Columbia, demanding payment of the five hundred dollars he still owed them. It took him eight days to reply to Columbia. "I belong to professions—Writing, Scholarship, Teaching—which are generally admitted, in this country, at present, to be poorly rewarded; and to a fixed-income class which suffers unreasonably under wartime inflation." He and his wife lived as modestly as they could. But "serious ill-health" had cost him dearly for the past five years. If he had ignored Columbia's earlier letters, it was only because he had no way of paying. He would pay them when he could find a job and start earning some money.

One piece of luck he did have, however, was the loan of Helen Blackmur's studio. Helen, Blackmur's wife, was working as second-shift supervisor in a war plant in Trenton, and had little time now for painting. The fifth-floor studio across the court from the Berrymans' apartment, furnished with green walls, a table, and Helen's paintings, turned out for Berryman to be a place of "light & colour & height & air & solitude." Here, he realized, he would be able to write poetry again.

In April he gave a three-week course on contemporary poetry at Briarcliff Junior College in Westchester County, New York. He called these talks "tentative judgments" on twelve men from English & American poetry. "The fact is," he told the young women enrolled in his course, "that if our time has produced in this country none and in England only two poets whom it is reasonable, already, to describe as 'great'—Thomas Hardy and William Butler Yeats,"—still, the period had been "unusually diverse in accomplishment." Only the early seventeenth century had been as rich in English lyrics. Besides Yeats and Hardy, he lectured on Bridges, Hopkins, Housman, Owen, Eliot, Pound, Robinson, Frost, Stevens, and Auden. He also touched on the poetry of Dylan Thomas, Delmore Schwartz, and—his favorite at the moment—Louis Aragon.

At the end of April he went to New York for an interview with two representatives of the Rockefeller Foundation. Yes, he hedged, he could do the intense work that would be demanded of him in editing *King Lear*. A week later he had the grant. It would run for a year beginning in June and gave him $2,600: $200 a month for a year for living expenses, plus $200 for travel to New York and the Folger in Washington. Suddenly, Berryman noted, Eileen had become "like a bird singing."

But Berryman himself suddenly felt trapped. An entire year had now been ransomed to Shakespeare, and he, a poet, nearing thirty, would have to spend precious time trying to reconstruct *Lear*. "Each year it is more plain to me that probably there exists no way of making a living (available to me) which will be either agreeable to my sensibility or convenient to what I pretend is my work," he complained to Mark. "It is very difficult indeed to live at all. . . . Each year I hope that next year will find me dead, and so far I have been disappointed." He despaired "of making anyone very happy," especially Eileen, so deep and ineradicable were his griefs. As for his "hope of writing something of value," that dwindled more each day.

His feeling of psychological constriction was one reason why he began now to study Baudelaire with a new intensity. After all, he noted, he and Baudelaire were alike in their "debts & oppressive awareness of hopeless obligation, in poverty & homelessness," in a father's death, a mother's failure to understand her son, in alienation from one's brother," in violent temper & razor sensibility to disgrace, in passion for privacy." There were other troubles too that spring. Bob's eighteen-month-old son, Charles Peter, drowned in a bathtub accident. Then, in mid-May, Berryman had a letter from Barbara saying Bob had left her for another woman.

The Lear project froze. Trying to find a way around his psychological impasse, Berryman decided to divide his work into two worlds. He used Helen's studio for his poetry and was given the Ball Room in the old library basement to work on *Lear*. This was a tiny room reached via a long tunnellike passage with exposed overhead pipes. Instead of using that route, however, Berryman took to squeezing himself in and out of the room through the basement window situated over his desk. In June he and Eileen moved into a larger apartment across the court from their old apartment. But since it too was on the exposed ground floor, he complained constantly that the whole world seemed to be looking in on him.

At the end of the month he sent the Rockefeller Foundation a final outline for his project. "To conservative readers who may object, plausibly, that *King Lear* is quite good enough as it stands," he explained, "it may be worth while to suggest an analogy: the cleaning of a Brueghel: which was sufficiently remarkable with its dirt, but hardly what the artist intended or painted,—and this Shakespeare has too in part to be restored." It seemed improbable to him that any of Shakespeare's punctuation or spelling or stage direction had entered the folio text. Moreover, layer on layer of assumption had been added by generations of Shakespearean scholars. He meant to record only those variants that, he believed, had "a reasonable chance of being right." Two weeks later he wrote to the secretary of the Clarendon Press's Oxford Shakespeare series, asking for the condition of the edited plays as they'd stood at the time of the death of McKerrow, the project's editor, at the same time informing the secretary that he was preparing a *Lear* edition with publication in mind. He should have suspected that such a letter would raise scholarly hackles on the other side of the Atlantic.

Finally, after several weeks of intensive work on the *Lear,* Berryman climbed out of the Ball Room in early August to take a vacation with Eileen on Cape Cod. They took the train up and stayed in Truro with friends from Princeton, going from party to party and renewing or forming new friendships with Dwight and Nancy Macdonald, Paul Goodman, and Edmund Wilson and his wife, Mary McCarthy. They spent one evening with Slater Brown, once Hart Crane's closest friend, and the "B" who had figured prominently in e. e. cummings's *The Enormous Room*. The hills were "full of writers & radicals to Eileen's delight," Berryman wrote Halliday, and it had been especially good to see Wilson and Macdonald. He was even writing poems again, and had done two sonnets on Scott Fitzgerald for Eileen's birthday.

After the Cape, however, Princeton looked very different to Berryman, especially in the August dog days, and he confided to his journal that he felt "Anti-Princeton in 50 ways." Eileen too seemed depressed at being back again. Moreover, there was no real reason now for staying in Princeton. He could work on *Lear* just as easily in New York. Nevertheless, stay on they did, and soon Berryman was back working in the Ball Room. Much of his time he spent reading *The Divine Comedy* (in Italian), Bartram, Doughty, Thoreau's *Journals*. But mainly it was reading the various texts of *Lear*. "*Text text text!*" he complained to Mark. "All scholars who are not to be saved should be set in Hell to edit 'King Lear,' the First Quarto."

In late August the Allies entered Paris. "I rub my eyes," he wrote on the twenty-third. "Can the war be really ending in Europe?" And two weeks later he wrote Halliday that, though he had been relieved of his teaching responsibilities, at least he was "not subject to the sort of leave which our fellow men are taking in large numbers on the Continent just now" as the war entered its last and most virulent phase. By then he was deep into "a new and exhilarating collation of the Second Quarto" and studying Elizabethan and Shakespearean shorthand methods. He wrote the librarian at the Gregg Institute about the various shorthand systems that might have touched on the practice of the *Lear* quarto of 1608: Bright's 1588 treatise, as well as those of two other Elizabethans, Peter Bales and John Willis, the latter of whom, Berryman believed, had invented the more likely system. At least the early quarto text, he was convinced, was "unutterably good from the early-stenographic point of view."

Early in October he wrote his mother to bring her up to date on his findings. He had finally decided that the irritating inconsistencies and garbledness in the *Lear* quarto were there because Shakespeare, "disloyal at heart and divided against himself, in a fit of amnesia, 'reported' his own play, sold the copy to the printer after carefully destroying all the distinctions in it between prose & verse, and is now merry with wicked joy peeping over Olympus at sorrowful scholars." *Lear* was indeed riddled with errors, he wrote Mark the same day. And although his renovation of the text was going rapidly now, his intense preoccupation with it had ruined him for anything else. He was, however, willing "to be destroyed in this cause," because rescuing Shakespeare's text was well worth the effort.

On his thirtieth birthday he wrote his mother that he was already feeling very old. "My talent lost, like my hair, sex crumbling like my scalp. Disappointment & horror. . . . Everything begun . . . everything abandoned. Every day I wish to die.'' His emotions had been ''white-haired so long that it is time really for their second youth; and this is what I count on, having wasted my first one.'' Realizing how black his mood was, he wrote her again the following day. That morning a letter—with money—had arrived from her, and he was ''tempted to use the gift to rush to New York to visit her for conversation of another sort altogether from the deadly institutional talk.'' But he was too busy writing poems and editing *Lear*. Oh, for some writers to talk to, he sighed, like Delmore and Bhain. He was stifling ''for lack of people of my own kind, *anti & literate*.'' But even if he could get up to New York, he complained, he had no money to do anything, and had even stopped carrying a wallet. He spoke briefly about his grandmother, eighty-one, whose health was frail and who had returned to Arkansas to live out her days. ''The qualities of joy and selflessness in those who are through age, or long & plainly fatal illness, really upon death, seem to me to redeem us if anything does,'' he wrote to console his mother.

At Halloween he wrote Halliday and told him he'd taken for his emblem a line from the fifteenth-century Scots poet Dunbar: ''Savour no more than thee bihove shal.'' Until just before his birthday he'd ''been speechlessly gloomy for a long time.'' Then, suddenly, he'd come out ''waving a pencil'' and was ''writing so busily'' he had no ''proper sentiments at all.'' He also mentioned that he and Eileen had had a visit from Halliday's wife, Harriet, who had come down from New York to spend part of the day. But Harriet had also written Halliday to say she and Berryman had had dinner one night in New York and that afterward she'd invited him up to her apartment for a nightcap, where he'd proceeded to down several and then confessed to her that she'd become ''an area of conflict for him.'' Suddenly he had run into her bedroom, calling after her that he planned to stay there until she joined him. It had taken all her wit to get him out of her apartment.

The two poems Berryman worked on that October—''Rock-Study with Wanderer'' and ''Canto Amor'' (originally ''Canto Eileen'')—show in their forms some of Berryman's recent preoccupations: the quatrain form of Pound's ''Hugh Selwyn

Mauberley" for the first; Dante's *terza rima* for the other. Such "formal" observations are easy to spot; other influences are more difficult. Clearly, however, Berryman's style was once again undergoing a metamorphosis. Yeats had given way to Rilke, and Rilke to Hopkins and John Crowe Ransom's sharp and sudden shifts in diction. In "Rock-Study," Pound was as much transformed by Berryman as Gautier had been by Pound. It was a difficult style Berryman had achieved, hermetic and jazzy at once, every effort being made to define himself by a distinctiveness of style that was too compressed for ready communication. Like "Mauberley," "Rock-Study" is a poem about war: war and the coming illusion of peace, war and "civil" war, and, finally, the terrible war within, which Berryman knew would be with him long after the war in Europe and the Pacific was finished:

> Waiting for the beginning of the end
> The wedding of the arms      Whose charnel arms
> Will plough the emerald mathematical farms
> In spring, spring-flowers to the U.N. send?

Years later Eileen would recall that early on in their marriage she had become "aware of the presence of a tall mute shadowy figure whose features I could not make out, a figure whose power over John was as strong as his mother's. It was the specter of John Allyn Smith." At the close of "Rock Study," Berryman allowed his readers a glimpse of this presence:

> a strange voice sometimes patiently
> Near in the air when I lie vague and weak
> As if it had a body tries to speak . . .
> I must go back, she will be missing me.

"Canto Amor" was written for Eileen for their second anniversary, then revised the following February and March. It was a poem divided between Berryman's anxieties about Eileen and his love for her. He blessed the "Unknown Majesty" for giving him, unworthy as he was, this woman, who had already kept him from giving in to despair, and sang of their marriage, having come at last to understand that in adversity the two of them had won through to something permanent. He acknowledged his "irresolute air," even as he tried to dance to the more spiritual music that Eileen had made at least possible for him. The poem's language and rhythms were racked, twisted almost beyond recognition, and caught Berryman's imperfect and needy love for his wife. He wanted desperately now to be her friend and, even more, to learn to love himself. But the only music he could make in his poems was a music fraught with fear and anguish.

With the new year, realizing that half his fellowship was gone, Berryman told Eileen that until June he would be able to give only one night a week to socializing. Otherwise, it was the Ball Room and textual emendation, or his study, where he managed a few reviews. Among them was one for *The Sewanee Review* of F. O. Matthiessen's *Henry James,* in which he guided his readers through James's work much as Pound had done thirty years before. Berryman knew, of course, that by 1945 the world Henry James had known so intimately was nearly lost, though James was *still* the great novelist of the twentieth century. There was something more in Berryman's essay, something unstated but driving it forward: a chance to speak his mind on equal if not superior terms about one of the leading figures at Harvard, Matthiessen himself. Several times in his review he corrected or refined what he took to be Matthiessen's coarsely formulated opinions. The new barbarism that James had foreseen had made itself felt everywhere, Berryman insinuated, until even the high priests of contemporary culture had been tainted.

There was news from Europe that January, the worst of it being the unfolding story of what had happened at the Battle of the Bulge, and a letter from a friend wounded in that action for a time stopped every thought for Berryman "like a fog of horror." Berryman's mother was married a fourth time, this time to a Swede named Nils Gustaffson, and Berryman wrote to wish them well. He sent them a book on Sweden as a wedding present, and visited them in New York with Eileen several times that winter. But by mid-June that marriage too was over. Nils had proven unstable and a drinker, Jill wrote her son, and Berryman was glad when his mother left Gustaffson for good.

Late in April, Berryman applied to the Rockefeller Foundation for a yearlong extension of his fellowship, citing the work he'd published or placed in *The Sewanee Review* and *The Ken-*

*yon Review* during the past year. When the foundation wrote back asking about his progress on the *Lear* and what he thought Shakespearean scholars would think of his work, Berryman asked them which Shakespearean scholars they could mean. After all, how many scholars could adequately judge the textual work he was doing? American scholars, he explained, would be hard-pressed to evaluate his work, for, while they worked hard, they accomplished very little and were committed to methods he was "trying to get rid of." He would, however, provide a list of the important changes he had made to two *British* scholars whose work he respected: Greg and Maas. A week later the fellowship was renewed for another year. Then he heard from Blackmur that, had the Rockefeller not come through, he was to have been offered a Hodder Fellowship at Princeton.

How distant Easter seemed now, Berryman wrote Mark on May 17. "Roosevelt, Hitler and Mussolini were alive, soldiers were checking out like flies in Europe, the cities falling." He mentioned how much he liked the *American Men of Letters* series Mark's colleagues at Columbia were doing, hinting that he would be interested in doing Stephen Crane's "crazy life" for the series. Mark lost no time in acting, and the invitation for Berryman to do the Crane came from the publishers within a month.

On May 22, there was a surprise party for Van Doren at the Algonquin Hotel to celebrate his twenty-fifth year of teaching. The Berrymans had dinner with Delmore, then joined the seventy people who had assembled for the occasion. Berryman was placed at the speaker's table along with Mark, Clifton Fadiman, Joseph Wood Krutch, and Lionel Trilling. Delmore sat off to one side, along with (Father) Steve Aylward, Jacques Barzun, Bob Giroux, and James Thurber. There were congratulatory messages from Tate, MacLeish, and Merton. Berryman kept his remarks short and ended by reading Van Doren's "Winter Tryst" and a poem he had composed for the occasion. The party had been like a roll call of his past, Mark wrote Berryman afterward, and called Berryman's remarks that night "the most beautiful discourse I have ever heard about anything."

A week later, with fresh reports of the concentration camps in Europe stirring in him, Berryman returned to New York and walked about Union Square, trying to evoke the ghosts of that evening four years before. Once again he listened to the tirades; only the subjects had changed. This time it was not right-wing anti-Semites but communists doing the haranguing, and when he engaged these haranguers in debate—as he knew he had to—he was glad to see that he fared better than he had four years earlier. Back in Princeton, he wrote from three till five in the morning, trying to recapture that summer night in 1941. This time it was prose, and what he wrote was a draft of his powerful and disturbing short story "The Imaginary Jew."

In early August he and Eileen went to the Cape again. It was there he heard the electrifying news that an atomic bomb had been dropped on Hiroshima. Who would have thought such a bomb possible? he wrote, stunned at what his civilization had created, "when the skill of Western science, the depth of our pockets, the energy of our industry, and the ferocity of our Army chiefs, enabled a Captain Parsons to destroy in a short time a large Japanese city." No "clear responsibility" could ever be assigned for this bomb or for any other bomb used in the future "to exterminate populations and cultures," he noted. The guilt for such an act had to be general, and he could only stare "upon the terror which in our name has been wrought."

Then came the second blast. "How extraordinary the end was," he wrote Mark on the nineteenth, "how horrible in the bomb and then how suddenly." He had been lying down, he would remember, when Eileen had burst into the room to say that the war was over. She had just heard it on the air. The war was over. Four-F status and all, the war had cost him, as well as Eileen. "She looked at me perplexed—the room was so dark that I couldn't see her eyes—and suddenly she burst into tears."

Proofs for "The Imaginary Jew" arrived from Ransom in mid-August with a note saying the story had won first prize in the *Kenyon Review*–Doubleday Doran Contest. When Berryman learned the news, he slipped to the floor and sat there, staring at the letter. The five hundred dollars he'd won was more money than he'd earned as a writer in the past ten years. He could not tell how good the story was, he wrote his mother, and was abandoning the question "to whoever reads it." The ending especially troubled him as perhaps a bit too literary, and when Dwight Macdonald noted the same defect several months later, Berryman sent him a postcard agreeing. How difficult to get that right, he told Macdonald, how hard to say exactly what emotions had swept him that summer's night. And then, all through the spring and summer of '45: the undeniable evidence of Auschwitz, Belsen, Treblinka, Babi Yar, Dachau.

"Heavier and heavier appeared to me to press upon us in the fading night our general guilt," he wrote at the close of "The Imaginary Jew." Unhappy as he may have been with these words, he had managed to evoke something of the tragedy of what had happened. "In the days following," he ended, "as my resentment died, I saw that I had not been a victim altogether unjustly. My persecutors were right: I was a Jew. The imaginary Jew I was was as real as the imaginary Jew hunted down, on other nights and days, in a real Jew. Every murderer strikes the mirror, the lash of the torturer falls on the mirror and cuts the real image, and the real and the imaginary blood flow down together."

Five hundred dollars. Enough to pay debts, including Clare College, so that he could retrieve his library, and also get Eileen a new coat. If anything was left over, he would buy some Shakespearean texts. And a Toynbee . . . and Chekhov. He felt "frivolously wealthy," as he had not felt since those first few exhilarating days when he'd won the Kellet. He and Eileen even went dancing. In two years he'd written two stories, both to some acclaim. Laughlin had reprinted "The Lovers" in his *New Directions* annual, and "The Imaginary Jew" was soon being translated into French and German. The following spring both stories were anthologized, one in the O. Henry Memorial Collection, the other in the O'Brien *Best Stories*. Yet he still found it hard to accept any sort of public recognition.

In October 1945, Berryman's brother remarried in New York, and Berryman and Eileen came up from Princeton for the wedding. Berryman's third wedding anniversary and his thirty-first birthday likewise came and went. That fall he began collecting materials for his biography of Stephen Crane. Mark, knowing how hard it was to collect Crane in 1945, sent Berryman his twelve-volume set of the author. But most of that fall Berryman worked on *Lear*. Then, in early December, he had a letter from the Rockefeller Institute saying they'd just learned that a Cambridge man from Edinburgh named George Duthie (who had the confidence of Greg and Maas) was about to publish his own edition of *Lear*.

The news came as a jolt to Berryman, but he managed to answer professionally. He thanked the foundation for the news and acknowledged that Duthie's edition would be interesting because of the man's extensive work with the bad quartos. He would write Duthie himself after New Year's. In the meantime, he assuaged the foundation, he too had made real progress, and now had some fifty pages of the textual introduction written, as well as a draft of the general introduction, and would show them the new work when he came to New York. But secretly he feared now that his edition would be unnecessary and that two years' work was lost.

He wrote Duthie one week into January, 1946, asking if Duthie might not "perhaps like to interchange opinions" with him. He wanted Duthie to know that he had finished a "provisional text and apparatus, with full commentary" the previous summer and was completing a textual introduction that would contain a study of the quartos and folios. He also wanted him to know that he'd photocopied "everything relevant in Willis' 1602 book" on contemporary stenographic practices and was now at work on the "Memorial-theatrical provenance" for the *Lear* quarto of 1608, studying the problem of memory failure in the actors who had performed in the original *Lear*. The letter was meant to intimidate Duthie as much as to share scholarly information with him.

With six months of his fellowship remaining, Berryman again resolved to do no more socializing until his edition was completed, and during this time Eileen came to believe she was married to a phantom. Making dinner in their tiny apartment, she took to singing, "All scholars' wives have rotten lives." Halfway through those last six months Berryman wrote again to the Rockefeller Foundation to say he had been in contact with Greg—the Shakespearean scholar for whom he had the greatest respect—about his own findings on the original staging of *Lear,* findings that went counter to Greg's in several instances. He had also sent Greg several textual emendations to the *Lear* text. Greg had written back to say that he now found himself in substantive agreement with Berryman's findings. At least, Berryman added, he had learned what to do with the text and how to do it, not only with *Lear* but with any Shakespeare text he might be given.

He also knew he had to find a teaching job for the fall, when there would be no more grant money. In March he went by train to the Women's College in Greensboro, North Carolina, to be interviewed for an opening there to teach writing. At least finding a job this time would not be a replay of 1943. With the war over and thousands of soldiers returning to college on the G.I. Bill, there were job offerings everywhere. He lost the Greensboro opening to Peter Taylor, but was offered a position at the University of Rochester. Then he heard from Tate, asking if he was interested in taking over as editor of *The Sewanee Review*. Berryman wrote back to say he was.

Berryman wrote Delmore Schwartz, asking what he thought about *The Sewanee Review* job. The salary was very good: forty-one hundred dollars. But for most of his life home had been the eastern seaboard: New York, Boston, Princeton. Living and working in Tennessee would mean "living a fortnight by plane & mulepack from civilization or what we call so." It would also mean being the very thing he had always despised: a professor. "There," he added, "one really pauses! There the abyss opens!" He was going to take the trip—"800 miles or something"—to look the Kenyon job over, but he was also crossing his toes.

But before a formal offer could be made by *Sewanee,* Dean Gauss made a counteroffer. Berryman could be Blackmur's "associate" in the new Creative Writing Program at Princeton at a salary of $3,750, beginning in September, and Berryman quickly accepted. He was drawn to Princeton, he wrote Delmore on April 26, with its accents of "a dying civilization," and where at least he wouldn't have to be "a professor but something fouler, an Associate in Creative Arts." To his mother he explained that he'd taken the job with Blackmur because it meant "very little work, access to my materials here in the library while seeing *Lear* through the press, access to Crane stuff in Newark, more money than I ever made before, and not having to move."

In early May he went to New York to attend a party at *The Nation* for Randall Jarrell, who was taking over as poetry editor while Margaret Marshall was on leave. It was the first time Berryman had met Jarrell, and he thought he might learn to like the man. Robert Lowell, who was also there, he'd met eighteen months earlier in Princeton under strained conditions, but this time Berryman took to Lowell immediately. Berryman knew Jarrell's work as a poet, and even more his formidable position as a critic, and had joked with Eileen that many poets, including those with established reputations, were holding on to their poems and praying for Jarrell's early death rather than run the risk of having their work shredded by his acerbic wit. Jarrell: tall, willowy, thin, dark-haired, dark-eyed, half a year older than Berryman, a man of stunning contrasts, a sentimental southerner, a hipster whose language was ten years out of date, a puritan who drove fast cars, a killer who could weep apologetically after his words had innocently sliced the heart from his victim.

Lowell was about to publish his second book of poems, *Lord Weary's Castle,* which would win him a Pulitzer Prize at age twenty-nine. At six three he was the most imposing of the three men, extremely handsome and rugged, a brilliant talker, comic, witty, and generous, a man who had already served six months in prison as a conscientious objector, a blueblood Boston Brahmin who had converted to Roman Catholicism, and a manic-depressive capable of lunging for the jugular. He was a critic very much in Jarrell's and Berryman's line: sharp, acerbic, honest, strict, unyielding. Like them, he had been influenced by Tate. But Jarrell and Lowell had been good friends since their college days at Kenyon, where they'd roomed together, and Berryman knew he would have to court both if he was to get closer to Lowell. For it was Lowell, he'd already decided, who was the better poet. Lowell left the party in *The Nation's* offices early, but before he did, he invited the Berrymans to come to Damariscotta on the Maine coast and stay with him and his wife, the novelist Jean Stafford, for a weekend that summer.

By late May, Berryman knew it was time to bring some kind of closure to the *Lear*. At a certain point, he wrote Sissam at the Clarendon Press that month, even work as apparently objective as textual criticism took on the temperament of the textualist. He had tried to read all fifty of the substantive texts of Shakespeare extant and had found the job a "nightmare." Five months had passed since he'd written Duthie, he explained, and he'd still to hear from him, but he had his own theories about the formation of the *Lear* text, and did not believe, as Duthie apparently did, that it had been dictated by Shakespeare or anyone else. Moreover, the work other editors had done on Shakespeare's texts showed them to be technicians rather than imaginative critics. In spite of Duthie's forthcoming edition, he was still willing to stand by his own work. A few days later he mailed "fifty pages of tough close argument" to Greg, and was, he told his mother, "now rushing through the text proper." That week alone he had written "twelve pages of text, five of apparatus, eighteen of commentary, and I mean to be done in a month of 15-hour days unless I break up."

Late in May he sent Tate a note asking for a thousand-dollar advance on the Stephen Crane volume. On the last day of the month, when his fellowship officially ended, he wrote to the Rockefeller Foundation that he expected "the Augean stables of *King Lear*" would be "more or less clean in another month," after which he would send his manuscript on to Sissam in England for his appraisal. At the same time Greg sent Berryman a "draft of a memorandum to *The Review of English Studies* withdrawing his theory of the staging to make way" for Berryman's. "A recent exchange of views with Mr. John Berryman, of Princeton, N.J., who is at work on a critical edition of *King Lear,*" Greg's note read when it was published in the July number, "has convinced me that at least some of the ideas on the staging of the play that I put forth . . . need modifying." At least Berryman had that small victory to hold on to.

Though the gap between what he had hoped to do and what he had done was wide, Berryman had been on his way to producing a reliable *Lear* text. Moreover, the poet in him, paying close attention to the inner workings of a master poet and studying the play's complex image clusters, had made some wonderfully imaginative emendations in the corrupt text. Something, however, stopped Berryman short of completing the text, perhaps his fear that—having published it—the future direction of his career as an academician would have been set. For, despite his having done little with his gift for the past two years, he was still first and foremost a poet.

In early July a letter from Duthie finally arrived. It was dated May 22, and informed Mr. Berryman that his—Duthie's—edition of *Lear* was "now in press" and would soon be published by Blackwell's of Oxford. Duthie outlined his arguments in favor of a dictation theory for *Lear,* asking Berryman, when he had seen the book, to please inform him if he had not quite "managed to refute the stenographic theory" that Mr. Berryman was arguing for. Berryman wrote back on the eighth, congratulating Duthie on completing his edition, and then went on—briefly—to explain that he had really been concerned less with mere textual issues and more with "recreating, justifying and explaining the text itself." Afterward, he wrote Sissam to say that Duthie had probably "scooped" him, and that he realized there might now be no need for his own edition of *Lear*. He still did not buy Duthie's dictation theory, but all he could do was wait and see what the man had to say. In the meantime he was "going North for six weeks to do other things." What he was going to do was see Lowell in Maine and talk endlessly with a real poet about poetry.

# chapter 11

# The Kingmakers

## 1946–47

Before they left for their summer place in Harrington, Maine, the Blackmurs too had invited the Berrymans to spend time with them. So had Nela Walcott, a wealthy Princeton friend, whose summer place at Blue Hill was near the Blackmurs. Berryman accepted both invitations and sent Lowell a note asking if he and Eileen might stop at their home at Damariscotta Mills, further down the coast. Lowell wrote back warmly, inviting them as well as the Blackmurs.

On the trip up to Harrington, the Berrymans stopped off in Cambridge to see Delmore, and over dinner he chided Berryman for not taking the *Sewanee Review* job and for electing instead to stay in Princeton, where he truly *was* in danger of becoming a professor. He also warned the Berrymans that they were in for some lovely fights between Helen and Richard. Nela, he warned, drank too much, and he was not feeling very kindly toward the Lowells. During the past winter they'd stayed with him in his Cambridge apartment, the three of them living in what Lowell would later describe as a mustard-gas-thick alcoholic maze.

There was some exaggeration in Delmore's manner, but he turned out to be right about the Blackmurs. Helen and Richard were constantly at each other, Helen aggressively, Richard passively, bickering from early morning until long after dinner. They seemed to enjoy fighting before an audience, Eileen would remember, as if their repartee were being scored. Far into the night the Berrymans could hear them through the thin walls, angry wasps stinging each other to sleep.

One night, unable to sleep, Berryman found himself up and reading long after everyone else had gone to bed. As he read, he could sense the shadows looming over him again. It had been twenty years to the month since a scene like what had occurred with the Blackmurs had taken place in Tampa. He stared out the upstairs window, across the fields, across the bluffs, toward the Atlantic. There was a huge, nearly human shadow out there, and it seemed to be waiting for him: the offshore island of P'tit Manaan. He could feel something tugging at him to cross the lawn toward the bluffs and then down into the water where he would begin walking out toward the thing that had been waiting so many years for him to meet it.

Some terrible presence he had managed to keep below the surface for twenty years had been triggered by Helen's assaults on Blackmur. Blackmur had lashed back, but Berryman could see that Helen was a woman with a tongue as sharp and destructive as his mother's. Only with first light was Berryman able to doze off. Later that day he told Eileen that he had had a strong premonition of the darkness tugging at him, and of his terrifying yet comforting wish to yield to it and simply let go. It was time, they realized, that they both got out of there.

The chance came when Nela Walcott came over for lunch shortly afterward. They took her aside and pleaded with her to let them go back to her house with her. That afternoon they packed hastily, made their transparent excuses, and left with Nela. The rift with Blackmur, with whom Berryman would be teaching in two months' time, had suddenly widened. Moreover, the stay with Walcott had its own problems, and soon the Berrymans left by taxi, headed for Damariscotta Mills and the Lowells.

What they found there was an early nineteenth-century white clapboard house with green trim sitting on a hill and Lowell waiting at the door to greet them. They were the first summer guests at the house Jean Stafford had bought with the money she'd earned from her novel *Boston Adventure*. This time the Berrymans enjoyed themselves. Berryman and Lowell took long walks and talked about everything. The Berrymans had planned to stay only over the weekend, but the visit was so easy, so compatible, that the weekend stretched into a week and then into two. On August 4, Berryman wrote his mother that the visit had turned out "lazy, agreeable, interesting & alcoholic; not conducive to correspondence." Not since Delmore Schwartz had he found anyone so pleasant to talk to as Lowell. It was for him a very heaven, Dante's circle of the philosophers busy with what mattered most—poetry and talk of poetry—two shadows on Damariscotta's hills, with the blue Atlantic behind them.

Lowell too would remember Berryman as all "ease and light" as they sat on the rocks by the millpond talking. All that work with Shakespeare had paid off, Lowell could see, for Berryman "could quote with vibrance to all lengths, even prose, even late Shakespeare, to show me what could be done with disrupted and mended syntax." Looking back to that time, Lowell understood that Berryman's preoccupation with broken syntax in the mid-1940s was "the start of his real style." Each day the three writers worked in different parts of the house: Lowell spread out characteristically on his bed upstairs, Jean sitting at her desk in the hallway, Berryman in the guestroom, fidgeting and staring at the blank paper before him. It was a wonderful moment: golden, impossible, the cementing of a friendship, and Berryman would come to look back at it as on the last summer of his innocence.

During the second week of August, Berryman and Eileen went down to the Cape. Between Truro, where they stayed, and Wellfleet, the home of Edmund Wilson and Mary McCarthy, they found themselves caught in the crossfire of "violently opposed political sects"—leftist writers like Dwight Macdonald and conservatives like Wilson—and Berryman soon found himself as bored as he had been with Bhain's earnest young communists. Still, he managed to avoid arguing except for one blowup with Macdonald, an argument which had arisen, Berryman wrote his mother, when Macdonald had repeated "some canard about Lowell."

But Berryman found it difficult to hide his disdain for the hangers-on, the hacks, the Hollywood sellouts he found among the Cape Cod literati and he "turned more monk than usual," spending his time, as he phrased it, sitting and scowling at the wall. He thought about returning to Damariscotta, but by then the Lowells' social calendar was filled, and he and Eileen returned to Princeton on the twenty-eighth. Looking back, he characteristically regretted spending so much time on vacation—eight weeks of it—and so much money accomplishing nothing beyond the writing of a few poems. One of these contained the line, "Delights, no more tempt my heart sullen with brume." Broom: the nickname he had given Eileen years before. He was beginning again to itch for "delights" outside his marriage.

In late September he began teaching creative writing. Among his students were Frederick Buechner, Sidney Monas, and Bruce Berlind, who would remember Berryman's peculiar, clipped speech, that strange amalgam of Brit lit studded with American slang. At thirty-one, Berryman looked very much the ascetic English don in bow tie and tweed jacket, with courtly, distancing manners. Berryman could be chummy one moment and vicious the next, and Sidney Monas never forgot how Berryman attacked him one evening at the Kahlers for holding what Berryman called "Stalinist" views. For weeks Monas avoided Berryman as much as he could. Then, one evening, he was surprised to find Berryman at his door, holding a copy of *Nassau Lit,* a Princeton publication with a new poem of Monas's in it. Berryman had read and liked it and had come over to discuss it with him. Monas understood that the gesture was meant to placate him, and the two of them talked poetry till dawn.

On the other hand, the rift between Berryman and Blackmur continued to grow. Having seen his hero in the cold light of his wife's attacks, Berryman now began to mimic Blackmur at social gatherings. But he also mimicked himself, unsure about his position as scholar, critic, and poet. It was that uncertainty that helped turn a visit from Lowell and Jarrell that September into a disaster. Lowell had just finished the revisions on his new book of poems and, separated now from Stafford, was living in New York. He was anxious to have Jarrell get to know his new "Scholar gypsy" friend better, and had insisted on Jarrell's coming with him to have dinner with the Berrymans. As it turned out, when Jarrell arrived, he was suffering from the effects of food poisoning, which made him more than normally touchy. Twenty years later, Berryman would remember that evening with affection and horror:

> So here's Randall walking up and down in my living room, miserable and witty. And very malicious, as he could certainly be, making up a brand-new Lowell poem full of characteristic Lowell properties, Lowell's grandfather and Charon, and the man who did not find this funny at all was Lowell. . . . At last we calmed Randall down. . . . We stationed him on the couch, and I gave him a book of photographs of the Russian ballet (he was very keen on ballet). While the rest of us had dinner, he lay there and made witty remarks about the photographs of the Russian ballet.

On the train back to New York that night, Lowell would recall Jarrell's mocking Berryman's high-pitched, excitable voice with his own excitable, high-pitched voice. For their part, Eileen and Berryman took turns that night mimicking Jarrell as they tried to cut through the chill Jarrell's visit had left. From that moment on, Berryman made sure he was never again in the same room with both men. There was much he could learn from them both, especially Lowell, but from now on it would be one-on-one.

When Berryman's poems were rejected once again in November, he decided—perversely—to send them directly to Eliot at Faber and Faber. By that point he'd lost all confidence in his work, so that the covering letter actually screamed with humor in its exaggerated self-defeat. "I can't suggest this precisely with enthusiasm," he wrote Eliot, "but if Faber were willing to take on my verse I should be glad." He would not trouble Eliot with a whole book, and so was sending him "ten poems, the earliest first, running from 1939 to 1944. If none of them interests you," he added, "their companions unsent probably wouldn't either." In fact, he had to admit that even he was "completely out of sympathy" with nearly everything he'd ever written.

Jarrell's long and brilliant review of *Lord Weary's Castle* appeared in *The Nation* in early January, a month after the book's publication. His praise was high indeed. "When I reviewed Mr. Lowell's first book," Jarrell wrote, "I finished by saying, 'Some of the best poems of the next years ought to be written by him.' . . . One or two of these poems, I think, will be read as long as men remember English." Berryman had just read Jarrell's assessment when he wrote his own review of Lowell. Here, he said, was a "thematic poet," capable of converting "a whole body of poetry" with transfiguring power. He showed in his review that he was as qualified as anyone (including Jarrell) to make such an authoritative judgment. "Set the simplicity and manliness of ["After the Surprising Conversions"] beside the mysterious frenzy of "The Drunken Fisherman" or the drenched magnificence of "The Quaker Graveyard" and you will observe," Berryman summed up, "a talent whose ceiling is invisible."

But what was fame, especially in a "comics culture" like America? A noise? A general clamor? And how many understood how to judge a poet anyway? Lowell had suddenly risen to the forefront of postwar American poetry, but what did that mean? "I don't wish to make a noise about Lowell," he added, "reviewers in other channels being equipped for this, and popularity in the modern American culture having proved for other authors not yet physically dead a blessing decidedly sinister." Fine poems, he noted, quoting from Hopkins, a poet from whom fame had been withheld as it had so far been withheld from himself, deserved to be "honoured and read." And though it was "one of the most dangerous things to man," fame was also "the true and appointed air, element, and setting of genius and its works."

In late December, Berryman's review of Grierson and Smith's *A Critical Study of English Poetry* appeared in *The Nation.* In reviewing the history of English poetry, Berryman made several comments on Pound's and Eliot's influence on the tradition, for their importance, he believed, was still underestimated. That was unfortunate, he added, for Modernism had begun with Eliot's *Prufrock,* and Pound, in spite of some of his literary judgments, had shaped the direction of much modern English verse.

Pound, under observation at St. Elizabeth's Hospital for the Criminally Insane in Washington, D.C., on charges of treason brought against him for his radio broadcasts from Mussolini's Rome, read Berryman's review and liked it enough to write him. He began by suggesting to Berryman that it might have been better "to treat humble vermin" like Grierson and Smith "with elaborate courtesy than with insecticide." As for Berryman's having called him up short for his literary judgments, if Golding's translation of Ovid's *Metamorphoses* wasn't the most beautiful book in the English language, as Pound had once said—and which Berryman had questioned—then what was?

Berryman rose to the challenge. For "most beautiful book" he suggested Chaucer's *Troilus and Crisseyde* or Spenser's *Faerie Queene,* "though Golding's matter, being Ovid," was "much more interesting than Spenser's." Other contenders were *Paradise Lost,* Joyce's *Ulysses,* half a dozen plays by Shakespeare, and Browning's *The Ring and the Book*. Berryman also took the opportunity to praise Pound for the pleasure his poems had given him over the years. During his stay in New York at Christmas, he added, he'd seen "a superb medal of Sigismundo Malatesta by Pisanello" at the Metropolitan Museum, made more real for him by his reading of Pound's portrait of Malatesta in the *Cantos*. Finally, knowing how hard it was for Pound to get good books where he was, he sent him his own copy of Golding's translation of the *Metamorphoses*.

Pound wrote back saying he was willing to admit Chaucer as a serious contender, but *The Faerie Queene* was merely "a bore" and *Paradise Lost* "a pest," both books being poison "for anyone under 60 who wants to write," and unreadable to anyone over that age. If Berryman could save only one book from a shipwreck—one—which would it be: Chaucer, Shakespeare, or Golding? When Berryman did not answer at once, Pound's wife, Dorothy, wrote, hoping Dr. Berryman would not wait to write again "till he has solved question of the whole of English literature posed in EP's letter," since there were more pressing matters to attend to. Thirty years earlier a magazine could be found to print Joyce, Eliot, Pound, and Wyndham Lewis together. Did such a review now exist, Ezra wanted to know. And if not, why not? Could, for example, Ford Madox Ford's "March of Literature" and the posthumous poems of J. P. Angold be published anywhere? Suddenly Berryman, like others, was being co-opted by Pound for the ongoing struggle to get the word out.

Berryman wrote back on February 14. "I've been walking

about New York, thinking, living like a hobo & writing, or I'd probably have written sooner though I wasn't sure you wanted to hear again until your wife's very good letter came.'' As far as publishers went, he told Pound, James Laughlin at *New Directions*—Pound's trusted disciple and publisher for the past dozen years—was, frankly, ''the most unreliable man in the country'' and assembled assistants as bad as himself. In the meantime Berryman had asked the editor of *The Sewanee Review* to send Pound a copy of the review so that he could judge for himself the current caliber of little magazines in America. But, he acknowledged, Pound was right about the moribund state of the intellectual quarterlies in America. There was nothing, for example, that could match the now-defunct *Little Review*. For the sort of writing Pound was after, independence was needed, and all the little magazines were now attached to universities. For all its faults, *The Partisan Review* was still the best thing available, largely because it was more open than most. The main reason, however, for the decline in the quality of the little magazine was money, especially the cost of printing, which had risen dramatically like everything else due to postwar inflation.

What was needed, then, was a magazine like Eliot's *Criterion*. Something had to be done to get away from the academic New Criticism one saw in all the reviews now—the sort of thing Ransom and Tate and Warren and Winters and Blackmur did so well but that was now ''stifling talent.'' It was time for new standards ''of life or form or power,'' though he had to admit he did not yet know where to turn for such standards. ''And for god's sake,'' he closed, ''don't address me as Ph.D., a thing I never was, despise, abuse, refuse to be, and have suffered very cheerfully not being now for ten years. . . . I only deal at the college here with some boys who want to write.''

Pound wrote back. Who were Berryman's contemporaries? he wondered. He had recently been in touch with six bright young men, and wondered if they might not form the nucleus of the new wave. He called off their last names as if anyone aware of the pulse of the times would know them: Allen, McLow, O'Neil, West, Olson, and now, of course, Berryman. Olson was Charles Olson, a six foot seven poet then living in Washington who took it on himself now to write Berryman at Pound's urging. He craved polemic, Olson wrote Berryman, but had ''got none from job on E.P. you may have seen [in] PR [Partisan Review] last winter), and grant to myself the rightness of his tactic, agitator he is, contriver, still spry agent of the lit. revolution.'' Olson was ''of another breed'' himself, but Pound had told him that Berryman was ''serious.'' He could grant that, knowing Berryman's work and respecting it.

He doubted Berryman would know his own ''stuff,'' especially since ''the Olson hand is little played as yet.'' But Berryman would be able to judge for himself if he looked at a book of his on Melville, *Call me Ishmael,* which would be out in a month. There were poems too, about to be published by the Black Sun Press. ''So—for papa—this opener.'' It was an invitation for a serious exchange, but Olson's jazzed-up tone put Berryman off. This was *not* the sort of exchange Berryman was after. Even the chatty missives from Dorothy Pound were wearing a bit thin by then. He did not answer Olson.

Instead, he wrote to Pound. His real contemporaries were not the group Pound had offered, but rather Dylan Thomas, Delmore Schwartz, and Robert Lowell. The best reviewer of his generation was Jarrell, though his generation had yet to produce a critic of major stature. Prose in the States had been ''dead for some time,'' although Jean Stafford was ''under way,'' and Malcolm Lowry's *Under the Volcano,* which he'd just read, had a subject—alcoholism and damnation—''worth treating.'' Most of the writers Berryman had mentioned were in their early thirties, and all had been set back (like himself) several years by the war.

At Pound's request, Olson answered Berryman's letter for him. What Pound had in mind was for five men of Berryman's generation friendly to Pound to keep in touch with one another to ''fight the fake'' and ''promote the serious—[Pound's] men [being] Kung [Confucius], Frobenius, Ford, Gesell, Fenellosa.'' Two of the five advance men would be Olson and Berryman. Was Berryman willing to ''do this for EP?'' Again Berryman ignored Olson.

But the thought of getting funding for a new magazine based on *The Criterion* particularly interested Berryman. He wrote Walter Marshall at the Institute for Advanced Study to see if the institute might back such a venture. In his letter, Berryman specifically addressed the issue of the southern critics and the omnipresent influence of Allen Tate on *The American Review,*

*The Southern Review, The Kenyon Review,* and *The Sewanee Review.* But even *The Partisan Review* was beginning to slip into "a cult-magazine" that "under an exhausted political impulse" was incapable of understanding Berryman's own brand of radically conservative thought in the tradition of Pound and Eliot.

He was proposing, therefore, a review that he could edit from New York to be called *The Twentieth Century.* At the heart of the magazine would be book reviewing, "to make known what is being done out there." Important articles appearing in the various quarterlies and reviews would be "noted and when profitable discussed." What he had especially admired about Eliot's *Criterion* had been the presence of radical and reactionary thinkers side by side. Berryman's own standards would be as high as those fostered by the *Times Literary Supplement.* He could get the review launched, he thought, with twenty thousand dollars.

In the meantime, Berryman's own poems had been developing along the lines of syntactic dislocation and its attendant deracinations, as in the complex and concealed poem on the loss of the father called "The Long Home," which he composed in April, 1947. There was also "A Winter-Piece to a Friend Away," a poem meant most likely for Pound at St. Elizabeth's. "I too the breaking blizzard's eddies bore/One year, another year," he wrote, remembering the Detroit winter when he had thought he was going mad. That April he also wrote a story about Bhain. He called the early drafts "Vain Surmise," a title lifted from Milton's "*Lycidas.*" Its final title, "Wash Far Away," would likewise come from that poem. In the story he thought back to his time with Bhain, when the two of them still thought they could revolutionize the world with what they had to say. Was the long preparation to become a poet a mistake then? he wondered, as Milton had before him. Bhain had struggled hard to become a writer, only to be cut off before he'd been able to accomplish anything of lasting value. And what of himself, locked into a deadening routine of teaching and scrounging for work, while younger poets like Lowell took the laurels?

In "Wash Far Away," Berryman caught the give-and-take of teaching the dull, the bright, the bored, the insistent. It was a series of skirmishes, teaching "*Lycidas*": opening with a prepared question, then the return fire of the unexpected question, and then—suddenly—seeing Milton's elegy become unsettling and strange before his eyes. Then, as one of the students rambled on, Berryman's narrator was suddenly back with his dead friend again. He could see Bhain laughing as he prepared to let himself fall backward off the edge of one of those huge, terrifying sand dunes at Grand Marais.

Bhain was showing him how to let go and fall down and down through empty space. First Bhain went and then it was Berryman's turn. "He shuddered, cold, came toward the edge, shrank. Feet moved by strong love on. Fought. He leaned erect off the world's edge, toppling, and stept! Through empty air straight down, terror of the first, the bounce and astonishment of the second. Pure joy the third, his eyes cleared. He rushed through the sunlight wild with delight in deep jumps . . . touching the earth, down and down" toward Bhain, who stood at the bottom waiting for him.

# chapter 12

# The Art of Adultery

## 1947

On the evening of February 20, 1947, Berryman attended a lecture at Princeton given by Arnold Toynbee. Standing around outside McCosh lecture hall afterward, he spotted an attractive woman whose name, he soon learned, was Chris. She was married to a graduate student and had a young son. Berryman saw her again in late March during an outing at the New Jersey shore, and again at a concert in Princeton. It wasn't his fault he'd noticed her, he told himself. After all, wasn't Bill Arrowsmith, one of his students, continually talking her up? And, regardless of how often he'd lusted after other women, he'd remained thus far faithful to Eileen. But he knew he was haunted by Chris's beauty. He began socializing with her in the company of others, joking, sharing confidences, drinking. Then, on the last Saturday in April, he kissed her.

Afterward he went back to his study and wrote a sonnet about the event—his first sonnet, he realized, in a dozen years. He tried thinking of good marriages and could come up with only one: Bhain and Florence Campbell's. But to what end?

Was not Bhain now merely "a bone sunned white"? Try as he might to write himself out of his obsession with Chris, he found himself gripped all the more tightly by it. To justify his obsession, he decided to elevate it to the level of art by writing a sonnet sequence that would record the progress of an affair, a sequence in the long tradition of Petrarch, Shakespeare, Philip Sidney, and Sir John Davies, but jazzed up to include Princeton and New York and the events of his own moment.

On April 30, he made his first visit to Chris's home. A few days later, he and Eileen met Chris and her husband for martinis and then went for a drive around the countryside. But Berryman's obsession grew, and by May 6, he knew he was in the grips of a "prolonged delirium." Was it possible, he wrote Chris that day, "that we first kissed just ten days ago?" He called her "a hedonist with a conscience about falling on people." He was mad to sleep with her and get "that blocking passion out of the way" so that they could begin "to speak slowly of what we are."

In the meantime the larger world outside went on. Eileen was busy working on her graduate degree in psychology, and Dorothy Pound continued to bombard Berryman with letters. The Pounds were depending on him to advance the cause of the Modernist revolution in the New World. So why, they wondered, didn't he answer their letters? On May 17 he took the train to New York to have tea with T. S. Eliot and Bob Giroux, Eliot's American editor, at Giroux's offices at Harcourt Brace. The talk moved from the *Four Quartets* and Eliot's upcoming lectures at Princeton, to Sarah Bernhardt, whom Eliot had seen when he was young, and on to Lowell's poems, which Eliot ...ught had "real punch." Perhaps, Berryman reconsidered, ...d too easily dismissed Eliot when he'd been at Cambridge ...ears earlier. Afterward he visited with Lowell. On the train ... that evening he wrote Chris that, though he had met that ... with Eliot and Lowell, her face was the one that kept ...ting him. "We move," he sighed, "down levels of under...ing into each other . . . until the separateness and the dis...ons dissolve."

...he following day he wrote his impressions of Eliot in an... sonnet. He noted the way Eliot had sat hunched across ... him, their easy talk, and how he'd been allowed to light ...reat man's cigarette. On May 23 he got back to Pound. He was sorry not to have written sooner, he explained, but there'd been classes, and then he'd had to finish a review for the summer issue of the *Sewanee,* on "Young Poets Dead," a review of the posthumous work of two young poets: not Bhain Campbell, but Samuel Greenberg and Sidney Keyes. The review was respectful, but ended by turning to the work of three young poets whom he admired even more, three British soldiers who had also died young: Wilfred Owen and Isaac Rosenberg during the First World War, and the Welsh poet Alun Lewis, who had died in the Burmese theater of World War II.

A few nights later, Chris stopped by the Berrymans' apartment for a talk on her way home. "Sky-high" on alcohol, she had talked "magnificently" for an hour and a half, Berryman noted. Afterward, he walked her back to her apartment "as burnt offering" for her husband, who was understandably angry at her condition. Toward morning—he afterward recorded in his journal—he slept with her. He celebrated the event in yet another sonnet, recalling Chris's husband's angry words and his own ambivalent feelings:

> —'Remorse does not suit you at all' he said,
> Rightly; but what he ragged, and might forgive,
> I shook for, lawless, empty, without rights.

Berryman kept telling himself that he still loved Eileen, was "in some way . . . fond of her, want greatly her happiness." But by early June he was "hopelessly in love with Chris" and wondered if he would ever stop loving her. Places had to be found where the two of them could be alone together: at their homes when these were available, at his office at 15 Upper Pyne, at the Ball Room, or in the surrounding countryside, off one of the back roads at a retreat they called the Grove. There were moments of soaring ecstasy in the strangeness and intense sensuality of the affair, but mostly what Berryman felt during that summer was guilt and depression, coupled with his need to create order out of the dreamscape in which he now found himself.

In early June Lowell visited the Berrymans again. They lunched at Lahière's, then spent the afternoon playing outdoors at Chris's house, where they drank heavily and romped shoeless in the grass. At one point, Berryman climbed the sycamore on Chris's front lawn, then watched Lowell race about below him, hunched over, grunting "like a caveman and throwing beercans and shoes." Suddenly Lowell was climbing the sycamore, pushing his way past Berryman to get to the very top to crown himself king of the mountain. Berryman tried to get around him, but failed. As a boy, Lowell had bullied his friends to let them know who was number one, and the meaning of Lowell's climb to the top of the sycamore was not lost on Berryman. Later that afternoon Berryman took Lowell aside to tell him about the affair. Lowell had been through this sort of thing; what advice could he give him? Say nothing about it to Eileen, Lowell told him, even if it meant lying, and then wait to see how he felt in six months' time.

Two days later Chris left Princeton with her family for a month's vacation, "five States away." Chris slipped Berryman a note, a daisy, and a photograph of herself with eyes lowered, hair bound back, lips shut. She'd suggested they toast each other at six that evening, and at six sharp Berryman found himself sitting in Burke's bar in Princeton, alone and unnoticed. Then, while the rain fell at the tattered end of a dull day, he puffed on a cigarette and drank her health. "My glass I lift," he wrote in Sonnet 13,

> my darling,
> As you plotted . . Chinese couples shift in bed,
> We shared today not even filthy weather,
> Beasts in the hills their tigerish love are snarling,
> Suddenly they clash, I blow my short ash red,
> Grey eyes light! and we have our drink together.

Separated from Chris, he turned with renewed intensity to the sonnets, ransacking older sonnet sequences for parallels to his own affair. He shuttled between the world of fantasy and the world of Princeton, anxious to ground his dream fever in the actualities of Princeton, 1947. On June 16, he wrote an imitation of Petrarch's sonnet, "*Passa la nave mia colma d'oblio,*" with its image of Ulysses driven "Between whirlpool and rock" while his "white love's form" shimmered from the ship's wheel. Sir Thomas Wyatt's powerful rendition of this, "My Galley Chargèd with Forgetfulness," only intensified the risks of Berryman's attempting his own imitation, as he struggled to fit the tradition to his own needs.

The following day he wrote a letter to *The New Yorker,* addressing the issue of how one went about reshaping a literary tradition to one's needs. He had recently noted in *The New Yorker*—under the heading "Funny Coincidence"—lines from Lowell's "Quaker Graveyard in Nantucket" juxtaposed with a prose passage from Thoreau's Cape Cod journal describing a shipwreck Thoreau had witnessed off the Cape. When Berryman saw that Lowell was being charged with plagiarism, he groaned. *Of course* Lowell had based his lines on Thoreau, but to impute this borrowing to plagiarism was to badly misunderstand how influence in poetry worked. Every poet borrowed. Consider Eliot and Pound. Had not Milton himself borrowed from Shakespeare? What mattered, of course, was how one turned one's borrowings into something new.

"Originality in poetry," he explained, consisted "less in the invention of materials than in the subsuming of materials into a moving and fresh unity. The poet invents some of his materials, and others he takes where he finds them,—from personal, conversational and literary experience; what he gives them is order, rhythm, significance, and he does this by means of style and the inscrutable operation of personality." It was the poet's personality, after all, that held a poem together.

That June Berryman attended several parties, including a memorable one at Erich Kahler's, where he met the artist Ben Shahn. Several times that month he also went to Manhattan, once to console Delmore Schwartz, who was in a terrible state after quitting his job at Harvard. Berryman and Schwartz drank heavily that evening, and Berryman returned to Eileen more moody than ever. And, as the amounts he drank increased, so did the ferocity of Berryman's arguments with Eileen. She worried about what was happening to him and could not forget how drunk he'd let himself get at Chris's house when Lowell had visited. "Eileen talked violently about my drinking now and during the past year," he confided to his journal, hurt that she'd taken his social drinking as a sign that he might actually have a problem with alcohol.

But he knew Eileen was right. A few days later—alone and sober—he began surmising how the affair with Chris would end. Was he going to remain a prisoner to his lady, some thrall to feverish sex, shivering before her every word and action? he asked in the mixture of archaic literary diction and modern lingo he'd invented for himself. The answer, he saw, was yes:

> I see I do, it must, trembling I see
> Grace of her switching walk away from me
> Fastens me where I stop now, smiling pain;
> And neither pride don nor the fever shed
> More, till the *furor* when we slide to bed,
> Trying calenture for the raving brain.

He could not shake his fantasies. That day he wrote four more sonnets, in one complaining of Chris's refusal to leave her husband for him, overlooking the fact that he himself was no more ready to leave Eileen:

> I stare down the intolerable years
> To the mild survival—where, you are where, where?
> "I *want* to take you for my lover" just
> You vowed when on the way I met you: must
> Then that be all *(Do)* the shorn time we share?

In early July, with Chris and her family due back shortly, Eileen asked him if she and Berryman might at least stay good friends. "I'll poison them off if we're not," she added, in a tone Berryman interpreted as "plaintive, half-humorous, and *mysterious*." Had Eileen meant only that he drank too much when Chris was around? Did she suspect? Was she asking him to try to preserve their marriage? He was too confused and terrified to ask her what she meant.

On July 3, he wrote six more sonnets, several of them in the grove where he'd earlier made love to Chris. "For weeks, for months, my will has been at the service of my passion and my imagination," he wrote with some irony on Independence Day. That weekend he had another terrible argument with Eileen (which he was careful to record in Sonnet 56) that had ended this time in talk of divorce. His greatest fear still remained that Eileen would find out about the affair, news he was sure would devastate her. He had no choice, therefore, but to lie to her, "a whole life of deception except when I say I love her, as I do." And yet wasn't loving Eileen "a disloyalty to Chris"? What in God's name, he wondered, was he raving about?

He waited impatiently for Chris's return on July 6. At dawn that day he was up, trembling as if a subway train were entering a station:

> As the undergrounds piston a force of air
> Before their crash into the station, you
> Are felt before your coming, in the platforms shake. . . .

By then he was sure Eileen knew. How could she not? He couldn't sit still, he made excuses, and when Chris at last stopped by on the seventh, he found himself shaking in her presence. Afterward Eileen told him he'd made a "damn fool" of himself.

A few days later, Berryman made love to Chris again and celebrated the renewal of the affair in his sonnets. "Drawing me suddenly into you," Sonnet 67 recorded,

> Your arms' strong kindness at my back, your weaving
> Thighs agile to me, white teeth in your heaving
> Hard, your face bright and dark, back, as we screw
> Our lives together—twin convulsion—blue
> Crest curl, to rest . . . again the ivy waving.

But the following sonnet marked a futile wait in the Grove—on a rainy Saturday morning—even though Chris had warned him not to expect her if it rained. The following morning he was at the Grove once more, waiting, and thinking of how mass was being celebrated somewhere at that very moment, the "dawn-priests applying/Wafer and wine to the human wound." He had his own sense of sacrament, though, and felt Chris's presence would cure him while innocent birds flew above them, bestowing their Franciscan benedictions on them. But when Chris failed to show up once more, everything went dead for him: his "delight in the sonnet, anxiety to show it her, all confidence, all . . . desire even."

On the last Friday in July he took a trip to eastern Pennsylvania to visit with Sidney Monas at his family farm. It was while at the farm that Berryman told Monas about the affair and about the sonnets. He spoke too of his recurrent dream of finding himself in an asylum, where he had stolen a quart of milk off a dumbwaiter and then tried to hide it among some copies of the *New English Dictionary*. Then Chris had come up to him (as he recorded in Sonnet 79) "in a matron's uniform/ And with a look (I saw once) infinitely sad/In her grey eyes" had taken the milk away from him. A matron's uniform? Was Chris then actually a substitute for his mother, a way of approaching the forbidden? And was hiding the milk among a plethora of words his attempt to translate his sexual theft into poetry? "Lord, the dream went exactly into a sonnet!" he noted in the manuscript of the poem, surprised at the power of the dream song he'd written.

But why, he asked himself, this obsession with a form as "exhausted and contemptible" as the sonnet sequence anyway? At first he'd been simply seduced into it and then had found himself "in the thick of it, with a dozen sonnets" before he knew what he was doing. Then too he had needed a form of some sort "to record (form, master) what happened . . . a *familiar* form in which to *put* the *new*." When Monas had objected to his use of local names, places, and events, he found himself defensively explaining that most of the sonnets had been written in haste, but that he would generalize them when the time came to revise. But the more he thought about it, the more he knew it was exactly this emphasis on the local in his sonnets that was new and distinctive about them and that would help make the sonnets memorable—if indeed they ever saw the light of print.

"Neither my fondness nor my pity can/O no more bend me to Eileen with love," he wrote with stone coldness in a new sonnet after his return home from Monas's farm. What, he wondered, was holding his marriage together? He even fantasized Eileen and Chris's husband pairing off like atoms into new constellations, the four making two new, happy couples. Then he discovered that he was enjoying himself once more in Eileen's company, and his guilt came crashing down on him with renewed force. But he was also angry and confused, and hated playing the devoted husband when he was obsessed by this other woman. He wanted no more of "this pretence-of-relation-we-don't-have-and-can't-have-again and this kindness more cruel than torture." Better perhaps to leave Eileen than continue this charade of a marriage. Then, one night, doing the dishes together, Eileen herself asked him why they kept up the marriage at all. Come fall, he promised her, if things didn't improve, he would move out. Then he stormed out of the apartment and wandered up to the lake, shaking at what he'd said.

In Sonnet 87, written a few days later, he used an acrostic, embedding his and his lady's name there for anyone to read: I CHRIS AND I JOHN. And, in another sonnet, which he would later remove from the sequence, he completed the sentence: ONE ANOTHER TAKE. Then, realizing that he had gone too far, he changed the last word to read, instead, LOVE. Here then was the mystical marriage of Berryman's sonnet sequence, first proclaimed, then altered, then partly erased by time and circumstance and the dissolution of the fantasy.

On July 30, he waited again for Chris in the grove and drafted Sonnet 88. The following day he waited for her in the Ball Room, and wrote number 89. By then he was ready to finish the sequence. He had little hope that Chris would ever see it all, and little hope of ever seeing the poems revised and reordered as he knew they would have to be if they were ever to be published. Perhaps, he thought, the best thing would be to finish the poems and then simply burn them. By then, clearly, they had taken ascendancy for him over the affair itself. He had written ninety sonnets in the past eighty days. Never, he told himself, had he worked so hard. With that kind of record, to feel guilty for neglecting work on the Crane biography was ridiculous.

Sonnet 91 signaled yet a further change. As their affair moved out of the turbulence of the falls into calmer waters, Chris was at last allowed to emerge in the poems less as an erotic force and more as an individual. She too had grown up in Oklahoma. Ten years before, at age seventeen, as the sonnet remembered, she and a boy had stolen horses and ridden across the plains through the night. She too had climbed oil rigs as Berryman had, and he remembered how the wind had blanketed him then "like a lyric." There were even shared domestic moments, as in Sonnet 95, where Berryman recorded listening to Chris accompany her small son to the strains of "On Top of Old Smoky." Sleeping with Chris, he noted ominously, had begun to seem rather like Ulysses' dallying with Circe, or—worse—like Oedipus' sleeping with his mother.

Then, in mid-August, Berryman's nightmares began to return. Early on the morning of the fifteenth he awoke, shaking from one in which a killer had chased him for twenty-six miles. Did the number, he wondered, refer to the year of his father's death? "Toss Jack a jawful of good August grass," the nightmare had droned. Toss this John a little affair, some splendor in the grass, so he could be lulled into forgetting what had really been eating at him for the last twenty years.

August 20 marked the six-month mark since he'd first noticed Chris. "1327, at six in the morning on April 6th, I entered the maze, and I still cannot see my way out," Petrarch had written six hundred years earlier, remembering the exact time and place he had first seen *his* lady. And Berryman, in Sonnet 106, imitating Petrarch:

At nine o'clock and thirty Thursday night,
In Nineteen Forty-seven, February
Twice-ten day, by a doorway in McCosh,
So quietly neither the rip's cold slosh
Nor the meshing of great wheels warned me, unwary,
An enigmatic girl smiled out my sight.

From the start, but without adequately counting on Berryman's obsessions, Chris had wanted to keep the affair simple. He had written of her as a goddess, an angel, the perfect woman. Now, however, he found himself adjusting his style to her "cruelty." "She must mean to torture me to my death," he confided to his journal on August 27. "As kind as a tigress, faithful as a whore. . . . 'Ring us up when you want to see us . . . anytime.' She knows I *can't* telephone . . . and when she'd gone I broke and wept. . . . *I am back on the rack.*" He felt rather like Moses pleading with some "SS woman" as she "put her whip and file" down and simply walked away from the affair altogether.

"A winter-shore is forming in my eye," he wrote that evening. Hadn't Chris invited him to swim out with her beyond the summer into a kind of death by water, to the

widest river: down to it we dash,
In love, but I am naked, and shake; so,
Uncoloured-thick-oil clad, you nod and cry
'Let's go!' . . white fuzzless limbs you razor flash,
And I am to follow the way you go.

The arc of passion, like the arc of the sonnet sequence, had finally iced over. In four months he had written 110 sonnets. It was time now to begin rebuilding his shattered relationship with Eileen. The following day, seeing his wife across the room—really *seeing* her for the first time in months—he wrote in a manic upswing of relief, "If we survived these four months, nothing can separate or destroy us. I *put away* despair." He was so elated she hadn't left him that he found himself dancing with joy around the empty apartment.

But even as he cursed Chris's "callousness," he could not get her out of his mind. She was the "cold and cocksure lover-murderer" who had snapped her fingers and dismissed him. Well, there was still his bald-headed, empty-eyed bride waiting for him, as once more he contemplated joining her in an ecstasy of death. Then a warm note arrived from Chris, and suddenly everything looked better.

On the Cape with Eileen early in September, Berryman noted that one of the Wellfleet crowd who had taken the train up with him had been drunk the entire trip. Strange, he thought, to see anyone actually live like that. He took walks along the ocean's edge with the Macdonalds and picnicked with the Cape "radicals" on the beach and at Gull Pond. He got into a ferocious argument over Pound with the black writer Emmet Coleman, and with others as well, and wound up retreating to his room to read Shakespeare. At one point, after he'd had an argument with Macdonald at a party, Eileen took him aside to warn him of his antisocial behavior. Angered, he stalked out and walked back to Wellfleet alone. But the following day he drove to Provincetown with Macdonald, apologizing and telling him about the affair, only to learn from Macdonald himself that Macdonald was having an affair of his own.

A few days later, as the Berrymans were preparing to go to a party at John Malcolm Brinnin's, Eileen received a breezy letter from Chris, and the entire weight of the summer suddenly slammed down on Berryman. As he watched Eileen reading the letter in the car, he thought he was going to throw up. Later, at the party, feeling sorry for himself and bitter toward Eileen, he began drinking heavily. By the time the party moved to another couple's for dinner, Berryman was drunk and seething inwardly. So, when the talk turned to Eileen's becoming a psychoanalyst, someone threw out the barbed question of how she as a Catholic could reconcile Freud with her religious beliefs. Suddenly, Berryman too was attacking her for trying to maintain that Catholicism and psychoanalysis could ever be reconciled. Eileen was hurt and confused.

That same evening John Dos Passos plowed his car into a parked truck, killing his wife and losing an eye. When Berryman heard the news next morning from the Macdonalds, he was stunned that a marriage could end so abruptly and so finally. That night, when guests came over for an evening of music, he vented his anxieties by insulting the choice of music—an "ugly Bartok sonata"—which he dubbed "extermination camp music."

Back in Princeton, he lost himself once more in his work. One of his first projects was an essay-review called "Frost and Stevens, and Others," which focused on two recent books of poetry: Frost's *Steeple Bush* and Stevens's *Transport to Summer*. Here, he noted, were two poets who had stayed in America. Both had "endured" Harvard and settled in New England; each had written poems unlike the other, Frost's concrete, Stevens's devilishly abstract. Both had begun writing relatively late, so that their work was fully formed by the time their poetry had become known, though—measured against Yeats and Eliot—neither had "exhibited a large development." Moreover, their prose was "infrequent & odd," Stevens's being "elaborate, rather inept," and "quotation-crammed," Frost's "racy & oracular." And while Frost had been ignored by the intellectuals, Stevens had been ignored by the public. Yet both—unlike himself, he noted—had managed to prosper in "a society inimical" to poetry, Frost managing five farms and Stevens earning his obscene "Egyptian salary."

Campbell's death still haunted him. "His visionary eyes," Berryman wrote that fall, "Hollow and ill, saw more then." He recalled the telegram from Florence informing him of Bhain's death and his sense then of having been deserted, and compared that desertion to what Chris was doing to him now:

Stricken I stood in Harvard Yard . . .
Holding the telegram—then I walked on, slow,
Walked on, and took my inevitable class.
The first desertion. Now the second comes,

Her chain falls from me, the delirium's
Dread heart slackens to zero—I can pass.

Berryman's depression, which had been deepening since August, now became so pronounced that he decided to seek professional help. He began seeing a psychiatrist in New York, a Dr. James Shea on Park Avenue, to help him uncover the reasons for his obsession with Chris. By then, he realized, even Eileen was treating him as if he were ill. He told Shea he was continually being abandoned by those he loved: by his father, by Bhain, by Chris. Up till then he'd been unwilling to examine his past, partly because all he could see when he looked there was some "hopeless fool," and partly because there were things he did not want to think about.

His epileptic attacks Eileen had long since dismissed as merely "hysteroid," his way of dealing with a difficult mother. Now, listening to himself and watching Shea's responses, Berryman began to realize that Eileen had probably been right. Wasn't that what he'd tried to work through in writing "The Lovers" and what he'd repressed for years: his mother's theft of what was properly his father's by taking on other suitors, first Uncle Jack and then those other men he'd caught her with, all of them spitting on his father's grave?

After that first visit in late September, Berryman took to jotting down things to tell Shea. He saw more clearly now that he hated women in direct proportion to how much he could use them, even for art, and soon he was showing Shea the sonnets he had written that summer, wanting some indication that they were too good to destroy. For the next few months, Shea advised him, it would be better for Berryman to stay away from his mother and work instead on cementing his relationship with his wife. After all, he had to remember, Eileen was *not* his mother. Berryman listened, though he also told his mother she was to tell no one of anything he'd intimated to her about the affair. "The summer, in general," he wrote her on September 27, "may be considered a nightmare from which I have partly waked up."

For the time being he decided to stay put with Eileen in Princeton and live as cheaply as possible until he finished the Crane biography. Eileen had been accepted into New York University's graduate program in psychology, and had a part-time job Mondays through Thursdays doing psychological research for a statistical survey sponsored by the university. She bunched her classes on Thursday night and all day Friday so she could be back home at least on weekends. For his part, Berryman hoped to make something during this year when he would not be teaching by writing journalism and lecturing while he worked on the Crane biography. Schwartz also came through with an offer to pay him for a regular chronicle of contemporary poetry for *The Partisan Review*.

Berryman also had his sonnets to finish. On September 28, he wrote Sonnet 111. He had talked with a Princeton colleague about his affair, and had again been advised to say nothing to Eileen for the present. He also knew that turning the affair into art was to admit that the affair had been played out for ends other than itself. More sober now, Berryman turned his energies instead to learning "God's will, give in,/ After, whatever, you sit on, you sit." Exasperated and exhausted, he promised to "freeze" his affections for his lady. For the moment he ended the sequence, still unable to "submit" to the hard lessons that the precursors to his own sonnet sequence had taught him: that sooner or later all affairs ended pretty much like his own.

The sessions with Shea turned now to an examination of Berryman's relationship to his father. Actually he could remember almost nothing of his father anymore, and most of what he did remember his mother had told him: that Daddy cared nothing about living, that he had almost no sexual vigor, and looked, with his little trim beard, rather like a French homosexual. But as the memories flooded in, he wondered if his mother might actually have killed his father, at least by insisting on a divorce at a time when his father's world was collapsing on him. And what of his own betrayal by taking Uncle Jack's name? But the more he looked at the hell within, the more he feared he might already be beyond Shea's or anyone's help.

As the fall deepened, Berryman again took up with Chris, even though he knew she was trying to put her marriage back together and that things between them could no longer be the same. Better, even he could see now, to put as much distance as possible between himself and her and to get on with his work. He began writing a play about adultery, calling it *Katherine Nairn* after an eighteenth-century adulteress-turned-murderer he'd read about when he was at Harvard. Soon he was working the play around the still-unresolved issue in his own affair of restitution for sexual transgression. He saw Chris as another Katherine Nairn, and Chris's husband in the role of Nairn's husband. When he realized that he himself was not a character *in* the play, he was delighted. Here, finally, was something he could share with Eileen as he'd been in the habit of doing until the sonnets had made that impossible. The play, on the other hand, was something he would have to keep from Chris.

That October the Berrymans managed to celebrate their fifth anniversary with "calm & affection." But the fever was still there, and a few days later Berryman again made love to Chris. "No one was ever more affectionate & gentle & devoted & womanly than Chris last night," he noted afterward. At first, Chris had told him, she'd hated him for cooling toward her and had wanted badly to hurt him. But the hatred had melted, and her affection for him had returned. They agreed not to make any plans or unrealistic demands on each other. If they were going to continue to see each other, it would have to be without the illusion of an "all or nothing" relationship.

But the first time Chris failed to show up for an assignation, Berryman went wild. By early November he was writing to himself: "TO HELL WITH LOVE. UP PLAYS!" He would focus instead on Eileen, giving "her confidence—in herself, in me, and in the marriage." But that same night he went to see Chris and made love again, afterward writing in his journal that they had been "closer tonight, as well as more *open*, and more deeply in love, than ever we were before." But later that day, when he read over what he'd written, he could hardly believe himself. "Try not to be so fucking self-important," he reminded himself. "Who the hell am I? It's not only unworthy & hideous, but silly." He saw Chris a final time a week later and then, except for the brooding, the affair at last burned itself out.

In retrospect Berryman calculated he had slept with Chris a total of fourteen times. There had, of course, been days of "unspeakable happiness," and there were also the sonnets, even if he could not bear now to look at them. He also believed the affair had given him a better insight into women. As for what that knowledge had cost his marriage, he had no way yet of gauging.

The sessions with Shea began to show now in his writing. As he developed an essay on the American intellectual, Berryman became uncharacteristically personal. His background, he noted, was mostly English, with some Irish and Scotch and German mixed in, so that by American standards, he was old stock. On the other hand, he'd been raised a Catholic in Oklahoma, which was surely an anomaly. How, then, had he been shaped by his culture? And what after all *was* culture? A matter of subscribing to *The New Yorker*? Was American glitter and hype simply a way of killing off English culture? And though he did not say so, his contempt for America, especially since his return from England, was directly linked to his rejection of that pure product of America: his flamboyant, wildly successful failure of a mother.

On November 20 he went to New York to see Shea, afterward stopping by to talk with Schwartz and William Barrett at the *Partisan Review* offices. What he found were two men harried with overwork, unshaven, and trying to get the next issue of the magazine out. Berryman had come to tell Schwartz that he still did not have the poetry review ready for him, but Schwartz told him to expand the review into a full essay, for which he would be paid accordingly. At first Berryman procrastinated. Then, beginning at half past eight Friday morning and working until noon on Saturday, he wrote a cogent and powerful piece on the contemporary scene in American poetry that he called "Waiting for the End, Boys." That afternoon he delivered the essay to Schwartz, who was so pleased with it he told Berryman he now had "a sacred obligation" to do many more such reviews.

In his essay Berryman noted that one kind of poetry seemed to be coming to an end just then and another kind beginning. What was ending was "Modern Poetry"; what was beginning was what Jarrell had called, in reference to Lowell's work, a "post-modernist" phase. Berryman began by reviewing his own generation of poets. "By 1935—referring only, for the moment, to this country," he wrote, "the Auden climate had set in strongly. Poetry became ominous, flat, and social; elliptical and indistinctly allusive; casual in tone and form, frightening in import." American criticism and a concomitant ignorance of the English tradition had acted to shape and misshape American poetry until only Stevens could offer anything like a counter-poetic to Auden. How insular American poetry had become since 1935 could be gauged by the handful of foreign-language poets American poets read in depth: Rimbaud, Rilke, Valéry, Lorca.

The main influences on American poetry for Berryman's generation, then, had been Auden and Stevens. Pound's influence had been "intermittent," "nobody of interest" was seriously listening to either Frost or Williams, and Marianne Moore's work had had its effect mainly on the two best women writers of his generation: Elizabeth Bishop and Jean Garrigue. The middle generation of poets, those now in their late forties, had already "gone to pieces." Tate had "published one booklet in a decade," Hart Crane was dead, MacLeish had "evaporated," and Van Doren and Robert Penn Warren had dead-ended. In short, his generation of poets had had to seek grandfathers rather than fathers.

As for Yeats, he knew from hard experience that the man's personality was "so distinct and powerful that few writers cared to submit to it in the hope of coming out themselves." The only exceptions had been Auden and Schwartz. But by the late 1930s, when Yeats's influence had been most felt, Auden had already developed a distinctive style and Schwartz had "drenched" his Yeats with heavy doses of Eliot, Stevens, and Rilke.

English poets presented an even less interesting case than the Americans. Most first-rate American poets, from Stevens to Lowell, were simply unavailable in England, so that there was an air of "unreality" to the English poetry scene, because Eliot, despite his British citizenship, was still an American poet, and Auden had left England for America. As a way of compensating for their wasteland, the English had "inflated almost to absurdity" the poets they still had. On the other hand, there was so much unthinking poetic activity, so easy an acceptance of Auden's "flat" sort of poem in America that it was even "possible for a hat rack" like John Ciardi "to write a perfectly presentable poem on any standard subject."

To demonstrate the kind of poem he was talking about, Berryman chose a sonnet by Howard Nemerov. Nemerov was clearly a gifted poet, Berryman began, but he wrote his sonnets in such an improvisational mode that it was as if he were not writing sonnets at all. At the other extreme was Allen Tate, who had obscured his early sonnets "frightfully" out of an "exactly opposite desire: *not to take it easy*." Either impulse,

Berryman considered, might prove "fruitful or sterile," though for the most part both had proved sterile in the hands of American sonneteers. He gave no indication in his essay as to whether he himself had added anything to the form.

The real find among the books under review, however, was the British poet Henry Reed. The renaissance Berryman hoped for in English poetry would be a repeat of what had happened three hundred years before: a reform of English versification, "giving it sweetness and regular pause and elegance," characteristics he found now only in Stevens. But in Reed he had been surprised to discover someone who could both outflat the flattest verse and yet write a poetry as elegant as Stevens's. In truth, he was attributing to Reed what he desperately sought for himself: a reimagining of the poem. Here was someone who had a developed sense of irony as well as a sense of humor—qualities Berryman was anxious to cultivate now in his own overly serious poetry so that he could learn to laugh at himself. He wanted a poetry that would be comic *and* tragic at once, a poetry too which could reshape the poetic tradition in one's own image.

At the other extreme from Reed was Robert Lowell, that pure product of America. For if Reed was all "anapests, feminine endings, extra-syllabled lines of all sorts," Lowell was all "spondees and humped smash." But Lowell and Reed both stood outside the poetic climate of the times, two non-union members interested in a myth-rich poetry. He did not know whether one or the other of these men represented the new poetry or was simply preparing the way for the new. But since Berryman himself had hopes of one day changing the direction of the English lyric, the identity of the new poet mattered very much to him.

A week later Berryman had a letter from the publishing firm of William Sloane. The year before they had agreed to publish a book of his verse, tentatively titled *Traditional Poems*. Now they wrote to say that the volume would be out in six months and they offered him an advance of $250. Ten days later Berryman at last heard from Giroux at Harcourt, Brace & Company, also offering to do the poems. It was too late now for that, Berryman wrote back. But there would be other books, including at least one on Shakespeare.

In December he wrote three poems, one of which, "The

Dispossessed,'' provided him with the title for his new collection. All three of the poems—''The Dispossessed,'' ''Narcissus Moving,'' and ''Fare Well''—attempted to bring to a close the difficult period he had just passed through: a period, he realized, which included his entire life since his father's death. ''Fare Well'' was yet another attempt to let the past go and begin again:

> O easy the phoenix in the tree of the heart,
> Each in its time, his twigs and spices fixes
> To make a last nest, and marvellously relaxes,—
> Out of the fire, weak peep! . .
> Father I fought for Mother, sleep where you sleep!
> I slip into a snowbed with no hurt
> Where warm will warm be warm enough to part
> Us. As I sink, I weep.

As the new year approached, he tried to be philosophical about the affair with Chris. ''It was Chris's marvellous vitality'' he'd been attracted to and not finally to Chris herself, he began to see now. One afternoon that month, sitting in the Balt coffee shop watching the snow falling, he thought back to the summer when he had waited day after day with an impatience bordering on madness for his lady to appear. Now, ''miraculously,'' he could begin to be his own man again. The ''mad sonnets'' were history, and he was busy now getting a book of poems ready for the printer's, glad to have Chris out of his life. He hoped never again to go through what he'd gone through with her. Still, he had to admit, for the first time in years he did feel young again, ''full of energy . . . & invention & judgment.'' In the long run, perhaps the most important thing about the affair was the poems and even the prose. He realized now that he was actually writing better than he'd ever written before in his life.

He ''celebrated'' the dying year with a poem, modeled in part on Yeats's apocalyptic ''Nineteen Hundred and Nineteen.'' In eight 8-line stanzas he wrote of the party dominated by German-speaking Jewish intellectuals he and Eileen had attended in New York on New Year's Eve, envisioning the final holocaust when ''brownshirt Time'' would order all workers—himself included—to lay down their tools forever:

Worst of years! . . no matter, begone . . .
We see now we had to suffer some day, so
I cross the dragon with a blessing, low,
While the black blood slows. Clock-wise,
We clasp upon the stroke, kissing with happy cries.

# chapter 13

# The Face in the Mirror

## 1948–49

All I want is *time* & I will be a great poet still,'' Berryman cheered himself thirteen days into the new year. Even if nobody else knew it, he knew that no one then writing poetry in English, with the possible exception of Lowell, could write better poetry than he was capable of doing. On the sixteenth he sent George Dillon, editor of *Poetry,* seven poems that he'd written over the past eight years in an order he characterized as ''reasonable.'' But in an office memo, practically on the eve of the publication of Berryman's first real book, Dillon noted that Berryman was merely ''a sensitive practitioner & one of the better exemplars of what someone called the school that writes 'to be analyzed by Brooks & Warren.' '' Berryman's real reputation rested rather with his ''harsh reviews of . . . other contemporary poets.''

To Dillon, Berryman was a synthesis of Thomas, Auden, and Yeats. Nevertheless, *Poetry* took five poems for its April number: ''The Dispossessed,'' ''World's Fair,'' ''Surviving Love,'' ''The Traveller,'' and ''Fare Well.'' Berryman managed to place other poems that spring: two recent ones in the

April issue of *The Partisan Review* ("New Year's Eve" and "Narcissus Moving"), and another—"The Long Home"—in the May issue, two ("A Winter-Piece to a Friend Away" and "Rock-Study with Wanderer") in *The Kenyon Review*, and another in *Commonweal*.

On February 13 he read four poems for the Library of Congress: "The Statue," "Narcissus Moving," "Rock-Study with Wanderer," and "New Year's Eve." He had arrived in Washington the evening before and phoned Lowell, who set up the recording in his office on the top floor of the Library of Congress, Berryman preparing for his reading by listening to the recordings Ransom and Jarrell had made earlier. Lowell and Berryman spent the weekend together talking of poetry and mistresses and went out to St. Elizabeth's to pay Pound a visit. It was the first time Berryman had met Pound, and Lowell would remember Berryman sitting on the floor and hugging his knees as he asked Pound to sing him an aria from his opera about Villon. For her part, Eileen would remember her husband, on his return to Princeton, imitating Pound's high-pitched voice with "great sadness." Two weeks later Berryman heard from Lowell about *The Dispossessed.* After discussing all sorts of literary matters, Lowell added offhandedly that Berryman's poems certainly demanded "a lot of reading." But that was all he was willing to say. Copies of the Library of Congress recordings arrived, but his "narcissism being of the inverted variety," as he explained to Lowell, Berryman could not bring himself to listen to them.

That winter Berryman busied himself with reviews for *The Partisan Review*, including one on Eliot, in which, having elected now to write a more personal poetry himself, he took the occasion to reject Eliot's theory of impersonality. "One observes," he wrote, "a certain desire in the universities to disinfect Mr. Eliot by ignoring his disorderly and animating associations." But he'd found in Eliot's poems evidence of a mind "grievous and profound beyond a single poet's," and in the end Eliot's poetry, "which the commentators are so eager to prove impersonal will prove to be personal, and will also appear then more terrible and more pitiful even than it does now."

On March 22, Berryman began a poem to another mistress, this one a woman dead three hundred years: the American poet Ann Bradstreet. He wrote out the first stanza and then stopped, trying to understand why he was writing about treachery and guilt again. So, he realized, he was still obsessed with his affair after all! If he was ever to work well again, he would have to rid himself of his demons. Since a Catholic confession was out of the question for him, he would write his way out of his dilemma, confessing his transgressions in his poems. If only he could get it right, he thought, the new poem he had in mind (since the sonnets would have to remain hidden from view for a long time yet) would reveal obliquely the story of his crime and subsequent return to society. Before him he kept vivid the great example of Hawthorne's Reverend Dimmesdale, with his public confession to the community against which he had sinned.

A week later, on March 29, Berryman's grandmother, Martha Little, died in Mena, Arkansas, at the age of eighty-three. Berryman and his brother flew to Kansas City, then took an all-night train to attend the funeral on the thirty-first. Jill took the loss hard, and Berryman did what he could to comfort her, but right after the funeral he pleaded deadlines and flew back to New York. The following day he wrote his mother to say he was back home safely and anxious to get back to the Bradstreet poem, whose real subject he thought he'd finally discovered. But now the poem refused to come. Forget the meaning, he counseled himself, and "luxuriate" in the writing. He knew he was too damned stiff. Better to "riot," and "with good conscience." But before he could allow himself the luxury of the Bradstreet poem, he knew he had to finish the Crane biography, now long overdue.

Advance copies of *The Dispossessed* arrived, but he was already unhappy with the book. He sent one to Van Doren, adding that he did not want to talk about it. Jarrell sent him a copy of his own book of poems, *Losses*, but Berryman wrote to say he wouldn't be able to get to it as long as he had the Crane hanging over his head. He knew Jarrell would be furious with the imagined slight and, what was worse, that Jarrell was about to review his own book.

So here it was at last, *The Dispossessed*, a dozen years' work, fifty poems in five parts, the book dedicated to his mother. Just how worried he was about the book's reception showed itself one evening when he went with Bill Merwin and Bruce Berlind to hear a lecture by Yvor Winters. Berryman was not predisposed toward the critic who had attacked Yeats and so many other other poets dear to him, but he promised himself not to lose his temper. After Winters's lecture, which Blackmur introduced, Berryman went with Merwin and Berlind to the Nassau Tavern. While Winters and Blackmur sat at the head table, Berlind would remember, "the three of us [sat] at a table some distance away. There was discussion, Winters . . . pontificated, and John got increasingly irritated at his remarks. Finally, John lost control, stood up [and] challenged Winters' knowledge of what he had been talking about." Winters turned to Blackmur and asked Blackmur who Berryman was. Was the fellow always this rude? This was "mild," Blackmur shrugged. Knowing he'd made a spectacle of himself, and upset now with Blackmur as well, Berryman stormed out of the tavern, taking Merwin and Berlind with him, and went back to Berlind's attic room on Bank Street.

On a table there Berryman spotted a copy of the current *Kenyon Review* with two of his poems in it, "A Winter-Piece" and "Rock-Study." As he thumbed through the magazine, he began shouting that John Crowe Ransom was a "son of a bitch" for reversing the order of the poems. Berlind and Merwin read the poems, but could not see what difference the change had made. Berryman was beside himself. Three people, he shouted, were "going to be mortally wounded" by Ransom's carelessness. They tried to calm him down, but he would have none of it. What was he bothering himself with these two amateurs for anyway? he sneered. In a year's time, now that *The Dispossessed* was out, he would be a "national figure."

For a moment it looked as if he was actually going to fight Merwin. Then reason returned and he realized he'd put too much of himself into a book of poems he no longer believed in anyway. It had been foolish to tell a critic of Winters's stature off, and he'd compounded matters by lashing out at his two friends. Still, he worried about Lowell's and Delmore's response to the book. As for Jarrell, there was nothing to do but let him have his say. Delmore broke the silence first by calling Berryman to say he'd been too despondent to write but had read the poems and believed they deserved the Pulitzer. He especially liked the recent poems, which showed that Berryman was moving in new directions. It was enough for the moment to placate Berryman.

Eileen too worried about the reception of her husband's poems. At the beginning of April she'd hurt her back in a fall from a bicycle, and there'd been talk of an operation. Yet in spite of her own difficulties, it was her husband she was worried about. Berryman felt guilt-ridden that he could not feel a similar concern for her. In fact, he was afraid he was incapable of feeling much of anything for anyone except himself. Then the nightmares returned: scenes of generalized guilt, especially one about his hacking women's bodies and leaving the pieces under various houses to be discovered. Eileen tried to persuade him to forget his nightmares and reassured him that he was indeed a good man.

In spite of misgivings about teaching, he signed on for another year as Resident Fellow in Creative Writing at Princeton. In June he had a letter from Paul Engle at the University of Iowa, offering him a salary of $4,500 to teach three to five hours a week, $750 more than Princeton had offered him. He took the letter to Donald Stauffer, his chairman at Princeton, hoping to renegotiate his salary, but got nowhere.

Six weeks after the appearance of his poems, he wrote a note to himself about what he'd tried to do in the book that represented ten years of his life:

> *The Nervous Songs* grew out of (as well as sonnet experimentation) my admiration for *Die Stimmen* [*The Voices*] of Rilke, though it was an accident that by the time I came to assemble the final ms., there were nine. . . . Two early poems show the deliberate influence of Delmore Schwartz, one late poem that of Wallace Stevens, and two late (not the latest) poems that of Robert Lowell. There may be some Auden left somewhere.

Pound and Eliot, he equivocated, had never interested him.

Finally, in July, the reviews began trickling in. The first one appeared in the *Times Literary Supplement* and noted that Mr. Berryman's poems, though "not always brilliant," were "thoughtful and friendly" and "invited re-reading." For younger English poets struggling with the problems of what to say and how to say it, Berryman's "range . . . , discipline and . . . confidence" made him "a useful pointer." Two weeks later Jarrell's review appeared in *The Nation*. It was as rigorous as Berryman had feared. Jarrell called him "a complicated, nervous, and intelligent" poet who had begun by slavishly imitating Yeats, with the result that the poems had about them a "posed, planetary melodrama" that could degenerate at times into bathos. When this happened, the poems sounded like statues trying to talk like books. And yet, Jarrell added, certain lines had about them a kind of "obscure magic." Too many "raw or overdone lines" coexisted with some "imaginative and satisfying ones," but in the end, Jarrell believed, Berryman would write poems better than anything he'd so far managed to do. Nor did Winters forget the rude young man who had attacked him. When his review appeared in the fall issue of *The Hudson Review*, he took Berryman to task for his "disinclination to understand and discipline his emotions." Until Berryman learned to think more and feel less, Winters ended, he would never be "a poet of any real importance."

In mid-July, Eileen had a severe relapse of her back problem and was moved to her sister Marie's home nearby on Linden Lane. It seemed now as if Eileen was going to require an operation for disk degeneration, and Berryman, chronically unable to cope with stress in any event, became more high strung than ever. Eileen, taking codeine and morphine daily, worried about having to postpone her degree and give up her internship. She tried to be stoical, but Berryman could not help noticing that even she was depressed. Broke, he drank more and more heavily and twice borrowed money from his mother to tide him over until he could begin drawing a salary again that fall. He avoided everyone he could.

Once more he tried to work on the Crane, and even managed an interview in a Newark bar with one of Crane's "few surviving friends," Dr. Walter Dunckel. He worked too on an introduction to Pound's poems for New Directions, as well as on a suite of poems he called *The Black Book* that he was writing in collaboration with a former Harvard student, Tony Clark, who had promised to provide him with watercolors or drawings to accompany the poems. The poems had as their subject the Nazi death camps, a subject that had occupied much of Berryman's thinking since the widespread disclosures about the camps three years earlier. In that time he had collected vast amounts of material on the exterminations. But the more he learned what the victims had suffered, the more he realized he would never be able to shape such evil into art. "One officer in black demarches here," he wrote, drawing for the Nazi officer on the darkness he knew lay within himself:

> cupshot, torn collar by a girl unwilling
> native & blond through the debauch
> that kept him all night from his couch,
> hurts his head and from the others' howling
> drove him out for morning air.
> Brooding over the water
> he reddens suddenly. He went back & shot her.

With Eileen ill, he was on the prowl after women again, mostly married. He continued his New York visits to Shea, who could see that Berryman was not taking care of himself. On one visit, when he and Shea were discussing Goethe, Berryman noted Goethe's lack of vision and Shea brought the discussion around to Berryman's own sense of grandiosity. Better, he told Berryman, to satisfy himself in his work than try to conquer every woman he saw.

For his part, Berryman knew that his trysts robbed his wife of what was rightfully hers, and Shea had said as much when he'd spoken of the affairs as thefts. So much energy expended in the arrangement of trysts, Berryman knew, without ever arranging any pleasures for Eileen. Perhaps he was even more of a monster than he had yet admitted to himself. Thinking this over in his empty apartment early that August, he suddenly broke down and wept. Again he promised himself to stop his mumbling self-pity and work once more at earning Eileen's trust. She would be coming home soon; there would be no operation for the present, though she would need a steel brace for her back. And she would be able to pursue her internship after all. At the end of the month, much to his relief, she moved back to the apartment.

By then Lowell's silence had become so deafening that Berryman had a nightmare in which he saw Lowell writing something contemptuous about him, and then telling him to assume the position as if he were undergoing some sort of humiliating fraternity initiation. Finally, he wrote Lowell asking if he'd received the book of poems he'd sent him in April. Lowell wrote back, studiously avoiding Berryman's question about the poems. It was clear he did want to talk about *The Dispossessed.*

By then Laughlin had been waiting for over a year for Berryman to choose the poems for Pound's *Selected Poems*. Now, he wrote Laughlin that he'd been "going crazy over the *nearly* finished Crane book" and would need a couple of weeks to figure out which of the *Cantos* to include. *"First day of the new regime,* he noted to himself on September 15, resolving to talk to no one, not even his wife, until the Pound was done. "With difficulty & uncertainty, like a dead man," he noted, "I reviewed my *Canto* selections & began the introduction: half a page (on Pound)." Eileen did what she could to accommodate herself to her husband's new silences. His depression deepened, but, broke now, he decided to stop seeing Shea.

That fall at Princeton, Berryman met Francis Fergusson, who was teaching modern languages ("very tentative & attentive, cackles when amused, large & slow, iron hair combed slick"), and Saul Bellow. Bellow he met at a friend's house, where he listened to him play Purcell "very sweetly" on the recorder. On their sixth wedding anniversary Berryman went to mass with Eileen, afterward thanking whatever God there was that the two of them had made it through the past year together. A week later he learned that he'd won *Poetry*'s Guarantors Prize for the five poems he'd published in the magazine earlier that year. It was, he noted ruefully, the first prize he'd won for his poems since his senior year at Columbia.

On November 2, Eileen had to return to New York for a back operation. Instead of staying with her, however, Berryman went down to Washington to give a reading and to visit with Pound on the third. At the hospital, Pound raced up the hall to greet him and told him to grab a chair. He rambled on, Berryman noted afterward, about the national elections for a while before he "sank down . . . buttoning a shirt he had thrust on . . . and began to eat a roll, after offering me one. Later when he went away to get some British illustrated papers about the removal of Yeats's body [from France] to Ireland to show me, he brought back bananas, was very surprised when I didn't want one, and rapidly ate both." Pound asked Berryman about the delays with the *Selected Poems* and why he hadn't written him, though he and Dorothy had both sent letters and postcards:

> Then he was very gentle, said I was taking much too much trouble with the introduction, and a look of pain went over his face when I mentioned E's illness. 'How *are* you?' when I asked, he put the query altogether away, saying that two hundred psychiatrists asked him this all the time. . . . He had been saying that he had gone to London to learn from Yeats how to write poetry, Yeats knowing more about it than anyone else. (Exactly as I did, a quarter-century later, but without Pound's brass; and like me had written five hundred sonnets, of which only the ten lines of 'Camaraderie' are rescued by Eliot; and Yeats's *height*—in the doorway at Woburn Buildings—astonished him as long afterwards it did me.)

A few weeks later, back in Princeton, Berryman would record something of this visit in his poem, "The Cage":

> O years go bare, a madman lingered through
> The hall-end where we talked and felt my book
> Till he was waved away; Pound tapped his shoe
> And pointed and digressed with an impatient look.
> "Bankers" and "Yids" and "a conspiracy". . .
> His body bettered. And the empty cage
> Sings in the wringing winds. . . .

On November 4 Berryman took the train to New York to see Eileen, and then went on to Bard College for a weekend poetry conference. He was horrified that even now he could give Eileen so little thought, and to make matters worse, he was involved with yet another woman. Again his thoughts turned toward suicide.

That same month he was invited by *Life Magazine* to take part in a group picture with other poets at the Gotham Book Mart in mid-town Manhattan, in honor of the flamboyant Sitwells, Dame Edith and Sir Osbert, the published photograph gaining notoriety for those present as for those absent. It featured Schwartz, Jarrell, Marianne Moore and her protégée Elizabeth Bishop, Auden, Gore Vidal, Richard Eberhart, Tennessee Williams, Stephen Spender, and others. Lowell had declined the invitation, but Berryman, who did show up, left the room when the picture was taken, refusing to be photographed with the likes of William Rose Benét "sitting there like a mummy," and Jarrell, "blazing . . . with ambition."

Eliot was at Princeton lecturing that fall, and Berryman invited him over for cocktails. Dwight Macdonald would be visiting, he explained, and he thought Eliot, who had met Macdonald in New York and liked him, might like to continue their conversation. Berryman also invited Paul Goodman. Eileen would remember Eliot's tall, stooped sixty-year-old public figure walking through the doorway into their apartment and Berryman congratulating him on winning the Nobel Prize. "High time," Berryman had said, to which Eliot had replied that it was actually too soon, since the Nobel was "a ticket to one's own funeral" and no one had ever done anything after receiving it. With the exception, Berryman noted, of Yeats.

Goodman arrived, all radical chic, clothes ripped and stained. Introduced to Eliot, he asked for his name a second time, but Eliot merely smiled, dismissing the slight. With Berryman, Macdonald, and Goodman all in the same room, the verbal fireworks began. Eliot left early, pleading he still had work to do on his acceptance speech, but not before Berryman saw him down five martinis, in spite of which Eliot managed to walk out of the apartment like a banker. As he left, Eliot turned to ask Berryman how Pound was doing. Couldn't Eliot help Pound get back to his writing again? Berryman wondered. Eliot shook his head. It was impossible. Not even he could get a word in with his old friend.

Earlier that fall, after visiting with Eliot at Princeton, Laughlin had stopped by Berryman's apartment to see how the Pound introduction was coming. He heard a faint croak telling him to come in, only to find Berryman hiding under the covers, muttering weakly that he was dying. Alarmed, Laughlin called in an internist, who, after examining Berryman, took Laughlin aside and told him he could find nothing wrong with Berryman. Laughlin knew then he would simply have to wait for the introduction until this difficult man was better. Finally, on November 30, after he'd finished teaching, Berryman returned to his apartment, flush with new insight into Pound's mind, and worked through the night to finish the piece for *New Directions*.

"The Pound is finished," a relieved Eileen wrote Dwight Macdonald on December 6, "and from a sea of Crane J[ohn] sends love to you both and so do I." It had cost Berryman, but the essay was worth it. If he overqualified his statements too often, still, the essay was closely argued, intelligent, and sympathetic, Berryman's major argument being that Pound's autobiography had come over the years to be Pound's real subject. "The *Cantos,*" Berryman summed up his essay on Pound,

> have always been personal; only the persona increasingly adopted, as the Poet's fate clarifies, is Pound himself. . . . The illusion of Pound's romanticism . . . has given him an inordinate passion for ages and places where the Poet's situation appears attractive, as in the Malatesta cantos, where Sigismundo is patron as much as ruler and lover. . . . Then he is anxious to find out *what has gone wrong*, with money and government, that has produced our situation for the Poet. . . . The rest of his heterogeneity is due to an immoderate desire . . . for mere conservation. . . . Once the form, and these qualifications, are understood, Pound's work presents less difficulty than we are used to in ambitious modern poetry. . . . The labour is similar to that necessary for a serious understanding of *Ulysses,* and meditation is the core of it.

In stressing the autobiographical element in Pound, Berryman once more went against the theory of authorial impersonality that Eliot and Blackmur had propounded. No wonder that, when he read Berryman's piece the following spring, Blackmur knew just how far Berryman had diverged from his own critical assumptions, and he remarked pointedly to Berryman that he wondered if Berryman didn't "really have much more against Eliot" and himself than he'd said in the essay.

With the Pound out of the way, Berryman turned his attention to the biography. December, he told his mother, would be a "nightmare month, one month, to finish *Crane* which is absolutely promised for Christmas." He would have to "work like a dog" before he could relax a bit and write verse again. His very soul was bored with teaching, but at least "it destroy[ed] only two days" each week. He also wrote to Van Doren, apologizing for the delay with the Crane and explaining that he'd had "no rest or peace of mind" for two years now.

he had "all the help science can give." Shea had done all he could, and Berryman was now on a diet of "dexidrine [sic] morning & afternoon; martinis before dinner; nembutal & sherry after midnight." He was both horrified and amused at what he was doing to himself.

A week later, poring over Stephen Crane's biography for the hundredth time, Berryman found what he called the "Primary Scene" in Crane's life. The long sessions of intense self-examination with Shea were about to pay off. In the final chapter of his biography, Berryman had decided to provide a Freudian account of the ground of Crane's motives. He was, of course, exploring himself as much as he was Crane, using his final chapter to confess—even exorcise—his behavior toward women. In "A Special Type of Choice Made by Men," Freud had discovered four conditions operable in the kind of man Crane and Berryman really were. "The woman loved," Berryman explained, "must involve, first, an 'injured third party'—some other man, that is, who has a right of possession, as husband or betrothed or near friend. She must be, second, "more or less sexually discredited . . . within the limits of a significant series" from a [flirtatious] married woman . . . up to an actual harlot. . . . Third, this highly compulsive situation [was] repeated." Finally the lover had to feel as if he were actually rescuing the woman even as he violated her.

Realizing that the rescue action in Crane was actually related to the taboo subject of the mother, Berryman became even more fascinated and afraid. Crane's theft of women, Berryman began to realize, was a way of getting back at the mother for depriving him of the father. The same thing, he knew, might be said of him. In his late short story "The Veteran," Crane had reinvoked the figure of Henry Fleming, the coward-turned-hero of *The Red Badge of Courage*, whom Crane now had enter a burning barn to save some children, knowing Henry would die in the rescue attempt:

> "Why it's suicide for a man to go in there!" Old Fleming stared absent-mindedly at the open doors. . . . He rushed into the barn. When the roof fell in, a great funnel of smoke swarmed toward the sky, as if the old man's mighty spirit, released from its body—a little bottle—had swelled like a genie. . . . The smoke was tinted rose-hue from the flames, and perhaps the unutterable

> midnights of the universe will have no power to daunt the colour of this soul.

Only when Henry young and Henry old had merged in the sacrifice of death, Berryman understood, would the son know he had been forgiven by the father.

"*The most important day of my life,*" he wrote in his diary that day, heady and depressed with having stared into the pit. Then he crawled out onto the terrace of his sixth-floor studio, his "brain ready to burst" with his terrifying discovery. He looked down; all he had to do was lean over and let go and at last he too would be reunited with his father. Never again would he have to worry about deadlines or anything else. He could labor, he knew, but he couldn't "come." Long ago he should have finished the Crane, but instead he'd let too many other things interfere. It was the story of his life, "first on Shakespeare at Cambridge then on Shakespeare here,—in my plays,—in my physical impotence—in my whole life." But standing there on the terrace, suddenly realizing what he was about to do, he steadied himself and then climbed back in out of the cold and telephoned Eileen. Once again he had faced down his demons. Now he could get on with the rest of his life.

# chapter 14

# Eddies & Backwaters

## 1949–50

On February 17, Berryman wrote the Rockefeller Foundation to tell them that George Ian Duthie's long-promised edition of *King Lear* had finally arrived. He was "still dead" from his work on the Crane and could not now put his head "back into Shakespeare," but he had taken an hour with it and wanted to send his impressions. The book had turned out after all to be "extremely different" from his own edition: merely "textual," "not exegetical, not illustrative, not critical and not aesthetic." Still, Duthie had gotten there first, and Berryman knew that it would cost his own edition—when and if it appeared—"a good deal of novelty," though novelty—as time went by—would matter less and less. Besides, the more he studied Duthie's text, the more his respect for it "faded." Duthie had ignored the very tradition Berryman had been at pains to exalt: a text with strong and well-reasoned editorial principles. He meant "to treat Duthie in public of course with more decorum," he closed. But privately he wanted to "kick his ass."

That same month, however, he was awarded the Shelley

Memorial Award for 1948 for his overall contribution to poetry. The award came to $650, money he found ''very useful.'' He bought himself some books and paid off some bills. He also treated himself to a bottle of Scotch and then demolished it at one sitting. He was drinking more and more heavily and talking nonstop, even as he tried to push through the Crane, until finally his doctor had to double his sedatives to slow his racing mind.

By then he had also been working for a year at his *Black Book*, trying to get some distance on the project by seeing it as a ''diagnostic, an historical survey.'' But in early April, ''reading of the murder of the Polish professors in *The Black Book of Poland*,'' he broke down and wept. He would have to let the book go, he at last decided. ''Lift them an elegy,'' he wrote by way of farewell:

> poor you and I,
> Fair & strengthless as the seafoam
> Under a deserted sky.

Except to salvage three of the poems for a pamphlet he published seven years later, the project was virtually abandoned. He hardly ever spoke about the book after that, as if silence were the only way to deal with the deaths of so many. It was hard, hard even for him, to bear adequate witness. And as the appalling truth of what had happened in the camps continued to be made known, the reality swept him under with it. When enough time had finally passed, he would speak of what he had had in mind for his abandoned book. It was to have taken the form of ''a Mass for the Dead'' and there were to have been forty-two sections. He had stopped only when he could no longer stare at the horror. Even the sections he had published were ''unrelievedly horrible,'' and he'd finally had to admit there was no way he could make ''palatable the monstrosity of the thing'' that had obsessed him.

Through the spring and much of the summer, he worked at the Crane and on the beginnings of too many other projects: poems, essays, even another biography. This one would be on Washington and would focus on the man's ''immense ambition'' as well as on his self-doubts and, finally, on his ''bottomless resignation'' in the face of death. The life of Washington was also to be a study in self-analysis. Meanwhile, he struggled to finish the Crane, bolstering himself with sedatives and alcohol and becoming more and more depressed. ''My conscience gets worse & worse,'' he wrote, ''mind & body fouled; and I cut myself off from my only source of help''—he meant Eileen—''by my bad conscience.''

At the end of July 1949, exhausted, he sent off the revised manuscript and then took Eileen to the Cape on vacation. They spent part of the time with the Macdonalds at Truro, and then with some young Princeton friends of theirs, Donald and Elizabeth Mackie, at Eaglis, the estate of Donald Mackie's grandmother. The year before, Macdonald had hurt Berryman deeply by commenting on Berryman's inability to finish anything with the result that Berryman had refused to speak to him until Macdonald had apologized. The apology finally came in February, and Berryman had written back accepting Macdonald's gesture of reconciliation. Now again at the Cape the two men quarreled, until Berryman refused even to join anyone for meals. On the evening of August 16, he and Macdonald got into yet another argument at a cocktail party, and Berryman stormed down the beach, walking directly into the ocean, clothes and all. For the next half hour the others searched the beaches, frantically looking for him. Finally he reappeared, sullen and thoroughly soaked, but alive.

During his stay at the Cape, Berryman managed to outline several essays. One was a response to Geoffrey Gorer's much-talked-about essay, ''The American Character,'' in *Life*. Berryman focused on the economic uncertainties of the American intellectual, especially the ''difficulty now of finding a job'' that would permit ''self-respect, much less build self-assurance.'' What did America do to her writers that made some—like Vachel Lindsay, Sara Teasdale, and Hart Crane—take their lives, and others—like Pound—go crazy? And why did Americans profess a passion for education, yet disdain those with educations? It was a strange sort of egalitarianism Americans practiced, insisting that they were as good as the next person, yet servile before the rich. As for himself, here he was, in his thirty-fifth year, being exploited by himself as well as others for very little money as he worked year in and year out, trying to make something of lasting value.

On September 1, he had an "angry, long, insufferable session" with his mother back in New York. Shea had warned him he would need at least a year of intensive treatment to deal with his mother fixation, and now Berryman could see that Shea was right. For the first time he spoke freely to his psychiatrist about his mother's flamboyant sexuality and about his own relations with women.

That fall Berryman also looked closely at Wallace Stevens's influence on his generation, wondering what to make of a Frenchified "holiday poetry," which was at once so "fantastic" and so "graceful-sounding." He also reevaluated Yeats's influence, wondering why it had not been greater. The truth was, he saw now, that Yeats had been " a damned bore until he was about forty," a truth borne out by a reading of Yeats's *Collected Poems,* which began with Yeats's early and mediocre lyrics and closed with his tedious early narrative pieces. True, Yeats himself had arranged the book shortly before his death, but "a good medium . . . might reach him easily" enough to talk some sense into him (though, as he'd noted in a letter to Bruce Berlind the year before, the "world-famous mumbling dim-sighted poet" had never really listened to anyone.)

How long, he wondered, before poets could get all of Yeats's poems in a single volume? Moreover, there was no good biography of the man. Joseph Hone's was "madly inaccurate" and Richard Ellmann's *The Man and the Masks,* "based on fifty thousand pages of Yeats's manuscripts," was a "spiritless affair, badly written, and very disappointing." Not much had changed since Berryman's days at Cambridge a dozen years before, when he'd complained that only six people had read Yeats more deeply than he had.

In spite of what had happened between Pound and himself, Berryman was still anxious to get Pound a fair hearing, especially as the Bollingen controversy over the awarding of that prize to the *Pisan Cantos* grew in intensity throughout 1949. So, when Berryman learned in February that Untermeyer might eliminate Pound from his anthology, Berryman wrote Untermeyer, legislating which of Pound's poems would have to be included. The heart of Pound's achievement, he explained, was in "The Seafarer," "The Return," "The River Merchant's Wife," "Exile's Letter," "Near Perigord," parts of the Propertius translation and *Hugh Selwyn Mauberley*, and especially, he added, several long passages from *The Pisan Cantos*.

Berryman knew that Pound was a "very uneven" poet, but he was also "extremely brilliant here & there in each of his periods." Pound's real strength could best be seen by making a judicious selection of the *Cantos*. Untermeyer wrote back to say that he'd been thinking along the same lines as Berryman, even though, as Berryman knew, till then it was Untermeyer who had led the attack against the Bollingen Committee's decision to give the prize to Pound. Berryman had often wondered "how these powerful fools felt," and now, watching Untermeyer scramble, he knew he had a more "accurate, depressing idea."

In November, as the critical furor over the Bollingen reached a crescendo, Berryman came to Pound's defense. He began a piece called "Antisemitism, Here," which explored the issue, and placed himself directly in the essay. He had a right to speak on such a delicate issue because, he reminded his readers, he was the author of "The Imaginary Jew," had been a contributor to *Commentary*, and had had a "continual relationship" with the Jewish community for years now. He began by admitting that he too had on occasion suffered momentary bouts of anti-Semitism, though all such incidents brought with them a sense of deep shame. Distrust, even hatred, of the other seemed endemic to the human condition, he realized. So "Dante hated Florence, Mark Twain hated Frenchmen, Baudelaire hated Belgians."

He thought back to Van Doren's 1932 *Anthology of American Poetry* spanning three centuries, which had contained one Jewish poet. Now, here was Oscar Williams's new anthology, with a fair number of Jewish poets. And how dissimilar these new voices were. Within Williams's anthology one found Schwartz's "enthusiasm for America" as well as Karl Shapiro's distaste for its culture. Berryman noted too the natural antagonism some Jewish writers felt "towards the elements which they cannot imitate in our older American culture—towards most of what [Van Wyck] Brooks, in fact, regarded *as* American culture." He was not surprised, therefore, to find most Jewish writers indifferent to Brooks's Protestant version of American culture.

He also sent a letter containing seventy signatures to Harrison Smith, editor of *The Saturday Review,* condemning Hillyer's attack on Pound that had appeared in the pages of that review. Smith wrote back to say he could not publish the letter because it had already been printed in a special pamphlet put out by *Poetry,* so Berryman had the letter published in *The Nation*. By then the Bollingen controversy had raged for half a year, and Berryman—having done what he could—went on to other things.

That Christmas he learned that he was being appointed Alfred Hodder Fellow at Princeton for the 1950–51 academic year, with a stipend of four thousand dollars. His only official function during his tenure would be to deliver several lectures on Shakespeare to a group of undergraduates enrolled in Princeton's Special Program in the Humanities. For the next nine months, however, he wondered how he was going to make enough money to cover his mounting debts. He continued to try his hand at essays for the paying magazines, but in each instance he got only as far as the outline stage before abandoning the essay for something else that interested him.

He contracted to write several essays for Philip Horton, Hart Crane's biographer and now senior editor for *The Reporter*, and wrote something on psychological biography, reviewing Francis Steegmuller's *O Rare Ben Jonson* and *Flaubert and Madame Bovary*, only to have the piece rejected—as the Pound had been—for being too esoteric. He began another on "Religion and the Intellectuals," abandoned it, then began another on Senator Paul Douglas of Illinois, whose hysterical scream on the Senate floor in the face of the increasing demands of the Defense lobbyists had caught Berryman's attention. He called his essay "The Hysteria of Honourable Men," but after several pages dropped that project as well. He would need something cleaner, faster, and sharper than the essay to register his reactions to world and national events. But when he tried to deal with public issues in his poetry, he turned awkward, verbose, bizarre. He had yet to find the form he needed.

In early February he received a letter from Van Wyck Brooks and the National Institute of American Literature of the American Academy, notifying him he'd been awarded one thousand dollars for creative work in literature. A week later another letter arrived, this one from a young writer named Robert Creeley, addressed from his chicken farm in Littleton, New Hampshire. Creeley was starting up a little magazine and wondered if Berryman would consider sending something, but Berryman did not answer Creeley's letter. Instead, he worked on a piece called "National Honour and a Future," which praised Orwell for blasting the debased state of the English language, noting that words like "honor" and "national pride" had been drained of their significance. He was dismayed to think how far Americans had fallen in their understanding of politics and international diplomacy when compared with the lucidities of a Henry Adams. The postwar years had turned out, he lamented, to be the Years of Mud.

All these were, of course, outward projections of Berryman's personal problems, for things did not go well for him that winter. The money from the American Academy helped, but he owed far more than that would give him. He needed to get away from Princeton, largely because he believed he was responsible for getting one of his intimates—a married woman—pregnant. So, when Robert Heilman, chairman of the University of Washington's English department, wrote to ask if he would be willing to take over Theodore Roethke's poetry workshop for the spring quarter—since Roethke had just had a nervous breakdown—Berryman jumped at the chance.

In mid-March, Berryman flew out to Seattle, staying in a small apartment on Shelby Street several miles from the university. For ten weeks he saw almost no one besides his students, complaining that his classes took all his time, since he had to prepare eight lectures a week on modern poetry. Instead, he stayed in his room and drank, stewing over his future. He managed a few poems, including one called "Seattle Breakdown" about his trip west:

> Came here tired thro' the air like lightning. Why?
> I'll dance a little. Hear you came for cash,
> With no high aim. No wish to be lavish!
> But to live on a while, take breath, and try.
>
> O the green hills & waters glistened from the air
> Circling down thro' mists. How does that follow?
> Work like a Soviet slave, and the work is hollow,
> Hard as I tried; so I flew to this last frontier

And I was full of hope: hope like a drain.
And I had other reasons to sit off still.
I ran from a rash of honour made me ill.
I ran from—and came to the hills of continual rain.

Some notes for a talk he gave that spring deal with the issue of an "English" as opposed to an "American" poetry, and it is clear from them just how far he still was from William Carlos Williams's kind of poetry. "The militant sense of an *American* poetry which was common a generation ago and persisted through the socially-conscious (& therefore more international) Thirties seems to have been dying away in recent years; as the need for it has died," he wrote. "When we (Americans) *had* very little that we could be comfortable with, it was necessary to assert the *value* and the *national* character of contemporary verse." But in the past thirty years American poetry had certainly proven as good as anything being written in England. The point was that a poet using the English language was by that fact an English poet, he believed, and none but "rabid nationalists and a few intransigent seniors like (say) Dr Williams will object to our (American) poets being called English poets." But it was better, he insisted, for Americans to "see themselves as part of an *English* tradition." What mattered finally was the perfection of a style, and that came only "by sedentary toil/ And by the imitation of great masters." Most of the masters of the English language remained, after all, English.

To acknowledge such mastery could only raise the level of American poetry, Berryman was convinced. If his two years in England had taught him anything, it was that even second-rank critics there knew the tradition better than America's frontline critics. And when he compared the *Times Literary Supplement* (which he'd read faithfully now for years) with the best of the American reviews, he found American criticism wanting because there was no audience for it. What the British needed from Americans was a sense of "hospitality," of knowing that their work would be carefully reviewed, much as the British provided a forum for American poetry in their reviews. And yet, while he was willing to hear what the English were doing, he was not willing to "fall in love with a dying woman." America was, in the final analysis, where the English-language poetry of *his* generation lay.

* * *

But as if to give the lie to that assurance, Dylan Thomas was making his first whirlwind tour across America, providing large American audiences with his Welsh declamations and naughty charm. On April 7, Thomas arrived in Seattle to give one of his reading events. In the thirteen years since Berryman had last seen Thomas, Berryman knew, the Welshman's poetry had flowered from the "inhuman" early lyrics to such extraordinary poems as "Fern Hill," and "A Refusal to Mourn the Death, by Fire, of a Child in London," the latter being, Berryman believed, "one of the profoundest elegies" in the language.

Berryman listened to his old friend's "fireworks with delight," then joined the party in Thomas's honor, not sure if Thomas would remember "his foreign fellow-tosspot." But Thomas did remember. "After many a summer," Thomas quipped as the two shook hands. He was heavier and even more untidy than Berryman remembered, and seemed more nervous. But then Berryman too was nervous. "We had had about ninety seconds' talk," he recalled in 1958,

> when our hostess, an affected and imperious lady known locally as the Duchess of Utah, crashed into and between us with "Well! Literary gossip, eh?" in a tone both injured and superior, meaning that we had no right . . . to seclude ourselves from the avid professors and professors' wives. . . . Thomas had already greeted everyone, incidentally. I kept out of the way until his chores were done. He was tired . . . [and] still on his first drink. Now he looked at our short hostess with resentment and contempt, and said slowly, "We were just discussing Hitler's methods of dealing with the Jews, and we have decided that he was quite right." An atrocious remark . . . and the reporting of this sort of thing *out of its context* would make it sound in the last degree impolite, or vicious. . . . But [the comment] had no context—nobody within earshot or eyesight was Jewish, and we had been discussing no such thing.

Thomas's vicious remark had been "an angry response to insolence," Berryman explained, for the Duchess herself "specialized in insult." Americans had "delighted in pinning Thomas to the wall," but

> measuring the response by the provocation, even in this instance of extreme response, I don't know that Thomas wants condemning. It must be remembered, too, that his weaknesses were often played on in order to get him into positions where he could be insulted with impunity; liquor was poured into him, and women not only threw themselves at him but were sometimes encouraged to do so by their academic husbands—I have myself seen this happen. It was an unbelievably difficult life he led on these tours. If his dignity, and his essential good-nature, sometimes suffered, it's little wonder.

Americans, Berryman knew, acted with a mixture of awe, bemusement, and contempt toward poets, and poets in turn often acted like clowns out of contempt and fear of their audiences and did things for which they were later ashamed. But it was important that those who judged the poet and told tales about him long after he was gone also understood the poet's extreme vulnerability, especially while the poet was on the public circuit.

During his time in Seattle, Berryman continued to practice his peculiar version of couvade. At the end of April he left his apartment for one on East Forty-third, closer to the university, but still he went nowhere and saw no one. In his first two months in Seattle he did not once leave the city. He did not even have a chair to sit in, and did his writing in bed. It did not occur to him to ask someone for a chair or to go out and buy one for himself. With the end of the rainy season and the return of better weather, his spirits began to lift. "It is very beautiful here after all on a good day," he wrote his mother at the end of April. There was "water everywhere, & green, & heights, & off to East & West the white great mountains: everything indeed Princeton has not."

But Washington had turned out to be "Wayne, & Detroit, all over again," and he had allowed too many outsiders into his lectures. He also realized that he'd expected too much from his students, pushing them "too fast" and "too hard," so that he had finally to slow down for them. He read his poems in Seattle and in Portland and even tried some easy mountain climbing. He was invited by some of his students to go skiing, but there he drew the line. He sailed Puget Sound and attended several parties and then, "tired & fed up," finished his lectures and flew home. The "Northwest rats" he'd had to deal with at the university had proven just too "big & boring."

A few days before he left Seattle, he wrote his mother, complaining that she'd never really loved him. Care and solicitude, yes, but not love. Whatever he hoped to elicit from her by that letter, however, he did not get. On June 9 she answered him. "It was because you did and do not love me that you accuse me of not loving you," she turned the issue around. She could not make her son love her, she told him, though she knew she would always love him. How did one answer that? he wondered.

Once home, he tried to get back to his own work but was plagued with insomnia and rage. In mid-June, Shea told him to stop taking sedatives and liquor and get more exercise. He took to bicycling and swimming, visited the Frick Museum in New York and studied the French and English paintings there. He worked on a play about Mirabeau. The galleys for the Crane arrived, but he merely threw them aside to read Pirandello and Ibsen.

He borrowed money from the bank to get through the summer until the money from the Hodder came due. By then he'd accumulated huge bills with his book dealers in England and in Princeton and owed his psychiatrist over one thousand dollars. He had hoped to get Eileen a car, but again could not see his way clear to buying her one. Nor could he afford to buy a house, though he and Eileen were nearly screaming to get out of their apartment. A few weeks later the baby he feared was his was born. Ironically, it was Eileen who unsuspectingly told him of the birth. Nearly fainting with anxiety, he locked himself in the bathroom until his nausea passed. When he tried seeing the baby in the maternity ward, he was informed that only parents were allowed in. He reread the "Canto Amor" he'd written for Eileen six years before, and thought he found in it a concealed wish for children. So here he was, after nearly eight years of marriage, his own wife childless and he probably the father of a child by another woman.

Once again he promised himself a new start. He would tackle one job at a time, the first being the Crane galleys. On July 20 he began working on them day and night, sending them back to his editor a week later, relieved to find the book better than he'd thought. Then he got back to work on his Shakespeare and began socializing again. As for the mother of the child, she managed to alleviate his fears, telling him the baby would be well cared for. He was so relieved he broke down and wept.

In November he won the Levinson Prize and a hundred dollars from *Poetry* for the eight poems he'd published in the magazine's January issue. Meanwhile, despite a promise to Shea and another to himself, he was still caught up in a series of affairs. Unlike what he'd gone through with Chris, however, he told himself now he felt nothing for these women, his indifference linked with his anger for his mother. Shea advised him to think better of her, but he could not find it in himself to forgive her. That fall, when the Blackmurs' marriage finally went to pieces, Berryman was deeply troubled. He might quip that his chasing after women was all part of his biography, but the joke was growing increasingly heavy on Eileen. He wondered just how long things could go on before she had had enough.

In December 1950, *Stephen Crane* was finally published. At least, Berryman sighed, that nightmare was over except for the publication-day luncheon in New York, which he so detested that he afterward refused to autograph copies of his book. His literary connection with Sloane—which had yielded two books in three years—was finally over. He was still writing poems, including one that Christmas in *terza rima* about the fighting in North Korea as hundreds of thousands of Chinese soldiers swept down upon American and U.N. forces, pushing them back to the 38th Parallel. It was a nightmarish piece about the death of Santa Claus, a poem about the nation's mythic lost innocence as well as of his own:

> Santa Claus with blood across his face
> Went past out of control; the reindeer cried
> Over the deep snow, and the dogs gave chase.
>
> Our youth spent that most bitter night outside,
> Deaf to the hurrying call, awake at one,
> Awake at three, clasping their metal bride . . . .

Now in the breath of the dogs the reindeer cry,
Blood dabbles the beautiful snow, and the slack
Reins suggest we have made someone die

No one believed in, who will not come back.

# chapter 15

# By Muleback Up the Foothills of Parnassus: 1951–52

Leafing through Untermeyer's new *Modern American Poetry* that January, Berryman tried placing himself in relation to his competition at midcentury. Masters, Frost, Sandburg, Pound, H.D., Jeffers, Ransom, MacLeish, Blackmur, Patchen, and Rukeyser were "through." Among those of the senior generation still active, he named Stevens, Williams, Eliot, and *perhaps* Cummings, Marianne Moore, Leonie Adams, Robert Penn Warren, Allen Tate, and Van Doren, the last added out of loyalty. Of his own generation, he named Roethke, Bishop, Schwartz, Karl Shapiro, Jarrell, Lowell, and himself.

Yet, when he wrote Erich Kahler a sympathy note for the loss of his mother at the beginning of February, he told Kahler his own spirits just then were so low that the best thing they could all do would be to follow Kahler's mother and die as soon as possible. The poem he'd done for Kahler, which he called "The Mysteries," he thought "poor, very poor," yet there was nothing at the moment he could do to make it better. All

Twenty-two-year-old Berryman on holiday in Heidelberg, Germany, July 1937, sporting his English beard

Berryman in Heidelberg, July 1937, with the "beautiful and vigorous and graceful" Beryl Eeman. "Heavenly hills," he wrote Halliday at the time, "& woods & river & shops & people & food & coffee & beer & the Schloss & plays & Beryl & Shakespeare." But he also warned his mother not to mention the Nazis or the state of affairs in Germany if she wrote him in that "Hitler stronghold."

An aging Uncle Jack and a vibrant Jill, together with Robert Jefferson, 17, on the roof of their West Side apartment on 115th Street, New York, September 1937

Berryman, Allen Tate, and his wife, Caroline Gordon, the novelist, at their home in the northwest corner of Connecticut in the summer of 1938, a month after Berryman's return from two years in England. Berryman is sporting the beard which Van Doren found so distasteful—along with Berryman's newly acquired British patois—that he could not bring himself to talk to his old student for several months to come.

Bhain and Florence Campbell in the summer of 1939

Berryman and Bhain Campbell at Union Lake, Michigan, July 1940, with Bhain's cancer in an advanced state. "Heretics," Berryman wrote in a poem addressed to his dying friend, "we converse/ Alert and alone, as over a lake of fire/ Two white birds following their profession/ Of flight, together fly, loom, fall and rise,/ Certain of . . . their mission."

An ascetic, inward-looking Berryman at 25, posing as the *poète maudit* at the Campbells' place at Union Lake, July 1940

Beryl Eeman in 1940, after her return to England and the war. "We picked, you and I, in history, a poor scene for our love," he wrote her at the beginning of 1941. "That it continues at all is a miracle."

Berryman, 31 (left, cut off), and Robert Lowell, 29, at the Lowells' home in Damariscotta Mills, Maine, in the summer of 1946. A "lazy, agreeable, interesting & alcoholic" time, Berryman would remember afterward with real happiness.

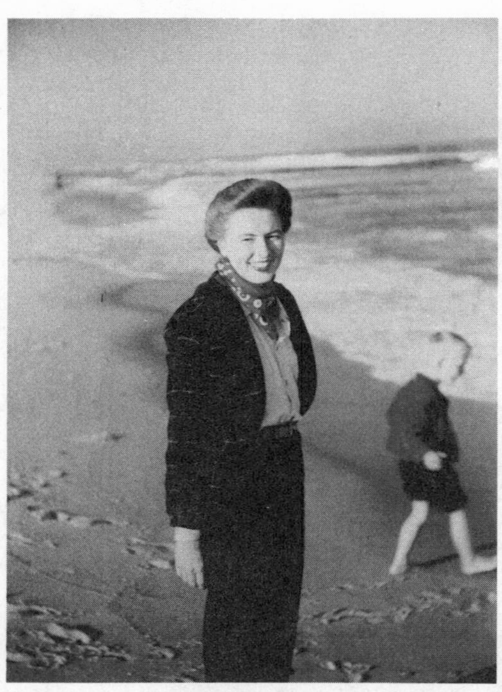

Berryman's Princeton student Bruce Berlind snapped this photograph of Eileen Berryman at the New Jersey shore in early October 1947, as Berryman was winding up his disastrous affair with Chris.

Robert Jefferson, cousin Shelby, and John Berryman at Robert Jefferson's third marriage, January 1949

Berryman with Sally Fitzgerald. In the early spring of 1953 he stayed with Robert and Sally Fitzgerald at their home in Ridgefield, Connecticut, making fast friends with their children and, fortified with pitchers of martinis, working feverishly on his "Bradstreet" poem in the same garage study that Flannery O'Connor had used earlier.

Anita Philips (1954) at the time she was involved with Berryman, following his separation from Eileen

Berryman, 43, sporting his beret at "a rakish angle" and posing for an informal family portrait with his young wife, Ann, and their son, Paul, eight months old. The photo was taken in the Murillo Gardens in Seville in late November 1957, following Berryman's stint with the United States Information Service in India.

he could manage was to signal toward the sacred grove from which he seemed to be expelled and write even more twistedly:

> At the trice of harvest to a middle ground
> I ascend and seek the hollow of my tree
> central in a grove and call: cherry sound
> swelling through swart night, near the sea, near sea,
> men aye did charm abroad . . . .

He sent a letter to Helen Stewart, his editor at Sloane, charging her with incompetence over the publication-day luncheon fiasco of the previous month as well as for the "nightmare of resentful non-communication" surrounding his queries about *The Dispossessed*. He was unhappy to learn that the book had sold only half as many books of poetry as Sloane usually sold. It was her fault that Eliot had decided not to publish the book in England. Moreover, Sloane had done nothing to advertise either his poems *or* the Crane, even though Edmund Wilson himself had endorsed the latter. True, he was no "big professor," but he was willing to bet his Crane would prove the most interesting of any of the lives published in the series. And while he did not read reviews himself, he would allow his wife to report to him the truth of what he said.

But he was still angry and out for revenge against the academic establishment, as his review of one of the biographies in the series for the *New York Times Book Review* showed: the redoubtable F. O. Matthiessen's study of Theodore Dreiser. Matthiessen had been a force at Harvard when Berryman was there, and had continued as such until, hounded and depressed, he had taken a suicidal dive from a Boston hotel window the year before. As "one of America's most respected literary historians," Berryman wrote, Matthiessen had done a merely creditable job in resurrecting Dreiser's posthumous fame. But it was H. G. Wells, rather, who had caught the central paradox of Dreiser, this most American of writers, when he'd written that *An American Tragedy* was "a far more than life-size rendering of a poor little representative corner of American existence, lighted up by a flash of miserable tragedy." One of the greatest novels of the century, it had caught "the large, harsh superficial truth" of America. What Berryman said about the moral impact of Dreiser's landscapes was what he was trying try to replicate in his own poems.

In March and April, 1951, Berryman gave four Shakespearean lectures, which were received with such enthusiasm that they made his reputation as a speaker. He was not, like Van Doren, "a natural" at teaching, for always there was the telltale trembling of the hands, the sweat-drenched shirts, the exhaustion afterward that lasted for days. Such public exposure, however, had its advantages. There was growing respect for him as a scholar, and for the first time people stopped him on the Princeton walkways to congratulate him for his riveting performances. Here, at 36, was a modicum of fame for Berryman. Eileen, knowing how much he needed such attention for his health and well-being, was happy for him.

The first of Berryman's lectures was called "Shakespeare at Thirty." It was a powerful and brilliant piece, which announced from its opening sentence the new authority Berryman had for his subject. "Suppose with me," he began, his phrases echoing down the hall,

> Suppose with me a time a place a man who has walked, risen, washed, dressed, fed, been congratulated, on a day in latter April long ago—about April 22, say, of 1594, a Monday—whether at London in lodgings or at a friend's or tavern, a small house in the market town of Stratford some hundred miles by miry ways northwest, or at Titchfield a little closer southwest, or elsewhere, but somewhere in England at the height of the northern Renaissance; a different world. Alone at some hour in one room, his intellectual and physical presence not as yet visible to us although we know its name, seated or standing, highlone in thought. He is thirty years old today.

Eileen, his loyal advocate, would afterward remember the power of that occasion, when he had masterfully scraped away "the layers of paint and clay on the 'complacent image of the Apollonian Shakespeare,' " to give his formidable audience a sense of a living poet. Standing before them, his thin, delicate hands shaking with intensity, Berryman held his audience spellbound.

His second lecture was on *Macbeth*, and by then the hall was filled to capacity to hear him discourse on a murderer—a regicide—who could still excite one's sympathy. The third lecture was a psychoanalytic reading of *Hamlet*, the fourth a reading of *The Tempest* as the closure to Shakespeare's brilliant career. But it was with the *Hamlet* lecture, when he examined Hamlet's complex of feelings toward his father and the hasty marriage of his mother to the man who would become his uncle, that the real drama in the lectures lay. Berryman had planned to have his mother sit in the front row, where he could watch her reaction to what he had to say. He would play Hamlet at Princeton, watching the play within the play, the audience unaware of what was unfolding before them.

His mother, however, had her own script for the pageant. While Berryman paced back and forth at the rostrum waiting to begin his talk to the packed hall, Jill's seat remained empty. Finally, when he could wait no longer, he began the talk without her. Only then, from the rear of the hall, did he hear the sound of high heels and sense the brilliance of a vivid dress. She walked loudly to the front of the hall, smiling at her son as she took her seat directly in front of him. Except for the stiffness of his neck, there was no sign of just how furious Berryman was. Afterward, back at the apartment, Jill carried on as if there had been no lecture at all. Berryman countered by refusing to write or speak to her for the next three months.

In early May he wrote the editor at Princeton University Press, responding to a letter asking if Berryman would be interested in publishing his lectures. The lectures, Berryman explained, were part of a critical biography of Shakespeare and were still very uneven. Those on *Macbeth* and *The Tempest* in particular still needed a lot of work. Moreover, he had promised "Shakespeare at Thirty" to *The Hudson Review*. In the end, he decided against Princeton's publishing the lectures as a series of essays.

In mid-June, Berryman began a two-week stint teaching at the University of Vermont's School of Modern Critical Studies in Burlington. He stayed in Waterman Hall overlooking Lake Champlain and the Adirondack Mountains and taught classes on Stephen Crane and Hemingway. His colleagues included Blackmur, Malcolm Cowley, Irving Howe, "a nervous bore from New Haven named [Norman Holmes] Pearson," and David Daiches, who, though perhaps "not a very good critic," had charmed Berryman—and others—with his delightful talk. In fact,

Berryman had to confess, he'd met no one "so pleasant for years." The drinks and jokes overflowed.

Berryman gave a lecture there entitled, "Africa," an essay actually about the state of the American novel at mid-century. "When not knitting or drinking," he began, "I often waste my time . . . wandering for hours in the stacks of the Princeton University Library, a comfortable building, reading endlessly standing up." In that way he'd managed to devour many forgotten novels, including thirty "published by Americans and Britons during the last two decades and dealing with Africa." Few of those novels had any permanency, but to write for fame, considering what fame amounted to in America, was foolhardy anyway.

One might write for the personal satisfaction it gave one, but even that made little sense in a profession strongly marked by manic-depressives and alcoholics. "When one thinks reluctantly over the lives of the writers with whom one is familiar," he noted, "they seem a chain of disasters and maladies." It was an old concern of Berryman's dressed up in new clothes: the discontent of American writers with their culture. Besides the strain of disillusionment in the older line of American writers, there was also the dissatisfaction being voiced by the immigrant populations. And to make things even more complicated, America itself had become so complex in the past forty years that even Henry James could not have dealt with what it had become.

As a result, many second-rate American novelists had resorted to dealing with no society at all, and a number had turned to Africa as they dimly understood it. They might have chosen the Far East, Berryman conceded, but things there had gone badly since the war, and South America hardly existed as a culture for North Americans. So, just as Shakespeare and other Elizabethans had been drawn to Italy as to an idealized and exotic place, American novelists had been drawn to Africa. True, the "three most impressive talents of the last ten years"—Saul Bellow, Norman Mailer, and J. F. Powers—had not been drawn to Africa, but that in itself was significant, for there was still a great deal of drama to be found in the complexities of the American scene, if only a writer had the necessary imagination to tap into it.

* * *

By the time Berryman returned to Princeton at the end of June, his mother's long silence had unnerved him. With her fifty-seventh birthday less than a week away, he wrote to apologize for his "stupid outbreak" after the *Hamlet* lecture. It was "dangerous," he'd decided, "to try to mix public and private occasions" with her, especially when he was tired. He explained away the silence between them as merely a case of nerves and too much alcohol and let it go.

But that summer, as Korea and the cold war continued to make themselves felt in the news, he worked sporadically on a play about treachery, turning the issue out from himself to the political arena. For models, he had James Connolly, one of the leaders of the Easter 1916 rebellion, Ezra Pound, and—more recently—the disclosures about two Englishmen accused of treason: Burgess and Maclean. Berryman's protagonist shared many of his own hatreds and fears, for he was someone "disillusioned w. Amer. capitalists *and* labor," angry with having been "taken in by . . . internationalism, & victimized by the exaggerated antipatriotism to which American intellectuals were schooled in the '30's."

In mid-July he and Eileen went to the Cape to visit the Mackies at Eaglis. He spent most of his time "loafing, swimming, eating & drinking," especially drinking. He revised his Shakespeare essays for the *Hudson* and *Kenyon* reviews and carried on long baby conversations with the Mackies' little daughter, Diane. He wrote Wilson, asking if there was any chance of his doing some reviewing for *The New Yorker*. He had no job for the fall, and was, he admitted, rather "brilliantly hard up" for money again. He even managed a few poems, including forty lines of something he thought "less stupid than usual."

Theodore Weiss wrote him, asking if he was interested in teaching that fall at Bard. But, job or no job, Berryman was not ready to leave Princeton. Then he was offered the Elliston Professorship of Poetry at the University of Cincinnati for the spring 1952 term, and the money and terms were so attractive that, after some internal debating, he decided to accept. Eileen would go with him, and Cincinnati would be the honeymoon they'd never had. Until then he would earn his income doing freelance writing and a biography of Shakespeare for Viking.

But he was drifting and he knew it. In late July he wrote

Macdonald that he hadn't written in a long while because he'd had nothing to report. Life had become "an endurance contest without prizes or plan." Perhaps Macdonald could help. After all, when Berryman had opted for a kind of selective amnesia of his past, it had been Macdonald who had spoken out for the importance of periodically reviewing one's past in order to understand where one was. And though at first Berryman had found the idea repugnant, the more he thought about it, the more the idea of looking deeply into himself was attracting him.

For years he'd thought that, like Edmund Wilson, he could make a living writing reviews and critical articles for the American intellectual community, but now he realized that he'd failed at that miserably. Nevertheless, he was convinced more than ever of the need for a critic like himself, more so when he realized that Jarrell *and* Schwartz had worn out their world-weary masks. What was needed in 1951 was a criticism that would be "active, learned, & fresh." He had hoped to fill that bill himself, but he could not forget what had happened to his hard and costly work on Pound. For every review or essay he published, five or ten had been stillborn, their remains filed away in one of his cardboard boxes. He had come to see now that the only way he was going to make a living was by eventually becoming what he had for so long tried to avoid, that despised thing itself: a university professor.

At the beginning of August he and Eileen left the Cape and returned to Princeton. He began an essay for *The Nation* on "The Character of Poets," looking again at the question of the relationship of the artist to his art. Was a poet's personal moral character so very important to the work he produced? It did not, as far as he could see, appear to be so. Even murder seemed resolvable in high art. Hadn't Ben Jonson killed his man in a duel and gotten off with only a branding? Hadn't Villon killed another poet?

At the heart of Berryman's probing was the question of where he himself stood. What was it going to cost him, he wondered, to become a poet? And how did one measure such a cost? Did one sacrifice one's life for one's art, as Hart Crane had, burning himself up until he'd gone out like a Roman candle at thirty-three? Or did one try to become a better person in order to write better poetry, as Hopkins and Eliot had done?

And what did a word like "better" mean anyway? Seeing no answers for himself, Berryman dropped the question to go on to other things.

That fall he worked on his poems and on another play, this one based on the Russian Revolution. He read John Reed's *Ten Days that Shook the World,* Shub and Trotsky on Lenin, a biography of Josef Stalin, Bert Wolfe's *Three Who Made a Revolution,* Edmund Wilson's *To the Finland Station.* His preoccupation with revolution and violent change reflected his inner restlessness and growing discord with the world of Princeton. The interest in communism had also been piqued by the intensity of the cold war as well as by the hot war still raging in Korea. In September he wrote out some lines describing how he seemed to be faring in all of this. Bad as the poem was, it recorded something of the malaise he had lived with that summer and from which he felt powerless to free himself:

> Skin & bones
> And eyes & hair
> The poet survived in 1951's
> American fun-fare,
> Nothing seemed to be what the Poet desired
> And his eyes were bright & tired.
> And his pocket was empty.
>
> His brain roiled
> With the Reds' lies,
> To his thin fingers came but what was soiled.
> Nothing, nothing to his eyes
> Awash as the ends of sticks up out of his brain
> Flashing in the sun with pain . . . .

At home too, another cold war took its daily toll. Jarrell was lecturing that year at Princeton, and living alone since his divorce. Soon after his arrival, he found Eileen eating alone at a local restaurant. Berryman was not with her, she explained, because he'd been playing tennis "all afternoon and was so tired he'd had some cold soup and gone to bed." For his part, Jarrell was glad to spend the evening "with somebody not professor-y or writer-y." He liked Berryman, but the man was just too "neurotic."

A week later Jarrell went over to the Berrymans for dinner, enjoying himself and staying late to talk, flattered that Berryman was still praising him for what he'd written about Auden. If anybody had captured him as well as Jarrell had captured Auden, Berryman quipped, he would have killed him since it would be "too embarrassing and disquieting" knowing someone else existed who knew one so well. Unfortunately Jarrell could still not bring himself to praise Berryman's poetry, though he did think the man was "very intelligent and nice and Disinterested," a quality very "rare among our Intellectuals." Besides, he was the only poet Jarrell knew who had written "one or two poems influenced" by himself, which in itself was enough to incline him to think well of Berryman.

In early December, Berryman attended an Anglo-American Poetry Conference at Bard, where he gave a presentation on the "Present Relationships Between Poetry and Prose." He wondered whether to view the relation between poetry and prose as friendly or antagonistic, and then moved to the example of Shakespeare, who had employed both genres with "great freedom and unselfconsciousness." Until the early nineteenth century, writers like Sir Walter Scott had employed both forms with dexterity, and the prose in *Emma* was so pure it actually approached the condition of poetry. But with the Romantics had come a rift, with the result that the century had come to belong to prose writers like Carlyle, Emerson, Thoreau, and Newman, as well as to scientific writers like Darwin and Huxley. As time had passed, Berryman lamented, poetry had lost more and more of its audience. Berryman's essay left the relative health of contemporary poetry hanging in the balance. Which was exactly where, at the moment, his own poetry was: pale, gasping, still waiting to be born.

At the beginning of February the Berrymans left Princeton for the University of Cincinnati. Berryman was scheduled to give seventeen lectures on Tuesdays and Thursdays at four: seven on Shakespeare and ten on modern poetry, beginning with Whitman and ending with Thomas and Lowell. On Fridays he would be expected to direct a poetry workshop. It was raining when they reached Cincinnati, and it continued to rain for weeks.

The university had found a residence for them in the downstairs half of a Victorian house at 256 Greendale Avenue, home of the Misses Resor (Sally and Marguerite), two elderly spinsters, one blind and bedridden, the other the puppet of the bedridden sister, who continually squeaked her orders from a darkened room.

The Berrymans were the first tenants the Misses Resor had ever had, and they were going to be sure their guests followed house rules precisely. There would be no smoking (this to a man who was up to three packs a day), and no noise after ten, and soon Berryman was complaining that what the university had actually found for them were rooms in a monastery. The rooms were in fact dark, walnut-paneled, high-ceilinged, bare. There were two uncomfortable beds, a "massively ugly table in the dining room," and a rolltop desk in the study. As for the prohibition on smoking, Berryman told Eileen to tell their landlords that what poets *did* was smoke. Only occasionally, very occasionally, the Misses Resor had to understand, did poets actually write poems.

Still, he was feeling better than he had in a long while. He gave his inaugural lecture, the "Shakespeare at Thirty" essay, and afterward he and Eileen went out to a "handsome bar" and took in the Cincinnati zoo. For the first time in his life, he noted, people actually deferred to him. The chairman of the English department—"a stalwart nervous Amherstman," he wrote his mother—had them to dinner the night of their arrival and Eileen had already met "20 biddies of this posh neighbourhood at a tea" and was very "funny about it." She was in good spirits.

Interviewed by the newspaper, he spoke of the decay of culture since the Elizabethans. In 1600, an "intelligent young man" could be interested in Shakespeare's and Jonson's poetry. He strongly doubted that one could say as much for the state of poetry now. It was too easy to blame the decline in culture on "radio, television, film stars, automobiles, world wars and political anxieties." Victorian poets could sell fifty thousand copies of a book of their poems; very few American poets could sell one tenth that number now. He had pictures of himself taken for publicity purposes and found them at least better than "the orangutang-with-anthrax image the N Y Times" usually confronted him with. He enjoyed being a local celebrity and having something he said in his lectures quoted—or even misquoted—each day in the papers. Even his dining out made the news. He had been told to expect about seventy-five people at his lectures; in fact he was drawing crowds of over two hundred.

There were also parties every week for him and Eileen, and he made some good friends that spring who would remain friends for the rest of his life. One was Van Meter Ames, a philosopher and an aesthetician at the university, "a charming guy," he told his mother, and "the only person in Cincinnati I had heard of when I came." At the conclusion of Berryman's lecture on Whitman, Ames had come up to him with tears in his eyes; after that he made a point of attending every one of Berryman's lectures, dismissing his own seminars so that he and his students could listen to Berryman.

Berryman's method of teaching poetry was to read the poem and then explain what he thought needed to be explained. He gave close readings of key texts, informed by careful attention to what the best critics had said about the poem. He began with a brilliant reading of Whitman's "Song of Myself," followed by talks on Hopkins, Yeats, Pound, Eliot, Auden, Thomas, and Lowell. He was even asked to give an additional lecture on Eliot, who by then had become for Berryman the "greatest living poet" in the language. The seven lectures on Shakespeare included even more effective versions of the four he'd given at Princeton plus three others, so that, taken together, they covered Shakespeare's entire development. After the preparation for those lectures, Berryman found his writing workshop mere "child's play."

In order to join her husband, Eileen had resigned from her job at a Rutgers clinic and delayed opening her own practice. Now, she introduced herself at the University of Cincinnati's medical school and attended ward rounds with the psychiatrists. She too enjoyed herself and quickly made friends. Besides the Ameses, the Berrymans' group of intimates included J. Alister Cameron, a professor of Classics, and his wife, Betty; Gilbert Bettman and his wife, Betty; and George Ford, a professor of English. Soon all of them had come under the spell of "Berrymania." Berryman loved it all and was in turn profligate with his time and energies; he read manuscript after manuscript and offered advice; he gave readings to every club and group that asked him; he listened for long hours to his new friends, offering a compassionate ear and, when asked, advice. When Allen Tate visited Cincinnati, he invited the Berrymans to lunch at his brother's country club and was surprised to see how well the Berrymans had taken to Cincinnati. He was also surprised to find out how quickly Cincinnati had taken to them. Indeed, Eileen would come to think of this time as hers and her husband's real honeymoon, and for a short while almost forgot why, a few months earlier, she had nearly decided to leave him.

It was not all idyllic, of course, for there were times when Berryman, believing himself unworthy of so much happiness, seemed bent on ruining things for both of them. When he drank too much, as he still did, he said things to Eileen in public that were calculated to hurt her. Women found him attractive; he did not control his compulsion to womanize, and, by his own admission, he had at least one serious affair that spring. Finally, when she could take it no longer, Eileen left Cincinnati for a time, ostensibly to visit with her sister, but also to get away from her husband.

In spite of the long hours he spent on his lectures, Berryman still managed to write a hundred pages of his Shakespeare biography and return to his Bradstreet poem. By early April he had read Helen Campbell's sixty-year-old biography of the poet, *Anne Bradstreet and Her Times*, from which he made thirty pages of notes, and had pored over John Winthrop's *Journals* and Perry Miller's *New England Mind*. But the poem itself still refused to "come." As the days grew longer, Berryman wondered if he would ever write his elusive poem. How could he write that *and* lecture, *and* run a workshop, *and* continue the scholarship necessary for his biography of Shakespeare? He was wearing too many hats. By the end of April, with classes ended and the Bradstreet still not finished, the strain began to show.

It had been four years since the publication of *The Dispossessed,* and, besides, he had long been unhappy with the book. No one had to tell him that he had yet to produce anything remotely equal to Thomas's "Fern Hill" or Lowell's best poems. In two years he would be forty, older than his father had lived to be, and he still had almost nothing in the way of poetry to show for fifteen years of work. Now he was trying to breathe life back into not one but two ghosts, Anne Bradstreet *and* Shakespeare. For years he'd believed he might actually discover in Shakespeare's plays the lineaments of a real man, and the Bradstreet was, really, another facet of that desire to breathe life into the dead.

So evident was this to his friends that one of them, Betty Bettman, began teasing him about his "necrophilia." At times he spoke as if he were actually inside the two poets, living their inmost lives. He thought he even understood how Shakespeare's own life had given rise to *Hamlet* and *Lear* and his other tragedies. When he spoke like this, as if from inside his characters, he seemed to Bettman to be almost on fire. Berryman was more determined than ever to follow Keats and erase his own miserable, fallen self to let the sublime voices of the dead speak through him.

For twenty years and more Berryman had hungered for the love of women, and, as he came into his own power and women responded to his intellectual and physical energy, he had found himself craving *and* hurting them. Afterward, when his head had cleared and he could survey the damage, he had felt intense shame. Then he would take pity on himself in gin and whiskey, first hating himself and then promising to reform. At such times he had no difficulty in identifying with the Tempter, carrying hell with him everywhere he went. The Bradstreet, then, was a logical extension of his restless preoccupation with women. It was almost as if he were in love with the dead woman, Bettman would recall. "She haunted his nights and days, and sometimes he could talk of nothing else. He worked in spurts. Sometimes he could go for hours on end, into the night without any sleep. At other times he would have a dry run that lasted for days" and left him more tormented than ever.

In mid-April he learned that, after four rejections, he had at last been awarded a Guggenheim. The fellowship came to three thousand dollars, and with part of the money he and Eileen would be able to go abroad. He wound up his lectures, read his poems in Detroit, gave his paper on *The Tempest* for the Jolly Boys, a Cincinnati organization of professionals, and attended several dinners and some "400 farewell parties" before heading back to New Jersey. So far had his reputation spread that even the president of the university came to hear him lecture on Eliot. By then he was very tired, but he could honestly say he'd done his job "properly."

At the beginning of May he went to Wayne University to give a reading to officially mark the opening of the Theodore

Miles Poetry Room. Miles had been one of the few people in the English department Berryman had respected when he'd been there thirteen years before, and it was to him that Berryman had addressed his poem "Farewell to Miles." At the time, Berryman could not have known that his "Farewell" would take on a meaning far different from what he'd intended when Miles, along with hundreds of other sailors, drowned when his destroyer, the *Indianapolis*, was torpedoed by the Japanese in the last days of the war. Well dressed and acting every bit the distinguished visitor, Berryman visited the Miles Poetry Room, escorted by the poet's widow. His reading, which ended Modern Poetry Week, began with a recitation of Yeats's "Easter 1916" and passages from Eliot's "Ash Wednesday," followed by a selection of his own poems. Afterward he went drinking with some of the local poets, who acted polite and deferential, though no one really thought much of his work.

Four days later, back in Cincinnati, Berryman gave his final lecture on Eliot. "I lay on my back this afternoon on the grass," he began, disarmingly, "looking up at the trees, the sky, the colors. It was all as beautiful as anything could be in an unreflective way. I felt it discouraging that poetry could not be concerned solely with this sort of thing, but must deal instead with the history and destiny of man on the earth; with the nature of desire, conscience, aspiration, and the fate of man's soul." With that introduction, he gave a reading of "Gerontion" that left his audience marveling at his brilliance. "I have workt here like a madman," he wrote Catherine Carver on May 14. He'd been "a great success," everybody had gone "off like fireworks" when he made his public and social appearances," and Cincinnati had turned out to be a "very pleasant city," perhaps even "too pleasant," because he was now in love with yet another woman.

Back in Princeton that June, he sent *Poetry* the twenty-fifth sonnet of his suppressed sequence for its fortieth anniversary issue and promised to send something from the Bradstreet as soon as it was ready. He still had no idea how long that poem would be, and might go anywhere "from 3 to 25 pages," though he was hoping to have it finished by early August. By June he had eighty pages of notes as well as "more than 125 draft lines of poetry," all of which amounted to the first substantial progress he'd made on the poem in four years. He even had his stanza pattern now: an eight-line form suggestive of the stanza Hopkins had invented for "The Wreck of the Deutschland," and he now had a sense of Bradstreet's life and the shape of her poetry. All that remained for him was to "POUR IN what-is-*already-done* FAST" before the poem "flapped away."

But the poem was still a series of fragments when the Berrymans left for Duxbury, Massachusetts, on August 3 to visit their Cincinnati friends the Camerons. A week later it was back to Princeton, where Eileen began her practice in clinical psychology and Berryman, now on his Guggenheim, plunged back into his biography of Shakespeare. In October, while working on the dating of Shakespeare's early plays, he "discovered" who the "W. H." was to whom Shakespeare had dedicated his sonnets. At once he rode his bicycle to the library and began going through the archives; by evening he was sure his hunch was right. The elusive W. H., he was convinced, was the actor William Haughton. Berryman kept this knowledge to himself, knowing it would be useful in reconstructing Shakespeare's beginnings in the London theater. It might also help him procure another Guggenheim somewhere down the line.

For Berryman's thirty-eighth birthday, Jill sent her son a stand for his Shakespeare folio; and for his and Eileen's tenth anniversary, tickets to a New York show. They'd needed the break, Berryman wrote, thanking his mother, because they'd both been working too hard. They were broke after a weekend away, but for the moment they were happy. Just after Eisenhower defeated Stevenson in the 1952 elections, Berryman took the train to Washington to spend a few days working on the folios at the Folger. A week later, in New York, he began group therapy, since Shea was hoping now to show Berryman that his problems were not all that unique. If he could see how others used similar masks, Shea reasoned, it might help Berryman better understand himself. At first Berryman was uncomfortable, but soon he was using the sessions as raw material for a novel he planned to write called *The Group*. He did not get far with the book, at least at the time and in that form, but the writing did help him to see better how he dealt with women. You *began* with "a sense of women being fascinatingly accessible," he wrote, but there they were, in the group setting, "utterly unattractive." As unattractive, he saw, as he himself was.

By then he'd been in therapy with Shea for five years and had become "an old hand" at talking about himself without getting anywhere. He wondered if he even respected his psychiatrist anymore. One thing was certain: he did not like working in a group setting. He was too good, too distinctive an individual, to be talking with such philistines, and that included Shea, with his ugly prints and bourgeois tastes. Magnanimously, Berryman tried to accommodate himself to the others in therapy, even joining them for coffee after the sessions. But he soon grew tired of trying to work with people he considered his intellectual inferiors.

That they were his inferiors had become apparent when, during one session, he had analyzed one of his dreams for the benefit of the group and someone had had the audacity to question "whether it was *possible* to have a dream involving a knowledge of Roman history" and that "of the most elementary sort." Exasperated, Berryman had asked Shea to explain to the idiot that *indeed* it was possible to have such a dream. Berryman lasted only two months in group before he lost his temper with the others and stormed out, refusing to return. By then he had decided he could do better on his own, analyzing himself through his poems.

At least culture hummed at Princeton. That fall Edmund Wilson gave his Christian Gauss Lectures on the literature of the Civil War, to which Berryman was invited, frequently engaging in cross-examining Wilson during the question period. Robert Fitzgerald, the poet and translator, who was then teaching at Princeton, noted Berryman's thin, "scowling, nervously intense . . . acidulous and combative" posture, ready at the slightest provocation to pounce on Wilson. Once he even attacked Wilson for resurrecting Grant's memoirs as literature. Why, Berryman demanded, read the memoirs of a monster whose war policies had led to the needless deaths of thousands? Wilson, whose critical eminence normally kept him above such treatment, was startled by Berryman's vehemence. But because Wilson respected Berryman's keen mind, the two managed to remain friends.

Delmore Schwartz was also at Princeton that fall, as a replacement for Blackmur, and had come down to Princeton with his second wife, Elizabeth Pollett. Instead of moving into an apartment near the university, however, Delmore bought a farm in Baptistown, miles from everyone. Already, as Eileen later remembered, there was a darting, haunted look in Delmore's eyes, something deeper than insomnia or liquor or drugs: the beginnings of paranoia. Moreover, between Berryman working on his Shakespeare and Delmore acting the recluse, the two seldom saw each other.

Delmore had brought Saul Bellow with him from New York to act as his assistant, and one night in mid-December Bellow had a party to which he invited the Berrymans. They arrived late, having come from another party, and as they walked up to the house, they heard the jazz growl of a sax on the record player. When they went to put their coats down in the bedroom, they found Delmore there with his wife in the middle of a fight. Convinced that Delmore was about to hurt Elizabeth, Berryman pushed himself between them. Delmore was upset because he'd seen his wife accept a light from the novelist, Ralph Ellison, and had pulled her into the bedroom, accusing her of flirting with him. With Berryman now standing between him and his wife, Delmore backed off. But Berryman was so upset by what was happening to his friend that he took Eileen and left the party.

It turned out to be the winter of the *Walpurgisnacht*. When Bellow left Princeton for the Christmas holidays, Roethke came down from New York and borrowed his apartment, anxious to meet Wilson. Soon Wilson was asking Berryman what he thought of Roethke's poetry. He had yet to meet the man, Berryman told him, but he had only praise for his poems. On the strength of that recommendation, Wilson invited Roethke to a party Christmas night. That afternoon three dozen anemones arrived from an exclusive florist's in New York, a gift from Roethke to Mrs. Wilson. Then, at nine o'clock that evening, Roethke's large, "aggressively sober" frame appeared in the doorway with several of his friends. When Wilson introduced Roethke to Berryman, Roethke acted as if he'd never heard the name.

Roethke began by swilling tomato juice and flirting with the female guests. But when he saw Wilson sitting on the couch, he plopped down next to him, demanding that Wilson "blow" the party and come upstairs so he could show him his poems. Wilson explained that as host he couldn't very well be expected to abandon his guests. Then Roethke was grabbing at Wilson's jowls and telling one of America's most powerful critics he was "all blubber." Wilson countered by calling Roethke a half-baked Bacchus and ordering him to leave. As he stormed toward the door, Roethke ran into Allen Tate's daughter, Nancy, and her husband, Dr. Wood. Mrs. Wilson, trying to make some introductions, awkward at best since Roethke was being thrown out, explained that Dr. Wood was a psychiatrist. Then, when Wood reached out to shake Roethke's hand, Roethke, thinking he was about to be restrained, lashed out and hit him. Roethke's friends hastily tried to explain that it was all a misunderstanding, that Roethke had never hit anyone before, even as they rushed him out the door and the tired year slammed shut behind them.

## chapter 16

# The Unmaking of a Marriage

## 1953

A new year and a new beginning. On Sunday afternoon, January 4, Berryman took a long walk around Lake Carnegie with Monroe Engel and Saul Bellow. Up till then he had seen Bellow only in the presence of other people. Now, he told Eileen, he'd finally had a chance to get to know Bellow better, and what he saw he liked. What a lovely, funny man he was. Walking around the lake, Bellow had picked up a log and thrown it into the water, bidding it with a flamboyant gesture to go and be a hazard. It was exactly the odd sort of thing Berryman delighted in imagining.

A few days later he came home with a typescript of Bellow's new novel, *The Adventures of Augie March,* having decided to take the weekend off to read it. Eileen would remember him sitting in his red leather chair, smoking as he went through chapter after chapter, laughing that "high-pitched *eeeeeeeee*" of his "so hard he couldn't get his breath," and exclaiming, "It's damn good," "Bellow is *it,*" a "bloody genius." He read it straight through, finishing the manuscript at 4 A.M. the following Sunday morning, then went over to Princeton Street and banged on Bellow's window to wake him up and tell him how good the novel was.

What he was particularly impressed with was how Bellow had let himself go in this novel, paying homage to Flaubert and Joyce and Yeats even as he jazzed up the writing. Most of all, however, Bellow had given him hope. Here was someone his own age who had produced something of value, something new. He saw now that the Bradstreet would have to be completely rethought. It would have to be braver and more ambitious and longer than anything he'd ever tried, longer than "Lycidas," longer than "The Wreck of the Deutschland."

Ten months after reading *Augie March,* unhappy that the novel had not received the notice it deserved, Berryman would write a short, dense essay for *The New York Times Book Review* in which he stressed, as Eliot had thirty years before in speaking of *Ulysses,* the book's wide-ranging and refreshing use of myth. It was Bellow's "recurrent allusiveness to masters of Greek, Jewish, European and American history, literature and philosophy" that had particularly impressed him, Berryman wrote, for Bellow had evoked these Overlords masterfully, letting their names resonate through the book. Together, these presences in effect constituted Bellow's version of the Sublime, providing him with a way of measuring the present moment against the weight of history.

As if that were not enough, Bellow had managed to employ these Overlords with a sense of humor, making it clear that it was he and not they who was in charge here. What a refreshing use of tradition this was, for Bellow's Overlords were like those "marvellous vast heads of statues in some of Watteau's pictures, overlooking his lovers," presences in a friendly landscape, larger than life but not forbidding: a tradition to be used for one's own purposes rather than the other way around. And that, Berryman insisted, was something new in American fiction. As for Augie, Bellow had created not so much a tragic figure as a survivor. For whenever another character in the novel tried to usurp Augie for himself, Augie's strategy had been to withdraw. In this way, Berryman saw, Augie had managed to avoid a disappointed life.

After ten years of marriage and five of therapy, after talking for endless hours with Eileen and with a succession of friends and mistresses, after years of alternately freezing out and confiding uxoriously in his mother, Berryman knew he still had a difficult time either accepting or understanding himself. He did not even know whether or not he wanted a child, if indeed Eileen could have a child. As for Eileen, if she was going to have a baby it would have to be soon. At the same time that Berryman was roaring over Augie March's misadventures, Eileen underwent a myomectomy to remove benign tumors that, the doctors believed, might be obstructing her from becoming pregnant. A few days after she returned home to recuperate, Berryman placed a copy of Lorca's *Yerma* on the table next to the couch for her to read. It was the story of a peasant woman who had wanted her husband to give her a child, but the husband, exhausted from working the land, kept finding excuses day after day for not having relations with her until finally, in exasperation, she had murdered him. Eileen did not miss the point.

That month, Berryman listed what he saw as the events that had led to his final breakthrough with the Bradstreet poem. Eileen's operation and its connection with Anne Bradstreet's five years of barrenness was one. Another was his aborted group therapy, which, he believed, had nevertheless helped him to understand some of his resentments about Eileen's failure to conceive. Yet another was the self-confidence he had gained from reading Bellow's portrait of a hero with "clay feet." There was also the example of Berryman's mentor, Allen Tate, who had recently passed the hurdle of writing his own long poem. Berryman meant to send the Bradstreet on to Tate for advice and—even more important—for approval. And finally, Berryman also had concrete recognition of his potential in the form of a Guggenheim. He was ready to take on Lowell by writing a poem even more ambitious than "Quaker Graveyard in Nantucket." After all, he reminded himself, Lowell, good as he was, was *not* "overpowering."

As soon as Eileen returned home, Berryman began writing the poem at white heat. Each day he went to his studio to write a single stanza: no more, no less. By then he had hundreds of detached lines and notes, and he worked each piece over, stitching lines together into eight-line stanzas on an erasable, glassine-covered wax pad. He placed the fragments he already had beneath the glassine and then worked at connecting his lines and revising each stanza. At lunchtime he descended to his apartment with his new stanza and read it over and over to

Eileen, then returned to the studio to work at it again. At dinner, elated and exhausted, he read the revised stanza to her again. Did she think he had the woman down properly? What did she think of the way he'd caught Anne's barrenness? Numbed by his insensitivity, Eileen lay there recovering from her own ordeal and offering her possessed husband what help she could.

On January 21, having just returned from Europe after more than two years away, Lowell paid Berryman a visit. And though neither had written the other the whole time Lowell was abroad, they talked nonstop now for twelve hours. Then it was back to the poem. By 6:00 P.M. on January 24, Berryman found himself halfway through the tenth stanza of the poem, and there it momentarily stalled. At that point in the poem Anne's despair over her long barrenness was at last coming to an end, and Berryman would need to talk with someone who had gone through the birth process. Eileen understood she could no longer help him; he would have to go to his women friends who had been through it. Now he sought out two young women in Princeton who had recently had children: Betty Hartle and Brenda Engel, the wife of his colleague Monroe Engel. Tellingly, he even interviewed his mother about his own birth.

At last he saw where his poem was leading him, for by then he had fallen in love with his creation and meant to seduce it too. Anne, though tempted by his advances, would at last reject him, for which "betrayal" she would be made to die slowly and painfully. He would also show, in the agony of Anne's giving birth, his own agony in giving birth to this, his first major poem. By noon on the twenty-seventh the "honeymoon" phase of the poem was definitely over; now he would have to cross "the Hump." He sent off the first ten stanzas to Tate, explaining that over the past two weeks the Bradstreet had begun at last "to shoot," so that he could neither read nor "even think of anything else" except his phantom mistress. He wondered if Tate, himself in the midst of writing a long poem, was also in a "tortured state of perfect happiness."

The following day Berryman wrote the twelfth stanza, about Anne's versing to please her father. All that "abstract didactic rime," all that poetry that Anne—like himself—had written over the years, he knew now had been dead even before the ink had dried on the page. Those poems had been written to please ghosts and were already "Drydust in God's eye." But the Bradstreet, with its fresh amalgam of styles ranging from the seventeenth century to the mid-twentieth, was a farewell and a new birth. No one, he believed, except perhaps Hopkins, had wrenched syntax as he was wrenching it. No one had caught the living and dramatic idiom of Anne's, and Shakespeare's, time as his syntax had. Now, in his new poem, he was far closer to achieving what he'd tried to do in his sonnets in merging the tradition to the present.

As best she could, Brenda Engel answered Berryman's "very specific and intense questions: how long did the strong labor pains last; what kinds of pains were they; what kinds of thoughts went through my head during labor; how [did] the pains change . . . as labor progressed." She could see Berryman straining to understand "*exactly* what a woman went through, both physically and psychologically, in the course of giving birth." Finally, unbelievably, after several days of exquisite self-torture, he managed to get something of the birth drama down on the page:

> So squeezed, wince you I scream? I love you & hate
> off with you. Ages! *Useless*. Below my waist
> he has me in Hell's vise.
> Stalling. He let go. Come back: brace
> me somewhere. No. No. Yes! everything down
> hardens I press with horrible joy down
> my back cracks like a wrist
> shame I am voiding oh behind it is too late
>
> hide me forever I work thrust I must free
> now I all muscles & bones concentrate
> what is living from dying?
> Simon I must leave you so untidy
> Monster you are killing me Be sure
> I'll have you later Women do endure
> I can *can* no longer
> and it passes the wretched trap whelming and I am me
>
> drenched & powerful, I did it with my body!
> One proud tug greens Heaven. Marvellous,
> unforbidding Majesty.
> Swell, imperious bells. I fly.

Mountainous, woman not breaks and will bend:
sways God nearby: anguish comes to an end.
Blossomed Sarah, and I
blossom. Is that thing alive? I hear a famisht howl.

Eileen would remember him coming in from his studio with the childbirthing stanza and handing it to her as she lay resting on the couch, then throwing himself on the floor next to her, exhausted by his ordeal. In that severe and unrelenting release in seeing Anne through her labor was a hint, perhaps, of the release awaiting him when his own trials were at last over.

By the end of January he was ready for Part Two. Here he would enter the poem himself as Tempter in a dialogue he had played out with many women since his affair with Chris. When he reached stanza 23—the little dialogue between Anne and her small son Sam that would serve as entrance song to the major dialogue between Anne and himself—Berryman called up the memory of uncle Charlie, who had given Eileen away ten years before. A year after their marriage, Uncle Charlie had died, and Eileen's sister, Marie, had written her about the exchange that had occurred between her and her son, Billy. If Uncle Charlie was gone, did that mean that Aunt Hilda had gone away too? No, Marie had explained; Aunt Hilda was still alive. Oh, Billy had asked, then God took us "one by one"? When Eileen had shared that story with Berryman, he had wept. Now he would give Billy's words to Anne's son.

Tate wrote, praising Berryman for the powerful stanza form he had created, and Berryman wrote back on February 3, sending along the childbirthing stanzas that, he explained, contained "the poem's first height." But, he added, the strain of the poem was killing him. "I feel like weeping all the time," he wrote, except that he was in too much of an ecstasy and too busy with "the hardest, most calculated work I have ever done." Every word he wrote felt as if it either made love to the poem or helped murder it, depending on whether or not it was the right word for the poem.

He also knew the dialogue between himself and his dead lover was, finally, an exercise in narcissism and autoeroticism. Perversely, around February 10, he mailed his close friend, Patricia Ann Hartle, two stanzas (25 and 26) without any other comment: "I miss you, Anne,/day or night weak as a child. . . .'' Soon afterward he took Hartle to Lake Carnegie and recited the poem to her. It was, she remembered, seductive and ''romantic & beautiful.'' But not so for Berryman's Anne, who, though tempted, remembered what her earlier rebellion against God had cost her. A young girl on the brink of her adolescent sexuality, she had been visited with the pox for what she took to be her sins of erotic fantasy, and the pox had left her permanently scarred. Now Berryman evoked the full force of that visitation:

> faintings black, rigour, chilling, brown
> parching, back, brain burning, the grey pocks
> itch, a manic stench
> of pustules snapping. . . .

Then he wrote an aria for Anne, a song of spring in New England, with hints of sexual awakening everywhere in nature. He sang of pussy willows wedging their way ''up in the wet,'' making notes to himself to check his WPA Massachusetts volume and his 1936 Almanac to get the New England spring right. The following evening, sitting in Carney's Bar on Third Avenue in Manhattan, he wrote out in longhand a draft of the fifty-third and the first half of the fifty-fourth stanzas, already preparing Anne for the horrible death he had in store for her and her unkindness toward him.

He knew he would need a recurring leitmotif somewhere toward the close of the poem to tie the whole together. And somewhere he wanted Anne to tell him she was actually afraid of him. There was also his recurrent nightmare to deal with, the one about taking the bodies of the women he had murdered and trundling them over heated grills in an attempt to get rid of the incriminating evidence. Something from his early Roman Catholic upbringing also began surfacing in the poem, evoked by his reading of Baron Corvo and Graham Greene, and he found himself calling upon a Byzantine image of the Virgin, begging it to refrain his lust, by which he meant both to keep it in check and ''refrain'' it, or—as with his sonnet sequence earlier—at least turn his lust into poetry.

He thought of Anne as trying to turn him back to God, but he would have none of it. ''I cannot,'' he wrote, ''feel myself

God waits. He flies/ nearer a kindly world; or he is flown." Experience had taught him that, if God existed at all, He was a cold and distant figure, a star in the winter night, and not a God of rescue. Human beings had been left "entirely alone" in an empty universe, and Berryman himself was merely "a man of griefs & fits/ trying to be my friend."

Toward the end of February, Eileen was able to get back on her feet again, though she was still unsettled with having to live daily with her husband's mistress. Then Berryman told Eileen that Anne had brought him around with her arguments and that he believed he was on the verge of a religious conversion. Remembering that the same thing had happened to Lowell ten years earlier, Eileen became alarmed. On February 10, Berryman had sent Robert Fitzgerald the twenty-six stanzas of the poem he had finished by then, telling Fitzgerald that his poem had lately begun to "blast & glow & head me for my grave." Then, on the twenty-second, Berryman called the Fitzgeralds at their home in Ridgefield, Connecticut, and asked if he could use the spare study over their garage to work on his poem. Eileen needed some space, and he was anxious just now to be around a family with lots of little kids, which was just what he needed to write the next section of his poem: Anne as mother, brooding over her children and grandchildren.

The Fitzgeralds' stone house at 70 Acres Road was on an upland, surrounded by woods, with New York City visible to the south. The living conditions there were primitive, but warm fires blazed in the large fireplace in the living room, where the family took their meals. For two weeks Berryman worked in the room over the garage—the same room Flannery O'Connor had used when she stayed with the Fitzgeralds—often taking a pitcher of martinis up with him to keep him company while he struggled with his poem. Sometimes he would come running into the kitchen where Sally Fitzgerald, pregnant with her fifth child, was working. As he had with Eileen, he would try out a new word, a phrase, an idea on her. Once, she remembered, it was the word "toof." Should he have Anne use it in speaking to baby Simon? Sally thought not. Another time it was a description of Anne's father (whom Berryman hated) throwing up "a yellow scum," a medical phenomenon he had discovered in his copy of *Merck's Manual*.

For the most part, Sally remembered, Berryman was a

wonderful guest, spending hours each evening playing with the children. He took a special liking to three-year-old Maria Juliana. And even though Maria did not take to strangers, by the time Berryman left the Fitzgeralds, the little girl was following him everywhere, "laughing, dancing about his feet, hanging onto his coattails, flinging herself on his neck every time he sat down." He worked hard to capture the prattle of children in New England's early spring. "Mother," he would have Anne's baby ask her, "how *long* will I be dead?" And Anne: "Our friend the owl/ vanishes, darling, but your homing soul/ retires on Heaven." And, on a more homely level: "Simon, if it's that loose,/ let me wiggle it out./ You'll get a bigger one there, & bite." He captured other images from the Fitzgerald children as well, transferring them to Anne's world: children climbing in a pear tree or fishing "down the brookbank/ . . . for shiners with a crookt pin."

Berryman found four-year-old Benedict especially captivating. Had Benedict ever read *The Wizard of Oz*? Berryman asked Sally one day. Benedict did not read anything, she told him. Oh, but Benedict *had* to read *The Wizard,* he insisted, and the next morning, when Berryman came down to the kitchen, he told Sally he was taking the train to New York to get something for the boy. When he returned from the city, he was waving his own copy of *The Wizard of Oz,* which he'd picked up at his mother's apartment in the city. There was no time to lose in acquainting Benedict with this masterpiece, he told her. Sally was touched by the gesture.

In the evenings, after he had finished teaching at Sarah Lawrence, Fitzgerald would join his family and Berryman for dinner and conversation, which—with Berryman—usually came round to poetry. Sometimes Fitzgerald, more often Berryman, would read aloud from their favorite poems. On several occasions Berryman even broke down while reading a poem, as happened once when he read Blake's "The Little Black Boy" and again when he read Wordsworth's "Resolution and Independence."

But two weeks into his stay, Berryman's behavior started becoming erratic and he lost his temper with his hosts. One night at dinner he bit into a stick of celery and broke off part of a tooth. Looking at it, he began to laugh hysterically at his physical disintegration. The following night he took offense at some comment of Sally's. "He pushed back his plate, and hissed," Sally remembered, refusing to eat any more of her "stuff." As for her jibes about his behavior, he knew more about his own "faults and misdeeds than anyone in the world," and didn't need her reminding him of them. The Fitzgeralds sat there, stunned, waiting for him to get control over himself. Then Fitzgerald came to Sally's defense, saying she'd meant no harm. Berryman knew he had overreacted, and though they were bantering back and forth lightly by the following morning, he realized it was time now to leave.

Twenty-four hours later he was back in Princeton, his poem nearly done. By then Anne had given birth to eight children, had seen several of her houses go up in flames, her oldest son emigrate to Jamaica, her daughter-in-law and her grandchild die. There was left now only Anne's death to enact. The inward fire of passion she had so long harbored Berryman would allow to consume her for having refused him. When he left the Fitzgeralds, he had got as far as the third line of Stanza 53, describing Anne on the very edge of her final disintegration. "Solemn voices fade," he had her say, "I feel no coverlet." Now he would watch her sadly, painfully die as her arms and legs began swelling and her skin turned red from dropsy. She would see her pain reflected in the faces of her family, who could do nothing but watch her suffer, so that, as with Berryman, language would have to be her only consolation.

But as he began to kill off his "mistress," Berryman seemed to die himself. From Eileen's perspective, he seemed at last also to be forcing an end to their marriage. One night, when his erratic, high-strung behavior became too much for her, she left the apartment and went to Lahière's, one of the few places open at that hour. There she ran into the Wilsons. Wilson, having seen Berryman several times that winter, knew that Berryman was "on fire" with the Bradstreet and seemed to understand what Eileen was going through.

The Berrymans' trip to Europe in April might make the difference, he told Eileen now. But Wilson's wife could see that Eileen was also getting ready to leave Berryman for good. When Eileen returned to the apartment several hours later, she found Berryman wringing his hands and worried sick about her. Never before, he told her, had he been so close to the edge of full-blown hysteria. He knew he had often used that very excuse, but whatever he'd suffered working on the *Lear* and the Crane were as nothing to what he was going through now. He had been left physically and psychologically exhausted by the poem, but it was almost finished. He asked her to hold on for a few more days.

Then he returned once more to face Anne's death, paralleling the travail of her dying with the travail of her childbearing. He was on the edge of some great mystery, he knew, the moment Henry James had called "the Great Change," when life gave way to nothing or to something totally different. When, a few weeks later, the ordeal of the poem was at last behind him, he would write Fitzgerald that, back in Princeton, he had gone through "bad times again." It had taken him thirty hours to get Anne's "first last lines done (that is, to let her die)—and before that, for several days I hated the world so intensely that I decided to abandon the poem where it was when you saw it and make her live forever in every sense." Somehow he managed to get over that hump as well and kill her off, and then write the last four stanzas—"the awful coda," he called it—"which I *hope* does not show the labour and excision it cost me."

On Sunday, March 15, he finished the poem. It was fifty-seven stanzas and 458 lines long, and he was so exhausted that he spent the following week in bed, getting up at the end of that time only to read the poem at a specially arranged Gauss seminar convened on March 23. Here he unveiled to the public the poem that had cost him his heart's blood, receiving in return an honorarium of two hundred dollars and many "golden" opinions and the pleasure of Delmore's claiming the poem for *The Partisan Review*. Wilson, astonished by Berryman's achievement, called the Bradstreet "the most distinguished long poem by an American since *The Waste Land*." He was so anxious to hear it again that he asked Berryman to read it for him at his house, and Berryman agreed. But on the night he first read it, Eileen told Pat Hartle how shaken she'd been by the words her husband had given Anne: "I am become an old woman." Berryman was not the only one who had come through the ten weeks' ordeal bleeding.

Slowly Berryman swam back into the present, to America with its racial issues, its cold war, its atomic-reactor piles, its Korea, its foxholes, and its wounded being flown by helicopter to makeshift hospitals behind the front lines. "Foxholes" and "piles": words that had undergone transformations so radical since Anne's time that she would have been able to make no sense of their mid-twentieth-century meanings. Out of a great silence in the winter of 1953, Berryman had managed to remake his poetry. For once he had made for himself a blameless "sourcing," a woman who could say no to him and mean it. He could not help marvelling at her, even as he turned her back into dust.

At the end of March, on "doctor's orders," Berryman went to Atlantic City by himself, and after a week of drinking and commiserating with his soul, began to feel, he was convinced, somewhat better. But walking along the boardwalk on April 3 (Good Friday), he came upon a display "of medieval torture instruments from Nuremberg, racks, pincers, shin-breakers, head cages, wheels, and—impassive, large, beautifully carved, horrible"—the Iron Maiden, shaped for swallowing and killing men. Unnerved, he went back to his hotel room, packed, and fled the city.

For a few days afterward he cut back on his drinking, then resumed sipping pitchers of martinis once again. On the fifteenth he wrote Nancy Macdonald to say it was time to "resume a friendship" with her and Dwight that he had "long missed" and did not "care to miss any longer . . . laying aside provisionally the burdens of resentment on the heart." Of his poem he said only that it was "much less bad" than his earlier work, and that the writing of it had left him feeling "less at the world's mercy." Even the drink he was holding seemed to mean something grand, though before he embarked "on a philosophy of martinis," he was going to "shut up & go to bed."

He wrote his mother, sending her a stanza sheet so that she could see "out of what trash beauty emerges," then sealed the letter and went back to reading Keats's letters, his yearly consolation. But ten minutes later, nerves "jumping," he wrote to her again. He had come on a passage in Keats that spoke exactly to his condition: "The innumerable compositions and recompositions which take place between the intellect and its thousand materials before it arrives at that trembling delicate and snaillike perception of Beauty." In spite of everything—and he had Keats's blessing for it—he believed he had created a lasting, shimmering thing of beauty out of the drumming agony of his existence.

But on the eve of his departure for Europe, he was inwardly still raging, and his right arm—his writing arm—still shook uncontrollably. He wondered if such rage as he felt always accompanied an ''intolerably painful, exalted creation'' such as he'd been through that winter. "Any artist not a saint," he absolved himself, ''that is, who loves humanity as much, while torturing himself as much as I did and was during parts of the composition of the poem, with that intensity over a protracted time, may be bound to take it out on humanity (any specimens that are unlucky enough to be by) afterward.'' It was his way of defending why he'd made life hell for Eileen.

On the morning of April 28, with the help of a loan of five hundred dollars from the Fitzgeralds, the Berrymans sailed from New York for France aboard a French liner. It had been sixteen years since Berryman had seen Europe. Louis MacNeice was another passenger aboard, and he and the Berrymans became such friends that the MacNeices insisted on the Berrymans staying with them when they visited London later that summer. On May 5, the Berrymans reached Paris and booked into the Hôtel des Saints Pères near the Louvre. They did some sightseeing, visited the museums, and saw a performance of *Elektra* at the Opéra. Berryman, realizing he was once again drinking too much, vowed to stick to vermouth, beer, and brandy, though he said nothing about how much of each of those he meant to consume.

Nine days later he and Eileen left Paris with the Camerons for a ten-day drive south through Autun and Avignon and the Côte d'Azur. On May 16, in Saint-Tropez, Berryman got drunk again, and after staying up the entire night, insisted on finding an audience to recite his Bradstreet to. As it turned out, the only person available at 5:00 A.M. on a Sunday morning was a baker, who dutifully listened to him recite his masterwork. After Saint-Tropez it was a ''delicious'' swim in the ocean and lunch at Juan-les-Pins, the sun a blue blaze off the Mediterranean as the two couples drove down the French coast into Italy, past San Remo, Piacenza, Bologna, Siena, and Florence, before arriving in Rome on May 25. There the Camerons stayed with the poet Denis Devlin, Ireland's minister to Italy, while the Berrymans took a room facing away from the street at the Pensione Svizzera. But if Berryman's disposition improved on the trip south, Eileen's did not. A broken rear spring in the Camerons' sports car, cramped sleeping quarters, and her husband's drunken behavior soon caused a painful flare-up in Eileen's back condition, so that, at some point on that trip, Berryman would later recall, he saw something in Eileen's face that made him understand that their marriage really was finished.

On the morning of June 5, the Feast of Corpus Christi, the Berrymans went to St. Peter's to catch a glimpse of the pope. They were among "the last of thousands to enter," Berryman wrote his mother, when suddenly he heard a voice and far up at the other end of the basilica he could just make out

> against a scarlet cloth, a small figure in white flanked by one in red & one in black. More mysterious applause. At last, men climbing up pillars, children held high to see, people w. backs turned looking in upheld mirrors, slowly [Pius XII] came towards us borne in his chair between aisle-barriers. He waved his palms slowly towards himself, leaning slowly from side to side down over the chair-arms—so Italians wave—while the part of the throng near him shouted. It was all alarmingly informal. A few feet from us he halted to ask who were a contingent of little girls in uniform. Then, a dozen feet off, at the end of the aisle before it turned out of the nave, the chair was swung to face the altar, he rose and solemnly blessed all parts of the congregation.

Eileen wept, and Berryman, seeing "a very white, kind, beautiful figure," felt "altogether astonished."

In early June proofs for the Bradstreet arrived from Catherine Carver at *The Partisan Review,* but it took Berryman three weeks to go through what should have taken him a day. When he did send the proofs back with one or two minor changes, he told Carver he was finally working again, had really quit drinking this time, and was at last "free of obsession" of the Bradstreet, through not yet well "in spirit." By then his money was almost gone, and he still had no idea what he would to do for a job come fall. So, when the Princeton art historian George Rowley offered him two hundred dollars to edit his manuscript on the use of space in piazzas, Berryman took the job and stayed close to his hotel room.

The Roethkes were in Rome that June, and Roethke also got Berryman to critique his poems for him. He had promised to do the same for Berryman, though it was soon obvious he was not really interested in Berryman's work. But if Berryman's behavior was unsteady, it was stolid compared to Roethke's. On one occasion, when Roethke and his wife of five months, Beatrice, and the Berrymans were finishing their meal at a German restaurant, Roethke suddenly suggested they all go out and have another dinner at another restaurant he was interested in trying.

At the end of June, her back still troubling her, Eileen took the train to Naples for some sun and rest and to get away from her husband for a week. Originally the Berrymans had planned to stay in Europe until early October, but two days after Eileen returned to Rome, short of funds, they decided to cut short their stay in England and return home in August.

On July 6, Berryman left by train for Paris, where he met Eileen, who flew up from Rome on the seventh. By then she was in so much pain that she spent her Paris stay confined to her hotel room. On the eleventh, at last reinforced with a loan from Jill, the Berrymans crossed the Channel and went on to London to stay with the MacNeices, who held a party in their honor on the evening of their arrival. But during the party someone jokingly pulled Eileen backward as she was going upstairs and managed to wrench her back. By the following day the pain had spread to her legs, and the MacNeices had to call in a doctor to administer sedatives. At the end of three days, however, the pain was still so intense that she was transferred to a hospital in the city.

Alone and depressed, Eileen became desperate now to get back to the States, but instead the doctors recommended she stay put for at least three more weeks. Berryman tried to put the best face on the deteriorating situation, but excused himself by insisting he was a "poor nurse" for whom the rudiments of daily living were still a mystery. Still, he remained sanguine. Something would turn up. Something always did. Through MacNeice's intercession, John Davenport offered Berryman money in return for reading his poems and giving a series of talks for the BBC's Third Programme. The talks would be on

Whitman, Stephen Crane, and Berryman's view of postwar Europe.

Berryman agreed to do the talks, but most of his time he spent drinking and visiting his old haunts in London and Cambridge (two days there, alone, speaking to no one, living "in a dream of sunlight"). At one point he even went to see Beryl, who was still living in London. True to her word, she had never married. Shaken by her old fiancé's appearance, and learning that Eileen was in the hospital, she went to visit her. But when Berryman went to see Beryl a second time, he made an awkward move, and Beryl was relieved to see him go. One night, soon after the Roethkes arrived in London, Berryman went with them and some others to a pub before they were to have dinner at Davenport's. Instead, Berryman got drunk and wandered out of the pub, not to be seen again that night. When asked later what had happened, he had to admit he could not remember.

He did very little in the way of work during his weeks in London, but at least he began his travel talk for the BBC. He called it "Three Cities," the cities being Paris, Rome, and London. The talk focused on the changes he'd noted since his stay in Europe before the war. And even in its unfinished state, the talk was a perceptive and comic piece of writing. What he had seen on his recent trip to Paris, he wrote, was an "increase in egoism, flamboyant smugness, and insincerity," even though the French had been beaten in the war. Rome too had suffered, though from talking with "artists, novelists, poets, critics and painters" there, he thought the city seemed "more vivacious and capable than Paris." As for British intellectuals, while he had been shown "great and almost continual kindness" during his stay in London, he could not help noticing a certain "resentment or scorn" in the way they kept standing him against a wall, holding him personally responsible for everything the Democrats and Republicans had done for the past twenty years. Nor was he very happy with American foreign policy. On July 31, he wrote Fitzgerald that, from a European perspective, Eisenhower and his secretary of state, John Foster Dulles, looked like the worst possible executives for a difficult time and that "the chief result of the Korean truce" seemed to be that it would result in a permanent split between England and the U.S. He promised "more good news" in his next letter.

Short again for money, he wrote Tate asking him to intercede on his behalf with the Academy of American Poets, which had a fund for needy writers. Tate saw that Berryman got a check from the academy and personally loaned him enough money to pay Eileen's hospital bill as well as Berryman's hotel bill, so that they could get back to the States. Berryman promised to repay Tate just as soon as he got back to a "more normal life."

But things were about to become even less "normal" than before. After four months abroad, the Berrymans returned via a long and grueling plane ride to New York. Jill celebrated their return with a party at her new apartment at 360 West Twenty-third Street, a few blocks west of the Chelsea Hotel, where the Berrymans planned to stay the night before returning to Princeton. Afterward, in their hotel room, Eileen told Berryman what had been on her mind for some time. She was going back to Princeton to get her things, and he was to stay with his mother. When she'd left the apartment, he could come down, get his books and clothes, and return to New York. It was better if they lived apart, at least for now.

Two nights after being told the news, alone in his mother's apartment, he jotted down some notes, trying to make sense of the worst disaster, as he would later phrase it, to confront an American since Grant's murderous assault on Cold Harbor. Still, when everything else failed, he knew there was always a list to bring some sort of order to things. He listed all the "broken-down bachelors" he knew, then those who already knew of the separation: himself, his mother, the Mackies, whom he'd telephoned that night, and Shea. By then, he figured, Eileen had probably informed her sister as well. Then he drew up another list of those who would have to be told the news, together with an announcement that captured perfectly the tragic denouement of his marriage. "John & Eileen Berryman," he wrote, not without a trace of dark humor even now,

> announce w. regret & agony
> their separation.
> Each begs to assure you of his or her undiminisht affection
> and hopes that you will be on his or her side.

# PART III

*1953–62*

# chapter 17

# Death of a Poet

## 1953–54

Contemplating the ruin his marriage had become, Berryman moved in imagination back to the falls at Tivoli he and Eileen had visited in July: the ruined temple above and two slender ribbons of water, each falling separately forever, like his and Eileen's lives from now on. Marriage was a godawful impossible ideal, he sighed, and his had turned out to be all "mildew, loss,/ ruin and sweetness."

And while he would lament the end of his marriage for years to come, he knew he still needed money and a job. With classes beginning all over the country, he set about writing to various colleges, looking for a teaching position. "I expect your staff is by now all arranged for this year but I send a note in case it isn't," the letter to the chairwoman at Queens College ran. If she was interested in seeing his work, there was, he explained, "a long Shakespearian essay" in *The Hudson Review* and the Bradstreet in *The Partisan Review*.

He wrote Lowell to tell him about the Elliston Professorship he'd held at Cincinnati and to ask if Lowell would be willing to teach there the following spring so that he could take his place at the University of Iowa. On September 26, Lowell wrote back that he was willing to make the change. The good news about Iowa was that the best students there were really hot, the bad news was that Iowa City was Iowa City, though it did have at least one "highbrow movie house." Lowell had already signaled the writing-program director, Paul Engle, that Berryman might be available as "someone permanent to alternate" with himself.

Berryman kept in close touch with Eileen, telling her how much he missed her. By then it had been seven weeks since she'd left him, during which time, he wrote her, he had really tried to change. He had tried being "good natured & helpful" toward others, and had been writing stories and articles to support himself. But he had had to borrow money to stay alive. Lowell had "presst" twenty dollars on him over dinner one night, besides picking up the tab, and his mother had also helped. Berryman had asked Bob Giroux at Harcourt Brace to take over his next four books, including the Bradstreet volume and the book he had in mind to do about Shakespeare's friend W.H., and Giroux had ended up lending him $120.

Suddenly, in the midst of his letter, he told Eileen he was seriously considering jumping off the George Washington Bridge. He would do it by climbing over the rail and staring down into the Hudson River until he became so dizzy he would finally let go. But even as he evoked the horror of the spectacle, he couldn't help giggling. "I believe one dies on the way down," he wrote, "but I don't wish to hit anyone or be splattered on the pavement, and in case my body is not found nobody has the bore & cost of burial." If his body was recovered, however, he wanted it planted "as cheaply as possible in Princeton, where I could not stay." He'd already "lost so much that few human beings dying can have less to lose." He pleaded with her to talk to him when she came up to New York again.

In early November his review of Jarrell's *Poetry and the Age* appeared. Jarrell's book, he wrote, was the best thing on its subject since Blackmur's *The Double Agent* and Winters's *Primitivism and Decadence*. And, he added, Jarrell, along with Delmore, was also the "ablest" American critic of his generation. Almost always, he noted, Jarrell's opinions were on target, his two essays on Frost forming nothing short of a brilliant upward revaluation of one of America's foremost poets. As for the early reviews he and Jarrell had done of Lowell's *Lord Weary's Castle,* he generously acknowledged that Jarrell's piece was by far the better and very likely "the most masterly initial review of an important poetic work, either here or in England, of this century so far." If there was still peace to be made with Jarrell, he made it with this review.

During October, Berryman rented a room in his mother's apartment house. Then, at the beginning of November he moved into Room 604 at the Chelsea Hotel, three blocks away, where Dylan Thomas was also staying. But if Berryman was drinking heavily once again, Thomas was about to drink himself to death. On the evening of November 4, Thomas fell off his bar stool at the White Horse Tavern in the Village and lapsed into a coma. An ambulance was called, and he was taken to nearby St. Vincent's Hospital. The following evening, returning from Princeton, Berryman found a note at the front desk informing him that Thomas was in the hospital. He rushed to St. Vincent's and positioned himself outside Thomas's room till one in the morning, then returned to the hotel, where he wrote Betty Bettman that "one of the greatest lyric poets who ever lived" had been in a "wet brain" coma for the past twenty hours.

He was hopeful Thomas might pull through, though "with how much brain damage" only time would show. If he could have, Berryman would have stood vigil outside Thomas's room till Thomas had either recovered or was dead, but he had to speak at Bard College. After he had lectured on *The Tempest* that weekend, Berryman attended a party ten miles from campus. Ralph Ellison, Saul Bellow, and Pearl Kazin were at the party, and Ellison would remember Berryman hovering near the phone, waiting for word of Thomas's condition. If Thomas died, Berryman wailed drunkenly, poetry would die with him.

The following night, as the conference ended with yet another party, Berryman and Kazin kept telephoning St. Vincent's, trying to get information on Thomas's condition. Ellison heard Berryman "relieve himself of a rather drunken recital of *Do Not Go Gentle into That Good Night*" and later that evening drove Berryman and Kazin back to New York. It was midnight when they reached the hotel, but Berryman insisted that he and Pearl go directly to St. Vincent's. Ellison dropped them off but did not go with them, "because their grief was so intensely private." Though it was late, the sister on duty let the two in to see Dylan, who lay in the darkened room under an oxygen tent lying eerily still.

At 12:40 the following afternoon—November 9—Berryman arrived at St. Vincent's to find Dylan unattended. As he looked at Thomas, he realized with a shock that something was wrong. He shouted for a nurse, who appeared immediately, and then realized that Thomas was dead. As Berryman walked out into the hall, he ran into John Malcolm Brinnin, the man responsible for organizing Dylan's American tours, just returning from lunch. Hysterical, Berryman screamed at him for abandoning poor Thomas, and then staggered out of the hospital.

That Friday Berryman attended the memorial service for Thomas. The day before, he'd had a note from Brinnin saying that Thomas's wife, Caitlin, wanted to see him before she returned to Wales. By then Berryman had heard about Caitlin's reaction to Dylan's death: how she'd gone wild at the hospital, smashing things, and had had to be restrained. But Friday night, after the services, Berryman spent several hours with her. She was still near hysteria, alternately crying on Berryman's shoulder and verbally lashing out at him, and—according to Berryman—trying to seduce him. The only thing that had saved him, he realized afterward, was the presence of ten other people in the room, so that he managed to save his neck and whatever chastity he could still claim.

The following afternoon Caitlin left a note for him at the front desk, asking to see him again before she left. By quarter past nine that evening, when she had not heard from him, she left a telephone message asking him to call her. But knowing how shaky his track record with attractive women was, and feeling honor-bound to Thomas's memory, Berryman did not return her call. As for Thomas, Berryman had no illusions about what had happened. "Dylan murdered himself w. liquor," he wrote Lowell, "tho it took years."

In the midst of all that turmoil, Paul Engle called, offering Berryman the job at Iowa for the spring. In a few months, Berryman cheered himself, he would be solvent once more. Yet, in spite of his protestations of grief, not everyone was convinced of Berryman's sincerity. When he heard that an Englishman at the BBC had called his reaction to Dylan's death a piece of "hysterical dramatizing," Berryman was so wounded that he went on a four-day binge. What particularly gnawed at him was his suspicion that the Englishman was right and that his hysteria was "unfortunately" an "actual aspect" of his character.

One of the reasons Berryman had agreed to the separation from Eileen was so that he could be "free" to write, but by December he found himself involved with no fewer than two women. One was a divorcée with a small child, the other was Anita Maximilian Philips, a close friend of Alexandra (Sondra) Tschacbasov, whom Saul Bellow was dating. Anita had been a classmate of Sondra's at Bennington College, and was now attending the New School. At twenty she had already been married and divorced.

A week before Christmas, Lowell returned to New York, and he, Berryman, and Giroux, dressed in formal attire, attended a performance of *La Traviata* at the Metropolitan Opera. Then Berryman went to Washington to lecture on Pound and went out to St. Elizabeth's to visit Pound for a third time. By December 23 he was back in New York, where he saw Eileen before she flew down to Nashville to stay with her sister's family. Christmas Eve, Berryman went to a party at Conrad Aiken's Manhattan apartment. Earlier that month he'd received a letter of congratulations from Aiken for the Bradstreet, a letter which had pleased and astounded Berrymore so much that he carried it with him everywhere he went, touching his vest pocket from time to time to make sure it was really there. It was Edmund Wilson who had given Aiken a copy of the Bradstreet, and Aiken had been so taken by it, he wrote Berryman, that he'd read it three times in three days. It was "far more than a tour de force of empathy and immersion in zeitgeist," Aiken told him. It was actually "one of the finest poems ever written by an American, a classic right on the doorstep."

But by the time Berryman arrived at Aiken's Christmas Eve, he was drunk. Afterward he claimed he could not remember what he'd said or whom exactly he had insulted, but soon the man who had so highly praised him was showing him to the door, minus his hat. Somewhere in New York that night Berryman managed to lose his coat and all his Christmas gifts as well. Four days later, he wrote Tate in Rome. By then he'd had enough of New York. He was tired of being used as "a clearinghouse for the worst news in the world, every madness & scandal imaginable, including my own true & imaginary." Since the incident at the Aikens', he added defensively, he'd gone on the wagon again.

Giroux, he told Tate, was anxious to publish the Bradstreet with Harcourt, but Berryman's old contracts with Viking had restrictive clauses in them, and he saw no way now of getting around them. He missed Rome and asked Tate to "eat a tartuffo" for him in the Piazza Navona. How much had changed since the summer, when he and Eileen had strolled through that same piazza together. A dozen years later he would still remember the loss that place signaled for him with a pain beyond what he would have thought possible, as if a man were to be "dragged by his balls, singing aloud 'Oh yes'/ while to his anguisht glance" the world and everything in it had suddenly been turned upside down.

"God damn the old year is dead," he wrote two days into 1954. He was getting ready to leave for Iowa as soon as his agent and publishers could advance him some money. By then he was actually glad to be getting out of New York. At six in the evening on February 4, his train arrived in Iowa City. He settled into his second-floor apartment at 606 South Johnson, then spent the rest of the evening drinking with some old friends from Princeton. By the time he got back to his apartment, he was very drunk. He managed to negotiate the stairs to his apartment, but as he came out of the bathroom into the dark hallway, he fell down the stairs and crashed into a half-glass door. His landlords, the Bristols, hearing the crash, came running, and managed to get him back upstairs and into bed. The next morning Berryman realized how badly shaken up he was. His teeth were chattering, his ankles were swollen, and his left wrist was broken. He had to be hospitalized, he told his mother, "for shock & exhaustion," but really so that he could get himself detoxified. He was so depressed over the way his life had turned out that he spent most of the next ten days in bed until classes began.

He decided now to study Hebrew with one of the Iowa instructors, Frederick Peretz Bargebour. Berryman's idea was to learn enough Hebrew to translate Job, but soon a new poem was pressing itself on him, so that by the end of the month he was working "unhappily & w intense reluctance" on it instead of his Hebrew. He called the poem "Letter from a Singing Man for Saul & Peretz,'' and he set it in Iowa City, using elementary Hebrew phrases to enhance the texture of his poem. It was an elegy ''for dead poets & their crazinesses when living,'' a way-down note struck for all poets who had lived too close to the edge.

By then he was also complaining that every ''proto-poet'' at Iowa was foisting his ''collected poetical works'' on him. Nevertheless, as Lowell had told him, his best students were so good that they were worth the trouble of his midwestern exile. In fact, his one consolation that spring turned out to be his Monday afternoon poetry workshop, which was often followed by an informal class at Kenny's bar. But, when he walked into his class at the beginning of the term, it was clear he was in no mood to suffer fools gladly. There were thirty students packed into the room, and he decided at once to pare the number down. He picked out a poem by a doctor's wife excoriating doctors, read it, then proceeded to tear the poem to shreds.

The slashing worked, for when the class met the following week, there were only thirteen students left willing to go through that sort of scrutiny for the sake of art. Those thirteen, however, made up an extraordinary assembly of talent. Nearly all would go on to publish serious books, and at least three would become part of the American pantheon in the next generation of American poetry. Among the thirteen who remained were Jane Cooper, Henri Coulette, Melvin La Follette, Paul Petrie, Shirley Eliason, Robert Dana, William Dickey, W. D. Snodgrass, Donald Justice, and Philip Levine.

Berryman proved to be an excellent writing teacher, who made ''the study of poetry, our god damned mediocre poetry, the center of the world,'' Levine would remember. He also took charge of his class in a way Lowell never had. Lowell's attitude toward his students had been something like, ''Your poems are killing me with boredom.'' But Berryman was all concentration, poring over his students' poems and spelling out ''in great detail where we went wrong.'' He was also more democratic than Lowell, and everyone had a chance at being both ''bashed'' and encouraged.

Berryman was quick, tense, nervous, even bombastic. There was no literary chitchat, no gossip, for it was serious business they were about. Once, at a gathering, Levine would recall, the talk had centered on Alun Lewis's war poem ''Song (On seeing dead bodies floating off the Cape.)" Berryman asked if anyone had ever seen the poem, and Levine, who'd learned it by heart the year before, recited it. Then one of those present—a big man, six two, two hundred and twenty pounds—began talking about Berryman's war poems in *The Dispossessed*. Far from being flattered, Berryman actually became enraged that anyone would compare Lewis's poem with his own apprenticeship work, and suddenly he was wheeling on the man. "Listen, you stupid shit," he screamed at him, "we're talking *real* poems here!" For a moment it looked as if there might be some violence, but the man simply stood there, stunned.

Berryman was continually measuring his students' work against "real" poems by Milton, Blake, Shakespeare, Keats, or by living giants like Stevens and Eliot, or by the contemporaries he most respected: Thomas, Roethke, Lowell, and Elizabeth Bishop. Often he quoted from poems in other languages: a nineteenth-century French poem, a poem from the classical Chinese. He was not showing off, for he was "used to being with well read people, and this was a natural manner of discourse. . . . He had incredibly high standards," and he judged his students by those same standards.

Once he asked them who the most powerful poet in the language was. He waited, and then told them it was Milton. Then he "went on to show us how rhythmic speed produced power and enjambment produced speed, that and the ability to control the sentence so it could sweep thru the lines. Then he showed us how Lowell derived from Milton, & that that was no accident, Lowell's stance was so similar, the stern Xtian damning the wicked. From there to the most lyrical, Blake, & how Dylan Thomas derived from him, & again, no accident with Dylan's mystical vision of creation & his political anarchism."

In his lecture course on modern poetry, Berryman spent a good deal of time explicating Whitman's "Song of Myself," his lectures spinning off the more formal lectures he'd given at Cincinnati two years before. He even began a minor Whitmania phase at Iowa. Levine remembered it as the best poetry he'd ever heard read, "& all readings since pale by comparison." It was the spring of the Army–McCarthy hearings, and once Berryman came into the class and read from a recent copy of *The*

*New York Times* an article in which Joe McCarthy was quoted as saying that he "stood behind" Roy Cohn and David Shine "to the hilt." Then he read from the morning edition of the paper a story in which McCarthy had just cut himself off from his associates. With that Berryman looked at his students. "Your language will always reveal what's actually there," he told them. The current fools and idiots in Washington would be replaced by other fools and idiots, but this—and he held up a copy of Keats opened to "Ode to a Nightingale"—*this* news would stay news.

Winter hung on. Berryman, his left arm still in his faded black sling, had difficulty even boiling an egg for his dinner. After two months in Iowa City he was once more contemplating suicide. One night at the end of March, he telephoned Donald Justice and asked him to come over to his apartment at once. Justice, sensing the desperation in Berryman's voice, called a taxi and went over to Berryman's as soon as he could. But as he climbed to the top of the stairs, he saw Berryman through the hall windows sitting on the couch in his living room, staring at his feet at an open case of old-fashioned leather-stropping razors. Justice let himself in and, realizing what Berryman had been contemplating, sank into a chair, nearly fainting. Suddenly Berryman became "all concern and consideration," fetching damp cloths with which to chafe Justice's wrists. Through the night the men talked. Then, around five, they went into town and had breakfast together, then went back to Justice's apartment, where Berryman fell asleep in the living-room chair. Justice never heard Berryman broach the subject of suicide again.

On April 7, a second, smaller cast came off Berryman's wrist, and the following day he was able to write a letter to Bellow. In all the time he'd been in Iowa, he explained, he'd written only to Eileen and Anita, though he could not bring himself to tell either of them what was really on his mind. Moreover, there was no one in Iowa he felt he could really talk to, so that he felt "completely isolated" from everyone. Now too there was this "thermonuclear business" of testing hydrogen bombs, which did not help his peace of mind any. He had not yet slept with anyone since New York, but at least he was not waking up in the middle of the night with nightmares. He was, however, afraid he was suffering from malnutrition, and he was having "violent diarrhea," so that he had kept to his bed for as much as "17 hours a day, days on end, not sleeping of course but not dozing, with an average of two nights a week winkless, as a rule not troubling to go to bed at all." Whatever his students might think, he was having trouble getting through his workshop and his lectures each week. If only he could write, he sighed, he could bear anything. He did not mention his drinking.

The following day he wrote to his mother. He was going to Grinnell College to read his poems and judge a poetry contest, and after Easter he hoped to be a changed man. With his cast off now, he could type again and had begun to answer "some of the fifty letters" he owed. Lowell had written, asking Berryman to join him in Cincinnati for a long weekend and some serious talk, but Berryman was in no shape to travel. Besides, he had no money. He was also surprised to hear from his mother that she was now seriously interested in the spiritual life. Writing to her now felt like old times, he told her, when he'd sent her long letters from England, filled with news of his latest enthusiasms. The difference was that now *he* was the adviser. The Princeton apartment, he'd learned, would have to be vacated, so now all his stern, elegant books would have to be stored in New Jersey till he had a place to put them. How he wanted those books by him now, for truly they made most modern writers seem "ephemeral & insubstantial."

Consider the Japanese masters, he told her. In studying Buson's death poem, he'd come to realize that the highest virtue in Eastern poetry was the gradual effacement of oneself. He had also learned something about substantive pauses in Japanese poetry, silences that reflected the idea of vacancy, "the most important factor in Japanese art." What mattered most in poetry was not the said but the sublimity and suggestiveness of the not-said. With this new knowledge he was going back to his long poem on Saul and Peretz and turn it into "the longest Japanese poem in existence."

In spite of his ambitions for his poem, however, which he now renamed his "Testament from In Here," it refused to yield itself. In it he had pictured himself as Job in the New World—in Seattle, Cincinnati, Burlington, Detroit, Iowa City. What was new about this poem was just how unabashedly autobiographical Berryman had allowed himself to become:

> Cast out, w boils: comes airmail kindness, for
> my friends across the smalled world kiss my sores,
> it does me good. Skin-solace
>
> Hall dark, steep stair down, travel blind, I crasht
> & snapt a wrist, landing in glass
>
> Peretz consoles my syntax, when I'd grieve
> in the ancients' tongue. Todah, Peretz. Look for me
> where cupshot Mars cases the Pleiades
> on winter's breaking: tiny, bored, withdrawing. . . .

He wanted the poem to be "more poetical" than the Bradstreet, but at the same time "clearer" and "weirder." Before he let it go, however, he realized he was writing yet another poem to his father, dead at thirty-nine. It was his own age exactly.

Part of that Good Friday Berryman spent meditating in the chapel of St. Mary's at Grinnell College, writing a poem in the evening called "Shrouds." The poem was in six-line stanzas of unrhymed verse and recalled Saul and Sondra and Anita and his other Jewish friends back East. It also served to remind him that, if part of him belonged to their world, some part of him did not:

> Shrouds have all saints, solely a vigil burns
> while early afternoon's light comes & goes
> as clouds must be shifting . . .
> Less I was lonely
> earlier, earlier: owing to those called Jews.
> Not real Jews. It seems now, & is better
> to act out what you are.

At the beginning of May, Elizabeth Hardwick wrote him that Cal had suffered a breakdown following the death of his mother in Genoa. At the moment Cal was at Jewish Hospital in Cincinnati, but he was about to be transferred to Payne Whitney in New York. It was the reality of bringing his mother's body back with him that had unhinged Cal, Hardwick explained. But what was worse was seeing some of their Cincinnati "friends" keep her husband from the treatment he needed. She added that she'd seen Eileen in New York and that she was looking beautiful.

Among the few bright moments for Berryman that spring was John Crowe Ransom's visit to the university. Another was Pound sending him the first installment of Fitzgerald's powerful translation of the *Odyssey*. But Berryman's chronic feeling was one of loneliness, and he took his consolation where he could. That, of course, led to problems. The problem with Berryman, Snodgrass would sum up, was that "as soon as he liked you he began making your life difficult by tampering in your love life and sometimes trying to tamper with your wife," and he managed to have at least one affair that spring, once again with the wife of a graduate student.

One of the most flagrant cases of Berryman's womanizing occurred late in the semester. Berryman had come to like Levine, fascinated as he was by his student's physical strength and working-class background. He also liked Franny, Levine's attractive fiancée, and so it was only a matter of time before he made his move. "We'd been drinking first in Kenny's & then we moved" to someone's apartment "where a hot dart match was under way," Levine would recall. But at last Berryman decided it was time to leave and he took Levine and Franny back with him to his apartment. "He sat on the floor, Franny on the floor, and I on the edge of the bed," Levine remembers:

> We were talking serious poetry stuff when I saw him shoot a hand up her skirt. I said, loudly, Did I see what I think I saw? Franny shook her head. We went back to our talking, & within a few minutes it happened again. I said to Franny, Let's go, she agreed, & we started to leave. I was pissed. John summoned me to his small kitchen; I expected him to apologize, but instead he told me that my woman wanted to stay there with him and wouldn't I be a good sport & just leave. I called him something & laughed at him, though I was deeply hurt; when we turned to leave Franny yelled something & I started to turn back to John, but before I could I was struck by the now empty Scotch bottle, a glancing blow but enough to put me down. . . . He stamped

on one of my hands, my left, & the next day the thumb felt broken.

But Levine outweighed Berryman by twenty pounds and had learned his fighting on the streets of Detroit, and though he'd been dazed by the bottle, he managed to get up and punch Berryman, knocking him down and splitting his lip open. "He was furious, yelling such outrageous things as, 'I'll get you back for this, Levine, you'll never publish in New York, I'll see to that." He was so awful that Franny & I just laughed at him, awful & corny."

It was ten days before Levine saw Berryman again and, when he did, Berryman was "incredibly apologetic." Berryman had had to meet his workshop with his lip cut and swollen. He could not even remember what he'd done, though he had managed to figure out that Levine must have hit him. Had he really acted that badly? he asked, astonished. When Levine told him what had happened, he had to smile at his own audacity. If Eileen had been with him, he explained, that sort of thing would never have happened. "He wanted to be forgiven," Levine could see, "& of course I forgave him."

After the final workshop, Berryman and Levine got drunk in Berryman's apartment, and when Levine awoke the next morning, he was on Berryman's bed, still in his street clothes, with Berryman sleeping under the covers in his pajamas. "A Western Union boy was pounding at the bedroom door, which opened directly into the stairway," and Berryman's glasses were still on the bedside table. "The kid said, Telegram for John Berryman. John put on his glasses & stared at me. Are you John Berryman? he asked me. No, I said. Then I must be, he said, & accepted the telegram from Bellow." Later that day Levine drove Berryman to the airport, "which was full of little schoolkids on an outing. John was utterly charmed by the kids & spoke quietly and wittily to many of them." Then, just before he boarded, he asked Levine for a good anti-Semitic joke, since he planned to see his publisher in New York later that day.

A week later Berryman was back at 120 Prospect Avenue in Princeton to help Eileen move their belongings out and pack his books for storage. Then he went back to New York and his room at the Chelsea Hotel to prepare for the Shakespeare course and the writing workshop he was teaching at Harvard that summer. Much of June he spent in New York, seeing old girlfriends, reading, and drinking. At last, on the Fourth of July, his mother drove him to Cambridge.

The following Tuesday he had lunch at the Faculty Club with some friends, held his first office hour, and went "pub crawling" with Irving Howe and his wife, Thalia. At nine the following morning he met his Shakespeare class in a "banked lecture hall like an operating theatre." After lunch he met the twenty students who made up his fiction workshop, the best of whom turned out to be Edward Hoagland, the future nonfiction prose writer. During the seven weeks he was in Cambridge, Berryman dated several students, attended as many parties and dances as he could, sat in movie houses watching his favorite, Danny Kaye, and once even attended the stock-car races and demolition derby. For exercise he swam. He taught one after another of Shakespeare's plays: the histories, the comedies, the tragedies. He taught them professionally, but without great enthusiasm. He also read dozens of fiction manuscripts. And of course he drank. Finally, on the last day of August, he left Cambridge in the midst of Hurricane Carol and celebrated his safe arrival that evening at the Chelsea Hotel by once again getting drunk.

A few days later he had a letter from Paul Engle saying he'd been assigned a novel course to teach. Berryman had assumed he would be teaching poetry again and was upset to learn about the change, especially with classes only a few weeks off. But he set about at once, preparing for the new course, listing the novels he felt comfortable teaching: one of Jane Austen's novels, *Pilgrim's Progress,* Gogol's *Dead Souls, Madame Bovary, Middlemarch, Crime and Punishment, Anna Karenina, The Wings of the Dove,* Proust, *Ulysses, The Castle, The Great Gatsby, As I Lay Dying, The Adventures of Augie March, The Story of an African Farm, The Power and the Glory, A Passage to India.* He would use an "experimental & inductive" approach, his main interest being in the problem of voice in the novel. Before long, enchanted with the riches the novel had to offer, he considered putting together a second course.

On the evening of September 17, he boarded the Pullman sleeper for Iowa City, and the following morning checked into the Jefferson Hotel and began looking for an apartment. At eleven the following night he telephoned Marguerite Young, with whom he would be team-teaching a workshop in the short story. There were seventy students enrolled in the course, and he wanted to get his bearings, he told her, as soon as possible, though he was not happy about having to share the workshop with another instructor, much less her. He spent the next two days registering students, then moved into an apartment at 409 East Jefferson Avenue. He was going through the motions, but his heart was not in it. John Montague, the Irish poet, had enrolled in Berryman's workshop and remembered seeing him eating alone at the Jefferson Hotel, a copy of *The Caine Mutiny* open before him, "nervous, taut, arrogant, uneasy."

By the end of September, everything had come unraveled for him. He liked some of his students, but he hated Young, whom he thought of as a prima donna who continually shielded her students from the criticism he felt they needed. But that was only part of the problem. He was drinking heavily and began calling anyone who would listen to him, including several of his students, reading his poems into the receiver at all hours of the night. The more unsure of himself he became, the more he crowed about his stupendous literary achievements. On the twenty-ninth, teaching the workshop for the second time, he made some remark that Young took as offensive to women and, in the "anti-Berryman barrage" that followed, Montague found himself "coming in on Berryman's side." There was a "nervous, fractious discussion," Montague remembered, that had more to do with "personalities than with anything substantive, and with Young's passionate, even violent defense of her students." When the workshop was over, Berryman retreated to Kenny's bar and began drinking heavily, arguing with anyone unlucky enough to get in his way.

Late that night he staggered back to his apartment, where, unable to find his key, he tried to force the door. When the landlord saw how drunk he was, he refused to let Berryman in. Upset, and desperately needing to go to the bathroom, Berryman began shouting obscenities. But when the landlord refused to let him in, Berryman squatted on the front porch and defecated. Upset, the landlord's wife called the police and had Berryman locked up for disorderly conduct. On top of that, Berryman became outraged when the police began jeering and taunting him. When several police officers exposed themselves to him, Berryman began screaming that they were nothing but "*homosexual* criminals." Still, there was nothing he could do but endure his night behind bars. For the first time in his life, he found himself stripped of everything, even of his glasses, as he stared in cold rage at his tormentors.

At eight the following morning he was released after paying two fines: $7.50 for disorderly conduct and another $5.00 for public intoxication. He spent the day planning to divide up his workshop (he would NOT teach with that woman again) and then moved his books from his apartment to the university. He wanted to forget what had happened as just another of his bad dreams. But this time it was too late, for by then the local papers had printed the story of his arrest. At six that evening he had a call from Paul Engle. Dean Strist and Provost Davis would see him in the morning.

The meetings began at ten and lasted until midafternoon, by which time Berryman found himself shaking with anger and helplessness. That evening he was informed that he would no longer be teaching at Iowa. Now he understood he really had hit bottom and wondered where he was going to turn next. At last he called Allen Tate at the University of Minnesota, who told him to come to Minneapolis and he would try to find a teaching position for him there. The following day Berryman packed his belongings and had dinner with three of his students: John Montague, Gertrude Buckman, and Emma Swan. Near midnight Swan and Buckman took him to the train. He was the same age his father had been when he'd left his son forever. Somehow, in the midst of his shame and utter confusion, Berryman had contrived to have another father rescue him and call him home.

## *chapter 18*

# Home

## 1954–55

Berryman arrived in Minneapolis on Sunday morning, October 3. It was raining, and he was astonished to see trees again after Iowa's flatness. He called Tate, then got in contact with a young friend of his mother's, Edwy Lee, who was doing graduate work with Tate and teaching part time at the university. That evening he had dinner with the Tates at the Rainbow, and Tate reiterated his promise to do all he could to get Berryman a teaching job at the university as soon as possible. If anyone could do anything, it would be that earth-shaker Ralph Ross, who headed up the Humanities Program in the Department of Interdisciplinary Studies. In the late 1940's and early 1950's, Ross had run the Humanities Program at New York University, where he'd brought together such luminaries as Tate, Bellow, Isaac Rosenfeld, Vivienne Koch, and George Amberg. When Ross transferred to Minnesota, he had brought Rosenfeld and Amberg with him, and then had helped bring Tate into the English department when Robert Penn Warren had left.

Monday morning Tate took Berryman to meet Ross, who

promised to find him something as soon as possible. For the first time in weeks Berryman was able to sleep soundly. The following day he located an upstairs apartment in a private home at 2509 Humboldt South just off the Lake of Isles and within easy walking distance of the Tates and Lees. He would start all over again, and since his drinking had led to his dismissal at Iowa, he resolved now to limit his intake to beer and an occasional martini. He even began keeping a record of his drinking. He promised himself to answer his letters and wrote a literary agent asking about free-lance work. Eileen wrote, anxious to know what had happened in Iowa, and he wrote back explaining. Within the week he heard from Ross. The new term would begin just after New Year's, and Ross was offering him a full-time job lecturing: a section of Medieval Literature and a seminar in Modern Literature. Berryman accepted.

"You see I am here, and not there," he wrote his mother four days after his arrival. The upshot of the Iowa fiasco was that he was now living "in this extremely agreeable city." It was very curious to be living so close to where Daddy had grown up, and he hoped to visit the family home in Stillwater soon. Could she send him any information on the Smiths, especially any of the names she could remember? It was also getting very cold, and he wondered if she could send him some gloves. A week after his arrival he went with the Tates for a long drive up along the St. Croix River, passing through his father's hometown, though he did not stop to explore.

Then the nightmares returned, and he found himself staying up all night until the windows began to turn blue. He kept busy writing through the long hours of darkness, but when he looked over what he'd written, he could see the stuff was hopeless. He wrote Shea in New York about his nightmares, and Shea wrote back. He pecked desultorily at his Shakespeare. In spite of his resolve to control his alcohol, he was soon drinking heavily again.

On Sunday, October 24, his twelfth wedding anniversary, Berryman wired Eileen, then called the Camerons in Cincinnati. The memories, sweet and painful, flooded in again. That evening, not willing to "celebrate" the eve of his fortieth birthday alone, he took a young woman to see a film about the life of Michelangelo. On his birthday he had wires of congratulations from both Eileen and his brother. "If you've ever had any worries abt becoming forty, don't," he wrote Bellow. "I made it today and I feel like dancing." It was "the first adult birthday anniversary" he could recall when he had not felt depressed, he wrote his mother. After all, he could hardly do any worse than he'd already done. More important, he was now older than his father had lived to be, and he could finally stop competing with that ghost. His character was "still far from being a desirable entity," he knew, but if he worked hard and *did* something, he reasoned, his human defects wouldn't in the long run matter.

He worked on several articles for *The Reader's Digest,* hoping in that way to make some money. He even returned to the darkness of his old *Black Book,* and thought now of incorporating a mixture of styles into his poem—the Classical, the Romantic, and the grotesque—to give the illusion of "a puzzle gradually revealed." The suite of poems would form a Mass for the Dead and he would be the poem's priest celebrant in which he would become, as in the Bradstreet, both torturer and victim. He planned to finish something every week, whether a story, an article, or a poem. He wrote letters daily so that he could tell himself he was getting something done. He had long, intimate, boozy talks with a number of graduate students. At parties he discussed literature with members of the English and Interdisciplinary Studies faculty, including several talks about the merits of his Crane biography. Especially now that rumors of his dismissal from Iowa were in the air, he needed to feel that his scholarly opinions mattered.

Lowell, back with Elizabeth Hardwick and living in Boston, wrote to say that he too had heard the rumors. "You got a lousy deal," he commiserated, believing the position at Iowa as Engle had defined it for Berryman had been "impossible from the start." Berryman was simply too good a writer to fit Iowa's system, too much the "scholar and professional teacher to find much in such a stop-gap job." Minnesota, he consoled Berryman, was bound to be "a hundred times better." Then Berryman heard from Van Doren. "So that is where you are," Mark wrote him in early November. "I never know. . . . And you are forty. And I am sixty."

But it was twenty Berryman was after, and he began seeing more of one young graduate student in particular, Elizabeth Ann Levine, a New Yorker and a friend of Sondra Tschacbasov's, going back to their days at Bennington together. Still, Berryman was not prepared to limit himself to any one woman yet, and he spent one Saturday night that November, after fortifying himself with a bottle of Scotch, reading aloud the whole of his Bradstreet to a group of young women. If he did fall in love with anyone that autumn, it was with a young woman he barely knew: a graduate of Vassar he'd met at Harvard the summer before. Her name was Sally Appleton, and she was a recent convert to Catholicism. She was also a friend of Father William Lynch, a Jesuit writer whose work Berryman respected, and she'd already spent time at Maryfarm working with Dorothy Day's Catholic Worker Movement. For "intelligence & sensibility & spiritual energy," he was soon writing his mother, Appleton was one of the "most remarkable young women" he'd ever met.

In November, Appleton wrote Berryman asking if he would look over something she'd written. Warming himself before his own fantasies and parsing the poem for whatever hidden messages about himself it might contain, Berryman completely misconstrued Appleton's intentions. For him, she was Bradstreet incarnate. At the end of the month he wrote her, saying that, while he knew he was "in a state of mortal sin" and had been "thro' my entire adult life," her caring might change all that. Then he enclosed a sonnet to her that ended, "nuns catch fire. Her beauty is in bloom."

The truth was that he was once more in serious need of rescue, for by November he had borrowed several hundred dollars from Tate and Edwy Lee, and at one point had become so desperate that he had gone over to the university to ask Tate for money, only to find that he could not bring himself to do it. "I am thoroughly ashamed of the nervewracking & evil complex I have got myself into," he berated himself. "Spare them! & myself! WORK."

As winter settled in, he became more and more introspective, and by mid-November he was systematically recording his nightmares. It was to be the most intense self-analysis he'd yet subjected himself to, as he now began scrutinizing his dreams to get at whatever secrets about himself might be hidden in the words he used to describe those dreams to himself. On the sixteenth he had a dream in which all he could retrieve were the words "St Pancras' braser" or "brazier," and that became the provisional title under which 154 dreams would eventually be catalogued and analyzed with Berryman's characteristic obsessiveness over the next six months. As early as his time at South Kent, he had been recording dreams, and then more systematically after he'd gone into analysis with Shea. But with Shea now ill and in any event separated from him by fifteen hundred miles, Berryman meant to enter into analysis with himself.

At the beginning of December Berryman at last heard from Appleton. She was, she made very clear, interested in Berryman's friendship only, and nothing more. On top of that blow, he heard from *The Kenyon Review* rejecting his application for a fellowship. And, since Tate had suggested he apply for the fellowship, he wondered now if Tate had somehow betrayed him! It was the last straw; that night he went out with Lee and got very drunk. When the two of them woke late the following day in Berryman's apartment, they picked up where they'd left off the night before. Twenty-four hours later, the blood pounding in his head and his breath still sour, Berryman managed to get over to the university and ask Tate straight out for a loan. Tate dipped into his wallet and gave him twenty-five dollars, with which Berryman paid his rent and some of his most pressing bills, then took in two British films. By the time he went to bed that night, he had sixty-five cents to his name.

When his head finally cleared this time, Berryman vowed once more to stop drinking and put his life in order. As long as he could work he was fine, he believed. But when at last he fell asleep, the nightmares began again to choke him. He went to Tate for yet another loan, then called Ross and pleaded with him to let him teach two sections of the same course rather than two new courses. Ross responded by giving him a beginner's and an advanced section of Medieval Literature. For the moment, Berryman whistled bravely in a letter to Catherine Carver, he was "very comfortable, very busy, and . . . gay as a bird." He was even looking forward to teaching courses that would "have some *material*" in them for a change—"the New Testament, Xtian Documents, Augustine, Aquinas, Dante—instead of pretending to teach people how to write."

But most of his prodigious energy went into analyzing his dreams, trying to come to some sense of what was actually driving him. The dream world, he was beginning to see, was not so much "a glory-hole" or Jungian treasure trove as it was a combination of "Maginot Line and . . . Strategic Air Command," defending the waking conscious against the threat of invasion. In fact, he quickly realized, his dreams were far more complex than any poem he'd ever analyzed, so that he was coming to have "almost a new idea of the mind's strength, cunning, & beauty."

Since October his mother had been helping him recall his early memories of his father. So it had been Bob and *not* him his father had swum out into Tampa Bay with, and Bob and not him "whom my father wished to drown with him." He began to put together the circumstances surrounding his father's suicide, though when he imagined his father's last days walking up and down the beach at Clearwater, he saw only the "final thrashings" of someone his own age and like himself out of control, a "rather cold & inexpressive man feeling . . . guilty and rejected." The truth was that he could no longer see his father's face and had to admit now that he had never really known him.

But, except for his fantasies of Sally Appleton, Berryman had little else to sustain him through the winter. Alone in a strange city, his rooms filled with Boschean visions, he had already transformed Appleton into the image of the woman of impeccable virtue whom he still hoped to win over and eventually seduce. His thoughts that winter turned constantly to the damned, among whom he had long ago come to count himself. The obverse of this fascination with evil was his desire to find a way past hell to a place, a time, where he might breathe easily again.

The answer came that fall while Berryman was preparing his classes. Reading Origen, he was stunned by that early Christian theologian's insight into the idea of a finite hell. Origen had called his insight "apocatasis," the idea that Christ's redemption had brought with it the abolition of hell. What a lovely consolation, Berryman sighed: that at some point all suffering had to end. He knew the Church had come to count apocatasis a heresy, but the idea had so astounded theologians that they could still "get as heated abt it now as they did in the 3rd century." Heterodoxy or not, Origen's "immortal and heart-shaking heresy" offered him the possibility of a way out of his own peculiar hell.

Psychoanalysis was the other way out of that hell, and he

worked hard analyzing and typing out his dreams, "improving" on them as he plumbed more and more into their strange logic, looking for the key that would reveal him to himself. On December 18, he recorded a breakthrough with his first dream in which the Shakespearean scholar Herschel Baker lectured while Berryman sat at his feet. "I still hero-worship establ'd people," he noted to himself. Had he not spent twenty years on Shakespeare, in fact his whole adult life? Yet what did he have to show for it? He analyzed and reanalyzed each dream, trying especially to uncover his preconscious years, as if the secret lay there. He began dreaming again of his father's death and of his adolescent awakening at South Kent. Other dreams went unremembered, except for a residual sense of horror.

For the first time in twenty years, Berryman spent New Year's Eve alone, working on his dreams right through the night. He was making no resolutions this year, he wrote his mother, for he was now "*all* resolution." On Monday morning, January 3, 1955, he taught his first class at the University of Minnesota. He spent most of that first week reading Saint Mark's Gospel, "the most primitive, reliable and astonishing" of the Gospels and therefore his favorite. When he studied Matthew, he had to marvel at the economy of the narrative of the Temptation in the Desert, which he read as a prologue summarizing the whole of Christ's ministry "in the refusals to take thought for himself, to give a sign, and to seek popularity by lowering the quality of the moral demands made on his followers." Clearly Berryman was once again fascinated with the historical figure of Christ. Besides his own courses, which went well, he also lectured on Thomas Campion for Tate's poetry course, and heard that those lectures too were being widely praised.

At Berryman's urging, Appleton had stopped by his mother's apartment in Manhattan on New Year's Day to introduce herself and borrow some books. When she'd gotten there, Appleton wrote him, his mother's annual party was already in full swing. Appleton spoke also of attending a reading given in New York by Lowell and Karl Shapiro, then turned to the subject of Rilke's poetry. Ten years before, Berryman wrote back, he too had been much taken by Rilke, but he was anxious now to warn her away. "I am down on Rilke and the hieratic boys just now. I don't deny his sensitivity and his marvellous melody," but Rilke had held back too much from mixing with real men and women, and it was imperative that the poet "get down into the arena and kick around." Then he added that he was becoming "a madman" about her all over again just when he'd thought he was over his intense feelings for her.

When Appleton received his letter, she realized it would be best if they simply stopped communicating with each other. Her tactic in dealing with him was to be understanding but firm. "You are the kind of person that sees things few people do and knows delicacy," she wrote, hoping he would come to his senses and realize what he was doing. She ended by quoting Mother Julian of Norwich that it was all for the best and that in the end (as he too wildly hoped) "all manner of thing shall be well."

Berryman was devastated, but he did his best to honor her request and not contact her. That did not, of course, stop him from thinking about her constantly. He wrote letters to her and put them aside, apostrophes addressed to thin air, just as his poem to Anne Bradstreet had been. Instead, he addressed Appleton's surrogate father, Father Lynch. Did Father Lynch know the passage in Kafka, he wrote, "I think it is in the conversations w. Janouch, where he denies that men ever are wicked deliberately: they only do not forsee the consequences of their actions: they are sleepwalkers, not evil-doers." He had *tried* to keep this in mind in his relations with Sally. "Give me that man that is not passion's slave," Shakespeare had written. But, Berryman noted, Shakespeare had managed to escape his passions only by hard work, responsibility, and—finally—by growing old.

Winter term moved smoothly, with lectures on Aquinas, the *Inferno,* and several medieval romances. Then there was a two-week break between semesters before Berryman moved on to the Renaissance. At the beginning of April he wrote a draft of a poem in four 7-line rhymed stanzas called "The Stone Empires," in which he examined the superpowers—Russia and the United States—from the larger, Christian perspective:

The stone empires confront each other, forever?
A Commons worries; sulks invisible
a Gloire. Cultures of Africans tremble, mutter,

> and littlest islands matter
> as of our great-grandchildren & kids. One gets dizzy. . . .

He got dizzy too walking around the still-frozen Lake of Isles, worrying about "the sons of Belsen in the Arctic" who dreamed about first strikes against America. He fretted over the secretary of state, John Foster Dulles, flying "here & there/ whom no one gives the right time to at home, who's of an elder world, like the Adams[es]." What sorrow to be an American poet in 1955, the hundredth anniversary of "Song of Myself," in this, the land of ice. "Disappointing & tiresome age!" he wrote:

> age heavy with horror:
> hope. Enable me, painful God. Free laves
> a foot of open water the edge of the land.
> All the forms smash, unmanned,
> in the Twin Cities, with Spring. A cock crows.
> As a man [Christ] followed, followed no longer, knows,
> I come. Age light of awe. . . .

He wrote Giroux, recently forced out of Harcourt Brace (a case of "ingratitude and bigotry," as Berryman saw it). Giroux replied, saying he'd gone over to Farrar Straus and had taken Eliot with him. He was ready now to publish Berryman's poems, including the Bradstreet. Berryman himself was ready to move, but, he explained, was helpless to do anything until he first paid Viking back the thousand dollars they'd advanced him for his Shakespeare biography. The biography was still where it had been for the past several years, he explained, with the result that all his work had suffered. Meanwhile, the Bradstreet, important as it was, remained "unreviewed and unavailable, with large parts of it appearing in anthologies in England & US." It was an exasperating state of affairs, especially when he was just beginning to recover his "energy and peace of mind from the chaos of the last few years."

Giroux wrote back, offering to buy off Viking and contract with Berryman for three books: the Bradstreet, the Shakespeare, and a third book. On April 24, a relieved Berryman wrote Giroux that Viking was willing to let him go as soon as the advance was repaid. As for the biography, that was already turning into something entirely different from what he had originally envisioned in his Hodder lectures. The audience for what he now had in mind would be Giroux himself (an amateur Shakespearean), Edmund Wilson, and a woman he knew. He did not name her, but he meant his elusive Muse, Sally Appleton. The third book, it soon turned out, would be *Shakespeare's Friend, W. H.* Working on the chronology of the early plays, Berryman was more convinced than ever about the rightness of his earlier hunch. As for the Bradstreet, he already had a prefatory note, notes, a dedication, and comments by Aiken, Allen Tate, and Jacques Maritain, contained in private letters, which might serve as blurbs. He remembered too that when he'd known Ben Shahn at Princeton, the artist had offered to do some line drawings for the poem.

As winter gave way overnight to summer, Berryman's depression lifted. Suddenly, he realized, with his "little girl students" trotting about half-naked in shorts and troubling his boys, nobody was listening to him lecture anymore except his "really good students," even though he had been "very cunning on Luther," from whom he had had to pass, "with unconcealed horror," to teach them Calvin. He continued to immerse himself in theology and Shakespeare and for weeks at a stretch saw "almost nobody."

When he learned that Saul Bellow's father had died, he wrote to say that he was in "a v[ery] g[ood] position" to empathize with Bellow since his own father had died for him "all over again this week in a terrible dream which when I analyzed it turned out to be about him not dying at once, as I was told he did . . . but living a while unable to move or call out for help." The death of the father was "one of the few main things that happens to a man," he understood, and it mattered "greatly to the life *when* it happens." To lose one's father at a young age left one crippled; losing him at forty was altogether different. True, there was "grief, remorse, loneliness," but there came with the loss "an entirely new strength." Reliving his father's death over the past year, he believed, had allowed him to live through both the adolescent and adult phases of the experience.

By the time classes ended in early June, Berryman was "amazingly tired." At first he simply collapsed and did nothing. Then he got back to work. One morning in mid-June he got up at half past four "in splendid weather" to walk around his beloved lake again, happy to be alive. On the twenty-fifth, contracts from Farrar Straus arrived, along with a two-thousand-dollar advance. "I really think I am going to die of happiness and excitement," he wrote his mother that afternoon, so pleased was he to have Giroux as his editor. Then Ross called to tell Berryman he had a job teaching Greek Civilization and Modern Literature in the fall. Berryman knew he would be hard-pressed to get ready for the latter course, especially as he meant to revise the texts his gifted predecessor, Isaac Rosenfeld, had offered. But again he prepared, and brilliantly. His salary was increased by five hundred dollars.

Reinforced, Berryman worked for the next two months at the Shakespeare biography, reading through "some of the most tiresome plays ever written" by Shakespeare's older contemporaries: *Alphonsus, Alcazar, John of Bordeaux, James IV, Jack Straw,* and *George a Greene,* studying them in relation to Shakespeare's *King John,* which he wanted to locate "solidly" at 1590–91, a date that would wreck and illuminate "everything" he had to say about Shakespeare's early development as a playwright.

That summer he wrote Catherine Carver thanking her for sending him some books, including Flannery O'Connor's short stories. O'Connor, he could see, was "a genius," and one "of the best natural storywriters living." She was so good, in fact, that she frightened him. As for Shakespeare, he was still stuck in 1590 and planned to be there for some time yet. "Everybody's gone, it's delightful," he closed, "I am dancing w. joy & in splendid order."

He worked again on *The Black Book,* thinking it might still be his next book of poems. He wondered if the narrator should be part-Jewish so that he could curse his tormentors. He knew the terrible difficulty of someone who had not actually been in the camps trying to write about them, but he was not willing to have what had happened there forgotten, and, besides, he felt "Jew enough." Had the Jews suffered for the rest of humanity? he wondered. And if so, then were Christians actually responsible for their deaths? Slowly, inevitably, a tidal wave of horror swept over him once more as he contemplated the evil of the Holocaust until again he had to abandon the project.

With the sharp-edged banter that characterized Berryman's relationship with Ann Levine, she and Berryman had taken to calling each other by the worst names they could imagine.

Thus Ann became Mabel; Berryman, Henry. When classes had ended she'd returned to New York to stay with her mother. But soon Berryman began bombarding her at home by telephone, one night calling her three times with her mother wondering what was going on, until Ann had had to slip out of the apartment and call him from a bar. He wanted to see her; he wanted to be left alone to explore his psyche. "Sometimes the burden of existence seems so heavy that one feels less like Husserl on his deathbed than like Thomas Hardy," he wrote his mother. On his deathbed Husserl had said that he thought Christ had forgiven everyone. But on *his* deathbed Hardy had asked to have read to him "the great quatrain of the Rubaiyat," demanding that God accept *man's* forgiveness for the lifetime of tricks He'd played on him.

By late summer Berryman could write his mother that he now had 120 dream analyses completed and was "unblocking gradually, or rather in violent painful strides." What he did *not* tell her was that in many of the dreams she and Uncle Jack had figured as those responsible for his father's death. By the time Uncle Jack had died in late October 1947, he had been out of Berryman's life for ten years. But it was impossible for Berryman to really forget his uncle Jack, and what his dreams had shown him was just how much he hated the man. He had always hated the silly "fake" name Uncle Jack had given his mother: Jill Angel. And what of his own name? Only Jill knew what had really happened that summer's day thirty years before. But while Berryman might scream at her in a drunken rage, he was still afraid to confront her directly, because at some level he did not want to find out what really had happened before he'd awakened "by the beautiful sea" to find his daddy dead.

On August 12, he began a draft of an entirely new sort of poem for him, in large part the result of the 650 pages of dream analyses he'd compiled over the past nine months. The poem began with three lines of something he'd written in 1947, which he now extended to form another sonnetlike poem in three 6-line rhyming stanzas. The poem was a blend of Christian allegory, punning, baby talk, and dreamlike slips of the tongue, and contained a suppressed wish to regress to childlike innocence, where such language seemed most natural:

The jolly old man is a silly old dumb,
with a mean face, humped, who kills dead.
There is a tall girl who loves only him.
She has sworn:—Blue to you forever.
Grey to the little rat, go to bed.
—I fink it's bads all over.

Goguel says nobody knew where the christ they buried him
anyway but the Jewish brass.
No use asking the rich man.
A story. Stories??
One of these bombs costs a fortune.
So at sweet dawn wás he gone?

A Bloody fortune!
Married her donkey? That can hardly be.
Magics sweat up & down.
Henry & Mabel ought to be but can't.
Childness let have us, honey,
so adult the hell don't.

On the twenty-first, Berryman drove out to the Apple River in Wisconsin along with Morgan Blum and some of his other colleagues for a picnic. It was on this drive, he would remember, that he first conceived of the title for the new poems he was writing: *Dream Songs*. It was "an idyllic afternoon," another colleague, Ray West, would remember. "Swimming in a small pool at the foot of a waterfall, eating our lunch on blankets spread out on the grass . . . drinking wine until dusk. When we arrived, John greeted both me and my wife warmly, and when he left he pressed a small poem into my hand—a small poem about a clown, as I recall." It was the poem about the jolly old man.

At the beginning of October the lease at 2509 Humboldt expired, and Berryman began looking for something closer to the university and to Ann Levine. On the sixth he located an "excellent" apartment at 1929 Third Street South, just off the west bank of the Mississippi. The apartment was in a seedy residential area in the notorious Seven Corners section of Minneapolis, but his offices were only a ten-minute walk across the Washington Avenue Bridge.

"I'm busy as sin & gay as virtue," he wrote Donald Justice, "working up my lectures on the Iliad and why the 20th century is so unpleasant to live in." The Greek Civilization course meant preparing lectures on Hesiod, the *Iliad,* the Book of Job, *Agamemnon, Antigone, Oedipus, Oedipus at Colonus, The Trojan Women, Lysistrata,* Plato's *Republic* and the *Phaedo,* and parts of Thucydides' *History*.

For his Modern Literature course there were readings in Lenin's *State and Revolution,* Koestler's *Darkness at Noon,* Orwell's *1984,* Wilson's *To the Finland Station,* Freud's *A General Introduction to Psychoanalysis,* Eliot ("The Love Song of J. Alfred Prufrock" and "The Waste Land"), *Ulysses,* Kafka, Anne Frank's *Diary of a Young Girl,* Whitehead, Hannah Arendt on the concentration camps, Arthur Miller's *Death of a Salesman,* and Beckett's *Waiting for Godot*. There were also suggested readings by Bertram Wolfe (*Three Who Made a Revolution*), Jung, Helen Gardner, Santayana, Sartre, and Monsignor Romano Guardini on social responsibility. The Modern Lit. course was to become his favorite. As he taught and retaught it semester after semester, he refined it, making it more and more distinctively his own. By the time he offered it a second time, he had one hundred students in a class that normally accommodated half that number. The students knew when they had a live one, and Berryman was, even when he was drinking, an extraordinarily gifted teacher.

On December 4, he wrote the earliest "Dream Song" that would eventually find its way into the book he had in mind. It was called "The Secret of the Wisdom," and its linguistic affinities were still with the Bradstreet. In it Berryman lamented his persistently childish behavior, examining—and still excusing—that behavior in terms of an "old hurt":

> When worst got things, how was you? Steady on?
> Wheedling, or shockt her &
> you have been bad to your friend,
> whom not you writing to. You have not listened.
> A pelican of lies
> you loosed: where are you?

In spite of his sins, however, he took comfort in the "secret of the wisdom" he'd discovered in Saint Paul's letter to the Romans, that "the more/ sin has increast, the more/ grace has been caused to abound."

In a note written late in the year, he considered the form of his new poems. Like his earlier Nervous Songs, the Dream Songs would also use the three 6-line rhyming stanzas, though he wanted them to be "*much* 'rougher' & more 'brilliant' " than anything he'd yet done. He wanted a coarse, demotic language to fit into the music of the poem without calling too much attention to itself. And he wanted the poems to deal with the human condition, but channeled through the life of one man. Each poem would also have at least "one stroke of some damned serious humour." He wanted "gravity of matter," but he wanted it wedded to a "gaiety of manner." He would avoid sentimentality at all costs, letting the emotions arise naturally out of the situations in the poems themselves. This time he meant to really let himself go, breaking at long last from the constraints of his overly intellectualized background, as Bellow had in *Augie*. He also meant to get all the sexual longing and lust into his poems he could.

He would do a book of these Dream Songs, perhaps as many as thirty of them, each based on his own experience, with Henry as their hero. He would begin the sequence with memories of his childhood and end with a poem about his daughter, when that event should finally happen. He would use the old iambic norm, but jazz it up and make it freer, mixing it with "rocking meter, anapests, spondees, iambs, trochees, dactyls" until he drove the prosodists "right out of their heads" with his weird riffs and sweet new music. He would rely on Christian symbols to gird the sequence, though he meant Henry to be closer to the picaresque hero in Apuleius' *Golden Ass* than to Christ. He would also leave the door ajar on the off-chance that some change of heart might yet someday visit Henry.

# Chapter 19

## Becoming a Professor

## 1956–57

Instead of spending Christmas with Eileen's sister's family, Berryman went off by himself to Atlantic City to rest and think for a few days. "I loafed a day," he wrote his mother in early January, 1956, "dodged invitations and got written almost the whole of an article I have owed *Poetry* for a whole year." He was happy just to be able to write again after the rigors of teaching that fall. He knew the piece for *Poetry* had no importance, but he'd become "so unused to sitting at the typewriter making sentences that are to be set up in type, that it filled me with bliss."

Then it was back to Minnesota. That winter, attacks against Berryman's Interdisciplinary Program intensified. Berryman had invested heavily in his teaching and had been virtually promised tenure. Now he found himself spending endless hours in committee meetings defending the very subjects he was teaching, and he could see that others in Interdisciplinary Studies were also becoming discouraged. He had hoped to see the Bradstreet with its design by Beilenson and line drawings by Ben Shahn out by then to show that he was still publishing. But the book would not be out till the fall, too late to help him with his tenure fight. At least his teaching and lectures had been widely acclaimed.

In early March, with winter term over, he flew out to the State Teachers' College at Bemidji in freezing weather to give the convocation address. Then he heard that Eliot at Faber & Faber had decided to publish his selected poems. He wrote Bellow and Sondra Tschacbasov to congratulate them on their recent marriage in Nevada, assuring them that it was "the most wonderful news since the Atonement." In spite of the departmental wars still raging, Bellow seemed willing to come to Minnesota, and Berryman stood ready to do what he could to make it happen.

Shortly afterward, Ross introduced Berryman to Antal Dorati, the conductor of the Minneapolis Symphony Orchestra, who was looking for someone proficient in French to translate Paul Claudel's "Le Chemin de la Croix" into English. The difficulty was that Dorati had composed his music to match the French text, so that the translation had to comply with an already completed score. Over the next several months Dorati and Berryman conferred together on the translation some dozen times, Dorati remembering Berryman "as a very introverted, rather shy person, trying to hide his timidity behind a certain 'roughness,' which was not convincing at all." The piece, with Berryman's text, was finally performed the following year under Dorati's direction.

On April 19, Berryman gave another public lecture, this one on Eliot as poet and critic. Eliot, he noted, had produced a surprising number of finished poems over a thirty-year period, besides producing a strong body of criticism, for which he'd perfected a voice "dispassionate & elegant & lucid." Now that Eliot's career was all but over, Berryman could see that Eliot had done what he'd set out to do. By the time Eliot was his age, Berryman realized, he had already produced "Prufrock," "The Waste Land," and most of "Ash Wednesday." But at forty-one, Berryman was still groping to find his voice.

As spring term got under way, the attacks on his department once again picked up momentum. On April 29, a worried Berryman wrote to Ralph Ross and Dean Cooper. He needed something more than the "day-labour situation" he found himself in. He now had his courses, "difficult & unfamiliar" as they had been, "well in hand," and was "steadily improving" in them. He appreciated not being saddled with committee work and advising responsibilities, though, he equivocated, he wanted to remind his chairman and dean that he had never had to perform such duties at any university where he'd been employed. But by July he was beside himself with worry over the fate of his tenure decision. "At the . . . last faculty meeting," he wrote his mother, those who had led the fight for the dissolution of the Interdisciplinary Program had "cut loose on us again; and after promise after promise, not only do I not have a permanent appointment, but neither of my two superiors has had the guts to tell me." But the answer came shortly after. Berryman's tenure decision had been delayed another year, until his case could be strengthened by the publication of the Bradstreet volume.

The Bellows showed up at Berryman's shortly after classes ended in June. They were on their way back to New York from Reno, and stayed with him for several days. The big news in Nevada had been Arthur Miller's staying with the Bellows for six weeks, ringing up Marilyn Monroe constantly, and it looked as if Miller and Monroe would soon be married. A month after the Bellows' visit, Berryman wrote to congratulate them on Sondra's pregnancy. He spoke about Bellow's novel in progress, *Henderson the Rain King,* and mentioned that he'd already sent along an advance copy of the Bradstreet, reminding Bellow that *The Adventures of Augie March* had been "one of its chief inspirations."

When Ann Levine returned from New York that September, she too was carrying a child: Berryman's. He was prepared to marry her, the only problem being that he was still married to Eileen, and Eileen was still hoping for a reconciliation. When Eileen, visiting the Fitzgeralds in Genoa, returned to Paris, she found a letter waiting for her from her husband asking for a divorce. Writing that letter had cost him blood, he confessed to Bellow, for Eileen had been terribly upset by the news, with the result that he'd had several "wild conversations" with her. By early October, however, seeing there was nothing for it, she finally agreed to the divorce.

Since, however, there was a "six months' non-remarriage business in Minnesota," Berryman and Ann would have to be married out of state. Then Jill stepped in. Since they would certainly need a car to get around in, she drove to Minnesota in her red 1951 Chevrolet convertible and offered it to them, along with the remaining car payments. Delighted, Ann and Berryman dubbed the car "Rudolph." Now all Ann had to do was learn to drive.

Since he held a joint appointment in English, Berryman counted on his friends in the English department to support his tenure case. But with three of his allies on leave, he was afraid Interdisciplinary Studies would be abolished before he had his tenure. Worse, the *Bradstreet,* officially published on October 1, was greeted only by "deafening silence," with the exception of a favorable review in the *Chicago Sun-Times* and Tate's letter to Giroux saying that the *Bradstreet* added "a fourth to the three first-rate long poems by Americans in this century—the others being by Pound, Eliot, and [Hart] Crane." *The New York Times* eventually reviewed it, but Berryman was not impressed. It would take time for the book to catch on, he saw, time he didn't have if he was to make his case for tenure.

Robert Lowell was to remark about Berryman that he made a good friend but you felt better knowing he lived in another city. Berryman had certainly made enemies during his two years in Minneapolis, but he was also blessed with good friends. Ross remained not only an advocate but an unswerving friend, and there were also Dr. Boyd Thomes and his wife, Maris, who lived in the Prospect Park section of the city. Boyd had become Berryman's physician (as he was Allen Tate's) and would remain that and much more in the years to come. It was he who would help keep Berryman going for as long as Berryman did. Maris too became Berryman's close friend. Phil and Ellen Siegelman were others.

In truth, Berryman needed all the friends he could get. "Dear Co-struggler," he wrote Bellow just before Thanksgiving. "I haven't written being gloomy & with no good thing to report." For starters, a few days before, the "bloody lawyers" had informed him that the thirty-day waiting period would begin only *after* the papers had first been filed a full thirty days. So the divorce would not come up on the docket until December 19, "which lovely fact" Berryman and Ann were still "digesting." But a few days later he was lifted out of his depression by a small, welcome miracle. "The baby kickt today," he wrote. "Her first act." (He was sure it was going to be a daughter.) He was also moved—nearly to tears—by news of the Hungarian uprising. The stark black-and-white images of men and women in the streets of Budapest, Stalin's statue toppled, the bodies of the NKVD, lime thrown over them to speed their decomposition, kids with Russian tommy guns, Soviet tanks. History seemed real again, and people truly people.

Just before the national elections, Berryman received a letter from William Faulkner, sent to a number of American writers on behalf of President Eisenhower's program to organize American writers in an attempt to rectify the image of the Ugly American abroad. Finally Berryman wrote Faulkner, at the same time sending along a copy of the Bradstreet. First of all, he began, the public had to know what was already being done by and for American writers. "Real writers," he suggested, should be sent by the United States to the various international congresses, writers of the stature of Cummings, Roethke, and Lowell. Funds should also be made available to allow American writers to travel abroad to see what was happening and to make their presence felt. Tax relief of some sort might also be provided, at least proportionate to what American businessmen were allowed, and something like the British Civil List might be established here in the States. For in spite of their occasional contempt for the American Congress, American writers worked "damned hard" for their government.

In November, Berryman's essay on Ring Lardner appeared in *Commentary*. What Lardner lacked, he wrote, as if writing about himself, had been a sense of purpose. Lardner seemed always to be trying to escape from responsibility through "alcohol and silence." He had taken "no satisfaction in his achievement," nor had he shown any "discernible belief or even religious sense," and he seemed always to have hated most of the human race. But—unlike Berryman—Lardner had also been "lowbrow," and "everything good in the end" was highbrow. Every artist who had ever lasted, Berryman was convinced, had been an intellectual. That included Shakespeare . . . and himself.

On the thirtieth he watched Floyd Patterson's "gorgeous fight" against Archie Moore on his friends the McCloskeys' television. But, while Boyd Thomes and McCloskey had rooted for Patterson, Berryman had rooted for poor old Archie Moore, calling Boyd and McCloskey "renegades" to their post-forty generation. Let old men flourish, he wrote Bellow. He also wanted Bellow to know that he'd just had a letter from *The Partisan Review* offering him a Rockefeller Fellowship in poetry worth four thousand dollars. He meant now "to write so good . . . the trolls of language will scream & come over to my side."

When W. B. Stevenson's lectures on the poem of Job had been published nine years before, Berryman had decided then he was "the man born to translate that great work into English verse." Now, in early December, he had finally got his "tone & rhythm right" and had written out the opening lines of the poem with lines "more literal than any transl into Engl I've ever seen, and therefore . . . simpler & more lucid & truer." He meant to build the meaning into the poem as he went along, so that it could stand on its own without more than a few notes of explanation. Then he quoted the opening lines he'd just translated—long, sinewy, and crackling with the story of himself:

> Perish the day's fire into which I was born, and that night's joy
> crying 'A boy!'
> That day let God enquire not for, no brightness burn there,
> But a dark of midnight claim, a black cloud seize it quite,
> Let all that stains & shrouds terrify that day.
> Disjoin out from its fellow days it, exiled from the toil of the
> months.
> Stony that night turn, joyless, empty of all song;
> Enchanters mark it curst, whose baleful power calls up Leviathan;
> Its twilight stars be dark, unseen the eyelids of its dawn;
> For it shut not the doors of my womb, but let me out to trouble.

He had resolved on a six-stress line with a pronounced medial break. The heart of the poem he thought would come to 750 lines, "accepting most of Stevenson's delenda, transpositions etc, and chiefly controlling him only w Reichert's commentary." He was hoping to see a draft completed by mid-February. But within weeks other, more pressing, events interfered, among them the legal and emotional aspects of his divorce.

Six days before Christmas Berryman finally had his day in court, the divorce being granted on the grounds that Eileen had deserted her husband "without justification." Eileen asked for no alimony until Berryman's salary should exceed ten thousand dollars annually, at which time she would receive 25 percent of said excess. In any event, as a clinical psychologist, she could earn a better living than he seemed capable of doing. A three-thousand-dollar life insurance policy was to be turned over to her. What it cost each of them personally to make this final separation was not recorded in the dockets.

Afterward Berryman and Ann headed for South Dakota and were married in Sioux Falls the morning after Christmas by a justice of the peace. At 12:17 P.M. Berryman sent off a telegram to the Thomeses that read: MYSTERIOUS UNION EFFECTED. HEADED FOR HOT SPRINGS BON VOYAGE. LOVINGNESS. Berryman was in no mood for a honeymoon, but that was the thing one did, and so, in spite of his nerves, he and his bride drove by bus across South Dakota for a few days among the Black Hills.

On the ride back to Sioux City, Berryman amused himself writing in a tiny notebook his impressions of the country. He called his jottings "Dakota Crossing," noting the stark, beautiful heartland he was passing through. He stared at America, and America stared back. How, he wondered, had men ever come to such a place as this? Yet there was a strength about this landscape, he felt, and a "life wholly unlike the complex, cluttered, interrelated, fascinating & tiresome urban existence we thresh about in, where nothing comes singly." It was three hours before he spotted his first car, and then "a church a car junkyard corrals a privy tilted . . . gas & oil tanks." Then the state capital at Pierre, only slightly larger, he noted, than Monmouth Junction, New Jersey. In 1950, flying home after his stint in Seattle, the land had seemed as "flat as a table cloth." Well, it was flat, flat as its names and its destination and its language. Highmore. Miller. Wessington. America.

In January 1957 Berryman began teaching a new proseminar—The American Character—in addition to his medieval course. The American Character course included readings by Santayana and de Tocqueville, Brogan's *The American Character,* D. H. Lawrence's *Studies in Classic American Literature,* Faulkner's "The Bear," Whitman's "Song of Myself," and Heffner's *A Documentary History of the U.S*. Berryman also expected his students to know Emerson's essays, Poe's short stories, *The Scarlet Letter, Moby Dick, Huckleberry Finn,* and James's *The American.*

By then Ann was driving and Berryman had gone so far as to take the written examination for his driver's license. With the baby due in two months, he made another New Year's resolution to take better care of his health, and for a while stopped his chain-smoking and his drinking. When his body reacted violently to the double withdrawal, however, he was sure it was because he was "on the mend" and his smoker's cough beginning to dissolve. It did not help that he was also having his teeth "ripped up" twice a week by his dentist and that the Bollingen had gone to Tate instead of to him. One small consolation, cold as it was, was knowing he'd at least beaten Richard Wilbur for second place.

He turned once more to his *Dream Songs,* still searching for the form and idiom that continued to elude him. On February 10, he wrote a draft for one that centered on his father's suicide. So impatient had Daddy been to cross over to the other side, he wrote, that he'd left no word of what he expected from his sons:

> His widow did feel bad.
> However it was only him,
> who *had* swum out with his younger son
> promising not to be a returning two or one,
> but he changed his mind & did.
> He swam strong, always had,
>
> thing he did best.
> Bequeathing the elder, upset son
> a seething, troubles less unspeakable than one
> vacant in-raging
> silence of the younger, lest
> a spilt word bomb the world.

On his fortieth birthday—March 1—Lowell wrote Berryman, commenting on a description Berryman had sent him of Ann. " 'A harmless and good woman, rather too young.' Your description is along the lines of Henry Adams's "She dresses badly . . . We shall improve her." But here he was at his age, with a ten-pound daughter of his own to look after. Surely Berryman could not match that. As it turned out, with a little help from his wife, Berryman could. Four days later, on Friday, March 5, Paul Berryman was born at Abbott Hospital in Minneapolis. Ann's mother came out from New York to help her daughter, staying at the Carling Hotel, five blocks from the Berrymans' new—and larger—apartment at 2900 James Avenue South. "I think of it as 'Peter' or anything—less Daphne—but BABY—I just did a crow, to my amazement, at the idea of holding it tomorrow," he jotted down the night after his son was born. "The Dream Songs might precisely end with *one on this,*" though he still had difficulty reconciling himself to the fact that his daughter had turned out to be a boy. "I see my son, but must not breathe on him," he began another Dream Song a few days later:

> I see his clampt-jaw, blowsy face, head, only
> He is a son?
> with both legs? fingers? I am docile,
> & do not even badger the nurse
> nor break the plate-glass down—
> All feeling has been civilized out of me. . . .

"The baby is all right," he wrote his mother on the twenty-second. "I cannot decide whether he is one continous howl, or on the whole a very *good* baby—yesterday he was the first, today the second." Ann's mother had proven "an immense help in the multiple labour of setting up the baby here, Ann's gaining strength, proceeding with the apartment's furnishing (it is largely now done)." Then Ann sent her own note to Jill, glowing that her husband had just been awarded the Monroe Poetry Prize and five hundred dollars.

For his son, Berryman had his own homecoming gift: a poem he called "A Sympathy, A Welcome." The sympathy was for having fallen into this evil world after having it so good inside his mother's womb. Still, no matter what happened, he was making a covenant now always to love his son:

> Feel for your bad fall how could I fail,
> poor Paul, who had it so good.
> I can offer you only: this world like a knife.

Yet you'll get to know your mother
and humorless as you do look you will laugh
and all the others
will NOT be fierce to you, and loverhood
will swing your soul like a broken bell
deep in a forsaken wood, poor Paul,
whose wild bad father loves you well.

A month before his son was born, Berryman gave a stunning lecture on Whitman's *"Song of Myself:* Intention & Substance." Then, in late March, having just completed Ellmann's biography of Joyce, he gave an "unfriendly" talk on the Irishman, noting that—except for Montaigne—he'd never found another important author who had proved as disappointing as a human being as Joyce had. True, Joyce was not as "distasteful" as Rilke, but then he also had less of a personality than Rilke.

Two weeks later he gave another talk, this one at the Walker Museum, on "American Letters & International Opinion." From the first, Americans had looked to Britain for their sense of themselves. Often England had had to show Americans their own treasures, reading Melville and Whitman and Stephen Crane when those writers had been "defeated here." Many of America's best books had even been written in England. Yet Berryman wondered whether England had ever really understood American literature. For centuries, he conceded, no "really important American artist had emerged," even though, as Pound had pointed out, the high point of American intellectual history had occurred 150 years earlier. Nevertheless, even among such luminaries as Jefferson, John Adams, Franklin, and Madison—figures who together made up the most distinguished society "since Elizabethan London, mid-15th Century Florence & Periclean Athens"—there had been no first-rate writer. But all that had now changed, for America in 1950 certainly had its share of good writers. For another fifty years England might hold a cultural edge over America, but the truth was that America's novelists, poets, and playwrights had already surpassed England's.

Now Berryman was going to show others what American literature really was about. For, within days of his son's homecoming, Berryman had decided it was time to go to India. He would lecture there during the summer, under the auspices of the United States Information Service. Tate had taught in India the year before and could recommend him. And since the baby would be too young to travel to India, Ann would stay behind to take care of him. In August she would take Paul and sail to Genoa, where the Fitzgeralds would meet them and get them settled until Berryman could join them in September. In truth, Berryman did not have the means to coexist with a baby in the same apartment. Moreover, there were already pressures on the marriage that Berryman would cope with as he usually coped when "worst things got": by running away.

The co-lecturer assigned him for the Indian tour turned out to be Howard Munford of the Department of American Literature at Middlebury College. Berryman wrote him in mid-May to say he planned to lecture on the American novel, beginning with Crane and Dreiser and working forward to *Augie March*. He also meant to lecture on modern American poetry, as well as discuss Hemingway and Faulkner. He passed on to Munford what Tate had told him: that the Indians knew "more than one wd expect" about American poetry.

Soon after, Berryman wrote the USIS officer in Washington, noting that he was unhappy with a report the USIS had released to *The New York Times* that had called him "a young poet." Well, he was *not* a young poet and did not wish to be called so again. He asked permission to fly to Japan for a visit to Kyoto before going on to India, and then to return to America at the end of the year via Spain. The USIS complied with both requests.

At the beginning of May he had flown to Chicago to teach a writing workshop. Still haunted by Dylan Thomas's death, he worked on a poem about him there, remembering the time he'd spent with Thomas in Cambridge and Seattle, and then his death in New York. The poem, written in seven-line rhymed stanzas, evoked vividly Thomas's last moments:

> I was the breathing nearest other thing,
> the body shuddered & fought, slashes & tubes,
> curled hair dript, I saw the body refuse
> five suns to go, and was saved from seeing it go
> by a speechless dozen feet of corridor
> & doorway & deserted ward. . . .

But the poem refused to ignite. "Nothing governs it yet," he noted, "it's like journalism: horseshit." Then, drunk, he slipped on a loose rug in his hotel room and twisted his ankle so badly he had to be hospitalized.

But there was other news to hobble his spirit as well. When Richard Wilbur won both the National Book Award *and* the Pulitzer for his poems that spring, Berryman was so filled with self-pity that he got drunk once more and then fired off a telegram to Wilbur that read: CONGRATULATIONS ON DOUBLE SWEEP STOP YOUR VIGOROUS STUFF WILL LIVE. Wilbur, thinking the telegram sincere, wrote to thank Berryman, adding that he had thought the Bradstreet should have taken at least some of the prizes. Compared to the Bradstreet, his own "slaughterhouse of grief," Berryman wrote back at the end of the month, Wilbur's work seemed "fireless." But, he had to admit, he really did not know Wilbur's poems well enough yet and promised to read them more carefully. Having cleared the air between them, Berryman hoped they might now become friends. He also reconsidered more coldly now his actual stature as a poet. At forty-two, he had, he believed, sixteen books to finish before he died. That came to a great deal of borrowing against the future for a man who had published, in the seven years since the Crane, a few occasional pieces and a book with one very good long poem in it, all of it written before he'd ever set foot in Minneapolis.

On June 1, he wrote his mother to say that the baby had magisterially cast a "cold eye on his first vegetable." He hoped she would come out soon to see her grandson and enclosed fifty dollars toward her airfare as a peace offering. Two weeks later the English department made what he called an "about-face" and asked for a joint appointment for him. Finally, he was granted tenure and promoted to associate professor. On his return to the university in January, his new salary would be eight thousand dollars.

But when he and Ann went to an English department party soon afterward, he was convinced he was surrounded by enemies. The Berrymans had left the baby with a sitter and, as he drank that night, Berryman began imagining that the sitter was hurting his baby. Soon he was turning on Ann, condescendingly reminding her of her failures and of his own importance. Then he slapped her. The next day, sober and contrite, he reminded himself that he was "a strange man, not unitary like other people." He was "really Henry Pussycat, and I am also a bastard, and I am hopeful & goodnatured, and I am a man insulted & injured." He really did "love Ann & the Poo," he thought, and could not understand why Ann would think he *didn't* love her. If they weren't "for each other," he sighed, life was "all pain & loss and grief."

Here he was, "on the verge of my best & happiest working in years," and now everything was in danger of turning to ashes. If only Ann "had some regular & interesting thing to do." But when his mother found out that he had slapped his wife, she warned him that if it happened again, she would advise Ann to take the baby and leave. Berryman listened to his interfering mother and smoldered.

As the time for his departure approached, he ordered one hundred copies of Oscar Williams's *New Pocket Anthology of American Verse* air-shipped to both Bombay and Calcutta. At the end of June he wrote Bellow that the past month had been the "wackiest" he had spent "for some time, partic w every known tropical disease in one arm or the other—my reactions, because I'm underweight—being heavy." Spring had taken a long time in coming, and he was hungry now "to see a temple . . . smell ancient blood, transmigrate." On June 30, Jill came to stay with Ann and the baby before returning with them to the East Coast. That same afternoon Berryman flew to Washington to be briefed by the USIS, then flew back two days later. Then, on the afternoon of July 6, he flew out of Minneapolis, heading west toward Japan and the delicious silences awaiting him in the gardens of Ryoan-ji.

*Chapter 20*

# The Holy Cities

## 1957

Berryman landed in Tokyo on July 8, exhausted. After settling into his hotel, he rewarded himself with a Japanese massage, performed expertly by a geisha, and later bought the services of a prostitute. The massage he found so relaxing he decided to have one each night he was in Japan. On the morning of the tenth, he crossed Honshu by train, headed for the old capital at Kyoto. Until he got past Yokohama, he noted, the ride had been about as interesting as passing through Trenton. Then, suddenly, the landscape was opening up on all sides, with "weird heights, terraced," on his left that ran down to the sea and, on his right, hills where peasants were planting rice.

But even that was as nothing to what awaited him in Kyoto. It was a big city with a population of some 1.2 million, shadowed by mountains on three sides and filled with a thousand years of history and beauty and its ancient splendid gardens. He settled into a room at the Tawayarain Kyoto and began his intensive study of the gardens "in a daze of happiness & attention," in the evenings reading D. T. Suzuki's *Zen Buddhism.*

Having prepared himself, he spent Saturday afternoon at the home of Mirei Shigemori, partaking in an elaborate four-hour tea ceremony with his host, a Zen priest, and an interpreter. How strange it was to be having tea with Shigemori, the man whose book on the Japanese gardens Berryman had read with such intense interest that he had come all this way just to meet him. But here he was, in the presence of "the greatest living authority" on both the Japanese gardens and the Japanese tea ceremony. For a time he could actually believe he was in the heaven of the philosophers.

He paid a visit to Nyo Castle and then went to see the fifteen stones of the fifteenth-century garden at Ryoan-ji. Ryoan-ji: a level ground garden so constructed that from no viewpoint could the observer see the entire pattern of fifteen stones at once. When, sixteen months later, he came to describe this garden in Dream Song 73, he recalled its austere beauty—"a sea rectangular of sand by the oiled mud wall." By then the place had become for him the aesthetic ideal toward which his own more frenetic and self-conscious poems might aspire. As with Ryoan-ji, so too his poems would demand to be seen from multiple perspectives and then held together—after long study—in the one place that could contain them: the imagination. The garden, then, would come to symbolize for him the deep form of *The Dream Songs,* his masterwork, as complete and unchangeable as Keats's Grecian urn, still there to contemplate and enjoy, long after their creator had disappeared forever:

> and the fifteen changeless stones in their five worlds
> with a shelving of moving moss
> stand me the thought of the ancient maker priest.
> Elsewhere occurs—I remembers—loss.
> Through awes & weathers neither it increased
> nor did one blow of all his stone & sand thought die.

On the evening of July 16, after several stops, Berryman landed in Calcutta and went directly to his hotel. But what he saw and heard and felt along the streets as the taxi drove him to his hotel stunned him. Besides the drenching monsoon rains and the stifling moist heat, there was the incredible crush of humanity, the thousands on thousands of homeless living on the sidewalks, the beggars with their tin plates, the sick and dying huddled on the curbs, boy pimps offering him his pick of women.

The next afternoon he flew to Delhi, where he was met by a USIS officer and taken to Claridge's Hotel. Here he finally met Howard Munford, tall, thin, clean-shaven, the man Berryman would be teaching with for the next two months. Alone in a strange country, the two took to each other at once. In the morning they were driven to 13, Golf Links for their briefings, which lasted all that day and into the next. Then they flew to Bombay. Their accommodations there were like those in Calcutta: air-conditioned rooms in a good hotel, but again there were the rains and the intense heat and poverty and misery everywhere. Sunday they were driven to Poona, four hours to the southeast, for their first symposium, which would last five days. Both men were afraid of being prostrated by the "ferocious" heat of central India. But after all their preparation, they were even more dismayed to find they had an audience of only twenty. It did not help to learn that the reason so few had turned out was due to the incompetency of the chairman of the English department at Poona, a Professor Sataqire, a "good-hearted man" but "the worst idiot" Berryman had "encountered for years." Like Berryman's mother, Sataqire turned out to be a nonstop monologuist, more willing to be listened to than to listen.

Munford opened the sessions by lecturing on the beginnings of a national literature in America, and Berryman followed with a lecture on Whitman and a film on New England writers. On Tuesday, Berryman opened with a lecture on Stephen Crane and Dreiser, followed by Munford on Hemingway and a recording of Faulkner reading from his novels. On Wednesday, as the twenty dwindled even further, Munford spoke on "The Organization of an English Department at a small Liberal Arts College" and Berryman on the differences between English and American universities. Crows settled on the branches and began their own discussions as the overhead fans whirred on. Thursday, Berryman lectured on modern American poetry, while Munford spoke on Frost and showed a film of the poet. On the last day of the conference, Berryman lectured on literary criticism and Munford on the nature of interpretation in poetry. Then Berryman read to a nearly empty hall from his own poetry.

"Oh servant Henry lectured till/ the crows commenced and then/ he bulbed his voice & lectured on some more," Berryman would write later (DS 24). "This happened again & again, like war." There were slights and antagonisms from several of the Indian professors, who could not see after all that America *had* a literature to speak of. "Above all," Berryman would write his friend Cameron, it was imperative, if one went to India, to avoid lecturing at all costs, "in which you wd be competing with the fans, the crows, and the 'summing-up' after the lecture, which might likely old boy make yr blood boil."

On the morning of July 28, Berryman and Munford left Poona by government auto and drove back to Bombay, where they had a chance to see something of the old city. Three days later they flew to Calcutta and were driven to Harington Mansions. Soon Berryman was taking notes again, trying to make sense of the spectacle of India he was witnessing. "The woman who bared her breasts on the East side of the square . . . The procession in Bowbazar." He noted with humor and amazement this time the salespitches of the young pimps outside the Grand Hotel near where he and Munford were staying: "young Chinese girl, schoolteacher, nice Indian student girl, nice boy massage, white girl, all white, nice French girl, dancing girl, come see . . . no pay if no like." Munford swore that one kid had even offered him a BOAC stewardess. And against that: the beautiful young Indian girl Berryman had spotted sitting cross-legged on the sidewalk staring passively up at him, her right foot quite gone with leprosy.

He could not help but be troubled by the contrasts he saw everywhere: on the one side the wealth of the old British sections of Calcutta and Bombay; on the other the primitive accommodations in Poona. He was in fact learning as quickly as he was teaching. For perhaps the first time in his life, he began to realize how parochial his Western vision of history and culture had been. Now too he better understood what Eric Kahler had told him years before: that Western culture—Hebrew, Greek, Roman—was "unintelligible" except in relation to the older cultures of the East, which had shaped the course of the West from the beginning. "Moslem domination links India & Spain," he jotted down. "British domination links India and USA." Two old empires—the Spanish and the British—one gone, the other disappearing.

But he was most deeply moved by the human misery he saw, underlining the kinship between these sufferers and himself. "If you knew—knew," he began another Dream Song;

you were going to lose a hand,
that wd be not so good.
And: if the other hand.
Or if you knew—knew—that yr power to love
wd wither in a second,
that would . . .

or a certain girl at her door in a red robe
wd never come again to let you in
& if it was known the pink thing wd never work after a certain
date,
discouraging.

And if you knew that shaking with nausea
& deep in pain, you wd have to rise
& open the door & go out
& walk alone into the lake, under the lake, forever:
Henry knows it all, all this, knows more,
something different.

Beginning Monday, August 5, Berryman and Munford participated in a three-day symposium at Ravenshaw College in Cuttack. This was an old missionary college in primitive surroundings, where the men were assigned a small bungalow with mosquito netting. During their time there, they managed to see Rajarani, Puri, Jaqarmath, and Bhubaneswar. Then, on the ninth, his lectures for the moment finished, Berryman braved the monsoon rains to visit the Cuttack Leprosarium. There were salaams answered by salaams, extravagant curtsies that only made the situation the sadder. The leprosarium was forty years old and had 490 patients, Dr. Prasad, the health officer, explained, and each patient received twelve rupees a month plus meals, but there was nothing to occupy a patient's time. Berryman, visibly upset by what he was witnessing, tried to ease his distress by talking with the health officer dispassionately. But somewhere, always, in the depths, he understood now, barracuda gathered and waited.

Back in Calcutta he gave a radio interview and was upset when he received a mere twenty-five rupees for his fee. Another sign of Indian greed, he told himself. When his wallet was stolen one night while he slept, then replaced, minus money, cards, and photos, his dislike of Indians intensified. He was also annoyed at his USIS officer in Calcutta, John Henry Stumpf, for not keeping him in adequate liquor, which he was taking —he told Stumpf—for medicinal purposes. When Stumpf delivered a "parcel" to Munford's room, it was, Berryman complained, too little too late.

But he had no complaints about Mrs. Stumpf. By then it had been five weeks since he'd had a "single conversation alone w. a woman," the longest Lenten period he could remember since his days at South Kent, and his "chat" with her proved "invaluable" to him. She was vivacious, funny, attractive, and she knew how to make Berryman and Munford feel more comfortable in a strange city. She sent them funny notes, watched after them, and later took them about the city. It was here too that Berryman had his first "endless & intimate talk" with Munford. The two men were, as Berryman had said in another context, "on each other's hands who cared."

Early on the morning of August 12, Berryman and Munford, still shaky from illness, flew out of Calcutta for Patna for yet another three-day symposium, identical to the one they'd given at Cuttack. Again Berryman was upset, this time by reading about the symposium in *The Indian Nation,* which was almost exclusively about the role Principal F. Rahman of the college would play in presiding over one of the sessions. Berryman tore the article out and scribbled, next to the presider's photograph, "the bastard." "Second Chairman at Patna, Principal Rainan or something (see newspaper clip)," he wrote in one of his notebooks, had been very nice the first time he'd met him, but not only had Rahman arrived thirty minutes late to chair his session, he had offered no apologies either to Berryman or to Munford but only to his audience. At least, though, three hundred attended these sessions.

All in all, however, Patna was not a happy experience and Berryman was glad to see the sessions end. On the other hand, he and Munford did have time to see Benares and the Ganges. In the predawn hours of the day following the conference, a guide took them through the streets of the holy city which was already teeming with pilgrims and holy men. Afterward they hired two boatmen to row them down the Ganges past the burning ghats and the bathing places. "A gigantic copper-red sun rose as we floated by the pilgrims washing away their sins in the holy river," Munford would remember, the holy men "in contorted postures of worship," greeting the sun "with a deep salaam" while smoke drifted from the ghats. Unreal as the scene looked, it touched a deep chord in Berryman. Benares alone, he would later record, had made the trip to India worth it all.

Then there was another five-day symposium, this one in Calcutta. Berryman, though ill by then with virus and a high fever, somehow managed to meet his lectures. During the final week of August, there was yet another weeklong session. After that the two men, both weak with fever, left Calcutta for Ahmadabad and their final three-day symposium. Unfortunately, for Berryman it proved one too many. By then he was ten pounds lighter than when he'd arrived in India and he was now totally exhausted. He and Munford were having lunch with their hosts when he suddenly got up, called out to Munford, and then collapsed on the stairs outside. Munford and the others got him to his room and Munford offered to cover for him, but Berryman told him to give his talk and that by then he'd be ready to give his.

As Munford finished his talk, he saw Berryman standing in the doorway, trembling, his face drained of color. Then Berryman walked up to the podium and delivered a lecture unlike anything he'd given so far on his trip. For six weeks, he told his small audience, he had been told over and over by his Indian hosts that America had produced no poetry and that the Indians were the most poetic people in the world. But what he'd seen of Indian poetry seemed nothing more than a loose sort of "spiritual sentimentality." Now he was going to tell them what real poetry was. He quoted a passage from Rilke in German and then a passage from Lorca in Spanish, translating into English afterward for his audience. Great poetry, he explained, sprang only from the pain and anguish of human experience. The audience sat listening to his stunning, fevered performance. If they felt angry or patronized, they did not show it. Afterward, several people came up to talk with him, but by then he was shaking once more and he had to excuse himself to lie down and rest.

On Saturday evening, September 7, the men flew on to Delhi. That Monday they were driven to 13, Golf Links for further briefings and interviews with their USIS officials. In the closing days of their Indian tour, news had reached them of Arkansas Governor Faubus's refusal to integrate Little Rock's schools and of Eisenhower's calling out the National Guard, and Berryman and Munford now found themselves bombarded with questions on the American race issue (this, Berryman noted, defensively, by the most color-conscious people in the world). He too was deeply disturbed by the race issue in his country, especially seeing it now from the perspective of India, but he did not enjoy being called up short on it, as if it were somehow his fault.

Early on the eleventh, he flew south to Agra to see the Taj Mahal before flying back to Delhi and then on to Rome. "Here is a performance devoted wholly to death," he would write of the Taj Mahal. Stunned by what he'd seen, he would insist that no photograph could capture the monument, which was "not white, but thousand-hued," all of it inlaid. The gardens at Ryoan-ji had been "a work devoted wholly to thought and purely symbolic," but the Taj Mahal was not a symbol, "embodying no protest of any kind, inspiring no sadness." He could understand something of the pain and fatigue, the "exasperation [and] agony" that must have gone into the building of this monument, and yet the total effect of this place, given over to death and loss, was strangely one of tranquillity. Somehow, the Taj seemed "free from all longing," a thing of beauty "beyond our Western quarrel with time."

Berryman arrived at the Rome airport early Friday afternoon, September 13, checked into the Hotel Regina, and slept for fifteen hours. A few hours later he was on a train heading for Levanto, accompanied by the Fitzgeralds, to be reunited with his family. He took long swims in the sea at Levanto and long walks with Fitzgerald, and spent lazy afternoons playing chess on the beach. He also spent hours telling Ann of all he'd seen in India and admiring his six-month-old son, who, he was amazed to see, looked exactly like him. "I'm out of Asia," he wrote his mother on September 19, "& fine except that I have no energy." Another week, however, would see him recovered. He loved Levanto, with its beautiful beach and surrounding mountains. And after two months in Kyoto and Calcutta and Bombay, everyone seemed "impossibly white & big & prosperous & energetic."

He visited La Spezia and Riomaggiore and revisited Siena in the company of the Fitzgeralds, then bought a typewriter and worked on a piece about his trip to the Taj Mahal that he called "Thursday Out." But if the Indian tour had soured him on the Eisenhower administration, he was outraged by the launching of *Sputnik* on October 4. Three days later he wrote a poem called "American Lights, Seen from Off Abroad." The only lights to be seen in the heavens, he noted sardonically, seemed now to be Russian lights.

On the eighth, as cooler weather settled in, the Berrymans said good-bye to the Fitzgeralds and sailed for Barcelona, accompanied by the baby's constant crying as he began now to teethe. From Barcelona the Berrymans went to Saragossa for the grand fiesta, and then on to Madrid. There Berryman began another travel piece, called "The Holy Cities." He read *Don Quixote* and visited the Prado, pouring over the Goyas, the Velázquezes, the El Grecos. On October 22, after receiving a rejection letter from *The New Yorker* for his *Sputnik* poem, he cheered himself by noting "that, lacking all plastic ability, w. poor colour-sense, ignorant of everything, still I can push & make real something—to the national honour & the glory of man. It's silly that this [rejection] shd seem anything to me, considering A Miller's and T Williams' fame & dough over all the world, but *so it is*."

Three days later he celebrated his forty-third birthday by writing an ode in Henry's honor while the bells in the plaza where he was drinking rang out the time:

> What's forty-two to forty-three?
> Certainly many things are over. . . .
> I find myself as ignorant & crazy as ever . . .
> I seem to have been alive a thousand years,
> two thousand, and I still can't see the end. . . .

But all of Henry was not happy. "Henry pickt up in Calcutta something or other," he wrote, something

viewed differently by doctors in Bombay & Ahmedabad,
Mabel something epidemic in Barcelona,
the baby is as healthy as Sweden, the hell with the old,
& howls half the night proving that he is perfect.

He sensed now—correctly—that he was on the verge of a major breakthrough in his poetry. At the end of October he left Ann with the baby for a few days to see Toledo. There, on the Feast of All Saints, he sat at a café table in the Plaza Todocover and wrote, "My gift is re-established. . . . I can do it, & do it. All I need is to be tortured, & then alone, & happy."

By the time he returned to Madrid it had become for him, in spite of the Prado and its wonderful shops, like "any big city in Europe." A "vellum ms. book of about 1600, containing a whole theological treatise" had cost him a dollar, a triple dry martini twenty cents. But he was bored and he knew it was time to be moving. He would visit a city a day. On Wednesday the thirteenth he saw the cathedrals at Valladolid, on Thursday the cathedrals at Segovia, on Friday those at Salamanca. Saturday he holed up in his hotel room in Salamanca and read Saint Teresa's autobiography in preparation for his trip to Avila. He could see that a whirlwind itinerary like his was not "conducive to the understanding," though he had seen some authentic glimpses of the country: men's faces "lonely and absorbing," women's faces among the most beautiful in the world. But they also had about them, these Spanish, "a self-ignorance so massive as to look like, & feel like, theological truth."

He was up early Sunday morning and bought himself a rakish beret before boarding the train for the trip to Avila. The following day he spent walking about Avila's "astonishing walls" and staring at "a few thousand churches, convents, hermitages, shrines" in a city where time had stopped in the year 1510. Reading Saint Teresa, he'd been struck by two things: the theological truth—more Hindu than Christian—that all was nothing, and by the psychological truth of the woman who leaped from the pages of her autobiography and who reminded him rather of his mother: a woman "shrewd, candid, vain, cajoling, domineering, piercingly wise, & vivid, & obsessed, & practical."

That day he wrote an introduction for what he thought of

as his *St. Pancras Braser* book, the collection of dream analyses he had worked on two years before. He now saw, however, that he could never publish the book while his mother was still alive. With that he put the book aside and turned instead to his *Dream Songs*. Why, he wondered, did the Songs always seem to be written out of pain? Ann had been right to complain about "the accidentalness" of his verse, remembering that Sidney Monas had said the same thing when he'd shown him his sonnets for Chris in 1947. Yet what else *could* the songs be about if not about himself: "Henry, separated, in hopeless marriage & Faith-problems, Henry—remarried w son & travel . . . the modern American divorced, wandering, not young, not old."

A week later he and Ann and the baby posed for an informal family portrait in the Merrillo Gardens in Seville. Wearing his beret to one side, Berryman held his son atop a wooden horse while Ann stood smiling beside him. In early December he flew to Tangiers to spend an afternoon shopping in the bazaars and old bookstalls. It was here that he picked up Frobenius' *Histoire de la Civilisation Africaine* and read it. Four days later, back in Seville, he wrote the man who had first brought the book to his attention: Ezra Pound. Frobenius was indeed as marvelous as Pound had said, Berryman wrote him, and had come as "an immense relief . . . after a long & fantastically variegated tour." The Indians had often asked him about Pound's long imprisonment, and he'd had to tell them "freely, whether I was on official business or not, that I thought it monstrous & a national shame besides what is wicked & ungrateful in the government's refusal to act." He wanted Pound to keep up his "marvellous courage" and he would try to see him when he got back to the States.

By then, with winter upon them, the Berrymans were ready to go home. But their last night in Seville, waiting for the ship, Berryman got himself so drunk he passed out in an alley, discovering only the following morning that he'd lost his wallet and his watch and had been hurt. He tried to remember what had happened but could not. Had he been with a prostitute? Had he been taken outside a tavern and robbed? He found himself staring into a blank even as his long pilgrimage came to a close.

A month earlier he'd tried putting on paper why he'd made

this pilgrimage in the first place. Hadn't he hoped to find out something about who he really was? Well, he was first of all a lover, especially of women. He also, except when it came to teaching and writing, "let people down." He knew he gave the appearance of being stuffy, and he still could not bear being "addrest by his given name by middlewestern shopkeepers & liquor dealers." He looked at what he was writing and he looked at the Beats and decided they were not the real competition. Ginsberg's "Howl," which had received so much publicity lately, was nothing more than an example of public masturbation.

Form, such form as his Dream Songs would need, would come to nothing less than a journey of self-discovery, without road signs, a journey such as blind Oedipus had had to undergo. One difficulty was knowing what a poor epic hero he made, "a man so ill-adapted that he made his way thro' American life in the middle of the 20th Century without a single angle." What he could not quite bring himself to admit was that in fact he'd been on a pilgrimage in search of the sublime to be touched in the holy places of Japan, India, and Spain. Nor could he admit to himself that he was an alcoholic with a bad temper and a proclivity for blacking out when he got drunk. But the stopover in Lisbon brought at least that bitter truth a bit closer to home.

On December 17, amid the silences of the Convento dos Teronymos, he and Ann had a terrible fight, marked by "extended & ultimate recriminations." As tempers flared, he struck her hard across the face and then left. That night, as he roamed the streets of Lisbon, he once again drank himself into oblivion. The next day, sobering up aboard ship, he became terrified at what he'd done. Why, he wondered, did he always seem to lose control of himself in foreign cities? Was it because he was at heart a small-town boy? He hated hotels as much as he hated having to move on, and blamed both on his abandonment and rootlessness as a child. He was even more terrified that the university would learn that he'd disgraced himself in a foreign country and that he would have to face the humiliation of the Iowa debacle all over again. He had worked hard to redeem himself at Minnesota, but if he lost his job there, it would be the "FINAL irretrievable disgrace" he knew he'd been "courting for years."

As they neared America, Ann and Berryman began getting along better. Even so, they both knew their difficulties were far from over. It had hurt Berryman when Ann had asked him if they couldn't be friends again, since it was hard living "in your enemy's house." But what had hurt most was her telling him how sad it made her, knowing that, while he loved their little boy, she no longer had any place in his life.

## *Chapter 21*

# Operating from Nothing

## 1958

The Berrymans disembarked in New York the day after Christmas, 1957, just in time for their first wedding anniversary. They spent the next few days there, visiting with their respective mothers and friends, before returning to Minneapolis. Five days into the new year, Jill Berryman began driving Rudolph back out to Minneapolis. But at Ephrata, Pennsylvania, Rudolph caught fire, ruining several rugs Berryman had brought back with him from India. As it turned out, the small disaster set the tone for Jill's visit. Jill spent the time in the apartment refinishing furniture and cooking and, of course, talking too much. Finally, in a long letter that she dated midnight on the ninth, she unburdened herself of her fears of insolvency, then left to catch the first bus back to New York so that her son could deal with her problem.

When Berryman found her letter, he was so distraught he sent a telegram at once to the Greyhound Terminal in Chicago, pleading with Jill to call him at once. Thank God, he told himself, that this time at least he'd been too preoccupied with his teaching to argue with his mother, or he would never have found out how things really stood with her. He was ashamed, he wrote her, that his own mother could not talk to him about her difficulties, for, hard as things were, he and Ann were "not without resources." As soon as he could scrape it together, he sent her eight hundred dollars. It made him feel good to still be off the bottle, off women, and reaching out to help another human being in need.

After the "Great Silence" with which his friends at Princeton had greeted him following his divorce, he was delighted to hear from at least one old friend, Ed Cone. "Dear Toner," he wrote back on January 17, "I am busy in the apparently unending way one is after being off for a long time." As it had turned out, Princeton had "lately figured in the most astonishing" ways for him. He'd heard from Ross that Blackmur was doing splendidly and that Eileen was apparently interested in someone, which he was glad to hear. He had not returned to Princeton, he explained, because it had turned out to be for him the scene of his "life-failure." Marriage breaks aside, at least Princeton had been spared the final catastrophe of deaths like Dylan's, James Agee's, and Isaac Rosenfeld's. As for his new wife, there wasn't much wrong with her except that she was still too young.

A week later he wrote his mother that he had to know more about his background. "Indian interviewers quizzed me constantly abt my ancestors," he explained, "and it's humiliating how little I knew." He went so far as to write a letter to the University of Oklahoma, asking about the possibility of giving a reading there, in a halfhearted effort to get back to his native soil. By February he was once again at work on the *Dream Songs,* trying to rekindle the renewal he'd felt in Spain. By then, realizing that he was headed for another fall, he addressed the subject head on in what he thought of as a new ending for the Songs. He called it "Waking Up":

Sober Henry hid his glass,
Henry wd have to be sober fr here out.
It was bitter cold out
& bitter cold in. . . .

His voluntary drug makes his brain swim,
he holds things that aren't here,
sees what never was. It's clear

Henry can't make it.
Somebody else will have to do the rest, or some
—the transferable parts of it

—some of the scholarship, father,
husband, maybe son—that's about all
transfers. As for the rest of it,
the hell with it, won't get done, the curse
of someone very strong was on Henry. . . .

On the twenty-fourth he flew to Washington to read his poems for the Library of Congress. The audience was small, though his mother was there. It was "a great pleasure not to be introduced," he began his reading, adding lightly that he was used to having all his friends' books attributed to him and all his important dates quoted wrong. He talked about Whitman's "Song of Myself" and then read from his own work. Six days later he wrote to his mother how pleased he'd been to see her, then thanked her for the documents she'd sent him concerning his shadowy father's existence, including his parents' marriage license. They were "strange to see," he wrote, and seemed to come from a world as far away as the Shakespearean documents he was used to working with.

By then the old war against his department had flared up again, and this time it looked as if the enemy would win. "No matter what happens to IDS on [March] 10th," he noted, "it's time to be out of it if R[oss]—as A[nn] says—is thinking of resigning." If that happened, he hoped to be reassigned to the English department, though he knew those prospects were slim. The day before the vote he wrote down some thoughts on the plight of "The American Writer." Interdisciplinary Studies had been established in 1944, when the United States was defending its way of life. Fourteen years later, the program was being disestablished before it had had time to attract many senior members. The truth was, he believed, that there were too many intellectuals in IDS for the program to be accepted by the university at large. But this disestablishment of communities of thinkers had happened before in history, he reminded himself. What mattered was one's work and that only. "Put word after word, & into word, as well as you can," he charged himself, "& take it easy."

This time the ax did fall, and Interdisciplinary Studies as a department was abolished, though the Humanities Program managed to survive intact, so that Berryman still had a job and tenure. The day after the vote, he wrote a savage poem aimed at those who had dogged him and his colleagues for so long. He read it to all his friends at all hours of the night, mostly with great success. "Three years, Ramses! you sank an aching tooth,/ neither in dignity nor scholarship," he began, singling out the member of the German department who had led the fight,

> but lip
> toward lip protrudes with jealous rage. Uncouth
> crept forth your fingering spirit, calling dim
> officious fellow-things, Von Witless, Clown,
> a boar-big boasty Grabbe, to howl down
> any man thoughtful, or dig under him.
>
> And so the vote sank into the violent dusk
> we dream's your mind. You won, waving them all,
> the fake philosophers & the history apes
> & many unclear scientists, gross shapes
> down mist, towards made-up ghosts. At the victory ball
> who danced to see the prize? "Open your mouth,
> great Ramses, yet! Flash them a joyous tusk."

He signed it "Chamaco," after the bullfighter he'd seen in Barcelona.

On March 19, he flew to Loyola University with Ann to give a reading. He began by reciting from Blake, Frost, Lowell, Roethke, Yeats, Basho, Issa, Wordsworth, and Justice. Then he read his own poems, including "Winter Landscape," "The Ball Poem," "American Lights," the Bradstreet, and two early *Dream Songs,* "Calamity Jane" and "The Secret of the Wisdom." Back in Minneapolis he returned to his *Dream Songs,* drinking heavily to sustain his "inspiration." He completed a draft of "Henry's Confession," expanding out from some early lines about his father's suicide, and then drafted "A Trail to the Hill-Fire" (DS5). It was a drinking song that began, "Henry sats in de bar & was odd," and recalled a glimpse of Mount Athos by air, where "a Virgin out of cloud" had "to her Mountain dropt in light'' to pardon Henry his many and unnamed offenses.

He entered twelve Dream Songs in the Wallace Stevens Awards poetry contest, explaining that they were ''stanzas'' of what he conceived of as one long poem, and which he thought of now as running to as many as ''50–60 or more.'' They were meant to be read ''as separate stages of a journey and a structure'' that the reader would not find very clear. He still thought of ''The Jolly Old Man'' as opening the sequence. Among the poems he sent, he included versions of what would become numbers 67, 75, and 77.

By then, however, his drinking had become so heavy and so constant that Berryman actually thought he might die. On April 1, Boyd Thomes had him admitted to a private room at Abbott Hospital, where he was treated for ''exhaustion,'' a euphemism for alcoholic poisoning. The medical staff tried to get his weight up and get him rested, then released him a week later. His plan for reform this time included doing ''only prose for months,'' since he was convinced that it had been the intense work his poems demanded which had landed him in the hospital in the first place. But his first night in the hospital he found himself drafting a new Dream Song. He called it ''Room 333'' (DS54), the first of many hospital poems he was to write:

guardrails up,
as if it were a crib!
I growl at the head nurse. . . .
I have been operating from *nothing,*
like a dog after its tail
more slowly, losing altitude.

The truth was that by then all he could think about were his Dream Songs. Well, then, he would ''restrict composition . . . to one every 2 days, say, & spend most of that time on construction,'' analyzing once more his extensive notes on his dream analyses. But, he wondered, would anyone ever understand what he was trying to do in these poems? ''Considering how unbelievably stupid were even the reviewers'' of the Bradstreet ''abt its plot & voices (and how, for instance, it took 2000 years for the form of *The Iliad* to be recovered (if Wade-Gerry's right),'' he would have to maintain *''a clear narrative-*

*&-meditative line.*" He considered adding footnotes to the Dream Songs as he had with the Bradstreet, since most of them would look like fragments or "interludes." Most of the Dream Songs were self-contained, like sonnets, one to a page, but, as with a few of the Bradstreet stanzas, he considered running the narrative over several pages. On the other hand, he still had no idea of how he was going to eventually string the long poem together. "I have not yet got the journey, action, structure," he admitted, but then he hadn't had them either with the Bradstreet until he'd been "5 yrs & 20 stanzas" into it.

That Good Friday, Dorati's *Cantata Dramatica* made its world premier on the university campus. Four thousand people heard 230 voices sing the music for which Berryman had provided the English lyrics. But Berryman, salted away in a hospital room two miles from the campus, was busy gestating a poem that would in time exceed the fourteen stations of the cantata many times over.

The following evening he fought with Ann and decided it was not good for him to talk with anyone at night. But the truth was that he raged at everyone: at Ann, the nurses, at anyone within shouting distance, which, in his case, meant several hospital floors. Sedated, he began examining his behavior, getting it wrong from the start. He could see no relation between his behavior and his drinking, which he did merely to lift his spirits so that he could bear other people. Why was it, though, that liquor began by calming him, only to leave him even more irritable than ever? He blamed the problem on his nervous system, his father, on the way Americans mistreated their poets. For all his self-analysis, he had learned nothing about the alcoholic mind.

Back home, he wrote a draft of "Silent Song" (DS52) and then a draft of the poem that would open *The Dream Songs,* a poem about Huffy Henry hiding from everyone like sulky Achilles in his tent. "I have been writing brilliantly," he wrote his mother, and had learned at last how to make his style so lean he could "make the reader's nerves jump" simply by moving his little finger.

A week later he wrote Macdonald in response to Macdonald's article on "Bright Young Men in the Arts." It was difficult to see how *any* of the new novelists really came up to the mark, Berryman wrote, for they all seemed to lack either energy or passion. He'd liked Styron's and Mailer's first novels, but he'd noticed a subsequent falling off in power. He also liked Edward Hoagland's *Cat Man,* but Ted had a long way to go. As far as he could see, Flannery O'Connor was the best of the current lot of prose writers, and she was not a man. The case with the poets was even more uncertain. Merwin and Hecht were "the most accomplisht" of the younger generation but wrote "as if nothing ever happened to them." Wilbur was better than either of them, but was also older. Of the unknown writers, the one he cared for most was Donald Justice. Actually, the really hot poets were all his own age. "Truth is," he added, "we are much more promising than the youngsters, as well as better. But don't say I said so."

His frustrations with the university continued. He held a joint appointment with English, but the department had ignored him from the start, except to assign him departmental chores like supervising teaching assistants, chores he usually did conscientiously and well. Moreover, after three years of teaching the same courses to the same state university undergraduates, he was becoming bored. He wrote another Song, "The Prisoner of Shark Island," about how the rats—Henry's enemies—were moving in on him from all sides, then woke Ross at midnight to read the poem in a drunken voice. He realized now that he would have to get his career going again if he was not to be "at the mercy" of those rats. He dropped into a fast-food restaurant for a hamburger, only to hear the Everly Brothers on the jukebox singing "Dream, Dream, Dream." Even their words, he believed, were aimed directly at him. But there were successes too, as when, that April 25, he read his poems at the university and Ross came up afterward to tell him that "nobody in the room had ever heard anything like it."

On May 1, he and Ross flew to New York, then on to Sagamore College in the Adirondacks to address a conference of some forty deans of humanities. Berryman gave a talk on American culture, during which he suggested that artists were no different from industrialists, scientists, and politicians in that they used their ideas about reality to organize and systematize experience. Through a Sparine, drunken haze he noted that the forty deans seemed attentive if somehow not quite human. He was there for the better part of a week before he and Ross flew out in a freak blizzard on the eleventh.

James Dickey wrote him to say he'd reviewed the Bradstreet in the current issue of *The Sewanee Review,* having performed what he called "a rather full-blown eulogy concerning your work in which I use you as a club to lay about me amongst the timid little souls." He also wondered if Berryman could give him any information on the poems of Bhain Campbell. A month later Berryman answered. He began by admonishing Dickey that he did not want anyone writing to him at his miserable university. As for Campbell, he was no expert on his work, "nor do or can I recommend it—I shd as soon think of beating drums for my own." He advised Dickey not to look for another Hopkins in Campbell, death in this instance having done its work.

On May 18, Berryman wrote a stiff letter to Giroux, unhappy with the way the Bradstreet volume was being handled. He had not been able to find a single copy of the book anywhere, and it distressed him to hear that the book was selling on the average of eight copies a month. Was this the same book Dickey had just described as having been written by the "marvellous John Berryman, who began quite ordinarily as one of the better disciples of Yeats and Auden, and after twenty years of wrestling with the problems of syntax as it operates within the poetic line, emerged to create, in the birth sequence of Anne Bradstreet, what is to my mind the most daring and successful rendering of human experience ever to appear in American poetry"? What was going on at Farrar Straus anyway? In the last six months his craft had developed so rapidly that he no longer cared even for the "American Lights" piece he'd written. The letter was a mixture of braggadocio, self-pity, arm-twisting, and reassurance that he meant to get the long-overdue Shakespeare biography to Giroux as soon as possible.

A few days later Berryman turned his prose skills to writing a short preface for the British edition of his poems. It was not calculated to endear him to the English:

> The great British statesman—Lincoln—the English sage, Walter Whitman; no doubt we encounter here a disordered mind, hospitable, grandiose, neglectful of developments since the Renais-

> sance. But let me assure any gentle English reader that the metrical stuff here reprinted is by a foreigner, who was not writing for him except as he is a human being and who cares nothing for his patriotic opinion of it. My passport, issued at Washington, is in order, so were my earlier passports, and there has been nothing British about my family for centuries.

He sent the preface to Giroux, who sent it on to Eliot, who was not—understandably—very happy with it. In early July, Berryman wrote his brother, whom he saw very little of anymore, asking if he might dedicate the English edition to him. But when Bob did not answer, Berryman took it as indifference and hostility toward him and at last withdrew the dedication altogether.

Suddenly it was summer once more in Minnesota. Berryman spent a day with Ann and the baby sunbathing and picnicking by the Lake of Isles and went for a swim, his first since Levanto. Mostly, however, he worked on his Shakespeare. When he heard officially from his dean that his salary was being raised to eighty-five hundred dollars, the dean adding he hoped he could count on Berryman in whatever new struggles might arise, Berryman wrote back saying that of course he could be counted on to "reinforce" the dean's party, though he wished the place "would calm down."

He sent *The New Yorker* two poems, "A Sympathy, A Welcome" and "Note to Wang Wei," and this time the magazine took them both. On the Fourth of July he wrote another Dream Song, "Of 1826," remembering the deaths of Adams and Jefferson on the fiftieth anniversary of the signing of the Declaration of Independence. By then he also had drafts of four essays for the Shakespeare handbook he still owed Crowell. But he was tired, the reason being, he told himself, that for a month he'd held his liquor intake to ale and wine, which was certainly no ichor for scholar-heroes like himself.

Then it was mid-July and summer classes were upon him before he'd had adequate time to prepare. "I am having to give up Shakespearean work," he wrote his mother, "in order to try to earn some money." On the plus side, he'd managed to send off the manuscript for a pamphlet of his poems that Claude Fredericks, Berryman's former student at Harvard, would handset for his Banyan Press in Pawlet, Vermont. The pamphlet, limited to an edition of 526 copies, took its title from a line in Dream Song 5, *His Thought Made Pockets & The Plane Buckt*. But, except for the middle stanza of that poem, none of the Songs were included. The pamphlet represented modest, interim work until a volume of *The Dream Songs* could be put together. He dedicated the pamphlet to his wife.

Reading through *Time* magazine, he came across the news that Mark Van Doren's son, Charles, had just had a daughter. "Hurrah for your grandfatherhood!" he wrote Mark on July 15. "I take my 16-month-old son for an hour's stroll every day and it reconciles me to everything." He caught his old teacher up on the news. Columbia had recently made him an honorary associate of their Seminar on American Civilization for no reason he could see. Eliot was at the moment "very very nervous" about the "very fine piece of Anglophobia" he'd written and wanted it removed. Berryman brooded over the request, then took the offending preface out.

That summer his dislike for Eisenhower reintensified when he learned that U.S. Marines had landed in Lebanon at the request of Chamoun and the Lebanese government in the wake of violent unrest in that area. "These weak, flailing fools in the State Dept & the White House look to be running the world in risk of being murdered," he complained. "Let's all die for Lebanon and petty tyrants wherever State can find them." A country as big as the United States *needed* good government, Berryman understood, and he was alarmed at the administration's "sudden and dangerous muscle-flexing" after its earlier "weakness & brainlessness."

Teaching began on July 20, and each day for the next five weeks he taught his Modern Literature survey. By then work on the Shakespearean handbook had completely ceased. Crowell wanted too much from him for the measly five hundred dollars he'd been given, he complained, so that there was no incentive to continue. Only Paul continued to flourish. At seventeen months the baby had taken "to looking up bitterly" at his parents "in odd frustrated moments, from under his lids in a lowered countenance." It was an absurd mannerism that delighted Berryman.

After he finished his classes in late August, Berryman flew to New York to meet his family and spend several days on

Long Island's south shore. From Bayport, facing out onto the Atlantic from Whitman's Paumanok, his head stuffed and miserable, Berryman wrote some lines, hearing much the same thing Whitman had heard facing these waters, that delicious word, death:

> Snuffle . . For Henry has a filthy cold,
> like a sea in the head,
> with slap & lurchings & a sense of congestion
> of weed just offshore, behind the eyebrows. . . .
> He isn't strong enough just now. He will be.
> Hoho, heehee.
> He cd put everything in order & perish. . . .

One of the reasons Berryman had come to New York was to see his publishers at Crowell to explain why the anthology he and Tate and Ross had promised was not yet ready, and this time there had been a scene. Berryman called Tate, who in turn called Crowell, but even that had no effect, "the same deaf meaningless shameless pressure" having "continued, solely abt their book." At last Berryman became so upset that he began drinking more and more heavily. Finally, Shea had him admitted to Regent Hospital in New York City for rest and observation. He had come East, he wrote the Thomeses, to think about the structure of *The Dream Songs*—"not writing: structure"—before he went back to teaching, and here he was, in this "nice hospital," lying on his back while he stared at the shiny plants and "polisht fronds of the jungle shivering over." He asked the Thomeses to tell Ross and Tate that it would be impossible now to meet with them to talk about the textbook.

Maris wrote back, bucking him up by telling him what he needed to hear: that he was loved, that he would pull through. He had yet to face up to the fact that he was an alcoholic. Instead, a new pattern of escapist behavior now offered itself. When things got rough from now on, he would check into a hospital and let the doctors and nurses take care of him until *he* was ready to come out. And from now on, he decided, things were going to get rough a lot more often.

A few days later he was back in Minneapolis, preparing to teach. On September 24, he delivered some general remarks on poetry at the university convocation and once more he was on fire. One's ideas about poetry came from one's home and one's school, as well as from society as a whole, he told his audience, and such forces tended to tame poetry's awesome power. The truth was that poetry was "too primitive & too realistic" for most Americans, who actually felt nervous before its nakedness. The best poetry made use of the basic rhythms of human life, so that it was a counterforce, a rebuke to those forces that threatened to dehumanize people. It cost everything to make a poem, which was a lot more than most people were willing to give to hear its true music.

Teaching the *Iliad* that September, Berryman pillaged through it looking for what he could use for his own epic. He read Tillyard on the Miltonic epic and Bowra on the Greek. His hero, Henry, would be based on a "deeply sympathetic, almost incredulous study of several of my closest friends and most venomous enemies," but really Henry would be based on John Berryman. If the "chief enemy" for Achilles had been Hector, he asked himself, then whose would Henry's be? God? He considered beginning the Songs *in medias res,* "late in a long war," a war that had been raging for thirty years now, for Henry had been often "deprived & insulted" and had learned long ago to take his revenge out by sulking. Instead of Myrmidons, his enemies were the philistine faculty who had led the fight to destroy him, as well as others he felt should be on his side but who weren't, like Ann and his mother. His odyssey through England, Italy, India, and Spain would replace Homer's catalog of ships. His lovers would also have their place in his poem. At last the poem was beginning to take a shape.

When he received advance copies of his poetry pamphlet in late October, he was troubled by the book's thinness and inconsequentiality. He knew he should have had more to show than this and the Faber edition of poems he'd written too many years ago. The day after he received the pamphlet, he wrote one of his best Songs, about his half-dozen readers gathered at the Cuttack leprosarium

> salaaming hours of a half-blind morning
> while the rainy lepers salaamed back,

smiles & a passion of their & his eyes flew
in feelings not ever accorded solely to oneself.

But, since he continued to write his Songs one at a time, discretely, in elegiac moments or as occasions offered, he wondered how he was ever going to order them into a viable sequence. To get chaos into his poems, he would offset the order of the strict triple rhymes in each stanza by including prose rhythms (irregularities, he called them) as well as rhymeless passages. The poem would begin with a struggle and gradually move "out into freedom," where the poet would at last be free to die.

Three days before his forty-fourth birthday, he sent a note to Samuel Holt Monk—an ally in the English department—with a copy to his dean, "aggrieved" that the department had decided not to use him. Surely he was capable of teaching Shakespeare or American literature or at least American poetry. He'd been elected to the English department unanimously, and five senior members of the department were "scandalized" that he had yet to be offered an English course. There was about all this, he insisted, "an air of insult" that needed "clearing up." But in spite of his brilliance as a lecturer, Berryman's reputation as a drunkard and a troublemaker were too well known. That he had insulted several of the department's members—including their wives—and that he had never taken the trouble to hide his disdain for most of the department did not help his case.

At the beginning of November he wrote Tate that he was still working on the anthology and hoped to be finished in another two weeks, having been "held up by an inability to stop writing verse." The same day he wrote Tate he drafted "Karesansui, Ryoan-ji" (DS73). A week later he wrote what would become number 26, on November eighteenth number 31, on the twenty-third another version of number 77, on December 1 a version of number 46, and two days later number 67. The real model for his epic, he realized now, was not the Iliad so much as it was "Song of Myself." If one did away with a strong story line, such as one found in the traditional epic, then it was the figure of the poet one was forced to fall back on. In the seventy-third Song, about the garden at Ryoan-ji, he tried to address the issue of the changing readers of his changing and unchanging texts:

> —from nowhere can one see *all* the stones—
> but helicopters or      a Brooklyn reproduction
> will fix that—
>
> and the fifteen changeless stones in their five worlds
> with a shelving of moving moss
> stand me the thought of the ancient maker priest.

From now on, he cheered himself, he would work in a more "withdrawn, methodical" fashion, "3 or 4 hrs a day," studying the poem to see if his hero actually was going anywhere himself. One of the problems was that some of the early Songs, laboriously worked on to the point of constipation, were beginning to look "lousy" to him, while some of the newer ones had been perhaps too hastily assembled. The only thing to do now, he decided, was to keep the Songs flexible and open until he was actually ready to put the sequence together.

The day after Christmas, his second wedding anniversary, he wrote Ross from a hotel in Atlantic City. He was alone and working on the anthology, and this time was really almost done. He planned to return to New York in two days and stay at the Hotel Wales until he flew to Minneapolis New Year's Eve. To save time, he was thinking of including as part of the book the lecture on "Prufrock" he'd given earlier in the year at the university. As it turned out, not only was that included, but a great deal of the poetry commentary Tate was supposed to have done and which Berryman soon wound up writing. Confined to his hotel room with the winter seas roiling outside his window, Berryman felt he'd "earned" his dinner that day and had actually enjoyed it, he told Tate, as he hadn't "enjoyed a meal for months."

# Chapter 22

## Another Drink, Another Marriage on the Rocks

## 1959

When Berryman returned to teaching in January, his mind was all on the snowballing Dream Songs. He wrote Van Doren and Edmund Wilson asking for Guggenheim recommendations, explaining that he needed the time for his poem. "I give lectures till my brain reels," he complained to Wilson on the thirteenth, in spite of which he'd managed to compose "half" of his volume of Songs already, by which he meant somewhere between thirty and forty sections. He was writing, he added, better than ever.

By then, however, life between Berryman and Ann had become an uncivil war, with charges and countercharges hurled back and forth continually. Paul, upset with the tensions he sensed between his parents, remained tense and untalkative. Ann's mother died, and Ann had a difficult time recovering from her loss, without much support of any kind from her husband. By then it had become clear to anyone who knew them that the marriage could not last much longer. "Henry hates the world," Berryman wrote on January 15, commiserating with his plight.

"What the world to Henry/ did will not bear thought." Nothing could make up for "the horror of unlove," he wrote in what would become Dream Song 74. "Kyoto, Toledo,/ Benares—the holy cities—/ and Cambridge shimmering": none of it could make up for the loss of love, as now with Ann, as earlier with Eileen, when he had looked into her face on the drive "south from Paris in the Spring/ to Siena" and knew. People, he told his mother, were very "unhappy & driven," though "most of them wish to do as well as they can but need love." He meant himself as much as anyone.

"Have not really slept for 4 nights," he noted to himself as he sat alone drinking in a Minneapolis bar one night at the beginning of February. He was dangerously on edge again and he knew it. He had to take it easy, do "as little as possible," "avoid all strain & decision." He was drinking far too much and feeling used. He felt he was there merely to supply other people's needs: his wife and the baby, Ross and Tate, students, "readers (here & abroad), publishers, editors, the English dept." No one saw him as a "human being" anymore, so that his roles as "husband, father, lover, friend" had died. He felt so bad for himself that one night he broke down in the Waikiki Room and a few nights later in another bar.

He tried connecting with one of the few truly stable individuals he knew, Mark Van Doren. What a teacher Mark had been, he wrote him, for it was quite possible he "would never have begun to write verse" if it hadn't been for him, though at this sorry juncture in his own life being a poet seemed at best a mixed blessing. Sitting alone in another bar a few days later, he wrote Dream Song 69, with Henry praying to the Devil to vouchsafe him "a personal experience" of the body of a Mrs. Boogry before he passed from lust. By then Ann had taken Paul and Rudolph and left him to work out a settlement with her lawyer. By then too he was feeling very tired and knew it was time to get back into the hospital. To get there, he drank until he began suffering from delirium tremens. Finally, on February 13, Boyd Thomes had him admitted to Glenwood Hills Hospital, Room 231, in the closed ward for alcoholics.

This time, however, his every move was monitored, so that he felt more like a prisoner than a guest. "Smoke on the frozen lake is freer/ than Henry," he wrote on the morning of the seventeenth in a Song he titled "Close Ward," wishing the struggle were over and that he could simply float away:

> It hovers.
> Something is being
> made, or is something—Henry—being no seer—
> he may go into that line—unmade
> Henry too is drifting away black.

He blamed his plight once again on the fact that he was a poet, a thing despised in his country. It was hard to believe, he sighed, that poetry had once been regarded "as important by men as different as Lincoln, Dante, and Shakespeare." Plato had thought poets so powerful he'd banned them from his commonwealth, "at pains to wipe our subject out." But what was so wrong with a little Bacchic frenzy and deracination of the senses now and then to brighten things up? If there was something to be said for sobriety, it wasn't much.

He liked bars, he noted the following day, though not cocktail lounges, which were so "damned middle-class." On the other hand, he had no illusions about the working class. He'd quit *that* egalitarian democratic stuff back in the thirties. No, he liked bars because he could think in bars. On the other hand, he hated telephones, which allowed wives and lawyers through, and which, if they could be "disinvented, the sudden advance in the quality of the national life wd kill many a sociologist."

On February 21, he began another Song (DS32), lamenting the boring status quo his life had long ago become. The following day it was another (DS48) based on the Little Apocalypse in Mark, the Gospel he was teaching that term. It was a poem about death and resurrection,

> a Greek idea,
> troublesome to imaginary Jews,
> like bitter Henry, full of the death of love. . . .

In the evening he wrote his mother. By then he'd been in the hospital ten days "trying to avoid a complete breakdown." He'd managed to finish the textbook, Tate having in the end written "12 pages altogether." For the moment, however, he was under strict orders "not to attempt to deal with any personal relations with anyone, even Ann," and so he had not yet opened his mother's letter.

On the twenty-third Boyd Thomes drove to Glenwood to see his desperate patient. What Berryman should do, Boyd suggested, was get out and buy himself some new clothes and spruce up, and maybe then he would feel better about himself. The shopping helped. One of the items he purchased was a blue raw-silk jacket that alone, he told Boyd, made him feel "3% more normal." He was grateful for Boyd's care. Who else, after all, did he have left?

But he was still plagued by insomnia and broke hospital routine continually to get on with his work. One morning he got up at five to try once more to arrange his Songs. This time he thought of them as "pieces of a novel (scenic, panoramic, descriptive, monologue)," his voice holding the disparate parts of the poem together. Most of the Songs he'd written too often struck the tragic note, and he considered now the need for counterpointing that darkness with something of the ecstatic and ceremonious about it.

Dream Song 75 and "Henry's Confession" (DS76), he saw, would come late, though they would not do to end the poem. For that he would need something that would grow naturally out of the sequence itself. He noted too that he'd written some fairly anti-American government Songs, and was afraid they might get him into trouble. To avoid that, he would have to scatter his political satires throughout the book and be sure to add some patriotic ones.

The theme he had relentlessly pursued in the Bradstreet—"love for a religious, inaccessible" woman—he meant to include as well. But he would also have to acknowledge Henry's lusts, the two forces creating their own tension in the sequence, as with the fragment he composed on March 7, when Henry had nearly fainted with lust watching the strawberry waitress on the sixth floor of the hospital, "running about on short legs/ with every hair in place, & crystal skin," her speech "laced with intensity."

After three and a half weeks in the hospital, Berryman was sent home. Most of that time he'd been able to meet his classes, going to the university by taxi to teach and then returning by taxi to the hospital, sometimes with a stop in between at a local bar for a pick-me-up. When he left Glenwood Hills, he was still uncured, still exhausted, still depressed. He moved into a small apartment at 1917 Fourth Street South, a block from where he had lived two years before. Once again he was within a few minutes' walking distance from his office, and back again in the Seven Corners section of the city with its twenty working-class bars to keep him company.

It was well he had not read his mother's letter while he was in the hospital, for in it she revealed several upsetting things about John Allyn Smith, Sr., and about John Angus, Uncle Jack. His father, she told Berryman now, had once told her that it would be "too expensive for [her] to go into hospital before Bob was born" and that "a funeral wd be cheaper." He had also been unfaithful. The only reason she'd remarried was so her sons "should never have to say they were fatherless," even though her marriage with John Angus had been a loveless one. In 1923, she'd fallen "desperately, instantly, totally, forever" in love with the man who would one day become governor of Oklahoma. But he'd "wanted a wife [and] not a mistress," and she had foregone her own happiness for her family's sake. As for her so-called precipitous marriage to Uncle Jack, Berryman was to know that Uncle Jack had filed for divorce before asking her to marry him. Then she asked her son to remove the dedication to her from *The Dispossessed* if the book was ever reprinted, since the gesture had been destroyed for her when, nine years earlier, Berryman had told her the book had really been meant for his father. She wanted no part of a "stolen" dedication.

It was only a matter of weeks, then, before Berryman was drinking heavily again. Once again he was alone and afraid. In his empty, ill-furnished apartment he wrote another fragment, which caught precisely his terrible despair:

> Immortal (maybe) Henry seized his head
> with both hands
> and half-knelt.
> Shall he pray now to the terror out there
> from the terror in here?

In mid-April he drafted another Song (DS17), this one a prayer addressed to Lucifer, the Sleepless One:

Muttered Henry:—Lord of matter, thus:
upon some more unquiet spirit knock,
my madnesses have cease.
All the quarter astonishes a lonely out & back.
They set their clocks by Henry House,
the steadiest man on the block. . . .

And Lucifer, answering, knowing his own by the smell of alcohol and fear on them:

—I smell you for my own,
by smug.—What have I tossed you but the least
(tho' hard); fit for your ears.
Your servant, bored with horror, sat alone
with busy teeth while his dislike increased
unto himself, in tears.

Four days later he wrote a sequel, in which Lucifer had left sweating Henry to reconsider the bargain he'd made for himself:

He's gone. Now I confess: it is eleven o'clock
and Henry's soul, after an effort, hangs
miserable in doubt
The giants have not made my peace. . . .

On April 20, the Berrymans had their day in court. There was a second hearing on the twenty-eighth, at which Berryman was neither present nor represented, and Ann was given temporary relief and custody of Paul. She was to receive one hundred dollars a month for Paul's support, then two hundred dollars beginning January 1, 1961, "payable until said minor" was twenty-one. Berryman was also to repay the money he had earlier borrowed from Ann: loans of three hundred dollars and fifteen hundred dollars respectively, the second so that Ann could terminate a second pregnancy begun after Berryman was convinced, as he told his mother, that the marriage was finished. Ann would get the furniture and the car. Berryman would get to pay Ann's lawyer.

Thinking over the reasons for the divorce, Berryman wrote another Song. Repeatedly, he knew, he'd "bombed" Ann's self-esteem by raging at her. Recalling his wedding vows in those ''winter hills,'' Henry wept. ''Shame & dismay,'' he wrote, ''flowered in my beloved. The things that mattered/ rounded a bend & were lost.'' When the first alimony payment came due, however, he found he could not meet his obligation.

Instead, he retreated under his bed covers, refusing to see his friends or answer his phone. Worried about him, Saul Bellow would recall, and Ross

> had to force the window of a house near Seven Corners to find out what had happened to John. We arrived in Ross's Jaguar, rang the bell, kicked at the door, tried to peer through the panes and then crawled in over a windowsill. We found ourselves standing on a bare gritty floor between steel bookstacks. The green steel shelves from Montgomery Ward's, meant for garages or workshops, for canned peaches in farmers' cellars, were filled with elegant editions of Nashe and Marlowe and Beaumont and Fletcher which John was forever importing from Blackwell's. These were read, annotated, for John worked hard. We found him in the bedroom. Face down, rigid, he lay diagonally across the double bed. From this position he did not stir. But he spoke distinctly. ''These efforts are wasted. We are unregenerate.''

Short of money and with back taxes to pay, Berryman took on another job. This one Bellow got for him with Putnam's: editing the Elizabethan writer Thomas Nashe's *Unfortunate Traveller* and providing the text with an introduction. He was offered a $750 advance and agreed to have the book ready by mid-July. With his background in Elizabethan literature, he was sure he could do the work quickly. But by the end of May he had written himself into a deathlike isolation. ''The grave's first night: this cold my body killed/ forever, wholly.'' On the other hand, he didn't suppose Henry would mind much once he actually got down under. Mercifully, in early June, a copy of Lowell's *Life Studies* arrived and Berryman roused himself enough to write Cal a letter, congratulating him on his achievement. He apologized for not having the time to review Lowell's ground-breaking book and thanked him for noticing his own meager Vermont pamphlet.

* * *

Since he would be flying to Salt Lake City on June 15 to do a workshop at the University of Utah, he thought it best, in case his plane went down, to leave Ann with a letter that would serve in place of a formal will. In it he bequeathed "everything, incl. literary property & mss." to her, except certain objects he wanted his mother, brother, and Eileen to have. The manuscript of *The Dream Songs* was to go to Faber & Faber, but he wanted all his "journals & diaries & all such notes destroyed at once unread; also my correspondence." He also expressed "the wish that there may never be a biography." When Paul was twenty-one, he should decide whether to publish the Sonnets of 1947 or destroy them. For literary advice Ann was to consult Lowell, Ross, and Justice. The Shakespeare material should be kept altogether, for he had done enough "to make someone famous." He did not wish to be buried in the Twin Cities, and certainly not in Iowa. He knew he was dying outside the Church. He did not wish to frighten her with his problems, but he had to let her know he'd had a strong premonition of death.

At Brewster Ghiselin's writers' conference in Salt Lake City, Berryman read from *The Dispossessed,* his "American Lights" poem, the first half of the Bradstreet, and a dozen of the unpublished Songs. He also gave a lecture on "Cross-Fertilization in International Poetry," in which he spoke of primary and secondary civilizations, the primary being few in number, and America not being one of them. The problem for the American poet was to find a way to release his energies by creating new forms rather than by merely copying or "plundering" the past as two of Berryman's models, Pound and Auden, had done. At the same time, he was aware that all poems, even the most "original," borrowed from the past. One could not really be taught how to write poetry in the schools. The only way to learn one's craft was through self-training, self-mastery, and a willingness to work without ceasing until one died.

He wrote jokingly about the "moral-religious atmosphere" at the University, summed up for him in the words of someone who'd claimed that liquor and sex were taboo at the conference because they might lead to swearing. Steven Spender was there, and the novelist Herbert Gold, and in spite of the altitude of the place, Berryman was happy to get a "fortnight away from a wretched apartment he called home," and to see the mountains in a part of America he'd never before seen.

On July 7, he read his Bradstreet poem at KUOM in Minneapolis for the BBC Third Programme. His poem, he explained, had been constructed "entirely in voices," and everything in it was meant to be spoken. The middle section was "a dialogue, imaginary & phantastic," between Anne and a narrator (himself) who was "hard, unscrupulous, suffering and guilty." It was a love poem whose subjects included "barrenness & child-bearing, irregular love, age & death," analogues "to colonial settlement," or—in biological terms: "plantation." The poem had been constructed on a series of strong antinomies: "rebellion & submission, creation & destruction, salvation." The poem, he added superfluously, was "rather compressed."

Six days later he wrote Ross with good news. Tony Alvarez, the British critic, had done a "brilliant" review of his Faber *Selected* for *The Observer* and the book had been discussed at length on the "BBC Home Service programme called The Critics," in which the British poets Betjeman and Larkin had "declared against" Mr. Berryman. The upshot had been that the *TLS* had asked him for some Dream Songs for a special issue on "The American Imagination." Finally, the English Shakespearean A. L. Rowse had written him, expressing "intense admiration" for the language of the Bradstreet. "All this," he sighed, "is encouraging to a man at the bottom of the universe."

On August 10, he sent Bellow his travel piece on the Taj Mahal for Bellow's magazine, *The Noble Savage*. The same night he wrote a second time, admitting he was feeling suicidal again and trying to write his way past it. He had come to the conclusion that, despite the cost, his work was still "trivial." Once, in the early forties, he noted privately, he'd waited in a Boston drugstore and contemplated jumping from a low bridge into the Charles. Seeing what the intervening years had brought, it might have been better to have done it then and had it over with.

Ann returned from staying with the Bellows in New York

to begin teaching journalism to eleventh-graders in Rochester, Minnesota, and Berryman took her out to dinner. But after visiting her the following day and bringing his son a wading pool, he left her once more reduced to tears and himself disconsolate at his own behavior. Once again he thought of suicide. Life, he decided was all "mad, cruel & mad."

But he was cheered to hear that the *TLS* had accepted all five of his Songs. Then he learned that Meridian was going to publish his Crane biography in paperback, for which he received a check for $750. He sent two more Songs to the London *Observer,* wrote new pieces of the poem, and continued to revise the old. Through it all, the drinking and the depression continued.

Fall term began. On October 1, he had himself readmitted to Glenwood Hills. For the second time in eight months the hospital became his base of operations, from which he was delivered by taxi to teach his classes before returning, again by taxi, to be fed and cared for by the nurses. "Four days in & I ain't well yet!" he wrote Boyd on the fifth. "Christ! Canst thou not medicine to a mind diseased? Yes? Yes?" It was all a matter of "nerves nerves nerves." He could barely stand the doctors and nurses who kept interrupting him. Nor could he sleep, and he needed ever heavier doses of Sparine to calm himself. He stayed put another ten days, until he could deal with the shock of his divorce becoming final. "God bless all married persons," he sighed. Released from the hospital, he went on teaching and working on *The Dream Songs*. When Putnam wrote in late October inquiring when his three-months-overdue Nashe might be ready, he simply turned the letter over and began another Song.

One night in late November he arose at 3:00 A.M., nervous about what he would say that day in class about Plato's *Republic*. He'd had a note from one of his colleagues whose wife had just seen his Dream Songs in the *TLS* and had found them so fascinating she'd read them aloud three times. After classes that day he went to the library to find out what he could about the history of the minstrel show to see how black dialect and the Tambo and Bones routine might be worked into his Songs. Then, at midnight, trying in a drunken stupor to negotiate the bathtub, he fell on his right arm and twisted it badly.

A week later he heard from Conrad Aiken, who was updating his *Twentieth Century Anthology of American Poetry* and wanted permission to publish the whole of the Bradstreet. Despite Aiken's having thrown him out of his house six years earlier, Berryman remembered the letter Aiken had written then praising his Bradstreet and decided to let him have the poem for a modest fee. In early December he completed the Nashe and celebrated by spending the evening with a graduate student at a bar. Once again he drank so much he passed out and could remember nothing of what he'd said during those "six hrs of dizzy talk & caressing." He was already seeing another woman, and here he was, trying to seduce a student whom he wasn't even sure he liked, much less desired.

As it was, he had more than enough company in his Fourth Street apartment with the visitors who flocked to him nightly, among them Campbell, Thomas, and others of his long-dead friends:

> Some good people, daring & subtle voices
> and their tense faces
> I see sank underground.
> I see. My radar digs. I do not dig.
> Cool their flushing blood, them eyes is shut—
> eyes?
> Appalled: by all the dead: Henry brooded. . . .

On the first day of winter he recalled the ghats at Benares and the burning of the dead:

> Weather wóuld govern. When the monsoon spread
> its floods, few came, two.
> Came a day when none, though he began
> in his accustomed way on the filthy steps
> in a crash of waters, came.

Pleased as he was by the warm reception his Songs were receiving in England, he worried constantly about meeting his obligations to Ann and his son. He worried too about his drinking and his argumentative spirit, which he excused by reminding himself that he was a genius and a poet. Needing some distance between himself and his troubles, he flew to New York at Christmas to visit his mother and some friends, but nothing seemed to alleviate his depression. He was anchorless and drifting more and more on the darkening waters westward.

# chapter 23

# A Perfect Marriage

## 1960–61

Berryman spent Christmas 1959 with his mother in New York, while she lamented the loss of another daughter-in-law and especially of her grandson. By the end of the day Berryman was ready to scream. "Ten hours of Mother's plangent babbling is about nine hours and twenty minutes more than I am able to stand," he told Ann afterward. Jill had chosen that day to show him the first pictures of his father he'd seen in thirty-five years, and the images had devastated him. The following day—what would have been his and Ann's third anniversary—Jill drove him to Peekskill to visit his son and give him a toy train. It was bad enough that the roads were icy and that his mother had talked the entire trip up, but when they got to Peekskill, he was so alarmed not to find Ann and Paul that he called the state police to report two missing persons. Ann, delayed by the weather, was furious when she learned what Berryman had done.

A few weeks earlier Berryman had been invited to teach the spring semester in the Speech department at Berkeley and had accepted. It would be a way of getting away from Minneapolis for a while, and the salary too was tempting: five thousand dollars for a four-month stay. At half past one in the morning of the last day of 1959, he wrote Dream Song 103, which described what he hoped to do with his Songs:

> I consider a song will be as humming-bird
> swift, down-light, missile-metal-hard, & strange
> as the world of anti-matter
> where they are wondering: does time run backward—
> which the poet thought was true; Scarlatti-supple;
> but can Henry write it?

Back in Minneapolis, he moved into a room at the Hotel Stone and began teaching again. Looking at the pictures in his bestiary calendar for 1960, he thought how the year just past had been his "Agony Year." By contrast, he hoped, 1960 would be his "Animal Year." He resolved to eat better and exercise and enjoy the San Francisco sun. He would order his life, plan his Dream Songs, make money. He would go to the San Francisco zoo and converse with the animals. Something like self-respect began once more to surge up in Henry's breast.

After classes on February 4, he packed and went to Rochester to say good-bye to Paul and Ann. The following day he flew to Salt Lake City, and from there to San Francisco, arriving in rain and darkness. He stayed briefly at the Faculty Club before moving into an apartment three blocks from the university at 2525 Durant Avenue. Afterward he went to see the acting chairman of the Speech department, Woodrow Wilson Borah. Tony Ostroff, his liaison with the Speech department and the man largely responsible for getting him to Berkeley, came by for a talk. On the eighth Berryman began teaching. He had three courses: one in the novel and another in lyric poetry, both of which met Mondays, Wednesdays, and Fridays, and a third course—another poetry section—which met on Thursday nights. That left him Tuesdays and most of Thursdays for his writing.

After classes that first day he went book hunting and took in Ingmar Bergman's *Smiles of a Summer Night*. Tuesday he received his first check from the university and went shopping for sheets, pillowcases, a jacket, some slacks, and shoes. He also heard from Henri Coulette, one of his workshop students at Iowa in 1954, and now teaching at Los Angeles State, suggesting a visiting professorship for Berryman there the following year. Berryman managed to put his house in order, but he had no one to talk to. Moreover, in spite of all his plans, he wrote nothing and did not see how things were going to change very much. He felt too tired even to read. His only consolations were foreign films and the "fabulous" bookshops around the city, where, among other treasures, he'd found "vol ix of the great 2nd ed of the Cambridge Shakespeare, 1893–1905, with complete apparatus to Pericles, the poems and the sonnets." But it puzzled him to hear "how wild everybody" in the speech and English departments was to meet him when in fact he was being invited nowhere.

In spite of his protestations of loneliness, however, he was not without female company. He met a young writer named Deneen Peckinpah and wrote a Dream Song about the afternoon they spent together, titling it "Deeper-up, with Deneen Pekinpah," managing to misspell her name:

higher in a West Coast late afternoon
on hills w cedar houses
above a campus Henry throve—when the bay
at last, short-breath'd, showed mountains all them miles each
   way
& the sun sank in fog like a moon

behind the golden gate, open to the sea
and happy as a refugee, among
the mad trees burn in lacy acacia
naked eucalyptus
O as his body dies (a cell by cell rout),
let it be climbing still, admissive peering out
between these redwood houses it could never own
over the strange bay, w Miss Pekinpah . . . .

On March 4 he was in New York to accept the Creative Arts Grant in Poetry from Brandeis University, disgruntled at being called a promising poet but needing the money the award gave him. The following day he flew to Minneapolis to be with Paul for his third birthday, then flew back to Berkeley. A week later he was invited to Tony and Miriam Ostroff's for dinner.

He arrived, as Ostroff would remember, "clean-shaven, lean, intense, humorous, a trifle wary," and grateful for the Ostroffs. But when Ostroff suggested a dinner party to which he would invite some of Berryman's old acquaintances—Mark Schorer and Ian Watt and their wives—Berryman bristled. Fuck *them!* he shouted. Where had they been hiding all this time? The dinner party idea was canceled.

Soon afterward his chairman held a party for him at which, drunk, Berryman recited from memory a litany of poems from eight till two in the morning. Then, on March 25, Richard Eberhart gave a poetry reading at the university, followed by a reception hosted by Thomas Parkinson of the English department. Parkinson had asked Ostroff to invite Berryman and Berryman agreed to go, but only if Ostroff got him a date. A date was found, with dinner planned before the reading. But when Ostroff's wife, Miriam, became ill and the dinner plans had to be scrapped, Berryman refused to attend the reception for Eberhart, telling Ostroff that he would not play second fiddle to a second-rate poet. Ostroff wound up taking Berryman's date, a young pianist, to the reading and reception himself.

But the comedy was not over, for after Ostroff left for the reading, Berryman came over to see Miriam, chatted with her, read her some of his Dream Songs, and was soon boasting of his sexual prowess. In spite of her protests, he began chasing her around the room. When she told him to get out, he suddenly became contrite and downcast and promised to be good if only he could stay. After a short while, however, he started again, until he finally browbeat her into letting him spend "ten or fifteen minutes reverently caressing her feet, while reciting poetry." Then, realizing that the house had windows and that someone might be watching, Berryman recovered himself, hailed a taxi, and went home.

Sometimes Berryman managed to get away with such outrageous demands with women. But when Ostroff got home and learned about Berryman's betrayal, he drove at once to Berryman's apartment. A big man, he seemed even bigger angry, and he did not mince words with Berryman, telling him to stay the hell away from the house. Berryman stiffened in his chair and, without looking at him, warned Ostroff that he'd been boxing champion of his class at Columbia. But when Ostroff took up the challenge, Berryman froze, refusing to say anything. There was nothing for Ostroff to do then but leave. Miriam never saw Berryman again, and Ostroff saw him only briefly during the rest of Berryman's stay. When he did catch a glimpse of him, it was usually in some bar where Berryman drank alone.

Berryman did manage to compose several poems for his son and occasionally wrote letters to Ann and to his Minneapolis friend Harriet Rosenzweig. In spite of his resolutions, however, he had arrived in San Francisco in bad shape and he stayed in bad shape. He saw no reason to make friends, surely not after having lost the friendship of the Ostroffs. Twelve of his Songs appeared in *The Noble Savage*, though no one mentioned seeing them. As money ran short, he moved from the bars to his apartment, drinking himself into oblivion night after night, telling himself that he was at least drinking less than he had in Minneapolis—bourbon, gin, and beer, and that was all. He read mostly pulp paperbacks. He refused to answer his phone or pay his bills. He took no exercise and missed most of his meals.

He called the Ostroffs to apologize, got Miriam, and learned that her husband was not in. He called again the following day, only to learn that Ostroff was still not in. "I live entirely in the Past (loss, regret, guilt—distance!) & the Future (fear, Death)," he noted to himself on April 8. "Naturally I am miserable and drink." He hid himself for days under his covers until he realized what he was doing to himself and tried once more to get hold of his life. Midterm break came in mid-April and Harriet flew out to Berkeley to stay with him for the week. Again Berryman tried inviting the Ostroffs for dinner and to meet Harriet, but they could not make it.

At the end of April he read Caryl Chessman's autobiography, *Cell 2455, Death Row*. Ten years earlier, Chessman had been convicted of kidnapping by a California jury and sentenced to death, but time and time again his sentence had been stayed. Out his window, Berryman watched Alcatraz Island drifting like a lost ship in the bay. Everyone, Berryman understood, was given a death sentence in the end, and he had followed Chessman's case from the time he'd arrived in San Francisco, fascinated. On April 26, with Chessman's execution just days away, Berryman wrote "An Open Letter" to him.

"You may be innocent of the capital charges on wh[ich]

you were convicted, but apparently few qualified persons think so,'' he wrote. He still expected Governor Edmund Brown to grant another stay of execution as he had in the past. And yet there was something terrifying and weird about the story he'd torn from the newspaper and underlined: that the condemned man might ''sleep, talk, sing, write or do anything else'' he wanted until 9:00 A.M., when he would be strapped down and his life snuffed out. ''The man leaving with his wife & child for his first vacation/ in 14 years,'' Berryman wrote now,

> my old clumsy friend, in rain,
> slips & dies under the train.
> Encephalitis is, & Goya etcht.
> Vanished his dialogues without a trace,
> Aristotle's . . . .
>
> Watching it steadily, unless he retcht . . .
> 'Endure'—one thinks of Faulkner;
> 'nothing,' of Papa.
> All the tundra of novels, bad & good
> unforgetting Henry's reeling mind withstood
> lined themselves up again . . . .

Then, on May 2, Chessman entered the gas chamber at San Quentin and passed out of his life forever. The following day Berryman racked his brain trying to decide whether or not Chessman had deserved to die before he realized it didn't much matter anymore and let the issue go.

On May 8, Mother's Day, Berryman wrote a guilty letter to his mother. There had been a blowup between them when he'd visited her in New York in March and it was time now, in the face of her terrible silence, to try to patch things up again. ''I have been very ill for weeks with the same prostrating business I had in India and am not better today,'' he equivocated, knowing she would forgive him more easily if he approached her contrite and ill. But he was too old, he told her, to allow himself to be ''smothered with talk'' by anyone. ''Thirty times I tried to make a conversation out of it. On you rushed.'' There was something, he insisted, ''intensely neurotic and aggressive,'' about her obsessive monologuing, against which he still had no adequate defense.

In truth, he told her, he ''almost never quarrel[ed] with anyone any more'' and in three months at Berkeley, in ''meeting hundreds of people,'' he had had only two arguments, and both of those had been with people notorious for their ''arrogance and effrontery.'' She would have to cease, he told her, her ''all-or-nothing'' approach with him; he could no longer bear to choose between ferocious monologues or cold silence. Life, he'd learned, consisted in getting along with others.

On May thirteenth, he attended the California Writers' Conference with Louis Simpson, Oscar Le Winter, and Rosalie Moore, and gave a talk on poetic influence. Poetic development was, as in his relationship to Yeats, a matter of having a master and then of developing past that master. Without Laforge, would ''Prufrock'' have been possible? Without Beethoven, could Eliot have so shaped ''The Waste Land''? Afterward Rosalie Moore brought his point home by quoting passages of his Bradstreet to him and juxtaposing them to lines from Hopkins. Since he had always denied Hopkins's influence on his work, the similarities astonished him.

His life continued to teeter between chaos and order, and he kept delaying his departure from California. He began making drunken phone calls to female graduate students. And when Ostroff finally came to Berryman's apartment to bury the hatchet, he got another quarrel instead. Friday morning, May 27, Berryman and the English poet Thom Gunn flew to Los Angeles to give a reading at the state college at Henri Coulette's invitation. Phil Levine, also scheduled to read with them, met them at the airport. ''He'd been telling Gunn what a hulk I was,'' Levine would recall, ''and Gunn, whom I'd known at Stanford, had insisted that both he & John were taller than I, which of course they were by several inches. ''Berryman,'' pretending to be shaken by the revelation, insisted on going to the airport bar to steady himself.

The reading took place in the college theater of a campus with ''maybe 20,000 students or more stuck in this awful smog belt & composed almost entirely of recently-constructed Mussolini-modern buildings.'' Levine, introduced by Coulette, went first, then Gunn, introduced by Christopher Isherwood, and finally Berryman himself. He was in "terrific form," Levine remembered:

> He opened with a very simple song from Blake, maybe "The Echoing Green," reciting it very slowly, breathlessly, lingering on the rhymes. Then he recited an ancient Chinese poem, first in the original & then in translation. He had the audience creamed, but still he held off his own work; he read—did not recite—Jon Silken's elegy for a son, aged one, who died in a mental hospital. I had read, or thought I'd read it, in the Hall, Pack, Simpson anthology NEW POETS OF ENGLAND & AMERICA, but in truth I'd missed it, hearing it only as a second-rate imitation of Dylan Thomas. Thru John I heard what an awesomely powerful poem it was.

Then Berryman read his own poems, including some of the Songs. The audience loved it. There were photos afterward and then the poets went to lunch, where there was a "very beautiful waitress" who "kept making eyes at Isherwood." Eventually "a car came for Isherwood to take him to a studio where he was working. . . . Then John, who'd been rather subdued during Isherwood's presence, began to bemoan the luck of the draw. He'd noticed that every woman in the place was attracted to Isherwood, who could care less, while he, John, lusted after a dozen of them, not one of whom would give him the time of day."

Later Levine, Gunn, and Berryman went to a bar, and Gunn asked Levine to do his Berryman imitation. "Like a fucking idiot, I did it," Levine would recall, "reciting a passage from Whitman in John's crazy, up-there-screech. Gunn roared, saying how I'd gotten it perfectly." But Berryman was so enraged he stalked out, returning a few minutes later with a box of large Band-Aids. "He tried to tape one across my mouth; he was seriously pissed off. My repeated apologies finally quieted him."

That evening, Levine, Berryman, and the Coulettes went to dinner and then to the Coulettes' apartment. Soon Berryman was talking about the Beats "and how Ginsberg totally failed to understand what Whitman was about & how that failure rendered his poetry impotent. He brought such energy to this rant I couldn't help feeling he felt somewhat threatened by the gathering cries of praise for the Beats & especially Ginsberg." When the evening was over, Levine took Berryman back to the Green Hotel in South Pasadena where he was staying. Earlier that day he'd bought Berryman a quart of bourbon. Now, back in his hotel, Berryman assured him, "he'd gotten this drinking thing under control." A quart a day was his absolute limit.

Next day Levine drove Berryman and Coulette to see the "gorgeous view" from the Poet's Corner at Forest Lawn. Then it was "a Beat haunt in Venice, a big, airy, dusty old place . . . near the beach," very *in* at the moment. Most of the people in the half bar, half coffeehouse seemed "in a stupor," and Berryman took it on himself "to coax two young people into talking to each other." Ha! he reminded his friends. Hadn't he told them just last night that not only did the Beats have "no smarts, they had no vitality either. What kind of bohemians were these anyway?" Afterward, driving to the airport, they saw a police cruiser pull a car over and police approaching the car with drawn guns. "One cop pushed this huge revolver into the bare abdomen of this big, shirtless, shoeless surfer type who got out." In L.A., Berryman shook his head, the police were no better than "fascist storm troopers."

He gave his finals, saw students, swam, and drank. One morning he awoke with a brain-pounding hangover and realized he'd attempted unsuccessfully to seduce his date the night before. While he swilled tomato juice, he wrote another Dream Song (DS 57), a poem about the hell he was daily living:

> I don't think there's that place
> save sullen here, wherefrom she flies tonight
> retrieving her whole body, which I need.
> I recall a 'coon treed,
> flashlights, & barks, and I was in that tree,
> and something can (has) been said for sobriety
> but very little.

The bar scenes persisted. On the evening of June 24, he checked out the "fag stuff" at a place called the White Horse Theater, then sat in a place called the Fugitive Kind and composed another fragment:

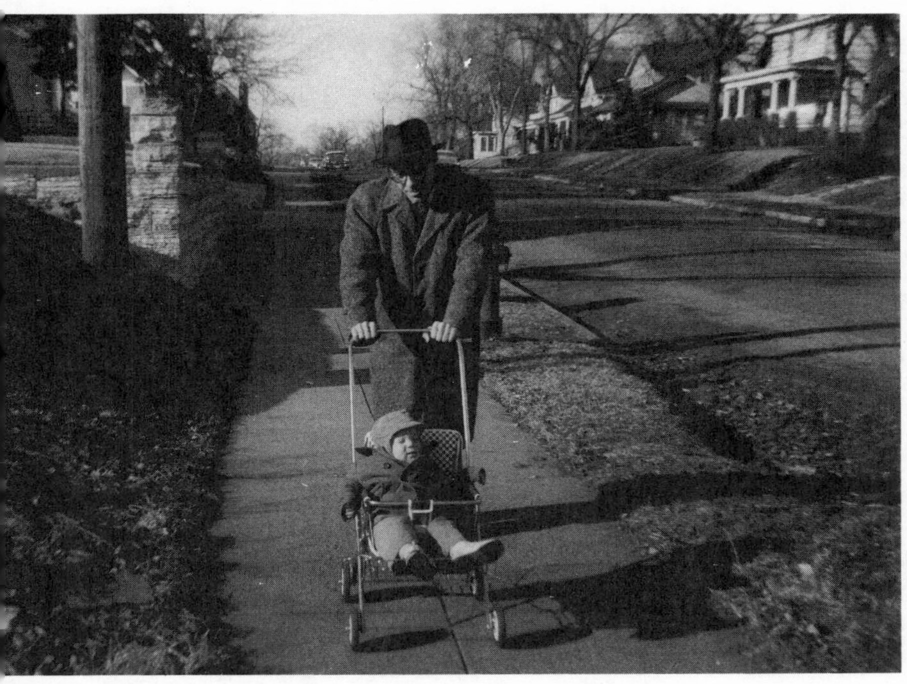

A proud Berryman wheeling his son, Paul, around the streets of Minneapolis in the spring of 1958

One of Berryman's closest friends, Saul Bellow, with his second wife, Alexandra Tscacbasov, in Minneapolis in the summer of 1959

Berryman, 46, on his first date with Kate Donahue, 21, March 25, 1961. Berryman signed himself out of the hospital to keep this date. On September 1 of that year they were married before a justice of the peace in Minneapolis.

Berryman and Kate at the rustic cabin they rented from Dulcie Scott from mid-August to mid-September 1962. The cabin is a mile from the Bread Loaf campus where Berryman taught that summer, with Robert Frost—"the Great Man," Berryman called him—living just down the road. Here, with Kate's indefatigable assistance, Berryman finally put together the first volume of his *Dream Songs,* which would win him a Pulitzer and a National Book Award.

Robert Lowell presenting Berryman with the Russell Loines Award in New York, May 20, 1964, apparently unaware that he had "betrayed" Berryman with his sharp review of the *77 Dream Songs* in *The New York Review of Books*. "I love him," Berryman had written in a Song (177) nine days earlier. "I may perish in his grins/ & grip. I would he liked me less." It took Berryman weeks to recover from the meeting.

Berryman, Kate, and Martha, the "Little Twiss," aged 2½, May 1965

Berryman, drunk, at the memorial service for Randall Jarrell held at Yale, February 28, 1966, at which, though he read brilliantly, Adrienne Rich was forced to take a bottle of liquor from him (for which act he later chided and thanked her). With him, standing, left to right: Stanley Kunitz, Richard Eberhart, Robert Lowell, Richard Wilbur, John Hollander, William Meredith, Robert Penn Warren. Seated, left to right: Berryman, Rich, Mary Jarrell, Peter Taylor.

The wild-bearded "whiskey & ink" poet, Berryman, 52, and Kate in front of the house they rented at 55 Landsdowne, Ballsbridge, Dublin, May 1967, where Berryman wrote most of the last book of the *Dream Songs* (*Time-Life*/ Terence Spencer)

Berryman and friend in Ryan's Pub, Ballsbridge, May 1967, Berryman's second place of study during his ten-month stay in Dublin (*Time-Life*/ Terence Spencer)

Berryman at work on his *Dream Songs* in Ryan's Pub, May 1967 (*Time-Life*/ Terence Spencer)

The Henry Adams historian, Ernest Samuels, snapped this picture of Berryman riding a donkey all the way up Mt. Athos on the island of Patmos, as though he were ascending Parnassus, "at the end of the labour" on the *Dream Songs,* August 1967.

Kate and Berryman, dressed as his grandfather, the Confederate General Robert Glenn Shaver, for a Halloween costume party in Minneapolis, October 1967

Berryman, 54, his wild, flowing "Irish beard" shaved off, with his daughter, Martha, 5, and son, Paul, 11, in front of his home at 33 Arthur Avenue, Minneapolis, in the summer of 1968

A bemused John Berryman at home in 1970, shortly after finishing *Love & Fame*

Berryman, 56, at home, in front of his book case, June 1971, at the time he began writing his unfinished novel with its wildly ironic title, *Recovery*. "Dear old thing," he wrote his friend and editor Robert Giroux at the time. "All's well, better than well, everything plunging ahead, especially the novel."

Probably the last picture of John Berryman ever taken. He is 57, has been in recovery and "dry eleven months," and is celebrating New Year's Eve 1971 at a neighbor's. A week later, on the morning of January 7, he jumped from the Washington Avenue Bridge to his death.

The femme, w. soft long hair & checkt slacks, & glasses,
in front of me, turned often to the butch
w. dark, bunned hair & shirt,
who never turned to her; then hand in hand
out of the film by the notorious fag
they tript to the little girls' room.

In Berkeley—where else? Well, the country over,
but most predictably here where the sick & queer . . . .
Mind you, I admire lesbians.
—Mr. Bones: I'm sorry?
—They do like women. They're not wrong in that.
If I was next one, I wd be that too.
Man, men are boring.

Three days later he wrote Bellow to confess that all that spring he'd tried writing something for *The Noble Savage,* but that nothing had worked out. "I have to be feeling really bad to write verse," he explained, "fairly well to write prose." The way he'd been feeling, he had stuck pretty much to verse. That day he also wrote Boyd Thomes. "I love the hills here, and some aspects of SF, and some people, but on the whole the Bay area bugs me." He admitted he'd been going "almost steadily downhill" since he'd been in San Francisco until he could neither think nor act. The times he'd dared to sit down and think it had taken all of five minutes "to abandon all three of my professions," and half an hour to become suicidal. The result was that he simply avoided thinking as much as possible. He would be home soon and needed rest. Could Boyd get him into Glenwood Hills or Abbott for a few days?

A week later he hobbled back to Minneapolis. From July 20 to August 26 he taught again: a section of James and Crane and a section of Humanities 54. He had two weeks free between late August and mid-September to write, but instead drank steadily, lost more weight, and began wetting his bed. Insomnia racked him. He took in some foreign films, especially Bergman. He read something in *Commentary* about several Jews who had escaped a ghetto during the war and transformed that experience into another Dream Song (DS 41):

The cantor bubbled, rattled. The Temple burned.
Lurch with me! phantoms of Varshava. Slop!
When I used to be,
who haunted, stumbling, sewers, my sacked shop,
roofs, a dis-world *ai!* Death was a German
home-country.

Late in October he wrote Ann, trying to explain that he'd fallen so miserably behind in his payments because he made so blessed little. She had to let up on him or he would go over the edge. "Mother, will I need haircuts in space," he began another Song on the twenty-second, obsessed with the stillness of death, "after I'm dead & saved"? And the mother had crooned softly back, "No dear, yr hair/ ever will hang the same."

Throughout the winter and spring of 1961, he continued his drift. John F. Kennedy was installed in the White House, and Berryman may have caught Frost on television reading his "Gift Outright" from the inaugural podium. He taught his courses, sometimes inspired, sometimes drunk. At least once that spring he delivered, word for word, a lecture on *Don Quixote* on a Wednesday he had already given that Monday. His students sat there, "pained and uncomfortable," one of them would remember, no one "moving or talking through the whole interminable hour. It would have been unthinkable to interrupt or stop him; there was too much dignity and bombast in him to allow for such a thing. It was very sad."

He received a letter from Robert Creeley, sent from Guatemala, saying how much he'd admired the Dream Songs he'd read in *The Noble Savage,* and especially praising them for their incredible "dislocations of syntax," idiom, and "great simplicity," pointing particularly to Dream Song 29. Creeley also enclosed a poem of his own to show how he too was dealing with similar poetic issues. Again Berryman did not answer. He may have linked Creeley with Olson and Ginsberg and the Beats. In any case, he had given up answering his mail long ago.

He saw several young women that spring, including one of his undergraduates. He kept notes on her as he had on Sally Appleton, idealizing her "strengths & subtleties & lovelinesses," realizing that to "take her wd be a shattering responsibility" for someone like himself who was "*older, sick &*

miserable-chaotic." An affair would be out of the question and marriage he was afraid of, especially since it would dilute his daimonic energies. Besides, he'd already failed that route twice.

In March he had to be readmitted to the hospital once more, but signed himself out to date a dark Irish beauty named Kathleen Ann Donahue, twenty-one and a friend of the young woman with whom Berryman thought himself in love. Since her mother had died, Kathleen had been the mainstay of her family, a family that included two brothers, a younger sister, and an alcoholic father. There are two photographs of Berryman and Kate taken a week apart at two Minneapolis restaurants. In both photographs Berryman, clean-shaven, in dark horn-rimmed glasses, holds a cigarette between the second and third fingers of his left hand, looking at Kate in the first picture and somewhere into space in the second. Kate, vulnerable, young, all anticipation, smiles toward the camera. Already there are three or four drinks on the table.

"My dear love," Kate wrote him on April 13, "last night was so sweet and lovely that today I feel all warm and glowing. . . . I want everybody to love everybody else." She was not jealous of his seeing her friend, and she did not like to think of herself as being in competition with anyone. It was enough to be with him, to listen to him. She had not yet been able to bring herself to tell her father about her seeing him and felt terrible about it. And—an absolute prerequisite for any of Berryman's friends—she liked his poems and wanted to hear him recite more of them. Whatever his shortcomings might be, she felt herself "coming to life all over the place." She was already in love with him.

On April 20, the airwaves were filled with the news that a young Russian named Yuri Gagarin had been hurtled into space and successfully retrieved. It took Berryman, as it took the nation, more than a few days to recover from the shock of the event before he tried a Dream Song on *that* one:

> Lo now we have a new name w. us forever:
> Gagarin—& suddenly—& they are writing poems,
> so the paper says—
> in an afternoon, it seems. Henry can't do that,
> sort of to order; you understand, pal, no?
> it's gotta slightly wait.

But—surely—the world-acclaim is offside?—
the teams, the teams deserve it
All he did was—like a many to
give up his life for??

Well. But black space, tho'. The 9/10's unknown.
Yes. And except in the pages of Life,
ours haven't got out yet.
So toss him, a few days late, heartache & hand-
shake . . . .

Berryman saw his old enemy from the German department stirring up trouble for him again and wrote a letter to the university newspaper, which published it on April 25. In the letter he tried again to explain the importance of a humanities curriculum for the university. It was an old and "tiresome and acrimonious controversy," this defending what it was he and Ross and his friend Siegelman did, though he would try. But there was a sense of autumn in what he was praising, as if he knew he was engaged in a struggle for the humanities in which the numbers were against him. He understood by then that the ideal of culture in America was too hard for even those in the profession to live up to.

At the beginning of May he moved into an ugly cinder-block apartment complex on the east side of the Mississippi at 415 Erie Place. At the end of the month he read his poetry at the Walker Art Center, the last in a biweekly series that had included Lowell, Spender, and Karl Shapiro. Then, even as classes ended at Minnesota, summer school began at the University of Indiana's School of Letters in Bloomington, and for a few days Berryman toyed with the idea of canceling out of his commitment. But on June 16, he finally left. His last act before leaving was to call Ann's lawyer to say that he'd finally come up with some money for her.

In Bloomington he stayed at the Indiana Memorial Union, a corner room on the seventh floor with "gorgeous views." He taught one course: a seminar in Deep Form in Major and Minor Poetry, centering on a group of lyrics and the two long poems crucial to his own work: "Song of Myself" and "The Waste Land." He thought his students—"15 of them—2 beards, a nun [the poet Madeleine DeFrees], & a Lebanese professor"—among the best he'd ever had. Then, on July 2, he learned that Hemingway had killed himself. So the "poor son of a bitch" had blown "his fucking head off," he told Robert Fitzgerald. Of course, Hemingway's father, he noted, had led the way.

Back home in Minneapolis, hiding in his Erie (eerie, he called it) Place apartment, he was troubled once more by his father's ghost:

> North Hell has telephones, which howl & yell
> all day & dark, where Henry hides in his own
> apartment; a *good* place to live.
> The pounding on his door stopped. Then (not with only
> it but) his bedroom door *opened*, and, well,
> a body stood there, speculative.

For weeks he refused to see anyone. He stayed in bed, drinking, refusing to answer the phone or the door except by prearranged signal. "For the first time since I got back here ten days ago I felt some energy today—eating breakfast at noon," he wrote his mother on August 10. He was exhausted after having taught six weeks at Bloomington and spending the rest of the time on his Dream Songs, "unpacking, separating thousands of papers in dozens of folders (& out of them)," including the six-inch-thick selection he'd taken to Indiana with him. He was glad Fitzgerald had seen them and, more, praised them.

On the evening of August 14, he began a Song about the U.S. Navy's nuclear strike force facing the Russians. By then the shadow of his miasmal exhaustion had lengthened across the globe:

> When a land seems both worn out, *both* worn out & fat,
> and the for (repeat: for) is both fresh & lean
> with a creed (to be sure, contemptible
> in theory *or* practice) easily understood
> & vivid, & dogma, one in the first land
> may really feel despair . . . .

"I am down with bronchitis, sparingitis, otitis and other goodies that have been building up," he lamented to Bellow on the thirtieth. Ross had told him that Bellow was thinking of remarrying ("What courage," Berryman had gasped), and now he was thinking of doing the same. In fact, he was supposed to have married Kate that very afternoon, but the event had been "postponed till Friday bec[ause] of my illness. Heaven help us, pal." He loved Kate and she was "a very very good woman, one of the sweetest-natured and most womanly and most loyal I have ever known." On top of which she was also "a raving beauty, tall, black-haired, shaped like a willow, like which also she moves, and elegant beyond praising." Also she was "a furnace." There were just two "little problems," he explained. She was less than half his age and she was a Catholic, "educated by the nuns for last 16 yrs.," so that her decision to marry him had destroyed "both her father and her best friend, according to them."

On Friday, September 1, Berryman and Kate were married in a civil ceremony at the District Court House. With them were Ralph and Alicia Ross and Phil and Ellen Siegelman. Berryman's hand was so shaky from fear and alcohol that the clerk made him practice writing his name several times before he allowed him to sign the register. In spite of his fears, however, Berryman was happier than he had supposed he ever would be again. "Hell is empty," he celebrated that Labor Day in what would become Song 56:

> O that has come to pass
> which the cut Alexandrian foresaw,
> and Hell lies empty.
> Lightning fell silent where the Devil knelt
> and over the whole grave space hath settled awe
> in a full death of guilt.

And if his father's ghost had stood there looking askance at him for his continual delay in meeting him, well, Kate was there too:

> So in his crystal ball them two he weighs,
> solidly, dreaming of his sleepy son,
> ah him, and his new wife . . . .

Having married Kate, he thought he could simply stop payments to Ann altogether. After all, she was working and living a lot better than he was. But when her lawyer came after him in October for three months' default, Berryman began several letters to her, threatening her again with suicide and arguing that, since "some peace of mind" was "essential to your son's father's work," it was *her* duty "as his mother not to crush his father to death." Meanwhile his publishers were clamoring for the books he had delayed so long. Everybody wanted a piece of the him:

The Man Who Did Not Deliver
is before you for his deliverance, my lords.
*He stands, as charged*
for This by banks, That cops, by lawyers, by
publishingers for Them. I doubt he'll make
old bones.

He was served a summons at the university by Ann's lawyer. Furious and abject, he wrote her, knowing he was "fearfully late," but surprised she would go so far as to have him jailed. The trouble, he explained, was that he'd had a desperate letter from his sixty-seven-year-old mother begging him for three hundred dollars and he had had to help her. He would send Ann something now and something more as soon as he could. Besides, it was only because of *his* training and largess that she was now teaching high school. He needed time to finish *The Dream Songs,* especially since many were convinced he was the only American who could actually write a contemporary epic. He was a poet "of some name, and of use," he reminded her. On the other hand, who had ever heard of her *or* her lawyer?

That evening he wrote his mother. He was sorry to have to say no to her request for a three-hundred-dollar loan, but he owed Ann twice that and the case was coming up in a week, after which he would probably be behind bars. To make some money, he worked on a selection of his essays for the Bush Foundation in St. Paul, which was offering a thousand-dollar prize for the best essay. He was thinking of calling his essay *The Freedom of the Poet* and it would include five pieces on *The Tempest, The Diary of Anne Frank, The Heart of Darkness, Job,* and *Don Quixote*. He was also "on the verge of putting the ms. of The Dream Songs in order, and firing them in all directions, esp The New Yorker where any single one taken wd be worth *fifty dollars*." Over the years he'd had several requests for poems and he meant to "satisfy them with Songs, quick."

He was ready to offer seventy-five Songs to Faber & Faber and to Farrar, Straus, & Giroux. There were "too many of them," hundreds in fact, and the work had "gone on too long without any public notice." He felt lost, he told his mother, "though an American poet [James Wright] tells me that his friend Donald Hall . . . . who spent last year in London, says the mere five I published in TLS have had an extraordinary effect on young English poets." For his forty-seventh birthday Kate had given him three handkerchiefs. You see, he added plaintively, "how we live."

That same day he wrote another Dream Song, in which he listed what the lawyers and the Fates would soon take from him:

> They weakened all his eyes,
> and burning thumbs into his ears, and shook
> his hand like a notch.
> They flung long silent speeches . . . .
> They sandpapered his plumpest hope . . . .
> They took away his crotch.

In mid-December, growing ever more anxious for time to complete *The Dream Songs,* he applied for quarter leave, ostensibly to write his book, *Shakespeare's Friend.* On the sixteenth he wrote to Delmore Schwartz. "How did we fall out of touch, all those years ago?" he wondered. "I can't remember that we ever quarrelled. It is this damned American geography; I haven't been east for two years; and of course money." He had just met several deadlines and had "spent the last 48 hrs largely in bed," so that for once his fevered brain was relaxed enough to think "of old friends." He expected to be "in and around New York next summer" and hoped to see Delmore then.

On the eighteenth he sent Ann's lawyer the support money he owed Ann for the first half of 1962, promising to pay off the rest unless she put him "in hospital or prison." Three days later he sent his son a poem called "The Poo & the Alphabet," which he hoped would help him with his analphabetism and strengthen a little boy almost as fatherless as himself:

A is for *awful*, which things are;
B is for *bear* them, well as we can.
C is for *can* we? D is for *dare*:
E is for *each* dares, being a man . . . .

Sick the entire week before Christmas, he could not get out to shop. Instead of a gift, he sent his mother a copy of the alphabet poem and a sheaf of Dream Songs and invited her to visit him the following summer up at Bread Loaf, where he would "bait Frost, who talk so good you forgive his megalomania." He also wanted to get over to Ticonderoga one day and see the place his father's fathers—the original Allens—had stormed in the name of the Continental Congress. With his Songs growing stronger every day, he meant to do some storming of his own.

## chapter 24

# My Heavy Daughter

## 1962

"Kate I think is happy, & I am, in her & with her; but everything else is CHAOS," Berryman noted to himself on February 10. For six months he'd been trying without success just to type and send off some of his Dream Songs. What was he afraid of, rejection? He knew he suffered a "monumental incompetent procrastination about taxes, bills, debts, insurance," and even about keeping in touch with the people he loved: Paul, his mother, Eileen, his brother, the Mackies, the Camerons.

Two days later he finally sent fourteen Dream Songs to Howard Moss at *The New Yorker*. He wrote Tony Ostroff about an essay he'd done on Lowell's "Skunk Hour" for him. He was ready to criticize Cal, he explained, but he had found it difficult to reveal what he'd seen at the heart of the poem: that it had shown Cal on the edge of another breakdown. "I am still riddled with ambitions," he told his mother. "And, worse, contradictory ambitions." Which would it be? "Art, letters [or] scholarship?" There was too the problem of moving. Soon the Erie Place lease would be up, and he and Kate would need a house. But where was he going to find the money to buy one?

His one consolation remained his Songs. On February 17 he wrote number 15 based on a story Bellow had told him years before about the courage of some "Polack broad" in a Chicago bar who had told some guy to kiss off. Women were better, braver, than men, he knew; they understood loss better than Henry, who took to the sauce when troubles came or retreated into the past or simply shunned the human race. Six days later he drafted another, asking himself if he had *ever* been happy. In early March it was a Song for John Glenn, celebrating his successful orbiting of the earth.

On March 14, a week after his son's fifth birthday, he sent belated wishes and a note to Ann explaining that nowadays he got birthdays "only approximately right." He was, besides, just then "swampt in term papers, reports for the En[glish] dept," visiting the classes of English teaching assistants, "and prep for a 2 1/2 hr seminar on Joyce's *The Dead* Friday." There were still "ten-foot snowbanks everywhere" so that he could hardly see out his windows and temperatures were still dipping to 20 and 30 below. He sent Paul two books: a Groddeck and Giuseppe di Lampedusa's *The Leopard*, "the most overwhelming novel" he'd read "for many years." When *The New Yorker* sent back his Dream Songs, he became so depressed he thought about "giving up the poem and verse" altogether.

Then, on March 18, with spring only three days away and the snowdrifts still looming, he wrote his son a man-to-man letter. "We must all be patient with one another and eventually rescue will come," he cheered him, as rescue had just come to him. Just that week there had arrived "from England a very pretty little Penguin book with poems in it, called *The New Poetry,*" and the only two Americans the book's editor, A. Alvarez, had included were Robert Lowell and Paul's daddy. In the same mail had also come a letter from Lowell himself, thanking him for what he'd written about his "Skunk Hour." True, it was not seemly to boast, but Paul's daddy was going to read from his poems at the university's convocation. Then he let his boy in on a profound secret, quoting the key stanza from the poem he had begun nearly fifteen years before, the poem that would one day stand as his *Paradiso*, "Scholars at the Orchid Pavilion":

Sozzled, Mo tzû, after a silence, vouchsafed
a word alarming:— We must love them all.
Affronted, our fathers' shades jumped.
—Yes.—he went madly on, and waved in quest
of his own dreadful subject.—O the father
(he cried) must not be all . . . .

"When you come to understand this stanza, and why I have now quoted it to you," he told his son, "you will be an educated Poukie or Paul-sensei." He wanted Paul to understand that everything that went wrong with Paul's life was not to be laid at his daddy's feet, any more than Berryman could blame his own father for the wretched way his own life had turned out. No father, he added, was strong enough to carry such a burden.

On March 23, Berryman sent Catherine Carver at *New World Writing* some of the Dream Songs that *The New Yorker* had rejected. He apologized for not writing, explaining that he *never* wrote to his friends anymore, although he was trying now to repair that oversight. He had recently called the Mackies to catch up on the news about all his old Princeton friends. *The New Yorker* rejection had hurt, but Alvarez's anthology, and letters from his friends, had oiled his troubled spirits.

When Lowell had been in Minneapolis the year before to give his reading, Berryman had shown him twenty sections of *The Dream Songs*. Now, out of the blue, Lowell wrote to congratulate Berryman on his splendid achievement, praise that meant much to him. Artists had to be there to help each other through the dark times as well as to celebrate the successes, he wrote Edward Hoagland on the twenty-fifth. Einstein, he remembered, had spoken of "*die unverliebaren Freunde,*" those "*un-lose-able* friends" of one's, the community of the living *and* the dead, bonded together by "the insights . . . they had achieved." He had benefited much from just such a community, and if he could be of help to Hoagland in that regard, so be it.

At the end of the month he greeted with relief and fear the news that Kate was pregnant. "Throng the Fates," he wrote, in what would become Dream Song 271,

he couldn't care less, being in love
with his own teeming lady,—whose dorsal fin
is keeping her nauseous. Wait till that kid
comes out, I'll fix her.
I'll burp her till she bleeds, I'll take an ax
to her inability to focus, until in
one weird moment I fall in love with her too.

His plans for the following year solidified. After teaching at Bread Loaf that summer, he would begin to arrange the Dream Songs before he began teaching at Brown that fall, replacing Edwin Honig, whose wife was seriously ill, and renting the Honigs' house during his time in Providence. At Brown he would teach two courses in the fall, but would have to teach three in the spring. It was a heavier load than he was used to, but there was nothing he could do about it. He was anxious to get back East—not New York or Boston but the "non-hectic East"—to see old friends and his son again. He needed money and hoped for some lucrative readings and whatever else might become available. A new location might also make it easier for him to change habits. There, in the rising East, he would work again with agents and editors, write, retrieve his library from its Princeton storage, maybe even learn again to drive a car.

On the twenty-ninth he wrote Lowell, thanking him for his good words and encouragement. He was taking his advice and planned to get off seventy-five of the Songs to Farrar Straus and to Faber as a sort of "dry run" for the book, which he thought would eventually swell to about twice that size. In another year he planned to be "rid of the bloody thing forever" and would then "go back to writing self-sufficient workable" lyrics. Lowell was "a lucky genius" to stay with the shorter lyric forms. He too had some shorter poems in the works, like his "Scholars at the Orchid Pavilion," his "chinese paradisal operation, scroll-style, fluent but abrupt," which he thought would eventually weigh in at sixty lines, though one could never be sure. After all, the Bradstreet too was to have been a lot shorter than it had turned out to be.

In May the Berrymans moved out of their Erie Plaza apartment and in with Berryman's graduate assistant, Lynn Louden, and his wife at 2230 Como Avenue, apartment 7. Since the Berrymans would be away from Minneapolis for over a year, they did not want another lease, Nor, in truth, could they afford one. Tired and drinking again, Berryman taught, waiting for the end of spring term. "A spattering/ pursued us to the orange old Chevrolet," he wrote in Song 249 on May 22, as Kate drove him to class to lecture on *Don Quixote* and a spring storm gathered momentum. By then he was tired of teaching wisdom to twenty-year-olds:

And sixty do not care
and they are bored with the electrifying air
& the Don & thunder-claps
And I am bored. That's a lie. But six are wild
quietly for the question of the length of the hairs
on the mole of his girl. Child . . .

He worried about his worsening alcoholism, his nightmares, his bouts of delirium tremens. "Reduce booze," he wrote despairingly in another Song:

Reduce . . . booze? Reduce. . . . booze.
—Why, Mr. Bones? —O they do say so, pal.
Frequent' they mention
walls made of spiders, fights you cannot lose,
campaigns gainless & horrid, Scott Fitzgerald
and Edgar Poe. Then

they speak of deterioration in the nerve centres,
and even a loss of personal dignity.
—That's heavy, Sir Bones.
I think so. Therefore I advised him to count to ten
*always* before his next one.—And did he?
—He got as far as nones

but the pit gaped for the unworthy man.
Singing the office, he was borne away . . . .

As the time for leaving drew near, Kate began suffering from morning sickness, not made easier by their moving and by the arrangements that had to be made for their trip east. Nor did it help that by then Berryman had lawyers after him for nonpayment of support to Ann for Paul. He also had the state of Minnesota after him for nonpayment of taxes. He wrote his mother to say that Kate's condition did not allow them to visit her in Washington on their way to Bread Loaf.

There was, however, the welcome news that he had at last been promoted to full professor. He had even managed to get free of the English department altogether, which meant "no more double chores & insolent nagging." Now he might at least be able to "rechannel" some of his paranoia elsewhere. He was also invited, along with a number of other poets, to read at the Library of Congress in October. When he wrote Roy Bassler at the library accepting the invitation, he expressed the hope that the occasion would have a certain seriousness about it. He did not, for example, "care to have anything to do with a circus where Mr Sandburg (whose poetry I happen to admire) and Jack Kerouac were the triumphant performing seals."

With a sheaf of Dream Songs two feet thick, the Berrymans arrived on the mountain on June 27, in the Chevrolet they called their "Orange Crush." Berryman's plans had called for the drive east in easy stages, but everything had in the end to be rushed. First they'd driven to New York to see Berryman's brother, then to Peekskill to see Paul, then to Connecticut to look in on the South Kent School Berryman had not seen for thirty years, where they visited briefly with the current headmaster, the junior Bartlett, son of the founder. There were two side trips as well: one to Falls Village to see Van Doren after so many years, and another to Cummington, Massachusetts, to walk about the Federalist homestead of William Cullen Bryant.

The important teaching for Berryman that summer would be his course in deep form, with its focus on Eliot's "The Waste Land" and Whitman's "Song of Myself," the first of which had informed his Bradstreet as the second was shaping his Songs. By the spring of 1957 he had begun to realize that *The Dream Songs* was going to be a heavier daughter than he had at first assumed. To help organize his poem, he began then to put down on paper how he believed Whitman's "Song of Myself" worked. "Song of Myself" was, he believed, the best long poem ever written by an American. And what a poem Whitman had wrought, managing it without relying on narrative to see him through. One moved through "Song of Myself" as through a symphony, swept into the paean's vortex and the bedazzling present without being distanced as narratives seemed to necessitate. All there was "conditional, open and astonished." Like Keats, Whitman had insisted on a disappearing self, the poet becoming a voice, "a mere channel, but with its own ferocious difficulties."

Each morning Berryman rose to teach his two classes, chat, or hold conferences in the barn, talking with his students on every conceivable topic, and he soon became the most talked-about teacher on the mountain, holding his classes spellbound. Perspiring and twisting, he sprayed the uninitiated sitting in the front rows with sweat and spittle, his voice a whisper one moment, then suddenly rising to an earsplitting crescendo. It was a strategy that intimidated and awed at the same time. Most afternoons he spent in his room in Maple, room 5, where he kept the shades drawn and wrote his Songs, chain-smoking his Tareytons and drinking. Oblivious to everything but the work before him, he burned circles in his manuscripts and clothes, sipping from a quart of gin from early afternoon to the early hours of the morning. His colleague, the poet William Meredith, one flight up, was his co-conspirator in the making of gin martinis navy-style, one reason among many why the two got on so well.

There was plenty to occupy his time: student papers, proffered manuscripts, texts to rehearse. Still, the Songs were his chief concern. And when he had a new one down on paper, he would race up to Meredith's room and read it to him. No respecter of hours, he unveiled his poems day and night, though 4:00 A.M. seemed to be his favorite time for sharing. Some nights he partied with his students, talking brilliantly into the early hours, and rolling in only as the northern summer sky began to lighten. On one occasion waiters on their way to the dining hall at 6:00 A.M. found him sleeping off a drunk by Johnson Pond. Nevertheless, that same morning he managed a stunning performance of "Lycidas." Keeping such hours took their toll, of course, and there were times when Doc Cook, Bread Loaf's administrator, would storm over to the Little Theatre or to the classrooms in the barn to chalk up on the board: "MR BERRYMAN WILL NOT MEET HIS CLASSES TODAY.

There were sponsored parties, lectures, teas, readings, a play, a smattering of musical performances, in all of which Berryman participated. On July 7, when news of Faulkner's death reached him, Berryman set about organizing a commemorative program to honor his passing. "The great ones die, die. They die./ You look up and who's there?" he wrote in his room that week. "With them all again & again I died/ and cried, and I have to live." Three weeks later he read from his own work, dedicating the event, as was his custom, to a woman, in this instance Professor Elizabeth Drew. He began with some early lyrics, read a section of the Bradstreet, and ended with some of the new and mostly unpublished Dream Songs. "Nobody knows enough to write poetry," he explained by way of disarming, so instead he would simply "mix a little of entertainer in" like "an old hand, a con man, and recommend nothing . . . and never apologize."

Though by then, with classes nearly over, he had enough to apologize for. Among those he had offended in the first weeks of his stay were Elizabeth Drew and Doc Cook, who had his hands full with Berryman, the man Cook also believed possessed the most brilliant mind of anyone on the mountain. There was also an ugly altercation at the Waybury Inn in East Middlebury with the inn's owner. But the most significant argument of the summer began the day the Berrymans arrived, when the Elder Presence and Grand Puritan Robert Lee Frost himself had fixed Berryman with a remark about his womanizing. Frost, great equalizer that he was, had treated other visitors to the mountain in much the same way, William Carlos Williams and Archibald MacLeish not excepted, and the old man meant no harm, other than to establish as quickly and as painlessly as possible that *he* was cock of the walk in Ripton.

Berryman, of course, was ready to accord Frost all the reverence and admiration due an elder statesman, and finally he and Kate were invited to the Homer Noble farmhouse where Frost lived. He turned out "to be utterly different from either his lecture or his party-styles, when you see him alone," Berryman noted afterward, and Berryman was "obliged, with love, to feel that he is a Great Man as well as (this I've known for twenty-five years) one of the best poets who ever lived."

Final exams descended on the campus August 8–9. Sitting on the stage in the Little Theatre proctoring his exams, Berryman felt "hinged and tired," like the foldaway desks at which the students wrote as they muttered their *sotto voce* damns.

While he sat up on the stage, one of his students, Blair Torrey, watched him scribbling madly at something. Berryman, seeing Torrey looking at him, waved back. Every time Torrey looked up, in fact, Berryman was looking directly at him, and waving. What Berryman was writing turned out to be Song 240, in which Blair Torrey makes a momentary entrance. The other person named in that poem, Nancy Jewell—"of the drooping eye"—also caught Berryman waving at Torrey, as she had so often seen him do to students as he walked across a field or on the walk. There was something very sad for her in the finality of that gesture.

The campus reopened on August 14 for the twelve days of the writers' conference. But except for an evening at Treman Cottage and another at a waiter's party, Berryman stayed away, quietly growing a beard (for the first time in twenty-five years), and hoarding the month to work on his Dream Songs. One of the few people he made an effort to see was John Ciardi, who, years earlier, had warmly reviewed the Bradstreet. Otherwise the Berrymans were content to stay in the small cabin next to Dulcie Scott's house, seeing no one, except Dulcie, for drinks. Kate, dubbed "The Whale" by her husband (whom she now outweighed by fifteen pounds), was content to rest, but Berryman worked hard, going through the manuscripts of the Songs, revising and cataloguing the poems, rediscovering what he had accomplished in the past seven years. Then he began scattering them: three to *The Atlantic Monthly*, then others to the *London Observer*, a little West Coast magazine called *Contact*, where Phil Levine had just published something, another to *Playboy*. He also planned to try the *Yale, Hudson, Kenyon,* and *Sewanee* reviews.

On September 1, his and Kate's first anniversary, he reflected on the sadness of Keats's "To Autumn," thinking of his own sense of finally having arrived at something. He understood too that for him winter was already in the air:

A small, soft rain, sweet on the summer's end.
The ringing mountains hide. Poplars & firs
& the sloping yard, & goldenglow, are all
his universe. Weak & still—his, hers,—

lie the dead, closed, across the mountains . . . .
And a new life will be here, later, in Providence . . . .

It was time now to reconcile with Giroux if Giroux was ever going to do *The Dream Songs*. "Three weeks ago," Berryman wrote Catherine Carver on the fourth, "when we moved over here after a wild six weeks of two lectures a day and so much social life that I counted nine parties in one week, the thing was nothing but a seven-year-mess filling a whole bag." But in the time they'd been at the cabin, he and Kate had made "a register of 130-odd revised & typed, so that I can find anything, plus alphabetized carbons of most of them, plus alphabetized mss., plus more than a hundred others deeply drafted, plus 8 or 10 folders of program notes & arrangements, plus (separated) hundreds of sketches in various stages of development. . . . Praise me." And then the question to which it had all been leading: Would she help make peace between Giroux and himself?

All he had left to do now was select the seventy-five he wanted and then order them. On Labor Day he listed whatever themes he could find in the poems, looking for direction: freedom, law, paranoia, entertainment, self-exploration, love, lust, art, war, politics, illness, loss, death, travel, place names, work, religion, wives. He'd used the theme of freedom in the song about "Seedy Henry" who "rose up shy in de world," ready to move on. As for remorse, he had plenty of that, too:

There sat down, once, a thing on Henry's heart
só heavy, if he had a hundred years
& more, & weeping, sleepless, in all them time
Henry could not make good . . . .

Of terror and paranoia he had more than enough to say, and planned to open the Songs with "Huffy Henry" hiding the day, "unappeasable Henry" sulking. As for the journey motif, he had place names galore: Kyoto, Benares, Toledo, New York, Minneapolis and Striding Edge, Saragossa and the Kremlin, Poona, Ahmadabad and the Congo, the greens of the Ganges and those delicious Texas Falls near Bread Loaf. There was also Henry's lust:

> Love her he doesn't, but the thought he puts
> into that young woman
> would launch a national product
> complete with TV spots & skywriting
> outlets in Bonn & Tokyo.
> I mean it . . . .

He meant too to deal with the imponderables, including his dim hope that suffering somewhere had its end. But in fact the themes did not fall singly, but knit rather like the constituents of a DNA molecule. For what really held the Songs together was what held Whitman's "Song" together: a distinctive and unstopped human voice, this one filled with laughter and sorrow in the same shuddering breath.

The Berrymans moved into 24 Congdon Street, and Berryman taught his classes or worked on *The Dream Songs*. Daniel Hughes, a junior member of the English department, would remember Berryman's time in Providence. At first he'd been unimpressed with Berryman, finding him stuffy, a man of fading elegance with "fierce feelings for the hierarchies," as if he'd just stepped out of the world of Henry James. But all that changed when Berryman called him one Sunday in November and asked him to come to the house and listen to some of the Songs. What struck Hughes was the evidence of "hard work everywhere: scraps of paper, the full ashtrays, the grey resistance of the light," all the signs of Berryman's "awesome concentration." He knew then what the Songs were costing Berryman and what he felt for him after that was something like love.

In late October, Berryman went to Washington for the Library of Congress readings. Louis Untermeyer, Poet in Residence that year, had brought together an impressive array of poets under the sponsorship of the Bollingen. Besides Frost, there was Langston Hughes, Ogden Nash, Kenneth Rexroth, Robert Penn Warren, Karl Shapiro, Gwendolyn Brooks, Louise Bogan, Eberhart, Tate, Meredith, Wilbur, Jarrell, Lowell, and Schwartz. In that gathering of poets Berryman had a chance to unveil seven new Dream Songs.

On the second night of the readings, Delmore, nearing another breakdown, went into a tantrum and was arrested and put in jail. Berryman was at a party at the home of Secretary of the Interior Stewart Udall when he and Richard Wilbur were informed of Delmore's whereabouts, and the two went at once to the police station to do what they could. Thinking he was merely drunk, the police released Delmore into Berryman and Wilbur's care, only to have Delmore lash into Berryman and then speed off in a cab, leaving his rescuers stranded. Then, back at the hotel, Delmore threw his girlfriend out of his room for expressing a liking for *The Dream Songs*. She could go and sleep with Berryman for all he cared. Berryman asked Kate to let the woman stay with her and he would stay with Wilbur. In the morning Schwartz demanded immediate payment for his reading and then left Washington. There was no mistake about it, Berryman wrote Meredith afterward, depressed by what he'd seen. Delmore was truly "in orbit."

On November 15, Berryman officially "unveiled" his Dream Songs at Harvard. When he had read the Songs to Bellow, he told his audience, he and Saul had cracked up laughing. Other people, however, found them unutterably sad. The truth was they were both, often at the same time, these songs by a "human American man"—black *and* white—who had suffered his first irreversible loss when he woke one dawn to find his father gone forever:

> All the world like a woolen lover
> once did seem on Henry's side.
> Then came a departure.
> Thereafter nothing fell out as it might or ought.
> I don't see how Henry, pried
> open for all the world to see, survived . . . .

Four of the Songs—numbers 27, 16, 36, and 71—appeared in the October issue of *Poetry* and a fifth (DS 51) in November. On November 12, he read his Songs for the BBC to introduce "Britain to Henry." On Armistice Day he wrote another (DS 61), echoing the eerie silence in the wake of the Cuban Missile Crisis. This Thanksgiving especially he was thankful that no white nuclear sun had flashed over Providence. "Far, near," he wrote, "the bivouacs of fear/ are solemn in the moon . . . tonight."

A week later he read at the University of Rhode Island.

He saw Paul Petrie, poet in residence, whom he'd known at Iowa, sizing up his "sweetnatured" junior and finding him wanting. He wished, he wrote in a new Dream Song, things could be different and that all poets could share in his own late mysterious excellence, but poetry was not, finally, a democratic process. Few made it, in any generation, to the top. Then, during Thanksgiving week, he managed to write fourteen new Songs.

The baby's arrival had been postponed for two weeks, he wrote his mother on November 25, and Kate was "tired of vastness (164 lb) but well." The Harvard reading had gone well and had served as Henry's "unveiling." Where better than there, where Ted Morrison, his chairman of twenty years before, had introduced him? The trouble was that the "violent emotional pressure of all these old associations" had nearly put him in the hospital again. He had rung Shea up in New York and made an appointment, but then, "too nervous for the trip," had canceled. "Whatever the cause—this, or Henry's formidable success at Washington & Harvard, or babywaiting"—he had managed another "breakthrough" in form, for the Songs he was writing now were "lower-keyed [with] *narrative* . . . as well as flashing units." At least he would not have to despair any more about Henry. Henry was now part of American poetry.

But the alcohol he'd consumed to fuel the new Songs had taken its toll. On the twenty-sixth he was admitted to McLean's Hospital outside Boston, where Lowell had been a patient several years earlier. By his third day in, Berryman was swearing never again to combine liquor with the writing of his poems. Sick and sweating, he tried once more to bring order into his frazzled life. That day he did a "coon" Song about "Disaster-prone" Henry "in observation room" asking why so much seemed to happen to Henry, to which his interlocutor had answered with another unanswerable question, like Job's God out of the whirlwind: "Mr Bones, as say de Book, when de waters swirled/ was you dere wid yo' sieve?"

Berryman was kept heavily sedated and slept much of the time. He played chess, had a physical exam, and was visited daily by the doctors. Then he had a bout of delirium tremens, which upset him deeply, so sure was he that he was getting better. He wrote Halliday, whom he had not seen for fourteen years. He was in the hospital, he equivocated, because of "violent overwork" on his long poem, though he expected to be out in time for Kate's "babying." Anxious about Kate's being alone, he called the house and was relieved to hear that his niece, Shelby, was there to help out. But he was not pleased to have the hospital psychiatrist tell him he would probably "crack up" when the baby was born.

On December 1 he was allowed to leave the hospital with a promise not to drink. "Our old set of cinches/ seem to've come down in the world—what's the phrase,/ I haven't drunk a drink in 7 days," he wrote the morning of his discharge (DS 246). Some of the other patients, he noticed, seemed incurable, but not him, for he was sure he was already on the mend. The following day Kate was admitted to Providence Lying-In Hospital where, after a labor of ten hours, she gave birth to a seven-pound four-ounce daughter with a head of black hair. "Martha was born an hour & a half ago," he wrote the Thomeses. "I just got out of hospital myself in Boston yesterday—payment for writing 14 Songs during Thanksgiving week." To his mother he sent a telegram celebrating his daughter's health and his wife's radiance.

On the fourth he went to see Kate and the baby, then visited with the Hugheses afterward. He was drinking, Daniel Hughes would recall, but did not seem drunk when they put him in a cab and sent him home. When Berryman got out, however, he was very unsteady, and the cab somehow backed over his left foot, snapping his ankle. Twenty-four hours later, around 11:00 P.M. on the fifth, Hughes got a call from Berryman's psychiatrist at McLean's. Berryman had missed his appointment that afternoon and was not answering his phone. Would Hughes go over to the house and see how he was doing?

When the Hugheses got there, they found Berryman in his upstairs bedroom lying immobile, his foot mangled and already beginning to fester. They called the fire department and an ambulance took him to the emergency room at Providence Hospital. Later, when Mary Hughes came to see him, Berryman told her not to give him "any tenth-grade Freud" about his being in one hospital while his wife was in another, as though he'd been competing with Kate over who was most in need of attention.

In the predawn hours of the sixth, he awoke from a series

of nightmares. In one a finger was pointed at him for desertion. In another he was being publicly denounced amid images of towers and flight and a terrible sea. But the nightmare that troubled him most included Randall Jarrell. He had been giving a party and Jarrell was there, telling him he just had "to stop writing these pseudo-poems." If Berryman would just "come back & write *real* ones," they would all be with him again. There were many guests about and all of them had heard what Randall was saying, though Randall had said it for his benefit, "sincerely, and I felt that he was right—all my work a stupid farce." He remembered promising "never to write again," was "even grateful to him—but no one was satisfied." The only way he could really expiate the offense of writing was to die. It was just a matter of figuring out how to do it.

On the seventh he was released from the hospital on crutches, his ankle in a cast. Early on the morning of the ninth, he wrote another Dream Song for his students in the deep form course he was teaching. The poem was addressed to Amy Vladeck, Riva Freifeld, and Ellen Kaplan, but especially to the quiet one, Valerie Trueblood, to tell them, humorously, that pain could be chastening and even redemptive:

That isna Henry limping. That's a hobble
clapped on mere Henry by the most high GOD
for the freedom of Henry's soul.
—The body's foul, cried god, once, twice, & bound it—
For many years I hid it from him successfully—
I'm not clear how he found it.

In spite of the dark humor, he needed to understand what was going to happen to him if he continued to drink as he was doing:

Tippling he toppled and his ankle cringed,
a hell of what to do to Pussy-cat.
For days he did not not walk.
Fusillades of pain Henry unhinged,
tippling anew. Devised a hobble that
was less a progress than a balk.

That day he also wrote Jarrell, who was putting together an anthology of American poetry for Dell and had asked him for some of his new Dream Songs. Berryman sent him twenty-five, including a transcription of the nightmare he'd had about Jarrell. "The worst feature" of the dream for him, he added, was that Randall's judgment on his work had been "delivered w. all the tender but grave authority of the author of 'I find no fault in this just man.' "

"During the period he was writing *Dream Songs* I grew to expect his drunken (sometimes) telephone calls," Ralph Ellison would remember. "Usually he wanted my reaction to his uses of dialect. My preference is for idiomatic rendering, but I wasn't about to let the poetry of what he was saying be interrupted by the dictates of my ear for Afro-American speech. Besides, watching him transform elements of the minstrel show into poetry was too fascinating. Fascinating too, and amusing, was my suspicion that Berryman was casting me as a long-distant Mister Interlocutor—or was it Mister Tambo? —whose ad lib role was that of responding critically to his Mister Bones and Huffy Henry."

When Berryman went to Washington to visit with his mother that Christmas, he called Ellison to read him "Dream Song 68," the song whose Muse is Bessie Smith. When, eighteen months later, he sent a copy of *77 Dream Songs* to Ralph and Fanny Ellison, he inscribed it, "Affectionally & with thanks for help on *68*." That Song he wrote the day after Christmas, while listening to "Yellow Dog" and "Empty Bed" on his mother's phonograph ("and empty grows every bed," the very first Dream Song had remembered). With bitterness he recalled how Bessie's fame had spread only after Bessie herself was gone:

> I hear strange horns, Pinetop he hit some chords,
> Charlie start *Empty Bed,*
> they all come hangin Christmas on some tree
> when trees thrown out—sick-house's white birds',
> black to the birds instead . . . .

As New Year's approached, Berryman once again addressed his father's ghost. "O journeyer, deaf in the mould," he sputtered, "consider me in my cast, your first son." How often he had tried to pay homage to his father. "We dream of honour, and we get along," he addressed that ghost now in what would become the forty-second Song:

Fate winged me, in the person of a cab
and your stance on the sand.
Think it across, in freezing wind: withstand
my blistered wish: flop, there, to his blind song
who pick up the tab.

Clear, there, just who'd been left to pick up the tab.

# PART IV

*1963–72*

# chapter 25

## 77 Songs 77

## 1963

The fame Berryman had so long dreamed of began now to seek him out. Toward the end of January he learned that the Songs he'd submitted to *Ramparts* had won their seven-hundred-dollar first prize. "I have been feeling low abt the poem, despite word fr an old friend in New York that Edmund Wilson has been praising it 'to the sky,'" he wrote the editor on the twenty-third. Then, early on the morning of the twenty-ninth, another old friend suddenly showed up at his front door. It was Delmore Schwartz, who had taken a taxi from Boston to talk to Berryman while he kept the taxi waiting. Schwartz was acting even more strangely than he had in Washington, Berryman noted, and kept hinting that Nelson Rockefeller had been plotting against him. Finally Schwartz asked Berryman to leave his job at Brown and come to New York with him; he would take care of all expenses. Shaken, Berryman offered him a drink and then downed one himself. Then Delmore was having difficulty even putting sentences together. Then, suddenly, he was gone.

Later that day Daniel Hughes came into Berryman's office

with the news that Frost had died. With the great man gone, Berryman wondered, who was "number one" among poets? Berryman suggested Lowell, hoping Hughes would contradict him and tell him *he* was. A few days later Berryman read what Philip Toynbee had said in *The Observer*: that Frost had been "the greatest American poet alive, even in an age which had produced Robert Lowell and John Berryman." Well, Berryman wondered, with Frost gone, where did that put him? That weekend he wrote three elegies in honor of Frost (DS 37, 38, 39). In two years America had lost Hemingway ("the shooter"), Faulkner ("the bourbon man"), and Frost. That left "the rest of us" either to be "fired" or "fired up." He prayed that Frost's spirit might inspire the poets left behind to "blow" their best:

> our sad wild riffs come easy in that case,
> thinking you over,
> knowing you resting, who was reborn to rest,
> your gorgeous sentence done . . . .

Three weeks later he went to Amherst College for a memorial service in honor of Frost. Bill Meredith was there, the Wilburs, the Morrisons, Van Doren, William Jay Smith, Earl Warren, Eberhart, Rolph Humphries. Berryman was delighted to be recognized and even hailed as the author of the Dream Songs by one critic in—of all places—the men's room.

Back in Providence, he found a letter from Catherine Carver. She had spoken with Giroux, and it was time for Berryman to write him directly. Now he wrote, without wasting any more time. He was working hard on the Songs, he told Giroux, "and doing public jobs here & elsewhere" until "the actual world" had grown "unreal" to him. Now he wanted an end to the "long estrangement" between them. Forty-five Songs had appeared in print, and he wanted to send Giroux seventy-five as a "dry run" for *The Dream Songs*. Afterward he wrote Carver. Giroux might or might not respond, he told her, but however it worked out, he would be grateful to her for whatever help she could give him. He knew he was asking for a lot, but he had good precedent. "As Frost grinned at me across the table last summer, after some outrageous piece of little behaviour," he explained, " 'I require special treatment.' " Now it was Berryman's turn for special treatment.

He watched carefully what the critics had to say about Frost's possible successors. Since 1946, he had been comfortable with the idea that Lowell was his "superior," but now Toynbee had virtually passed Frost's mantle on to him as well as Cal. Then he heard that James Dickey had been calling *him* "the greatest American poet." Soon he was playing his game with outrageous false modesty, acknowledging what everyone knew, that Lowell was king. Or was he? "Industrious, affable, having brain on fire," he wrote on March 1, in what would become "Dream Song 58," "Henry perplexed himself; others gave up." He prayed that Apollo might "damp" him down, reminding him that he was servant Henry, a "serf, if anyfing." He dedicated the Song to Edmund and Elena Wilson and then sent it to them, hoping Wilson, as the one "surviving American man of letters," would use his influence to get the Songs a wider hearing.

In late March he began work on a poem called "The Other Chicago." He was writing it specifically for a contest that *The Chicago Daily News* was running for the best poem about the Windy City. By April 7, after staying up every night for a week, he finally had the poem sketched out, its "under-conception" plotted and its ending nailed down. He'd yet to do any research on Chicago, except to mention his friend Isaac Rosenfeld, his own hospital stay there several years before, the Great Chicago Fire, and finally Chicago's race relations betweem the sick "white coons" and the blacks.

But while he admired the work of Ralph Ellison and James Baldwin, he was ashamed to have to admit that, mostly, he didn't care for "Negroes." His "race stanzas," he was sure, were going to cost him Gwendolyn Brooks's vote. Besides, Paul Engle was another of the judges, and he hated Berryman as much as Berryman "thoroughly dislike[d] & despise[d] him back." He told himself it didn't much matter whether he won the contest or not. What was important was that writing the poem had shown him that, even after eight years of working on *The Dream Songs,* he could still write outside their framework.

In early April, Charlotte Honig succumbed to cancer and the Berrymans attended a memorial service for her on the tenth. The service, Berryman confided to Meredith, had proven depressing to him and Kate: the culmination of living since September with "a dying woman's things." Edwin Honig would move back into his house at the end of the school year, which made it necessary for Berryman to find another place to live. He wrote Dulcie Scott to see if he could rent the Ripton cottage for another summer, having worked so well there on the Songs, but when that plan fell through, he found a mill house, primitive but picturesque, at Chepatchet, Rhode Island, on the Connecticut border, complete with outdoor water pump, outhouse, and private waterfall. In May he corrected finals and read manuscripts. He also sent off a blurb to Hill & Wang for Mark Van Doren's *Collected and New Poems,* noting that Van Doren had been "the first modern poet I seriously read; and I have never recovered, or tried to recover." On the nineteenth, Martha was baptized at a Roman Catholic church in Providence. Jill made the trip up from Washington to see her granddaughter, and Fitzgerald came from Perugia to stand as Martha's godfather. He'd stood there, Berryman noted, "learned-looking, belly out, w his missal, to catch the priest out."

On the twenty-sixth an article entitled "John Berryman on Today's Literature," appeared in the *Providence Sunday Journal.* When the reporter had interviewed him earlier that month, Berryman had been sporting a bow tie and had reminded her that he had an appointment to see a doctor in half an hour. He seemed to pretend "to an air of vagueness and diffidence," but she could sense his energy and enthusiasm. "I teach and I write," he told her. "I'm not copy." Still, he'd spoken on a number of topics: his own work, the "dearth of anything good in the literary magazine field" in the United States. Then the interview turned to American writers, and the doctor's appointment was forgotten. Frost, he noted, had been "as shrewd and as cruel as a Medici." And though he found "most women writers too personal," he greatly admired Flannery O'Connor. He praised Bellow and J. F. Powers, but felt that Mailer was beginning to go "to pieces." People who wanted to write, he added, should not take so-called Creative Writing courses. If they were going to write, they would write. Better to study "history or language or mathematics." As for his Dream Songs, they were "still hopelessly unfinished" and filled a suitcase.

On May 31, he wrote Henry Rago that he was sending some Dream Songs for the fiftieth-anniversary issue of *Poetry* as well as a revised version of his Chicago poem, which he asked Rago to pass on to Bellow so that he could tell him what was wrong with it. Then he wrote Bellow directly, disconsolate over Pope John XXIII's death, over which he had "cried & prayed" when he'd heard the news. "He was like a good man," he added. "The jerks"—he meant the assembled cardinals—had "put him in as a compromise, decrepit," but "ha ha! he bombed them."

A week later he wrote Ross to say that he and his little family were leaving Providence and moving "to the country, I don't know how." Six months after the cab had cracked his ankle, his leg was "still UGH." He had been considering his options—returning to teach, with full pay and the winter quarter off, or a yearlong sabbatical at half pay, and had decided on the sabbatical. He would supplement his income however best he could, for he needed all the time he could find to finish *The Dream Songs*. In order to save, he would stay at the mill until cold weather forced him and Kate and the baby to leave.

His third day at the Grist Mill, June 11, he wrote Song 228, with "the Father of the Mill" surveying "his falls,/ his daughterly race, his flume." A week later he wrote number 66, which described, among other frightening events, the self-immolation of Buddhist priests in the streets of Saigon in protest against the escalating Vietnam War. Then, on the twentieth, he began an autobiographical sketch that he called, "Toward 48." Something, he wrote, had happened once that had forever after changed him: the death of his father by suicide. And yet his father did not seem to him to be the "suicidal type." Why *did* one kill oneself? he wondered. Who knew, really, "whether the reason he gives himself in the final instant is the same one he wrote down?" He let the piece go to continue with the Songs.

When an unexpected check showed up in the mail from Brown at the end of the month, Berryman did his "Super-Extra-Dough dance," then wrote another fragment:

> Praise we then, barefoot, after no dear thought,
> days when one thousand extra bucks arrives
> already earned, known about
> by any counting boob but Henry
> who just is was to plunge down debt again
> like his earlier lives . . . .

A few days later he wrote Boyd to thank him for the lovely flashlight he'd sent so that he could grope his way to the privy at night. His mother had come up from Washington to spend the week of her sixty-ninth birthday with them, and her presence had once more kept him from sleeping or getting anything done. "Throw me more, please, 50 mg Sparine," he begged Boyd. He did not enjoy gorging on drugs, but he was going crazy watching his mother's interaction with his daughter. He and Kate took Jill to Boston to see the Chinese collection at the Fine Arts Museum and then got her on a bus headed back to Washington. Only then was he able to get back to his Songs. "His mother goes," he wrote, in what would become Dream Song 11:

> The mother comes & goes.
> Chen Lung's too came, came & crampt & then
> that dragoner's mother was gone.
> It seem we don't have no good bed to lie on,
> forever . . . .

On July 15, he wrote Giroux as to exactly how many Songs he should give him. Whether he gave him 75 or 130, it would take a tremendous amount of energy to get the manuscript to him, since Berryman was still having "enormous" problems with the order of the Songs. On the other hand, he knew there were legitimate pressures to publish a group of them now. Maybe, he suggested, "the thing to do [was] stop exacerbating, pretend to satisfy myself on some sort of Ms. (not the Poem of course), send it to you, and come to NY for a chat." Giroux had mentioned Donald Hall's recent Penguin paperback of *Contemporary American Poetry*, which had begun with 1914 and had included William Stafford and then Lowell, but not Berryman. It had even included, among the younger poets, three of Berryman's former students—Merwin, Justice, and Snodgrass—and another, James Dickey, whom Berryman thought of as "a sort of disciple." With the younger poets making their little ripples, he added, maybe it was time for him to come out and make his great big splash.

On the thirty-first he sent Rago at *Poetry* some Songs, adding that he'd just learned of the suicide of a young American poet named Sylvia Plath in London five months earlier. Berryman asked Rago if he could get the American rights to her final poems as well as find a biographical piece on her to reprint in this country. Those poems, he added with admiration, were "rare." "Your face broods from my table, Suicide," he had written two days before, in what would become Song 172. He could understand Plath's wanting to leave it all behind. What he found hard to accept, however, was her abandoning her children:

> I brood upon your face, the geography of grief,
> hooded, till I allow
> again your resignation from us now
> though the screams of orphaned children fix me anew.
> Your torment here was brief,
>
> long falls your exit all repeatingly,
> a poor exemplum, one more suicide
> to stack upon the others
> till stricken Henry with his sisters & brothers
> suddenly gone pauses to wonder why he
> alone breasts the wronging tide.

But worse was to come. On August 1, three thousand miles away from Chepachet, Theodore Roethke dived into a pool and swam toward the shallow end. Moments later several women sitting at the pool's edge saw him floating face down. They managed to pull him out, and one of the women tried mouth-to-mouth resuscitation. But Roethke was dead. Isolated as he was, Berryman did not learn of his death for four days. When he did, however, he was badly shaken. He had not known Plath, but Roethke was his contemporary, part of his special company. Three days later he composed his powerful elegy (DS 18):

> Westward, hit a low note, for a roarer lost
> across the Sound but north from Bremerton,
> hit a way down note.
> And never cadenza again of flowers, or cost.
> Him who could really do that cleared his throat
> & staggered on.

He sent it to the editor of the *Times Literary Supplement* with the wish that a copy might somehow be sent to Dylan Thomas, "our crony-potman," who had unfortunately left no forwarding address. Roethke's death had brought it all back.

In mid-August Berryman had a note from Ross, telling him to listen to Kate and stop writing his Songs for a while and get the book out. He wanted Berryman to know he was loved and missed at the university and that he had just been awarded an eleven-hundred-dollar increase in salary, by "far the largest increase of anyone in the Humanities Program." Berryman also learned that he and Hayden Carruth would share the prize for the Chicago poetry contest (though Berryman's poem was not published). But by then Berryman had come to despise the poem and would "have gone into hermitage on Athos with embarrassment" had he taken the prize alone. In any event, he thought Lucien Stryk's poem far better than either his or Carruth's.

On the twenty-third he mailed Giroux sixty Songs. It was "not the poem, of course. But a heavy proportion of what so far is best in it. I don't count on collecting any fame from these sixty pages but I shn't be surprised if some of them proved more or less immortal." He was not yet sure of the exact number he would publish by way of trial run, but a hundred he thought too many. He had decided against notes; better to let the reader supply his own. On September 4, he increased the sixty to seventy-two, and then a few days later, to seventy-five.

For their second wedding anniversary Kate drove Berryman to the Cape to see some of his old friends and attend a party. It had been twelve years since he'd visited the place, and that had been with another wife. In mid-September he heard from Lowell, who had learned from Meredith about Berryman's "fine" elegy for Roethke and wondered if he could have it for *The New York Review of Books*. He'd also heard that Berryman was thinking of going to Dublin later that fall and wondered if they might not get together at least once before Berryman set sail.

On September 20, Giroux wrote Berryman that the Dream Songs were "terrific." He wanted to publish them all—the first volume, and then the whole book—and a check for five hundred dollars was on its way. Four days later he wrote again that they were already looking for the typeface. Meanwhile Berryman continued to tinker with the manuscript. The day before, he wrote back, he had put "the Japanese one (The taxi) [73] through major repairs," so that there were now seventy-six Songs. He was sending along "the front matter": the dedication—"To Kate, and to Saul"—and the four epigraphs (from the Book of Lamentations, Carl Wittke's *Tambo and Bones,* and another from Olive Schreiner's *Dreams*). He was giving a reading from them on October 31 at the Guggenheim, where Lowell would be on the same bill, and hoped to talk with Giroux then.

Bellow wrote Berryman, pleased to have the book dedicated to him. Then Wilbur wrote saying how much he liked the Songs. "From a writer as conservative & elegant as Wilbur this is a little tribute," he told Giroux on October 7, "and I like it because I pretend to be conservative & elegant myself." He was considering calling the seventy-six poems "The Lay of Henry," though "the sexual implications" of that would have to be "sternly . . . put down." Giroux wrote back at once, pleading with Berryman to let the title be.

On the ninth the Berrymans drove to Boston, where Berryman read his Dream Songs for fifty dollars. At one in the morning, unable to sleep, he wrote Song 225, focusing on the missile crisis and the U.S. missile installations in Scotland and the question of who had provoked whom first in the cold war. So too with the problem of who had said what first in poetry, as if that could be recovered now. *"Pereant qui ante nos nostra dixerunt,"* he called it, considering his poetic antecedents: "Let them perish who used our words before us."

A week later he wrote Meredith that he'd been ill "practically every day for weeks" and was very tired. His reading in Boston had gone all right, but something was gravely wrong: "My thought drags, is uncertain, and inventionless (though I've written some new Songs), and I can't make prose." As a result he was "badly behind" with several "prose jobs" he'd promised various editors. He'd even had to give up his Dublin plans because he was broke again. In fact, by then he'd given up almost everything but the writing of his Songs, and those only because his head would suddenly fill "once twice thrice" and he would be reaching for a pencil. With cold weather setting in, he'd soon have to give up his little retreat and head for New York. They had a puppy now as well, "half-beagle, toward whom the baby is very brave." He asked Meredith if he could go over the seventy-six Dream Songs and tell him "every damned thing" he didn't like about them. Meredith consented.

At the end of October the Berrymans moved to the Chelsea Hotel, by which time Berryman was drinking almost constantly. He read with Lowell that Halloween and made several trips to Princeton, hoping in some vague way to find living accommodations there and get back to serious work on Shakespeare. But too much had changed, and Blackmur raged at him, telling him to go stay with "those rich friends of his," the Mackies. New York too had changed in the eight years since Berryman had spent any appreciable time there, and this new sense of isolation did not make matters easier. So much for the East he'd been so anxious to get back to.

When President Kennedy was assassinated in Dallas on November 22, Berryman rented a television and sat stunned and mesmerized before it for the next four days, horrified by what he was witnessing: the telescopic rifle found on the sixth floor of the Depository, news of Patrolman Tippit's death, Oswald's murder. "Scuppered the yachts, the choppers, big cars, jets," he wrote in his "Formal Elegy" for the fallen president three years his junior. He knew as well as anyone Kennedy's failings, especially the Bay of Pigs fiasco. He even wondered if he would have voted for him in 1964. But he was numbed to learn that schoolgirls in Dallas had actually cheered when they'd heard that their president had been struck down.

In mid-December the Berrymans drove to Washington to the two-story apartment Jill had found for them and herself at 103 Second Street, N.E. When they got there, she was waiting for them with a pitcher of martinis. The Berrymans would have the upstairs apartment, and Jill would take the downstairs. Forgetting what his mother's obtrusive presence could do to him, Berryman believed that things might actually work out between them all. Jill would help with the baby and prepare meals, and he would work at the Folger and get on with his Shakespeare. But all he found over the next few months were the local bars. Never once did he make it to the Folger.

Still, he managed a few good Songs. On December 19 he composed what turned out to be the last poem he would include in the *77 Dream Songs*. It was called "The Elder Presences" (DS 72). He wrote it from the perspective of the little park opposite the Supreme Court, where he could swing his daughter from a rope while he saw "the high statues of the wise" lining the court building. Christmas Day he returned to the scene. His wife's candle, he noted in what would become Dream Song 200, was "out/ for John F. Kennedy." So no one, neither he nor the nation, had escaped that fall, in spite of the tiny splendor of Christmas. Once again a leader had been murdered. Well, wasn't that what the Christmas tree inevitably led to: that other tree on which had hung a fallen hero? A flash of tinsel, Berryman sighed as another year burned out, "by the terrible tree/ whereon he really hung, for you & me."

# chapter 26

# Henry's Success Story

## 1964–66

On January 11, Berryman got back the corrected manuscript of *77 Dream Songs*. Still dissatisfied, he reworked thirty-nine of the poems, then called Giroux to apologize for so many last-minute corrections. The problem, he explained, was that too many of the Songs had lacked sufficient form in their new setting. By the fifteenth, still sorting and revising, he reached the bottom of his manuscript bag. He felt "brain-worn" with work. What helped pick him up was the news that he'd just received a four-thousand-dollar grant from the Ingram Merrill Foundation to write his Songs and work on his biography of Shakespeare.

A month later he had proofs for the poems. These too he corrected and sent back. "I do feel no confidence that the stuff is any good," he told Giroux, even as he planned this time to take all the prizes. He wanted an "utterly plain" book binding, "blue-black if possible," and was prepared to send along some of his own skin for that purpose. Late in February he ran into Stephen Spender, who took three of the Songs for *Encounter*. A few days later, Berryman received corrected proofs, and these too he went through immediately, checking in a final time with Giroux. The book was finished.

On March 3 he learned that he'd won another prize: the Russell Loines Award of one thousand dollars from the National Institute of Arts and Letters. The prize would be formally awarded in New York on May 20, with Lowell as presenter. With *77 Dream Songs* arranged in three books, he now began a fourth book: an "Opus Posthumous" sequence that would hinge the first three and the last three books of his poem together.

A few days later he left Washington for a reading tour through California. But by then he was in terrible shape, down with bronchitis and an ear infection and hallucinating from too much alcohol, and on the flight out he suffered a burst right eardrum. He telephoned Boyd to get him back into Abbott just as soon as he was done with his readings. But on March 16 he collapsed and had to be rushed by ambulance to Riverside Community Hospital, where he was diagnosed as suffering from "influenzal syndrome, complicated by acute infection of the left ear and chronic exhaustion." But this was *not* the hospital Berryman was interested in staying at, even with the care of Miss Cienfuegos, whom he'd met on his tour and whom Song 188 would remember—

> Convulsed with love, who cares? There is that hair
> unbuttoned. Loves unbutton loves, we're bare,
> somewhere in my mind.
> When this occurs I begin to think in Spanish
> when Miss Cienfuegos, who looked after me
> & after me in Pasadena.

After three days at Riverside Community, he promised the doctor there to return home immediately "for further hospitalization and treatment" and was discharged. Back in Washington he stayed in bed, waiting for Boyd to find him a hospital room at Abbott while he nursed himself on whiskey. He heard from Faber & Faber, offering to bring out the *77 Dream Songs* in England, but he held off answering as his health deteriorated. On March 27, his left eardrum ruptured. He solaced himself by working on his "Opus Posthumous" sequence in which Henry had finally been allowed to die.

A week later he flew out to Minneapolis and was admitted to Abbott for rest and recuperation. There he was kept sedated and isolated. But after four days, when an advance copy of *77 Dream Songs* reached him, he felt the need to celebrate. With "Boyd's express permission," he left the hospital and went shopping at Dayton's, stopping at the Brass Rail on the way back for four martinis. The spree and the drinks had left him with "an electrical sense of liberty, restoration, normality," he wrote Kate.

The Siegelmans sent him roses and the Tates a pot of tulips, and this event too became the basis for another Dream Song, one that would eventually be placed at the start of Book V, his first post-"Opus Posthumous" Song, with Henry at last restored to life:

> Tulips from Tates teazed Henry in the mood
> to be a tulip and desire no more
> but water, but light, but air.
> Yet his nerves rattled blackly, unsubdued,
> & suffocation called, dream-whiskey'd pour
> sirening . . . .

He spent his time jotting down ideas for organizing the rest of his poem. The new volume would contain an additional eighty-four Songs and would be titled *His Toy, His Dream, His Rest*. Thus there would be a symmetry to the whole: 77 plus 7 "Opus Posthumous" plus 77: 161 Songs arranged in seven books. Book IV would be Henry dead, and solemn. Book V would enact a "resurrection." Book VI would be a "reconciliation," like that between Achilles and Priam, desolate over the death of his son, a reconciliation "ironic & pathetic as well as happy." He still did not know how he would end the poem. But, he noted, if the Bradstreet had centered on the mother, *The Dream Songs* would center on the father.

"With 150 mg of Thorazine in me and after five hours' sleep," he wrote Giroux on April 17, he was reading light stuff for the moment: old newspapers, *Time* magazine, *Holiday*, and a few pages of *The Tin Drum*. Moreover, he was still writing Songs. He was taking extra dosages of Thorazine and leaving the hospital each day for a few drinks to help steady himself.

A trickle of letters congratulating him began arriving at the hospital. There was one from James Merrill and another from Dudley Fitts saying he'd been "dazzled" by the "wit, the resonance, the pity, the exuberance, the faultless, absolutely faultless ear." Berryman was overjoyed. "Your letter has almost broken my heart with pleasure," he wrote Fitts on April 20. In fact, it was "the most important letter from a stranger" he'd received since Aiken had written him about the Bradstreet. Kate wrote to tell him that Howard Nemerov had called to see how he was doing and that he too was enjoying the Songs. She missed her husband, missed their laughing together. "It's true that when you were sick here your sense of humor was about as good as a tiger's but I think it has come back," she wrote. On the twenty-third he wrote back. The day before he'd gone to the bank and to the university, got himself "quietly loaded alone at the Brass Rail," and then "slept brilliantly from six until ten, then again from four in the morning until eight. He was beginning to see that "maybe a toot every fortnight or so" was "a sound conception," as long as he kept out of trouble. He was even eager to get back to teaching again. He'd been over to his office and it "looked good, desirable." He'd even bought season tickets for them to the Guthrie Theater.

April twenty-third was also Shakespeare's four-hundredth birthday and Berryman celebrated by rereading *The Taming of the Shrew*. The official publication of *77 Dream Songs* was scheduled for the following Monday, and he began making plans to fly to New York for a party. But later that day he changed his mind. He wrote Giroux that if he stayed in Minneapolis, he planned to spend that evening with six of his closest friends. Instead, he celebrated in advance by going on a two-day drunk from which he woke in the hospital at one in the morning, still dressed, unable to remember where he'd been or what he'd done.

He tabulated the literary chores he had outstanding: a piece on himself for Voice of America, a piece on Stephen Crane, the introduction to Dreiser's *The Titan* for New American Library. He talked with Phil Siegelman about buying a house in Minneapolis. But after three weeks in the hospital, he was still so excitable he couldn't even watch television. Why did he drink so much? he asked himself in another Dream Song (96):

> That last was stunning,
> that flagon had breasts. Some men grow down cursed.

Why drink so, two days running?
two months, o seasons, years, two decades running?
I answer (smiles) my question on the cuff:
Man, I been thirsty.

He managed to convince Boyd that he was never going to get off booze unless he got more drugs, and Boyd put him back on the higher dosages. When Berryman wrote Kate that evening, he complained how "dead tired" he was after working forty-eight hours on two new Songs with only two hours' sleep. He had just heard from Denise Levertov that Adrienne Rich was reviewing his book for *The Nation*. He was relieved, he told Kate, for Rich was someone he'd "admired for ten years or seven at least and never met or written about," the "best of the women younger than Miss Bishop." He knew too that Lowell was reviewing the book, though why he wanted to, Berryman still couldn't figure out. What made him particularly nervous was not having yet heard as much as a whisper from Lowell about *77 Dream Songs*.

On publication day, April 27, Berryman lay in bed, his brain still "boiling" with Songs. In the afternoon he received unwelcome reviews from Tate and Van Doren in letters and from Lowell in *The New York Review of Books*. He was especially disappointed with Lowell. "One would need to see the unpublished parts to decide how well it fills out as a whole," Lowell had written. "As it stands, the main faults of this selection are the threat of mannerism, and worse, disintegration. How often one chafes at the relentless indulgence, and cannot tell the what or why of a passage."

Berryman stayed awake all that night going through his book, convinced Lowell was wrong. Even Giroux, he consoled himself, had called Lowell's review stupid. He tried to take the edge off his bitterness by treating himself to a new suit and counting stars with his Japanese binoculars. Kate wrote to say that she and the baby were both ill with colds. She would be happy to get back to Minneapolis and—she hoped—into a house of their own. She commiserated with him over Cal's betrayal, but she was also upset that her husband seemed in no hurry to get back to Washington.

Worse, the longer he stayed at Abbott, the more paranoid Berryman became. On the thirtieth, standing in the elevator, he asked a police officer why there seemed to be so many police around the hospital. The officer turned and stared at him. Enraged at having been fixed "insect-like" by a man armed with a gun, Berryman returned to his room to write Dream Song 95, damning the guard to hell:

> A meathead, and of course he was armed, to creep
> across my nervous system some time ago wrecked.
> I saw the point of Loeb
> at last, to give oneself over to crime wholly,
> baffle, torment, roar laughter, or without sound
> attend while he is cooked
>
> until with trembling hands hoist I my true
> & legal ax, to get at the brains. I never liked brains—
> it's the texture & the thought—
> but I will like them now, spooning at you,
> my guardian, slowly, until at length the rains
> lose heart and the sun flames out.

"DO NOT CALL ME, damn it," he ordered Kate three days later. "I am sick, I am to be left alone." Even "five minutes' anger" was enough to set him back. In answer to her question as to how he felt, he told her he'd just written another Song in which Henry was "a parachute that does not open." Finally, on May 8, still unsteady, he paid his hospital bill and was taken by Lynn Louden to the airport for the trip back to Washington.

A few nights earlier James Wright had stopped by the hospital to tell Berryman how much he admired the songs and, not finding him, had left a note. The book, he wrote, was "almost blood-curdling" and "truly magnificent." Back in Washington, Berryman heard from James Dickey. The Songs "ought to make all tiny poets like myself run and hide," Dickey wrote him, for Berryman had written "the best poetry book" he'd seen in ten years and Berryman himself was "the best living poet in English." Then he heard from Merrill again, calling the Songs "the most valuable poetry written in years, in any language." Even the best of Berryman's contemporaries seemed safe by comparison.

An advance copy of Adrienne Rich's glowing review reached

a groggy Berryman and left him feeling overjoyed. What struck him was the gap between the glowing private letters he'd received and the cooler—except for Rich's—public reception of the Songs. Exasperated by the fundamental lack of comprehension he found in the reviews, he decided to provide a "Note to the Second Ed[ition]" of the 77. The poem, he explained, was "about an imaginary person named Henry, and all but entirely about him, as Miss Rich's brilliant review in *The Nation* fully understands." Other voices were "signallized by initial dashes, as in Continental fiction." There was, besides Henry, also Henry's friend, who called him Mr. Bones. And, while several "editors and readers urged the printing of notes on the Songs," although he knew where to start them (with the first line of the first poem), he was not sure where such notes would end.

He wrote Rich to thank her for what she had written, especially "for such insight, sensitivity & generosity that you make me wonder." It was, in fact, "the most remarkable American verse-review . . . since Jarrell's study of *Lord Weary's Castle*." "From under the cloak of the dreamer," Rich had written, "the poems take their often surrealistic quality, apparently rambling, recollective . . . [where] scraps of memory and nightmare shoulder for room. But it is the identity of Henry, inseparable from his several tongues, which holds the book together, makes it clearly a real book and not a collection of chance pieces loosely flung under one cover," so that Henry was enlarged "from poem to poem." Berryman had written a courageous book, an original by its own "inner necessity and by the force of a unique human character." Long ago this poet, writing of the loss of Bhain Campbell, had written, "Nouns, verbs do not exist for what I feel." Now, Rich understood, Berryman had brought those words into existence.

In spite of its being Lowell who would present the Russell Loines Award, Berryman decided to fly to New York to attend the ceremony. Ralph Ellison and Ben Shahn were there, as were Sir Kenneth Clark, John Updike, Truman Capote, James Baldwin, Bernard Malamud, and Edward Hoagland. Berryman invited Ann and Paul, as well as Bill Meredith and Giroux. The following day he took Kate to Flushing Meadows to see the World's Fair. Then it was back to Washington. Through mid-May into early June, new Songs kept coming. His reading of *The Tin Drum* led to number 270, fantasies of fame to number

190: "The doomed young envy the old, the doomed old the dead young." He even managed a Song (DS 120) on Lowell and his other enemies the day after the academy affair.

He bought a car so Kate could make the trip to Minneapolis with the baby. Once there, she found an apartment at 3209 Lyndale Avenue South, while Berryman, prostrate, lingered in the Washington heat. The Dream Songs shrank to a trickle, then stopped entirely. That June he wrote for Howard Nemerov a "slight exploration" of his development as a poet that appeared the following year in *Shenandoah* under the heading, "One Answer to a Question." It was "the statement of a man nearing fifty," he began, a man "less impressed than I used to be by the universal notion of a continuity of individual personality." He analyzed some of his early work—"Winter Landscape," "The Ball Poem," the Bradstreet, and two Dream Songs: numbers 1 and 29. As for the diction of Dream Song 29, whether or not it was "consistent with blackface talk, hell-spinning puns," and "coarse jokes," and whether the end of the poem was "funny or frightening, or both," he left for the reader to decide.

By August 13, he was back in Abbott for another two-week stay. On the twenty-third he wrote Ann. Young Paul had looked well when he'd seen him in New York and had "behaved brilliantly, neither forward nor shy." But it had been a "great mistake" to attend the ceremony. He had gone, really, because in the past thirteen years the academy had come to his aid on three occasions. He was supposed to have taught that summer, but had had to turn his first summer-session classes over to Lynn Louden and his second-session classes over to someone else. The upshot of all this was that he had no money to give Ann.

Slowly his health began to improve and he found himself walking up and down the five flights of hospital stairs. It was the first time he'd been able to do anything like that since breaking his ankle. In mid-October he moved his family into a turn-of-the-century two-story house at 33 Arthur Avenue, Southeast, in the established Prospect Park section of the city. Monthly payments came to $130, about, he figured, what an apartment would have cost, and for that price he had a roomy study where he could at last put his library. Unpacking and teaching kept him so busy he did not get to his typewriter until the end of the month, but when he did, his poem roused to greet him once again.

Besides his own courses, he gave lectures for Ralph Ross and James Wright, both of whom were in the hospital, and Wright never forgot Berryman's suddenly appearing by his hospital bed, this "shockingly great artist . . . asking me if he could help me. As long as I live on this earth, I will never forget his request. I answered: 'Will you please take care of my students while I'm ill?' And he did." Berryman helped him out again a few months later, when Wright taught an intensive interim course at Macalester College in St. Paul on The Comic Spirit. Richard Furze, who took that course, would remember Wright and Berryman at the back of the room, laughing uproariously as they showed old films of Charlie Chaplin. Wright, himself an alcoholic, his thick hands shaking, chain-smoked throughout the long afternoon, pacing the class while Berryman sat up front and lectured.

That fall Berryman learned of Oscar Williams's death, "one of my oldest literary friends," and then, soon after, of Morgan Blum's, and he was called upon to be one of the speakers at the memorial service held for Blum that October. His friend had died, he said, "unfulfilled—like most of the rest of us—as a poet, critic, & teacher." He remembered with affection Blum's lecturing on *War and Peace* and the long review of his *Stephen Crane,* which turned out to be "the most intelligent American notice that book received." But mostly he remembered the drive north in the summer of 1955, when Blum had been "at his happiest & best," "on the way to Apple River for a picnic at the falls" and Berryman had just "invented the title of the long poem already underway." Blum had "followed with generous interest the murderous course" of those Songs until sickness and death had intervened.

Death. What was most real, he asked in Song 195: history's bitter message of death, or the promise of the resurrection, "the growing again of the right arm/ (which so we missed in our misleading days)/ & the popping back in of eyes"? He wondered too about his students. Did they really *know* what effect literature could have on someone? Did they even begin to understand the real frenzy of something like the *Bacchae,* as he stood in front of them and lectured on it to them?

I think the elder statesman stance will do.
I will wear my bearded difference with rue
before the damned young things
flashy for knowledge of they dream not what
until I drop the Bacchae in its slot:
take that! and that!

He flew with Kate to Chicago on November 11 to read at the Annual Poetry Day benefit. "I'm tugging with Ted's ghost," he wrote that day, "wrestling in a pal's way/ with Cal's self, for prizes which never mind." He gave a press conference, and the following evening he and the others read from their works in Orchestra Hall before an audience of two thousand.

Despite the sodden end to the year, the new one began auspiciously enough. Early in January 1965, Berryman learned that he and Nemerov were among thirteen members added to the roll of the National Institute of Arts & Letters. In the Minnesota winter he wrote out of his drinking, isolation, and pain, his chest racked with bronchitis. Eliot died that month, a loss that distressed him greatly, and then Blackmur on February 2. So distant had he and Blackmur grown in fifteen years that Berryman did not learn of his death until the nineteenth, when he composed an elegy (DS 173) for this "older friend of three" who had now "blackt out" on him. Was it possible that the mouth of this magnificent speaker could be stilled forever?

Richard is quiet who talked on so well:
I fill with fear. . . .
I blow on the live coal. I would be one,
another one.
Surely the galaxy will scratch my itch
Augustinian, like the night-wind witch
and I will love that touch.

The following day he called Ed Cone in Princeton. "Toner!" he cried into the receiver. "Richard died and I didn't know it!" Then he read him the elegy he'd just written and apologized for not keeping up with his end of a correspondence. "But now all that will change," he promised. It was, however, the last time Cone ever heard from him.

In late March, Berryman began a Song about Henry's complicity in the evils of the world. Had he had more power, he realized, Henry would have been even badder than he was. As it was, he had added a sufficient measure of hurt to the world's store:

> Tottered thro' his remorse many Bigger Ones—
> the maximum leader, the Secretary, Mao,
> Il Duce, El Caudillo
> Soon full backing
> helped out his hoores & coccyx. His beard hurled
> one deal across the world. . . .

In the April 15 issue of the *Times Literary Supplement,* a favorable review of *77 Dream Songs* by A. Alvarez appeared. "John Berryman's virtuosity is the product of twenty-five years of inventing a highly distinctive idiom," Alvarez wrote, discussing the interlocking of themes in the book and the limitations of any modern antihero such as Henry. As much as the review pleased Berryman, it paled compared to what he felt when he heard in early May that he'd finally won the Pulitzer.

Invitations and congratulations poured in. "We had reporters & photographers in & out of the house like flies," he wrote Giroux ten weeks later. "There was a vast picture of Kate & me on the front page of the main [Minneapolis] paper," and *Time* magazine had even commissioned a story, for which he had given an interview and been photographed. Even *Time,* he added, had to be "getting uneasy that they have never reviewed any of my five American books of verse." So many letters! "The articles! the wires! the phone calls!" Real fame, he added, "must be intolerable."

But by early July the drinking had again taken its toll, and he was readmitted to Abbott for "exhaustion." From there on the sixth he wrote a short note to his mother, wishing her a happy seventy-first birthday. It was, he told her, the first "letter" he'd written *anyone* since he'd written his son for Christmas. The drug dosages once again proved "inadequate," and Boyd had to double them. His spirit completely exhausted by the struggle with alcoholic withdrawal this time, Berryman lived on Sanka and longed for nothingness. So regular had his hospital stays become by now that no one came to visit him anymore. Instead, he passed the time writing Songs and sent three of them to *The Atlantic Monthly,* one of the few magazines that had yet to succumb to Henry's charms. He was careful to add a note that the three were to be published as a unit, though he had "no reason to suppose" *The Atlantic* would like them any better than the earlier Songs he'd sent them.

His fierce pride was wounded when *The Atlantic* sent him a routine rejection slip. So the Pulitzer, after all, didn't matter "a straw," he grumbled to Giroux. Of course it mattered, Giroux reassured him. Just fourteen months after publication, the 77 were already in their third printing. In fact, they had actually outsold Lowell's *For the Union Dead* the week before by a single copy. No news could have sounded sweeter to Berryman's ears. The night of his discharge from the hospital he wrote another Song (DS 223) about the poems themselves, which had by then taken precedence over everyone and everything. What were the Songs after all, he wrote, but "mysteries" he kept "rehearsing in the dark" to trouble "brighter minds" when he was gone.

While he taught in the sweltering heat of Minneapolis that summer he dreamed of visiting lost places—Campidoglio, Bhubaneswar, the Andes—and drank ounce after ounce of Ouzo. He listened to the reports coming out of Vietnam, as "bombs bombed on empty territory beneath." When he finished teaching, he went back into Abbott for another two weeks to recover. A week after being discharged, however, he was in again. "I've been in & out of hospital so often lately I'm dizzy," he wrote Meredith in mid-September. Because of his poor condition, he had arranged to teach only one course that fall.

But worse was awaiting Berryman. On Thursday evening, October 14, walking to the Chapel Hill campus, Jarrell seemed to lunge into the side of an oncoming car and was killed. He was fifty-one, and had already slashed his wrists during a breakdown earlier in the year. "One of Henry's oldest friends was killed," Berryman wrote that Sunday in another Song:

> it came on a friend' radio, this week,
> whereat Henry wept. . . .
> every little while

you can count with stirring love on a new loss
& an emptier place.

"Randall's death hurt me," he wrote Meredith the following day. "Shock and sorrow to Mackey, please." Finally, on the 30th, he wrote Mary Jarrell, "stunned" by her husband's death. He had learned that state troopers at the scene had called the death a suicide, but could not believe it. "He was just not the man to kill himself," he told her. But on All Souls Eve he wrote another Song for Jarrell, calling his death, in spite of what he'd told Mary, a "suicide,"

which dangles a trail
longer than Henry's chill, longer than his loss
and longer than the letter that he wrote
that day to the widow. . . .
My air is flung with souls which will not stop
and among them hangs a soul that has not died
and refuses to come home.

The following day, walking in his socks, he slid on the wooden floor of his home and broke his left arm. "When will you make do like the moon/ cold on a placid sea," he wrote that Thanksgiving, "with three limbs" taking along the other limb "for a cruise,/ like an elderly lover not expecting much."

In December he flew east to read at Bennington on the third and then at Columbia on the sixth. He wrote another Song (DS 168) in which he compared himself once more to Hamlet, obliquely accusing his mother for his father's death, then wrote another (DS 169) in which he noted how he was kept busy packing his suitcase with "books drugs razors whiskey shirts" to give five-hundred-dollar readings that went to help pay for the insane war raging in Vietnam.

At one in the morning on January 8, 1966, he called Tate to tell him, through a drunken blur, that Lionel Trilling had called him—John Berryman—a great poet indeed. Tate answered shortly, then hung up, but the following morning he wrote Berryman, telling him that, while he regretted his brusque tone, he did *not* like being told what a great poet Berryman was, especially by Berryman himself. And while he was at it, he wanted Berryman to know that his "lack of consideration for other people" had become "scandalously notorious." Last spring, he reminded him, when Robert Fitzgerald had been at the Tates', Berryman had rushed in and monopolized Fitzgerald. Such conduct in public places was not "an organic necessity of genius," Tate reminded him. Berryman did not answer Tate's letter for eleven weeks. It felt too much like Blackmur's earlier dismissal of him.

Although he had the winter term off to work on his *Songs,* Berryman applied for another Guggenheim, which he hoped to spend abroad "for a change and cheapness" to finish them. He wrote a belated Christmas Song celebrating his own virgin birth, then another early on the morning of January 13, sitting "in the dawn, if it can be called dawn/ of mid-winter in Minnesota, scribbling." In yet another he caught the Minnesota cold as it began to smother him: "Sixteen below. Our cars like stranded hulls." In late February he read at Harvard, and then, on the twenty-eighth, at Yale, in honor of Jarrell. Besides himself, Eberhart, John Hollander, Stanley Kunitz, Peter Taylor, Robert Penn Warren, Wilbur, Meredith, Rich, and Lowell were also there. Though he was again drinking heavily, Berryman managed to read a splendid short prose memoir and some of the Dream Songs he'd written for Jarrell. He ended with an anecdote about Jarrell up at dawn changing wickets in order to beat some children at a game of croquet. Randall was not someone, he closed, "who liked to lose at all."

After Yale Berryman flew on to the University of Rochester for another reading. Bruce Berlind, Poet-in-Residence there, was shocked at how awful he looked. He had gone to meet Berryman at the airport, and when no Berryman disembarked, wondered if he'd missed his plane. Finally, he saw "a doddering trembling old man with a cane" hobble down the ramp. As Berlind greeted him, Berryman squinted at him, demanding, "And who are *you*?" When Berlind told him, Berryman snapped, "You've gotten old, Bruce, and you've gotten fat."

When he got back to Minneapolis at the end of the first week in March, having again failed to circumvent the airport bars, Berryman went back to Abbott. A week later, home again, there was a letter waiting for him from Rich. She'd loved the new Songs he'd read at Yale; there was about his poetry "a shock-relief quality" that nobody else possessed. But she hoped he would get the hospital care he needed. A few days later, another concerned letter arrived, this one from Lowell. "This is really just to say that I love you, and wonder at you, and want you to take care," he wrote. Berryman's reminiscences of Randall had been "the height of the evening," and what he'd achieved in his Songs was a "freedom for us too, if we had the nerve." Berryman had at last proved that he was now the "boldest and most brilliant spokesman for our common profession." "If anything happened to you," Lowell ended, "I'd feel the heart of the scene had gone."

In mid-March, Berryman was awarded his second Guggenheim. Now he could take Kate and his little Twiss and go off to Dublin at the end of August. "Do you know anybody in Dublin?" he wrote Henry Rago on March 21. "I am thinking of spending next year there but don't know a soul." The people he knew were either "all dead like [Dennis] Devlin or departed like Brian Boydell." Rago wrote back suggesting he get in touch with either Thomas Kinsella or John Montague. When Berryman wrote Montague, he asked if he was the same man he'd known at Iowa in '54. Montague wrote back from Paris saying that indeed he was. He would be back in Dublin at the beginning of 1967 and would see Berryman then. He thought Berryman's "best bet" would be to take rooms at "a slightly dotty place called The Majestic on Fitzwilliam Street." From there he "could case the possibilities through the good house agencies." He also suggested Berryman get in touch with Liam Miller of *The Dolmen Press*. Brian Boydell, from Berryman's Cambridge days, still lived in Dublin, out near Howth.

At the beginning of April, Berryman wrote Tate. "I hope you have forgiven that phone call," he apologized. "Infernal alcohol: I have been off it, more or less, for some months, and very gradually, under a heavy drug regime, am feeling better. Your angry letter was a bitter pill to swallow but I swallowed it and I daresay am the better therefor." He'd lost enough friends through one means or another and could not afford to lose Tate as well. But by the time he flew out to give a reading at the University of Wisconsin later that month, he was fully drunk once more. Daniel Hughes was there and, despite his affection for Berryman, knew the reading was a disaster.

At the end of June, Berryman "tossed a farewell party for

his pals,'' the Rosses and the Siegelmans, who were leaving Minnesota to take teaching positions in California. Minneapolis would never be the same, he knew. Heartsore, he wrote three Farewell Songs over that weekend for them, ''leaving Henryville bereft, carnivals-/ cum-intellect closed down now, off in pairs' as they flew away ''to lead fresh lives.'' Well, they would miss him too when he was in Dublin making ''shanty-talk.'' He could try to be brave about it, but in truth he was heartsore and afraid.

He tallied his chases after women, found them fewer, more talk than action. Mostly he admired his Muses via the mails, as with Amy Vladeck and Valerie Trueblood. He studied his Song bag again and found he now had 259 Songs from which to make his final selections. He did not look forward to teaching two courses each day during the second summer session. He wrote his mother for her birthday and enclosed a check. Vietnam—Johnson's War, he called it—was also on his mind that summer. The conflict, he wrote, now resembled ''The Hunting of the Snark'' as the war bogged down with no end in sight, and where even the shape of the negotiations table had become a little war of their own. He wrote his frustrations about it out in a Song:

> a war which was no war,
> the enemy was not our enemy
> but theirs whoever they are
> and the treaty-end that might conclude it more
> unimaginable than *Alice's* third volume—eee—
> and somehow our policy bare
>
> in eighteen costumes kept us unaware
> that we were killing Asiatics, daily. . . .

Then, on July 14, *The New York Times* ran a belated obituary for Delmore Schwartz. Alone in the predawn hours of the eleventh, dressed in bathrobe and pajamas, Schwartz had left his shabby apartment at the Columbia Hotel on Forty-sixth and Sixth to put the garbage out, wandered onto another floor, and suddenly felt a pain in his chest. He may have tried to cry out for help, before he slid to the floor, strangling for air in the oily dark that engulfed him. Now Berryman's grief poured out in a series of fourteen Dream Songs, a "solid block of agony" that consumed him over the following weeks. "I can't get him out of mind," he wrote in one. What terrible changes he had seen in Delmore since the time when, a young man filled with "surplus love," he had thrilled Berryman and so many others with his "electrical insights."

But even as he wrote his elegies for Delmore, Berryman considered publishing his old sonnet sequence at last. On August 11, he called Meredith, asking if he would read through the poems and advise him whether or not to publish them. If he liked them, he was to pass them on to Giroux. So, that August, in addition to teaching and his other tasks, Berryman arranged his sonnets and added several new ones as he reworked the ending of the sequence. He also went through the manuscript changing the names of persons and places, especially "Chris" to "Lise."

When classes ended on the eighteenth, he was interviewed by several young men, "armed with taperecorders [and] cameras," while his two telephones rang constantly. But already his mind was on the delicious fogs of Ireland. Exhausted by his creative outburst, he tried to rest. On Sunday morning, August 21, with five days to go before sailing, he composed Song 256:

> Henry rested, possessed of many pills
> & gin & whiskey. He put up his feet
> & switched on Schubert.
> His tranquillity lasted five minutes
> for (1) all that undone all the heavy weeks
> and (2) images shook him alert.
>
> A rainy Sunday morning, on vacation
> as well as Fellowship, he could not rest:
> bitterly he shook his head.

He took care of the business end of things, making the necessary arrangements and preparing his manuscripts for his year away, while Kate took care of packing for the three of them. There were the usual tensions, exacerbated by his compulsions, and at one point he became so angry with her that he stopped talking to her. Who was *she,* he demanded, to argue with *him*:

> When I trained my wives, I thought
> now they'll be professional:
> They became professional, at once wedlocks went sour
> because they couldn't compete with Henry, who sought
> their realizations. . . .

Moved to it by a student's handing in a late paper on one of Jarrell's poems, Berryman realized with numbing finality that Randall would never write a single word again. "Does then our rivalry extend beyond/ your death?" he asked, "our lovely friendly rivalry/ over a quarter-century?" Strong as was his desire for death, Berryman understood, it was not yet "strong enough," though he might be willing to be coaxed to Randall's side if the arguments could be made just a little stronger. Besides, what kind of God could let Randall die? Maybe God really was a slob,

> playful, vast, rough-hewn.
> Perhaps God resembles one of the last etchings of Goya . . .
> Something disturbed,
> ill-pleased, & with a touch of paranoia . . .
> Perhaps God ought to be curbed.

At two in the morning, listening to Schubert and Beethoven with the rest of the house asleep, he tried to figure out how these masters had managed to commit such intricate and compelling forms to paper when he was having such difficulty managing a form for his epic. "You go by the rules," he sighed, but at the depth where forms like Schubert's and Beethoven's operated, rules no longer mattered. There was no one, after all, to tell him *how* to put his Songs together, or when, or even why.

# chapter 27

# Dublin's Shades

## 1966–67

At last Berryman was ready to leave "the country of the dead" behind and sail to Ireland. The house at 33 Arthur was rented at the last minute and, on August 26, he, Kate, and little Martha embarked on *The Carmania* from Montreal. The "war for bread" had a little ceased, he noted, and "the war for status" had "ceased/ forever." He would keep a journal of that fall in the only form he now felt comfortable with, his Dream Songs, and the last part of his epic would be a shining record of his return, after thirty years, to his beginnings as a poet, when he had yearned to become another Yeats. But this time he was returning more on an equal footing—like Achilles—to have it out with the "father."

But by his fifth day out at sea, he had become a familiar face at the bar. Figures of authority with "large heads & gold braid" brushed past as his mind went back to that earlier time with Pedro Donga when all the world still lay before him and he had stayed up all night, too "in love with life" to sleep. But what he saw staring at him now from the mirror behind the ship's bar was wreckage. The following afternoon he found his

Lady of the Northern Sea, "Parisienne, bi-lingual, teaches English, at 27 unmarried," her name Yvette. She was even more beautiful than his own Kate, and he planned to say more about this and his other Muses in the months and Songs to follow.

After a mild crossing, the Berrymans disembarked on September 1 at Cobh, where they were met by journalists and photographers. They took the five-hour train trip up to Dublin, arriving at the Majestic Hotel in midafternoon. By then they were exhausted, and Martha was ill with flu. One's first day in Dublin, Berryman sighed, was always one's worst. There were letters waiting for him from Valerie Trueblood, calling him the master of "grace & fear" for his *Dream Songs,* from Meredith, who wrote to say he liked the '47 sonnets, and from Van Doren, honored to have the second volume of Songs dedicated to him and to Delmore.

By his second day in Dublin, Berryman had already adapted to his surroundings. He listened while, with "barely credible kindness," his pub friends at the Majestic discussed how to find a place for the Berrymans to live. Yet what a difference between these people and the romantic heroes of the Easter Rising who had filled his imagination for so many years: "The O'Rahilly, Plunkett, Connolly, & Pearse," those "fatuous campaigners/ dewy with phantastic hope." On the sixth day the Berrymans found a small house at 55 Lansdowne Park in Ballsbridge, very near the American Embassy, for $140 a month.

Ireland: so full of "the lovely good," he wrote in another Song (DS 313), a strange place surely, made by heaven and by "men,/ great men & weird," a place where ghosts moved "past/ in full daylight" and where the spirits of "holy saints" could make "the trees' tops shiver." His Muse flourished here, and by September 19, he'd written thirty to forty Songs since leaving America. Martha began nursery school in the neighborhood, but lasted there only two days. She had sobbed for her mommy and daddy and had had her bottom spanked for her efforts. Her parents would not tolerate that. For the present she would learn at home.

Shortly afterward, Berryman sent Maris Thomes a copy of his just-completed "Opus Posthumous" poems, the short Book IV, "in all of which Henry is extremely dead/but talkative." Maris had helped him out with his financial affairs when he had been defeated, and he praised her for running her daily life so well. "We get on," he sighed in a new Dream Song, "better than/ most husbands & wives." He also wrote Meredith, thanking him for reading the Sonnets and for the "noble letter" he'd sent Giroux at the end of August, advising Giroux to print them. He was also sending Meredith Book IV, most of which had been written three years ago, "just too late for *77,* but extensively reconsidered ever since." After Meredith was finished reading the new poems, he was to pass them on to Adrienne Rich. He planned now to go directly on to the final book, VII, and then shape Books V and VI, "to be constructed out of 300 unpublished." He also planned to "send the whole of IV to London *(TLS)* fr. whom I had a special invitation some months back, & see what happens." Within weeks he had a cable from Lowell. Meredith had shown him the "Opus Posthumous Songs" in New York and was stunned by what Berryman had achieved there. The poems, Lowell wrote, were "a tremendous & living triumph." He signed the cable, "Love." "An unexpected & triumphing cable/ when least he hoped for hope," a delighted Berryman wrote in another of his many Songs.

In late September an invitation arrived from President Johnson to have dinner at the White House. Unfortunately it had been sent by surface mail and the reception—in honor of General and Mrs. Ne Win of Burma—had taken place three weeks earlier. "Some boob in the White House saved 3 cents by failing to take in that I might be abroad," he complained to his mother, "& cd not have gone anyway." Dismayed, Berryman wrote the White House at once to explain that he had not boycotted the affair. True, he hated the war, but he also felt President Johnson was doing all he could with an impossible situation. A week later there was a letter signed by Lady Bird Johnson, apologizing for the mix-up.

In early October, Berryman had a surprise visit from his old fiancée, Jean Bennett Webster, and her new husband, Sidney Lanier, who ran the American Place Theater in New York. They were in Dublin for the opening of William Alfred's play *Hogan's Goat,* and, after telephoning, called at 55 Lansdowne to see the Berrymans. Berryman could not help feeling a twinge of envy when he saw the cut of Lanier's suit, though, he added, he would never trade his writing with its "moments of supreme joy" even for a suit like that.

Giroux wrote to say he was planning to publish the sonnets. There would be an advance of five hundred dollars on signing and another five hundred dollars on publication. "I knew a bit," Giroux hinted as to the story behind the poems, "but most I did not." These poems might reopen wounds, Berryman knew, but in his new introductory Song he had said all that could be said in defense of publishing them:

THE ORIGINAL FAULT
WILL NOT BE UNDONE BY FIRE.

THE ORIGINAL FAULT WAS WHETHER WICKEDNESS
WAS SOLUBLE IN ART. HISTORY SAYS IT IS,
JACQUES MARITAIN SAYS IT IS,
BARELY. SO FREE THEM TO THE WINDS THAT PLAY,
LET BOYS & GIRLS WITH THESE OLD SONGS HAVE
  HOLIDAY
IF THEY FEEL LIKE IT.

The sonnets would be out in nine months, Giroux explained, and then in 1968 he planned to publish the second volume of *The Dream Songs*. The 77 were still selling briskly; sales for September alone had been $306, and a check for that amount was on its way. The terms for his sonnets were fine, Berryman wrote back on October 8, but he still wanted a fall 1967 publication date for the new volume of Songs, "which unfortunately, owing to incessant production of new ones—some 40 in the last month alone," he felt "less & less confident of controlling at 84." It was the first public sign that he was thinking of expanding *The Dream Songs* beyond the original 161.

On October 4 he wrote Adrienne Rich about Book IV, calling her one of America's three best living female poets, along with Marianne Moore and Elizabeth Bishop. Soon Rich was writing back praising the "Opus Posthumous" sequence and co-incidentally confirming Lowell's opinion. How could she speak of weaknesses in poems that were "lengths ahead even" of Berryman's own "past victories"? The sequence as a whole was "as far along the lines of daring and intelligence" as anyone was likely to get in the twentieth century.

On the eighth Berryman wrote Valerie Trueblood to say that she too was very much on his mind. That fall he would dedicate three of his Songs to Rich and at least one to Trueblood, besides mentioning them both in several others. "Hard lies the road behind, hard that ahead," he wrote in the one addressed to Lady Valerie, making himself her protector:

> but we are armed & armoured & we trust
> entirely one another.
> We have beaten down the foulest of them, lust,
> and we pace on in peace, like sister & brother,
> doing that to which we were bred.

WHY DO YOU HONOR ME? she cabled Berryman, when word reached her that Berryman had dedicated a Song to her. The truth was, he told her, that he had seven American readers and wanted her to be the eighth. The reason for the honor was simply that he thought about her a good deal. She would hardly recognize him now with his "full Irish beard, part brown, part grey," having grown it, he quipped, because he was "tired of being taken for a graduate student." He was very hot just now, with several European journals hailing him and Ian Hamilton eager to interview him in London.

In spite of his regimen, Berryman and Kate did manage to visit around Dublin. On September 8, they saw the tombs of Swift and his lady at St. Patrick's, the stones looking much the same as they had when Berryman had first visited them thirty years before. On his fifty-second birthday—October 25—he took Kate to revisit Dublin Castle. They took in several plays, including *Hogan's Goat* and, two weeks later, a play about Dylan Thomas, which they thought in terrible taste. They got a picnic and some salmon fishing in on the Fane River in mid-October, as guests of their "*very* rich American friends." Berryman caught nothing, lamenting, as he did in Song 346, that it was "in the nature of Henry to catch nothing."

At last, at the end of October, the blaze that had fired Berryman for the past four months began to subside. By November 15 he had written seventy-five Songs in Ireland and felt now "invincibly tired." Lowell wrote again, this time to tell Berryman he'd won five thousand dollars from the Chancellors of the American Academy. Among the Chancellors were Auden, Bishop, Tate, Wilbur, Meredith, Lowell, and Louise Bogan, who, having declared Berryman the English language's public enemy number one, was "a bitter enemy" of his work. Still, he had won the prize. He wrote Meredith to say he was "working like bloody hell" on Book VII, which alone stood at seventy-four Songs, besides "12 or 15 always destined in order for the absolute end." Did Meredith "know of a warm cave" where they could go and hide and write short poems "in happy emulation"?

In mid-December Berryman finished VII, and—except for a handful of Songs added late—he was finally finished with the poems he was willing to include in *The Dream Songs*. On the fourteenth he wrote Meredith, apologizing for sending him new Songs after he'd already asked him to read the sonnets. All he had really wanted from him was an "Okay or No Good or Kill x & y & z." Now, he confessed, without his Songs to occupy him, he felt "remote and lost." In truth, they were still coming at him unbidden, so that he had "fifty new ones" in his head. Moreover, he still had "the very heavy editorial & administrative labour of Bks V & VI," which he looked forward to with about as much pleasure as cutting his throat. He began killing some of what he called his Irish poems, but realized he needed most of them to tell his story. He knew the last twelve or fifteen Songs in the collection were good, but he still wasn't sure about the ninety he'd done in Ireland, though he realized he'd already passed judgment on them by allowing them their place in his book.

The BBC was anxious to do a film of him, and sent Alvarez to talk to him about it. There was also talk at the American Academy of having Berryman read in New York in the spring, which he thought he would do, if they paid enough. The best thing about the five thousand dollars from the academy was that he wouldn't have to teach summers for another four or five years. He had too much other work to attend to, and too little time. He also made his peace with a number of ghosts that fall, including William Carlos Williams in September (DS 324). He envied Williams his zest for life, the good sounds he'd made over a lifetime, the "girls" he'd had, and the wife he'd loved through half a century. What he envied him most, however, was his being finished with his labor, having earned the right at last

to lie down
in your sweet silence, to whom was not denied

the mysterious late excellence which is the crown
of our trials & our last bride.

But the main reason he was in Ireland was to have it out with Yeats, take his true measure, and move on. For all his grand rhetoric, Berryman saw now, Yeats had understood "nothing about life." The trouble, as Berryman saw it, was that Yeats's overweening ego had turned everything he came in contact with into a symbol:

Yeats on Cemetery Ridge
would not have been scared, like you & me,
he would have been, before the bullet that was his,
studying the movements of the birds,
said disappointed & amazed Henry.

In his own willingness to confront the terrifying and unadorned facts of life and death, Berryman had long ago moved beyond the Master. Now he was ready to get on with the hilarious tragedy life had become for him.

Without friends, Berryman found Dublin at Christmas thronged with other ghosts too, especially that of Hopkins, the man who, like Berryman himself, had so loved "his own lovely land," only to wind up in Dublin. Hopkins: with his eye on heaven, one of the few artists who, Berryman feared, had died sane. He had died here in his forty-fifth year, exhausted and ill, though he had kept his witness, teaching and writing as he could, until death had washed over him.

Berryman placed the elegy to Hopkins near the end of *The Dream Songs,* between a Song that remembered another good man, Christian Gauss, dying alone at Christmas, surrounded in Penn Station by strangers, and a Song about suffering. That Song—number 378—was a rewriting of Hopkins's terrifying Dublin poem "Spelt from Sibyl's Leaves," and it recorded Henry's giving some "woman & her child ten shillings," even if only because he could not

bear beggars at my door, and I
cannot bear at my door
the miserable, accusing me . . .

When death came for him, Henry understood, the way the scales of justice tipped for him might well come down to a matter of those ten shillings.

New Year's 1967: At midnight the Berrymans could hear ships blowing their foghorns through the mists like lost ghosts. Berryman knew it was time to be going through the three hundred Dream Songs he'd collected. If he kept to a schedule of five a day, he would get through all of them by March 1, the deadline he'd set for finishing his second volume. But that night he fell again, hurting his right side so badly that at first Kate thought he'd broken his back. Thorazine and not alcohol, he complained, was responsible. In spite of the pain, he stuck to his schedule, passing judgment on which of the new Songs would live and which had to die.

Often Martha and Kate took a taxi out to Sandymount to collect shells, though Berryman did not accompany them. He was tired of Dublin, having discovered no new genius to supplant Yeats. Nor had he made any real friends, telling himself he was too old for that sort of thing now, though he did have all the pub acquaintances he needed to share a many few with him. Finally, toward the end of January, Kate had him committed to Grange Gorman, the forbidding-looking Dublin mental hospital he'd first visited thirty yers before. The place was no Abbott, and after a week of it, Berryman was begging Kate to sign the papers for his release. "I love my doctor, I love too my nurse," he wrote on the thirtieth,

> but I am glad to leave them, as now I do.
> Too long it's been
> out of the world, away fr. whisk', the curse
> of Henry's particular life, who has pulled thro'
> too & again makes the scene. . . .

And in another Song (DS 286), he recalled dropping a lit cigarette and knew that, if he did not find it fast there would be hell to pay:

> Henry walked the corridor in dark, drug-drunk, smoking
> and dropt it & near-sighted cannot find.

Nurses will deal hell if the ward wakes, croaking
to smoke antic with flame. . . .

In mid-February, out of the hospital now a week and trying to control his drinking, he heard again from Giroux. It was too late to include the two new poems Berryman had sent him for *Berryman's Sonnets,* and it would be better to let them go. Besides, there was other business to attend to, including reprinting *The Dispossessed* and *His Thoughts Made Pockets* in a single volume to be called *Short Poems,* which could come out at the end of the year. They would talk of this and other matters when Berryman came to New York to read in April. Alvarez came to Dublin to film Berryman reading his Songs and talking at the house and at Ryan's pub nearby, and that program aired on March 11. When he saw himself on television, Berryman wrote another Song (DS 298), which he swore would be his last. This one was for Martha, his "almost perfect child," his heart sinking at the thought that one day he would have to leave his "lovely baby" to become a blank. There would be nothing for it then but for her "to study him in school, at most,/ troubled & gone Henry."

"We have been burdened with Dream Songs all winter and now everyday is a day of reckoning," a tired Kate wrote on March 9 to Maris Thomes. She was being kept busy typing all of Berryman's handwritten Songs, with "John organizing and not writing any more which is a good thing since there are over 300 contenders for *His Toy, His Dream, His Rest*." Their lease would be up in two months, and John was eager to see Jerusalem and Greece. In the meantime they traveled to western Ireland to see the rugged promontory at Achill, and then Sligo so that Berryman could make his pilgrimage to Yeats's grave.

On April 24, the day *Berryman's Sonnets* was published, Berryman was back in New York. One of his former students, H. Wendell Howard, would remember walking through Kennedy Airport and being frozen by Berryman's voice roaring at him. He'd just spent a year in Ireland, he told Howard, "right on the edge of Europe," a place "crawling with delicious people who all speak English and are blazing with self-respect." He wished ol' Howard had been with him in those pubs "where everybody sings—they do not sing well but they sing together,'' and where he had been received ''like Sam Johnson in the court of the Dauphin.''

He read his Dream Songs at the American Academy and then at the Guggenheim, his jacket clearly indicating where he had walked all over it before putting it on. But shortly after his reading at the Guggenheim, he was rushed to French Hospital with alcoholic poisoning. The flight and then being on his own in New York had once again proven too much of a temptation. In mid-May he returned to Dublin with Jane Howard, who was doing a feature story on him for *Life* magazine. For four days she stayed with the Berrymans, gathering the material for her feature story, which would appear two months later under the title ''Whiskey & Ink.'' ''Writing,'' he told her behind his gleaming, trapped eyes, was ''just a man alone in a room with the English language, trying to make it come out right,'' and no one else, *no one,* could do that work for you. The interview and the photographs were certain to make good press. Here was one of the last Romantics in the tradition of that other boozer and roaring boy, Dylan Thomas. After Howard and the photographer left with their story and their thousand photographs taken in every setting from pubs to the ruins of ancient monasteries, Berryman found himself once again exhausted.

At the beginning of June the Berrymans were still in Dublin. Unable as yet to organize his Songs to his satisfaction, he gave up on the idea of publishing them that year. He also gave up on the idea of going to Jerusalem, and focused his attention instead on Greece. On the nineteenth, shortly before leaving, thanks to John Montague, he gave his only organized reading in Ireland in the ten months he'd been there.

The Berrymans spent five days in Paris, during which Berryman visited with John Montague on the Rue Daguerre. Then they traveled on to Italy, and the places Berryman saw gave rise to a number of new Songs. In Venice he admired the ''Byzantine beauty'' of this most impossible of cities with its Grand Canal and Bacino di San Marco, and listened to the throng of the ''murdered & distraught'' ghosts inhabiting the city. It was hot and humid when they arrived at the beginning of July, and they rowed up the Grand Canal in a gondola trying to cool off, while Berryman wondered if, like Saint Mark, he too would be "cut off/ just ere he finisht his work."

From there he traveled alone by train to Ravenna to visit Dante's tomb and the mosaics at St. Apollinare that had so profoundly shaped Yeats's vision of Byzantium. Then he moved on to the festival at Spoleto to give two readings of his Songs in the company of Neruda, Auden, Spender, Empson, Charles Olson, and Ungaretti, though the recording made of his reading would reveal how very drunk he was. Allen Ginsberg, who shared the podium with him, would remember finding Berryman a cab afterward because he was too drunk to get one for himself. A few days later Berryman flew to London "to perform more tricks" for two more poetry festivals. In the meantime Kate took Martha and went first to Rome and then on to Athens, where friends helped Kate find a furnished apartment.

Finally, on July 22, Berryman joined his wife and daughter. He quickly made friends in the local cafés, downed vast amounts of Greek brandy, and at last organized his Songs. His face appeared in the July 21 issue of *Life,* though there were few on the streets of Athens who recognized this strange American poet. How things stood between him and Kate at that point he registered in a Song written for Kate's birthday on July 28, baffled by her "mountain-top" standards and by the shouting matches that he found, to his amazement, erupting now around him.

In mid-August they took a five-day cruise of the Greek Islands. Ernest Samuels, a professor at Northwestern University and a historian of Henry Adams, and his family were also aboard the boat, and soon he and Berryman were having long conversations. Both, it turned out, had won their Pulitzers the same year. On the island of Patmos, Samuels watched Berryman ride up the narrow, winding mountain track to the monastery on a donkey, while Kate and Martha and the Samuelses took a taxi. As they passed Berryman, Samuels took a snapshot of him, beer-bellied and wild beard flying, grimly determined to make it to the top.

Back in Athens at the end of the month, Berryman wrote out a Table of Contents for *The Dream Songs* and a Note meant to open the new book, in which he explained that the poem was not about him, but "about an imaginary character (not the poet, not me) named Henry, a white American in early middle age sometimes in blackface, who has suffered an irreversible loss." "Requiescant in pace," he ended, thinking of the many faces of his hero. He composed one more Song and numbered it 383. "August in Athens," he wrote, exhausted, "at the end of the labour."

## chapter 28

# The American Bard

## 1967–68

By late August, Berryman was so ill that a doctor was called in and, seeing at once how things stood, prescribed massive doses of vitamins. The Berrymans had to cut their Greek holiday short and flew from Athens to Liverpool to embark for the return trip to Montreal. For three days and three nights Berryman remained confined to his room, suffering from delirium tremens and muttering through his vomit while the steward tried to get into the darkened room to clean it.

Back in Minneapolis, Berryman was admitted to Abbott Hospital, and on his release returned to his classes—and drinking—once again. He spent the second week in October reading and lecturing at Trinity College, Hartford. The first night, Monday the ninth, he read from his work in the Goodwin Theater, where William Meredith introduced him. It was not until the Dream Songs had begun appearing in print, Meredith began, "or perhaps until the summer of 1962 at Bread Loaf when I got used to having them sung to me," that Meredith had become what he now was: "a true believer in a genius I never made."

Wednesday evening Berryman read the poetry of four "major figures": Roethke, Schwartz, Lowell, and Bishop. There was a coffee hour Thursday afternoon, and his lecture on *The Tempest* the following evening. Interviewed for the school newspaper, he spoke warmly about his "family": Saul, Cal, Meredith, and Fitzgerald. Between performances, he stayed in his room drinking.

When he got back to Minneapolis, he heard from Giroux, ecstatic about the manuscript for the second volume of *The Dream Songs: His Toy, His Dream, His Rest.* What the manuscript needed now, Berryman insisted, was some hard criticism. Again Meredith was recruited to weed out the weaker poems. At Halloween, Berryman attended a costume party dressed as his great-grandfather General Shaver, his great gray-red Irish beard flowing to his chest.

He read at Northwestern, and Michael Anania would remember him leaning over the podium, "as though he were stretching himself into an intimacy with the audience," as he shaped his poems "with his hand the way a sculptor might describe a figure." He seemed, almost, to be "reclaiming the act of composition." Later that evening he and Anania talked about movies, and Berryman rhapsodized over the Marx Brothers and then Bogart's and Bergman's performances in *Casablanca,* recalling the details of the film with amazing attention to detail.

Shortly before Thanksgiving Berryman learned he'd just been awarded a ten-thousand-dollar grant from the newly established National Endowment for the Arts. But when a local reporter called to ask what he thought of the grant, Berryman told him he'd never even heard of the damn thing. In no time Berryman's dismissal made its way back to Washington, where one of the grantors wondered why the government wasted its time on such ingrates. "Henry under construction was Henry indeed," Berryman noted wryly in yet another Song.

Just after Thanksgiving he was back in Abbott's Mental Health Unit. Terrence Collins, an English major at the university who worked at the hospital, was on duty when Berryman was admitted. "He was fairly well intoxicated" that night, Collins recalled, but as he followed the "routine admission procedures of blood pressure, temperature and the like," Collins began talking to him about literature, "specifically about *The Scarlet*

*Letter,*" for which he had a paper due the following morning. Amazed, he listened as Berryman talked about Dimmesdale's crisis and his realization of his hidden guilt. It was, Berryman assured him, "the high point in American fiction of the 19th century." On his break, Collins wrote down everything he could remember about what Berryman had told him. He got an "A+" for his paper.

Five days before Christmas, Berryman was released, still "very nervous." On New Year's Eve he wrote Meredith, "burning to know" which of the Songs he did not like. He was anxious to get some hard criticism, as if daring Meredith to find any weakness in them. Go ahead, he told him, and "crucify them."

"After the pains & glories of the Fall," Berryman wrote, still relying on the Song stanzas to speak for him:

> dead winter: snow car-high, snow shoulder-high,
> snow cinema-high:
> hope shoulder-high for death . . .
> Death all endeth, Henry to Sybil said.

He wondered what such sounds as he made had to do "with his failing life," his "whiskey curse," and his problems with Kate, who was growing more and more unhappy with him. He flew to Skidmore College to hear fifteen young women read the *77 Dream Songs* to an audience of seventy-five. As he listened to his words flow back on him, he wondered if, after all, they had been worth all the pain. Would it not have been better, he asked himself, if, instead of singing the blues, he had simply knelt "in a far corner, unknown," and begged God to help him?

Back in Minneapolis, he tried again to stop drinking, hoping to allay his nightmares. Ross wrote to commiserate with him, amazed at Berryman's constitution, knowing that most other men would have succumbed long before. But Berryman was ashamed of the body he had helped destroy, and as fear began to condense "on him like ice," he realized that all he had to warm himself with now were his Songs.

That Valentine's Day he wrote another (DS 255), with himself as Sir Henry, Knight, watching Martha in kindergarten exchange cards with the other children. They had all had a ball, Henry noted,

> save one got none at all
> & tears, like those for the Roman martyr shed
> & the bishop of Terni who suffered the same day,
> so ancient writers say.
>
> I say, said Henry (all degrees of love
> from sky-blue down to spiriting blood, down to
> the elder from the new,
> loom sanctuaries we are pilgrims of,
> the pierced heart over there seems to be mine) this is
> my Valentine.

He wrote another on the twentieth, confessing to his ignorance of so much that was happening in the world:

> Its source obscure, the river make its way
> all the same seaward, and animals can't count,
> puzzling Henry.
> Some insects can, and birds, and the amount
> of organisms is over a million, say
> the author of these books driving Henry crazy
>
> with their zooids & their interfascicular cambium.
> Did he after all take the wrong courses?
> How can a man be so ignorant & live?

He managed a month of drinkless days, going over the Dream Songs a final time at the rate of ten a day. He organized his books, read Shakespeare, cut back on cigarettes and coffee, exercised. But he knew now that arranging his life in this manner was like arranging deck chairs on the *Titanic*. Fifty, a hundred times in his life he had made similar resolutions, held to them for a week, two weeks, a month, and then found himself drinking again, always with a new vengeance.

"I'm going crazy waiting over Meredith," he wrote Giroux on March 1. He had said what he'd wanted to get said and it was time to "get the show on the road." He should never have saddled William with the job, he added, knowing how "over-conscientious & self-overworked" he was. The worst was that he'd begun writing Songs again, "very reluctantly, having resisted the daily or hourly impulse for months," and had "about a dozen new Songs, some bad, some good," which he would use "to plug the gaps left by you & Mark & me." It was, however, important that there be exactly 385 Songs in all, for he was "superstitious about the numeration," which had cost him "such hell for years to effect." He would be "in & around New York" in mid-March and wanted to see Giroux to go over the book one last time.

Reading Chief Justice Warren's decision on the Adam Clayton Powell case in *The New York Times* in mid-March, Berryman was struck by one sentence in particular. When power centered on any one branch of the government, Berryman quoted, it was not difficult "to conjure/ the parade of horrors" that might follow from "unreviewable power." So with *The Dream Songs* he was about to unleash on the world. Did he really expect readers to follow Henry through a poem as long as his that seemed to go nowhere? He was afraid of being misunderstood or, worse, ignored, and began to put his bets on his imaginary future readers. They would have to work hard, he admonished, to understand what he had to tell them, not about Henry but about themselves. But maybe the Songs had nothing to do with his readers after all. Maybe they were "something just between" Henry and the language.

On March 18, Berryman had a letter from one of his ex-students, Rita Lux, who was living at home in Havre, Montana. Despondent, she had sought a priest for counseling, only to have that turn into a more intimate relationship. Now all she did was sit and stare at the darkness, living like Henry in a world of dreams. By the time Berryman received her letter, Rita was dead. She had gone down to the basement the day before, "where the jukebox & the guns were," and shot herself. It took Berryman two weeks to address that loss in a Song, imagining the soul of this young woman "wandring shuddering thro' the air" or simply "vanisht." The following month he called Rita's mother to tell her he had established a Pulitzer Prize Award fund at the high school in Chinook that Rita had attended. In return he asked her to send him photographs of Rita's grave.

He had the satisfaction of having four of his Dream Songs published at last in *The Atlantic Monthly*. Other publications in prestigious magazines followed: three in *Harper's;* four in *Tri-Quarterly,* three in *The New American Review*. In April he won the Emily Clark Balch contest sponsored by *The Virginia Quarterly* for a group of eleven Songs, including ten of his elegies for Delmore Schwartz. When interviewed that month by Catherine Watson for the *Minneapolis Tribune,* he told her, half-jokingly, that he'd sent the galleys for the new volume of *The Dream Songs* in because Kate had "threatened to leave" him if he "didn't stop finishing it." He no longer taught summer school, so his plans for the upcoming summer included staying at home, swimming, playing tennis. Mostly he just planned to sit in his rocking chair "in the middle of my living room with a glass of bourbon in one hand and a cigarette in the other, rocking and thinking."

He made another trip east in late April, reading at the Guggenheim on the twenty-seventh and at SUNY Binghamton five days later. "Unprotected, Henry took off east/ & west," he wrote in Binghamton, lonely in "this town of 9,000 souls." Well, to hell with the world. Henry had his own problems, trying to deal with

> That terrible booze bruising his future, dear,
> solo, with accurate money
> & a brain, a brain, that should have left him clear
> years ago, honey, of this *stuff* he drinks
> & of every damned thing he thinks.

With the good weather he picked up tennis once more, Kate playing as his partner. But his body was hardly up to it, and it annoyed him "to be continually beaten by somebody absolutely no good." He wrote and received love letters through the mails, trying to fire himself in any way he could. But the alcohol and drugs had rendered him a very old fifty-three. What was this extra-marital sex thing after all, he wrote, but a matter of two minutes where one lowered the lights and let the genitals have full play, where "I go up & down, you go up & down," and nothing much really happened after all. The real issue was alcohol and drugs. "Haldol & Serax, phenobarbital," he wrote that June:

> Vivactil, by day; by deep night Tuinal
> & Thorazine,
> kept Henry going, like a natural man.

"Old codger Henry," he wrote on the Fourth of July, at last a success of sorts, with money in the bank for the first time in his life:

> Old codger Henry contain within hisself
> Henry young, Henry almost beautiful
> Henry the seducer
> Henry the mad young artist, with *no* interest in pelf
> whereas now he takes steps to keep both his bank accounts full
> just like: you, Sir!

By midsummer, as the sense of crisis in the country intensified, he wondered when the end would come, not just for him but for the nation. By then Martin Luther King and Robert Kennedy were dead, and the Tet Offensive of January and February had brought home just how unwinnable the Vietnam War was. Over the nation also lay the threat of nuclear annihilation. When would "the fire be turned on," he wondered,

> and by whom?
> heating the memory & soul alike
> until both crisp.
> Not soon, I wonder, but in some lead-shielded room
> mistakes are being made like the Third Reich. . . .

Late that summer he wrote "Henry's Fate." It caught wonderfully the comic distance between Henry's tragic sense of himself and the domestic world in which he lived. Here was the Pulitzer Prize winner baby-sitting the Twiss and her friends while Kate did the errands. He might have been any other bumbling American father trying to maintain peace, except that it was his fate to sigh great thoughts. What did the Twiss understand about the angst of the existential soul in near despair?

* * *

At seventy-four, Jill Berryman had already begun to exhibit strange new behavior patterns. She was becoming reclusive and managed to lose large sums of money—probably in scams—after which she asked Berryman to help her with her difficulties. As it was, he was already supplementing her income. In June she asked for a loan of twelve hundred dollars, which he sent her. When she sent him small checks in partial repayment, he refused to cash them. At the end of August, Paul flew out for a visit with his father. It was amazing, really, how much his son looked like him, he thought. He tried, difficult as the role was for him, to act like any ordinary father. For Paul's part, he was delighted to be with his father, even for so short a time.

That fall Berryman taught two seminars, one on The American Character, with readings by de Tocqueville, Santayana, D. H. Lawrence, D. W. Brogan, and others; the second on The Meaning of Life, with readings from the Buddhist texts, Saint Mark, Tolstoy, Freud, Norman O. Brown, and *The Tempest*. At the start of the semester Daniel Hughes spent a weekend with the Berrymans. There was no liquor in the house when he first arrived, he remembered, but soon a "substantial delivery" was made. An advance copy of *His Toy, His Dream, His Rest* had just arrived, and Berryman insisted on Hughes having it. But in spite of Berryman's friendliness, Hughes did not feel comfortable. There was too much smoking and drinking, too many long silences interrupted by Berryman's sudden availabilities and quick retreats. Nor could he help noticing the tension between Berryman and Kate. And yet there was Martha, not quite seven, who sang and colored with crayons and played house and was Daddy's little Twiss, blossoming before them.

When Lowell received his copy of *His Toy,* he wrote Berryman at once. "They add up enormously and are much clearer, are perfectly clear," he wrote Berryman on August 19. "Either they are really so, or I am much more at home with your idiom." He was in Berryman's debt and had said so in the preface to his own long poem, which he was completing and which he was tentatively calling *Notebook of a Year*. His poem too was a sequence, made up of "fourteen line rough, unrhymed blank verse sections, full of autobiography, elegy, events, surrealism." His book and Berryman's shared, he thought, much of "the same world," though their styles were unlike and they seemed to have only the character of Jarrell in common. There were 172 poems in Lowell's book, and he had just handed the manuscript in to Giroux. Lowell's sequence would be out in March.

But three days later Lowell wrote again, "dumbfounded at how many of the same things" the two poets shared. They both used "rough iambic lines, often pentameter," "short sections" of a page, and their list of characters did, after all, extend beyond Jarrell. Moreover, the Irish poems made Berryman "the best Irish poet since Yeats." What particularly astonished Lowell was how Berryman had continued to grow even as time ravaged them both. The difference in their visions, Lowell had found, was that his was the more tragic, Berryman's the more comic.

Other letters of congratulations flooded in, including one from Elizabeth Bishop, who told him she liked his (and Cal's) poetry better than any other contemporary's. In late October he heard again from Conrad Aiken. "Woids fail me about HIS TOY," Aiken told him. "You're a new invention—a comic strip tease *in poetry*" and "the answer to our poetic predicament, as of now, just as St Thomas [TSE] was in 1914." If the earlier Dream Songs had been oblique, the later ones showed that Berryman had invented nothing less than a "totally new kind of narrative poetry." Psychologically too the poems worked. "And o christ, the humor."

Giroux had scheduled the official publication day for *His Toy* to coincide with Berryman's fifty-fourth birthday. He threw a party for Berryman at Luchow's, and showed him an advance copy of Helen Vendler's favorable front-page review in *The New York Times Book Review*. Berryman had never heard of Vendler, but reading what she had to say, he decided she was one "smart cookie." The following day he read his Songs at Brandeis. Then he read at Harvard and was interviewed for *The Harvard Advocate*.

He was a master at giving interviews, and enjoyed giving this one. Yeats and Auden had been his early influences, he told them, and Keats and Hopkins had helped him understand that poetry was a matter of creating a personality in one's poems. *The Dream Songs* did have a plot of sorts, and the poem's central emotions were hope and fear, through which Henry had

had to pass as he made his way in the world. The references to blues and minstrel songs he'd picked up from records and from his college visits to the Apollo. As for the national election, less than two weeks away, he no longer much cared. He'd been interested in Rockefeller and McCarthy, and both of them had been "bombed." That summer he'd watched Hubert Humphrey on television repudiate "every position" he'd ever taken. It was clear to him that Nixon, a man he'd long feared, a man who had "never held any position" at all, was going to win in November.

On November 3, Berryman composed two Songs, one of them a rewriting of Yeats's great death poem "Cuchulain Comforted." "The world has ended," he lamented, and two days later Richard Milhous Nixon was elected president of the United States. Berryman continued to teach, and once more the snows settled over Minneapolis. On November 12, he wrote another song for Rita Lux, considering her death and his own. "I bore my birth. What more do I have to bear?" he asked. Then he rehearsed her suicide once more, this time making the gunshot echo with his name:

> Her mother was in the kitchen after breakfast. Why,
> Rita went downstairs, where the jukebox & the guns were.
> She used to hit the punching-bag
> in hospital gloveless till her knuckles were bloody,
> calling my name with each blow. Her mother runs
> at the shout, but then there's a shot.

*Time* magazine wired, asking for a poem on the flight of *Apollo 8,* which would circle the moon that Christmas Eve. (The people at *Time* would read it, scratch their heads, and pay him a kill fee for it.) He watched as the astronauts—Borman, Anders, Lovell—disappeared behind the dark side of the moon then reappear, the craft's "incredible circuitry" intact. So this was what the moon looked like, its desolation stripping the viewer of his comfortable myths about the heavens. That Christmas, for the first time in history, the moon lay revealed for what it was. Berryman shuddered. It too was a place from which the gods seemed to have long since disappeared.

*chapter 29*

# An Archaic Sea with Craters Grand

## 1969

In early January, Berryman learned that he and Karl Shapiro were co-winners of the Bollingen. Shapiro sent a telegram congratulating him, adding that he'd just reviewed the new Dream Song volume and loved it "awfully." The judges for the Bollingen had been Richard Wilbur, M. L. Rosenthal, and Louise Bogan, and the prize was five thousand dollars, halved. Late in the month Berryman was back at Skidmore reading and talking about his poetry to a class that was focusing on him and Philip Larkin as opposite tendencies in contemporary poetry.

By that point Berryman was congratulating himself on having stayed out of the hospital for the past six months. Once again, he shaved his beard, then grew another, which he promised to take better care of. He increased his monthly checks to his mother. Martha sailed through first grade, and Kate took courses in education at the university to certify for teaching elementary education. On March 12, Berryman was in New York to accept the National Book Award in Poetry for *His Toy, His Dream, His Rest*. It was a chance to make a few jibes, especially at one "eminent critic" who had once accused the Bradstreet of lacking "inherent imaginative grandeur. . . . Think of that!" he shouted. "I wonder I dared ever lift my head and trouble the public again. 'You lack inherent imaginative grandeur,' I said severely to myself over my Grape Nuts: 'down with you!' "

At the end of the month he was interviewed at home by Richard Kostelanetz. Dressed in an open button-down shirt, gray slacks, and brown slippers, he paced or sat, hands trembling as he sipped glass after glass of wine. If something happened to Henry, he told his interviewer, Henry thought of it as lasting forever. But nothing lasted forever, not even Henry, for he had now abandoned Henry for good. When Kostelanetz asked if that wasn't a new Dream Song on the table next to him, Berryman answered that it was, and that in truth he just couldn't bear "to be rid of that admirable outlet, that marvellous way of making your mind known to many other people."

He talked about his generation of poets. Why so many of them were "so screwed up" he didn't know, though they had "every right to be disturbed." America could "drive anybody out of his skull," especially its poets. He was deeply upset by the constant lies being promulgated by the Nixon administration about what was happening in Vietnam. But as bad as the protests against the war already were, he knew they were going "to get worse and worse and worse" until something was done.

The major problem with the Songs, he saw now, was that Henry had never got around to solving his problems. The other major problem was the lack of a sufficiently all-inclusive language. If Henry was going to use blackface and the language of the blues, there were limits to the range of language one could realistically use in the Songs. How could Henry discuss "Heisenberg's theory of indeterminacy, or scholarly questions, or modern painting"? In that sense, the Bradstreet, with its seventeenth-century language and twentieth-century interpolations, had been even more restricted. The new poems he meant to write, then, would need a more knowledgeable persona. Over the years he had learned to loosen up and sound more like a real man talking. There had been no lightning leaps in his development; every step had meant years of hard work. As for what he wrote about, it was as if the universe—or God—actually sent him signals. He knew it sounded ridiculous speaking like this, except that it was true: the universe sent him signs that he had learned to snag the way an outfielder positioned himself to snag a ball.

Scheduled to read at Notre Dame on April 5, he checked into the campus inn two days early. When John Matthias, teaching creative writing there, learned where his former teacher was, he went to see him. "His suitcase was full of cigarette cartons and bottles of Jack Daniel's, and he had been smoking and drinking alone for a long time," Matthias recalled. He managed to get Berryman to eat something, and then took him for a walk around the campus lakes. By the night of the reading Berryman was at least in somewhat better shape and read well, dedicating the evening to Matthias's wife, "with whom he had flirted in his courtly way during dinner."

A few days later Berryman was at Michigan State in East Lansing, where he read before a crowd jammed into Kellogg Auditorium. Before the reading he was interviewed for the Sunday edition of *The State Journal,* an interview that began in his room but soon moved to the bar. Berryman raged against the spiraling dehumanization of America and its preoccupation with sex. Then he raged against the war. "Many students come to me before running to Canada to avoid the draft," he told his interviewer. What a terrible cost it was to the young, whether they decided to serve or to oppose the draft. Better to get out of Vietnam now, though he was glad *he* didn't have to figure out how Nixon was going to do it.

He scheduled another reading for Monday, May 19, at the University of Illinois. There was bad weather that day, Lawrence Lieberman would remember, and Berryman's plane was delayed. Finally, Berryman called to say he was in Chicago but that the plane to Urbana had been grounded. Lieberman was to hold the crowd until he got there. At seven-thirty he called again. He'd found a cabdriver at O'Hare who'd agreed to drive him the 140 miles to Urbana, and he was already on his way. At nine-fifteen he called again, this time from a bar, roaring into the receiver to hold that crowd. When he called again at ten, he was at the registration desk. But by then the crowd had all but disappeared. Lieberman found him downing shots of whiskey to steady himself. Then, together with a small group of students, they went to a private house for the reading. In the crowd was a disturbed Vietnam veteran, and when Berryman saw him, filled with compassion for the man, he stopped everything to talk to him.

On the twenty-third he was in Detroit to read at a community college, and the following night at Wayne University. After the first reading he stayed up late, drinking. Then, around noon on Saturday, Dan Hughes picked him up at his motel. "He looked sicker" than the previous fall, Hughes would remember, "and, in fact, a fragility I had not seen in him before seemed to dominate him; he was warm to us, tired in his bones, a kind of walking, ill-clad nerve." Berryman's reading was to be the poetry event of the season—"a thousand dollar job," Berryman called it—and there had been some hostility to his coming at all. "He was heroic and frail; soaring and slumped; finally triumphant." Given the condition Berryman was in, the reading was for Hughes "an act of moral grandeur." Afterward a "Women's Libber" told him she had parodied all his poems. Berryman stared at her. It was "the worst thing," he informed her, anyone had ever said to him. Ill as he was, actually sweating alcohol by then, he was going on to the University of Washington to give another reading. He was doing it, he told Hughes, because he needed the money for his family, which now included his ailing mother. At the airport there was a tense half hour while Berryman's body trembled, whimpering for the bar to open. By then even Hughes needed a drink.

When Berryman arrived in Seattle, William Matchett was at the airport to greet him. Having heard the horror stories about Berryman's drinking, Matchett had brought along another teacher, Paul Hunter, to help him. That night Berryman went to Hunter's house. He seemed a "painfully shy man," Hunter recalled, who seemed to blink "out through the mask of his beard" as he shouted out the places he'd been and the people he knew. He would never forgive "that young upstart" Bob Dylan for stealing *his* friend, Dylan's, name. Oh, Bob Dylan was certainly a real-enough poet. All he had to do now was learn how to sing.

Next morning, when Jean Cox, a staff member, called for Berryman at 7:45 for his television interview, he was still drunk from the night before. What he needed, he told her, was whiskey to straighten himself out. Then she remembered what *Life* had said about his consuming a quart of whiskey a day. Luckily the stores were closed. Luckily too the interview was taped, for Berryman could not focus his attention on the questions and rambled on incoherently. After the interview, he insisted once more on getting a bottle, and Cox had to drive him to two liquor stores to show him they were still closed.

But the poems themselves Berryman would not violate, and he read them impeccably, his powerful voice keening and filling the auditorium. "The effect of such precision and music (and tenderness, and dirge-like elegiac intonation)," Matchett recalled, "was to convince me very soon on in the reading that the drink was probably an unconscious strategy. By the time he reached the last poem . . . the overflow crowd was breathless, most eyes were wet."

"An eye-opener, a nightcap, so it goes," he wrote afterward, looking back on his exhausting tour:

> One for the road, eight to pass out, so it goes.
> So it goes.
> They say if the Harvard Provision Co. shut down
> there wd be no more excellent teaching in that town.
> Full professors wd come to blows.
>
> Too much can hardly be made of the eccentric view
> that sees liquor in quantity as a sedative
> & for poets dissociative.
> I won't linger over that. That's up to you.
> Like the 3 kinds of marijuana I was recently offered
> in Illinois, like a bird
>
> of passage, bard of passage, oh well I somehow refused
> them all & got home safe.
> Also a "sexy" fat woman
> was offered me, whom likewise I refused, I
> with my intent to be true beyond belief,
> which is merely human.

He was not surprised to learn that he had been passed over for the Nobel Prize. After all, translated into "Polish, Italian, German," the Songs "all came out in a lump." He knew his work depended on the American idiom and the mastery with which he manipulated its nuances and rhythms. That summer he had hoped to get to his translation of Sophocles, the "giant Sophocles/ in his heights & final peak/ of weirdness & blood, like the mysteries of the sea." But in early June he crushed a nerve in his neck during a spasm brought on by his drinking. He lost thirty-five pounds that summer and spent several weeks in the hospital, then for months after had to return daily for physical therapy.

He found it physically impossible that summer to write anything; he wrote no letters, and even the Dream Songs dwindled to almost nothing. Finally, on September 5, he broke his silence by dictating a letter to Kate addressed to Lowell, thanking him for sending him a copy of *Notebook*. "Dear Cal," he began, "With those two words I plan to disappoint the summer of my pain and re-enter the normal world." One doctor had told him it would take "150 days, another says that the nerve regenerates itself 1 mm. a day and it is a very long nerve." He'd read *Notebook* through twice in twenty-four hours, and whatever objections he'd had at first had "dropt to the ground." It was a book that *needed* to be read twice. He had given up rhyme in his later Dream Songs, and knew Lowell was right to do so too. As for the "disjointedness" he'd first noticed in Lowell's sequence, even that had disappeared, and the poems had come together for him as his Songs had: into "one poem."

Lowell answered at once. He too was ill, and at fifty-two was already having trouble with his blood pressure. "One day in Israel I couldn't get my coffee cup to my lips, my hand shook so." He was still revising his *Notebook* and adding poems all the time. He had seen the "new and top Dream Songs" in *The Harvard Advocate* and was glad to see that Berryman had not abandoned the Songs. "If you can go on that way," he added, "why stop ever?" He was teaching at Harvard and living pretty much alone. Was there "anything more last man alive," Lowell mused, "than a dinner with one's self?" Then he added; "I think anyone who cared for your book would for mine." Anyway, we're accomplished beyond jealousy. Without you, I would find writing more puzzling."

On the eleventh Berryman dictated his second letter, this one to Adrienne Rich. He was disappointed in her new book, *Leaflets,* he told her, for he'd expected her to be another Sappho, and instead she'd turned out to be "only a struggling and beautiful and gifted lady." But, he added, slight as the book in some ways was, Rich was still "queen of ladies," second only to Elizabeth Bishop. "Branch out!" he cheered her, "Ransack!"

He was still going for daily hospital visits for his neck injury when classes began that fall. On September twenty-second he wrote to a bibliographer of his work to say he would help her in any way he could. "Various people are writing various books & papers on me," he explained, and "a very bad" first booklet on him by William Martz was due out at any moment. She was the first, so far as he knew, willing "to undertake the necessary preliminary [task of bibliography] . . . (I speak as a Shakespearean scholar, where chronological and textual studies are basic)." There was much to be done to get his story straight, he knew, and he would begin by filling her in on the early years.

There were other recognitions too. On October 2, he was named Regents' Professor of Humanities at the university's convocation ceremonies. The honor carried with it an extra five thousand annually in recognition of his "outstanding contributions to the teaching profession, to the university, & to the public good." Dean Ziebarth would remember Berryman telling him that he would go through with the ceremony only if Ziebarth "stood by his side and told him what and what not to do." "I am v nervous today, so I write briefly," he wrote to Meredith on the eleventh. He did not believe he was improving, except that the pain in his neck and back had subsided somewhat and he was lecturing only "w. great difficulty." He had "got through the v. elaborate ceremony" for his professorship and had received the same day "a royalty cheque for—expecting maybe $600—nearly $8000." All five of his books were selling briskly.

At Halloween, "dealing out treats" for the little ghosts clamoring at his door, he wrote a Song for his Twiss. So the little girl on whom he doted was getting ready to go it alone:

> This is the end of Daddy, the shallowing of the depths
> of her childhood, when bearded Daddy was any.
> Daddy, parked at the curb,
>
> will watch his baby, muttering in Latin,
> scrambling up the steps of Smith or Vassar saying
> 'I want a Yale man with a yacht

after my degrees, whereon, me in satin,
my Daddy can spend his last years without paying,
revising his works or not.'

By then Kate had suffered through eight years of Berryman's drinking. In Dublin she had taken John Montague aside to tell him she didn't think she could go on living with Berryman the way he was much longer. Now, she gave her husband an ultimatum: either he stopped drinking or she left him. Berryman became terrified, for he knew now he was helpless to stop his drinking on his own. "Great flaming God," he wrote on November 2,

My thought ceases to flow
forward to drinks & cigarettes & such
and sticks in the now. Where I must be
for years, for years, for years.
I am not myself, it suddenly appears,
but horrible habits. . . .

The following morning an advance copy of *The Dream Songs* arrived. He began thumbing through the thick volume of 385 poems from back to front, studying it again. Bellow would later speak of the thinness of the human dimension he found in Berryman's work. Now Berryman asked himself the same question. Had he created a fully developed human personality in Henry? he wondered, then answered himself in one of the last songs he ever wrote:

A human personality, that's impossible.
The lines of nature & of will, that's impossible.
I give the whole thing up.
Only there resides a living voice
which if we can make we make it out of choice
not giving the whole thing up.

A week later he was admitted to Hazelden with acute symptoms of alcoholism. He had taken Thorazine and Tuinal and, disoriented, had fallen down and hurt himself. X rays were taken at St. Croix Falls Hospital, and then he was transferred to Hazelden, where the admitting doctor described him as "a well-developed, poorly nourished bearded male," weak but "alert and cooperative." He was suffering from chronic severe alcoholism, alcoholic peripheral neuritis, drug abuse, and the beginnings of acute withdrawal.

For a week Berryman remained in the intensive-care unit. This time there would be no more trips to the Brass Rail. At the start of his second week, he was assigned to Thiboult Hall with twenty-one other recovering alcoholics. At first he followed the regimen patiently, but soon he was insisting on getting back to his teaching. This time, however, he was told flatly that he would have to stay put. He'd already paid for the treatment, and if he chose to leave the hospital early—as he had every right to do—he would not be permitted to return. He would also forfeit his five hundred dollars. Berryman roared, but then submitted.

By the end of his second week in, he was convinced he was feeling better than he had in years. Sunday afternoons Kate brought Martha out to visit with him. On November 16 she wrote Meredith asking for a favor. John was in the alcoholic rehabilitation unit at Hazelden and having a very hard time of it. Almost no one knew he was there, and she asked Meredith to write to him. Finally John had been made to understand that he would have to give up drinking. Then she added that God alone knew if the treatment would actually work.

At the end of the month Berryman was assigned a counselor, who began to uncover Berryman's history of alcoholism. It was not until 1947 that he actually realized he might have a drinking problem, Berryman explained. That was at Princeton, during a time when he was having an intense affair. Since then, the longest he'd gone without a drink had been three months, and that was from September to December of the previous year. As for drugs, he had taken sleeping pills "irregularly" since 1949, and pills for his nervous condition since 1955 on an irregular basis. It had all seemed so natural at the time. He had seen psychiatrists from 1947 to 1953 and every other week for the past year for marriage problems and alcoholism. He was willing finally to admit that he was indeed an alcoholic.

On December 19, six weeks after being admitted, he was released. "I feel marvellous," he wrote Ross that day, "better physically mentally and spiritually than I've felt for many years.

The programme is almost as much interested in your character defects, personality disorders, as it is in your drinking problem, and I corrected some of my wrong thinking about myself, helped by the lectures (3 a day).'' There had also been group therapy sessions, reality therapy sessions, as well as ''various excellent books they give you to read, and interviews with a counsellor, a psychologist, & a priest.'' The first four days, he confessed to his mother after Christmas, had been ''pure hell,'' and it had seemed ''hard & ridiculous to expect to reform one's character, morally & spiritually, in just 3 weeks' time.'' Nevertheless, he was convinced, it was his fellow alcoholics, his friends—eight or ten of them, regular, nondescript people he normally would have ignored or avoided—who had helped him pull through.

He spent Christmas at home with his family. Kate gave him a kimono and sandals to replace the ones he'd bought in Kyoto, and Martha gave him ''a hideous turtle, modelled, baked & painted by herself.'' When Kate's ''lousy & worthless brothers, with her sad grandmother'' had made their annual visit that afternoon, he'd become so upset he'd considered having a drink. Somehow he'd managed to stick to coffee.

''As one who took a bottle away from me in New Haven,'' he wrote Adrienne Rich, ''you deserve to hear that I have just spent a whole month in intensive treatment . . . and am a new man in fifty ways.'' He was preparing his proseminar on *Hamlet* for the winter term, his first-ever regularly scheduled course for the English department, and he was anxious to do a good job. When preparations for that were out of the way, he would begin ''branching out'' into a comprehensive overview of the current studies of Shakespeare to bring himself up-to-date on the subject. He still had that critical biography of Shakespeare to finish and this time he meant to finish it.

# chapter 30

# Revelations of a Locked Ward

## 1970

Berryman's new sobriety lasted just twelve days. He took his first drink at a party New Year's Eve, explaining away the horror of what he was doing by telling himself that he needed a stiff one to get some work done and that this time he would drink only in moderation. Kate, having watched her husband begin to recover and then return to drinking, was almost in despair. At first he did appear to keep his drinking under control, telling himself he was happier that December and January than he had been in years. He taught his two seminars and ordered giant quantities of scholarly books from his English booksellers. He read up on Mexico, planning to vacation with Kate there that summer. He went through his essays and some of his unpublished stories, arranging them for a book to be called *The Freedom of the Poet* that Giroux planned to bring out in a year.

Organizing his magazines, he came upon an essay by Richard Wilbur called "Poetry and Happiness." "I have just shelved it with Criticism, in a case behind this chair," he wrote Wilbur. "You come between Valéry & Edmund Wilson, and you dignify the company. I wish you wrote prose more often, my friend; you make most critics, including me, look like drudges." He was working on his Shakespeare biography again and had written three new chapters. Years before, he explained, he'd drafted 250 pages, but too much time had elapsed and he'd had to start all over again.

"Blessings on yr endeavours; let me hear what they are," he wrote Meredith on February 1. "I am having the best winter within memory—mostly very hard every day at Shakespearian scholarship and criticism." There was nothing "like *work* in good causes, for man's soul. . . . Off here in the Middle West I suffer a little from the feeling that I am working in a void. The death of Sir Walter Greg, who was kindly & expertly privy to my editing of *Lear* 25 years ago, has rather isolated me. Help me," he pleaded, "with your advice, to bear my great burden!"

Then, without warning, the Muse interrupted Berryman's scholarly plans once more. He had been rereading Emily Dickinson's poems when he began, on February 2, to compose a new kind of poem, which he titled "Her & It." It was written in unrhymed four-line stanzas, the lines expanding and contracting as needed, the diction and range of reference were a continuation of the Dream Songs he'd written since Dublin, but with an even greater freedom. What he was composing turned out to be a bildungsroman: a portrait of the artist as a young man. Against the nostalgia of those tea dances and classes at Columbia and Cambridge, he placed the more strident jazz of the older poet looking back in mock disbelief:

I fell in love with a girl.
O and a gash.
I'll bet she now has seven lousy children.
(I've three myself, one being off the record.) . . .

Time magazine yesterday slavered Saul's ass,
they pecked at mine last year. We're going strong!
Photographs all over!
She muttered something in my ear I've forgotten as we danced.

He stared at what he'd written. "Intoxicated with it," he wrote "another, and in the evening two more." The following day he wrote another two. On February 5 he wrote a draft of "Cadenza on Garnette," recalling Wordsworth's regret that he wished he might have "said out passions as they were." Against that, Berryman placed Allen Ginsberg's admonition to him at Spoleto to tell it all. "A revolution. I swear no less," he wrote Meredith on the sixth. Never had he written better, and he was sending some of the new work on to him to see if he didn't agree. "Be candid though," he urged, "and if you find any blunders or numb spots for Christ's sake point them out. These poems aim at nothing short of *perfection* of tone."

Over the next two weeks he worked "madly" on his new poems, drinking more and more heavily and asking the alcohol to relax and excite him. Then he sent the poems on to his privileged handful of readers. This craving for approval by a writer as distinguished as Berryman troubled Meredith, and when Meredith expressed reservations about the new work, Berryman retorted by calling him obtuse. By the thirteenth, feeling the need for a break, Berryman wired Valerie Trueblood in Chicago. I HAVE BEEN OVERWORKING MADLY, he shouted in capitals. MEN NEED A BREAK. FLYING TO CHICAGO TOMORROW TO SEE YOU, IF YOU AGREE. CALL ME AT MINNEAPOLIS 338-3353, COLLECT. The wire went undelivered.

Instead, he continued to work at the poems and to drink. At the end of the month he flew east to read at Fairleigh Dickinson. At the airport, in his room, on the trip back, he drank. On his return he was taken to Abbott once more, unable to stand, his shins black and purple, his liver palpating. The doctors did what they could to detoxify him, then released him on March 6. "We are both disappointed," Kate wrote her mother-in-law, trying to control her bitterness. Again she gave Berryman an ultimatum. Either he stopped drinking or she took Martha and left. "Is Kate really going to take the baby away?" Berryman asked himself in a poem two days after his release:

> She shook my hand: "It's been nice to be married to you."
> The (unexpected) end.
> Ah Kate to leave me at this time
> When I am nearly through. . . .
>
> It cost me a month, hard, hard on you
> harder on me—our fates are terrible—

The bad work must be done.
Otherwise what will the future think of us?

On March 17, he was back in Abbott again, once more suffering from delirium tremens. He stayed a week, made no real progress, and left. He did, however, use his stay to write poems for the third section of his new book, *Love & Fame*. The first poem was written his first morning in, and he called it "Death Ballad." It was about two young women on the locked ward with him, both of whom seemed intent on killing themselves. A second, written a day later, he called "The Hell Poem":

It's all girls this time. The elderly, the men,
of my former stays have given way to girls,
fourteen to forty, raucous, racing the halls,
cursing their paramours & angry husbands.

Nights of witches: I dreamt a headless child.
Sobbings, a scream, a slam.
Will day glow again to these tossers, and to me?
I am staying days.

On the twenty-fifth he wrote Giroux that his new manuscript was "one of the beautiful, original & powerful works of the age." He wanted copies sent to twelve friends for their criticism: Van Doren, Meredith, Ransom, Aiken, Rich, Wilbur, Wilson, Franklin Reeve, Tate, Hoagland, Albert Gelpi, and Deneen Peckinpah. A thirteenth copy was to go to Ann Berryman. *Love & Fame* would be divided into three parts—the promise of 1) Columbia and 2) Cambridge set hard against 3) the disenchanting alcoholic present. The entire book, he added, had been written in the past seven weeks.

The following day he wrote Arthur Crook at the London *Times Literary Supplement,* saying that some of his closest friends and critics had expressed "hostility and ambiguity" toward some of the new poems and that it was taking all his "courage to go on." He was "a wreck, but Sir a gorgeous wreck." He was sending along six lyrics, two from each of the book's three parts. Oxford men from "all over the world" would be "jealous about *The Other Cambridge,*" no poem of comparable worth on the subject of Oxbridge having been written since

Hopkins's "Duns Scotus' Oxford" ninety years before.

In early April, as Kate began student-teaching sixth grade, Berryman went through another bout of drinking. He was lethargic, uncoordinated, and walked about as if in a dream. On the seventh he had to be readmitted to Abbott, this time for three days. Kate handed him a final ultimatum. He *had* to understand that alcoholism was a fatal disease. If he continued to drink, he was going to kill himself and destroy his family. Either he went back to Hazelden for treatment at the end of the spring quarter, or she really would take Martha and leave.

Berryman agreed to return to Hazelden. But first he had to go east to give a series of readings he had promised months before. His first two stops were Vassar on April 16, then the International Poetry Forum in Pittsburgh the following evening. Nancy Willard, on the Vassar faculty and pregnant at the time, would remember his concern over her condition and of how he spoke with authority and compassion about the birth process. The Vassar reading went well. But back in his room that night, he flicked a live cigarette into the wastebasket and had to stamp the fire out.

When Samuel Hazo met him at the Pittsburgh airport the following day, Berryman's left thumb and right foot were both bandaged. At a restaurant that evening, Berryman told Hazo he would read from his new manuscript, which he was calling *Love & Fame* because that was what life had been all about for him when he'd started out: the search for love and a name. When Hazo commented on how much he was drinking, Berryman told him not to worry, that he would do "a creditable job" for him. Again, in spite of the alcohol, he came through, reading before a crowd of six hundred, his words coming, as Hazo phrased it, from some place deep in "his racked soul."

When Berryman got back to Minneapolis, there were letters waiting for him from Rich and Wilbur, both of whom felt the new poems were a falling off from *The Dream Songs*. Wilbur would not be bullied. The book, he told Berryman, seemed to have been thrown together much too quickly. For her part, Rich felt the book wanted to be a prose volume rather than a book of poems. There were some fine moments, but not enough of them.

As long as classes continued, Berryman felt free to drink. Afterward he would enter Hazelden and get cured again. But his nervous system could not wait. Late Saturday night, May 2, he was rushed to the Intensive Alcohol Treatment Center at St. Mary's Hospital. Chris Fall was on duty that night, and saw a drunk with a ragged, untrimmed beard and large, raw blisters on his hands from cigarette burns, looking like "a dishevelled Moses." He sat there in the nursing station, quoting from various Greek and Japanese poets, then stood up and, in a loud voice, sang one of Bessie Smith's blues.

Berryman spent the next three weeks going through withdrawal again, by turns arrogant and abject, until he feared he was actually going insane. He paced up and down in his room all night long, threatening to kill himself because he could not eat, then because he could not sleep. But by May 12, he felt strong enough to have a taxi take him to the university so that he could lecture on Saint John's Gospel, before being brought back to St. Mary's to continue his treatment. But at ten that morning permission to leave the hospital was withdrawn.

There had been disclosures that American troops in Vietnam had widened the war by crossing into Laos and Cambodia, and the news had resulted in an outbreak of student uprisings around the country, including the University of Minnesota. Berryman was horrified to learn that some of his students were actually wearing red arm bands in support of the Viet Cong. In spite of his own collapse, however, Berryman was not about to witness the collapse of the one place left for reasoned debate and dialogue. He *had* to get over there to do what he could. His counselors, however, knew he was in no condition yet to leave. Seeing Berryman's terror and helplessness, Jim Zosel, one of his counselors, offered to take over his class for him. As an Episcopal minister, he had had training in New Testament theology and would do what he could to help Berryman.

Suddenly something happened that Berryman would later call "a sort of religious conversion," explaining it as a sudden and radical shift from a belief in a transcendent God—a formal principle of sorts holding the vast complicated harmony of the universe together—to a belief in a God who cared for the individual fates of human beings and who even interceded for them. Beginning on May 21 and extending over the next two weeks, while he continued his recovery at St. Mary's, Berryman wrote a series of poems that became his "Eleven Addresses to the Lord." The middle poem, the sixth, spoke intimately of the conversion experience itself, especially of Berryman's exhaustion in having tried for so long to go the journey alone. Ever since his father had abandoned him, he wrote, he'd had signs of God's presence and care, but nothing like this. Now he had the sense of some incredible weight being lifted from him, and he found himself talking not in Henry's voice but in a voice closer to his own:

> Under new management, Your Majesty:
> Thine. I have solo'd mine since childhood, since
> my father's suicide when I was twelve
> blew out my most bright candle faith, and look at me.
>
> I served at Mass six dawns a week from five,
> adoring Father Boniface & you,
> memorizing the Latin he explained.
> Mostly we worked alone. One or two women.
>
> Then my poor father frantic. Confusions & afflictions
> followed my days. Wives left me.
> Bankrupt I closed my doors. You pierced the roof
> twice & again. Finally you opened my eyes.
>
> My double nature fused in that point of time
> three weeks ago day before yesterday.
> Now, brooding thro' a history of the early Church,
> I identify with everybody, even the heresiarchs.

The "Eleven Addresses" turned out to be a complex orchestration of responses to the Lord, ranging from awe and qualified belief to a new understanding of love and fame from a less ego-centered perspective. Let him only get on with his work, Berryman prayed, and let God decide its worth. After all, the poems had always been a gift. He understood better now something Hopkins had spoken of: the Pauline mystery of kenosis, that Christ, though of the Godhead Himself, had emptied Himself out of love for others, even to undergoing death by crucifixion. Now Berryman asked that he might be witness to the father's mercies in his own modest degree, so that he too might also be made "acceptable at the end of time."

Nevertheless, Zosel for one could see that Berryman was

holding back from surrendering himself to the higher power those in Alcoholics Anonymous had finally to call on. At the end of five weeks of treatment, Berryman still drew the line as to how far he was willing to change. He was willing to counsel others in whatever way he could, but for himself he still saw suicide as the only way out. Zosel noted in particular Berryman's unconscious habit of playing over and over a low, tuneless version of some song, he discovered, that dated back to 1926, the year Berryman's father had killed himself.

On June 7, Berryman wrote his mother a long letter from St. Mary's. He thanked her for sending clippings of the student strikes, including those about the killings at Kent State, which had hit him particularly hard. In his Christian Origins course "only a third of my 70 kids showed up for the mid-quarter exam, and only about ⅔ are taking the final or writing a paper (the option I gave them)." He'd been told by his doctor that it would be another year before his nerves were restored. What had frightened him was that, three weeks into withdrawal, he had had a seizure, which was very "unusual & threatening." This time his body had warned him he might not "survive another such period" of drinking.

On June 12, he was discharged uncured. He had lost nineteen pounds in the hospital and could sleep only sporadically. Zosel planned to have him return for group therapy for at least two more weeks. He would need a great deal of exercise and rest, things he was not in the habit of giving himself. There had been some progress, Zosel noted, but Berryman had already begun to retreat into his former "hostile, arrogant & defiant behavior."

Berryman now became an outpatient of St. Mary's AA Squad 2 and was given a sponsor named Ken. If he felt the urge to drink, he was to call Ken—himself a recovering alcoholic—at any hour of the day or night and Ken would be there to help him get through the crisis. But six days after being released from the hospital, Berryman walked into a bar and drank for three quarters of an hour. "Christ!" was all he could say when he realized next morning what he'd done. It was, he hoped, only a "slip."

By early June he had decided to add the "Eleven Addresses" to the end of *Love & Fame*. The book, at fifty-nine poems, was now "finished" and he hoped to see it published in time for his fifty-sixth birthday. By then the *TLS* would have printed six of the poems, *The New Yorker* his "Death Ballad," and *The Atlantic Monthly* his "Hell Poem" and "Olympus," his long-delayed tribute to Blackmur. Then he plunged at once into yet another book of poems.

In late June he wrote "Somber Prayer," with its evocation of Uccello's "The Flood and the Recession of the Flood":

> Uccello's ark-locked lurid deluge, I'm
> the brutal oaf from the barrel stuck mid-scene. . . .
>
> A twelve-year-old all solemn, sorry-faced,
> described himself lately as 'a lifetime prick.'
> Me too. Maladaptive devices.
> At fifty-five half-famous & effective, I still feel rotten about
> myself.

By the time he wrote his mother on July 6, he was sounding more optimistic. Bellow had just sent him his latest novel, *Mr. Sammler's Planet,* "the wisest artwork of my generation so far," he whistled. Since his doctors had urged him not to travel, he suggested Jill fly to Minneapolis for a visit. He felt confident he was up to such a visit, "better physically & busy w many things—esp: new poems every few days." His next book, with his Washington and Beethoven and his "Scholars at the Pavilion" poems added, was, he calculated, already "a quarter done" and might well be published in two years' time. He was also working on a "vast gorgeous anthology" of poetry (beginning with the Rig-Veda and ending with Richard Wilbur), which would "render all existing ones superfluous & evil." Having worked that hard, he rewarded himself with a drink the following afternoon, then another and another, until once more he was drunk.

This time he found the strength to right himself. At least, he congratulated himself, he had managed to get back to work at once. The following day he sent *Poetry* ten of his Addresses, hoping they could publish them before *Love & Fame* appeared. But there was not enough time, and the poems were returned. He worked again on his biography of Shakespeare. Then he received "an able thesis" from Susan Berndt on the eight epigraphs to *The Dream Songs*. Much research, he noted, had gone into the thesis, "all relevant," though the piece was at times "over-ingenious," as when she'd argued that the elegiac form had been "influenced by the prosody of ancient Hebrew laments." As far as he knew, it hadn't.

On Sunday, July 26, he read from his poems in a "people's park" in Minneapolis near the west bank of the campus. Peter Stitt, who had been Berryman's student in 1962, reintroduced himself, and Berryman agreed to be interviewed by him for *The Paris Review* in October. Eight days later Berryman wrote Meredith at Bread Loaf, thanking him for sending along his new poems. He'd been much taken with them and hoped Meredith took the prizes away from his own book. He included the Pulitzer—from the judging of which he had withdrawn, knowing that his own *Love & Fame* would be one of the contenders for that.

"I heard Dickey read a beauty on TV the other night," he added. He'd also heard from Tony Alvarez that Cal was not doing well, and he was worried. He'd just received a letter from Chris, the first he'd had from her since 1947. "That bold remembered hand!" She'd talked first about *The Dream Songs,* then about the sonnets (she had no objection to their publication). Her son, who'd figured in several of the sonnets, was married now, and her husband had left home the previous September "in a fog of invective, evid'ly looking for the adolescence he denied himself 30-odd-years-ago." Bellow had called from Chicago to say that the poems Berryman had written in Abbott—"The Hell Poem" and "Death Ballad"—had actually changed Bellow's life. With that sort of approbation Berryman was "ready now for what anyone else" might say. "I really write mostly for him," Berryman told Meredith. And sometimes for Bhain Campbell.

But at home there was tremendous friction that summer, and Berryman was terrified as he felt his old supports pulling away from him. Suddenly he felt very old:

> Age, and the deaths, and the ghosts.
> Her having gone away
> in spirit from me. Hosts
> of regrets come & find me empty.

I don't feel this will change.
I don't want any thing
or person, familiar or strange.
I don't think I will sing

any more just now;
or ever. I must start
to sit with a blind brow
above an empty heart.

Back in March, when he'd written "The Home Ballad," he'd praised Kate for making the new poems possible. Now, he felt his own fate unraveling from hers. He carried on affairs of the imagination, warming up the mails with letters to young women. What he needed if he was really going to change, he reasoned, was a change in routine. So, in spite of his doctors' warnings, when Loyola University of Montreal offered him nearly twenty thousand dollars for three months' teaching that fall, he seized the opportunity. Deneen Peckinpah was there now, and he planned to fan out from Montreal to see his friends and the world. Kate would stay home and begin teaching.

In mid-August he was still making changes on the galleys of *Love & Fame*. That week alone he wrote three new "political poems" to replace three poems he'd killed. One of the new poems was "To a Woman," which he thought "an exquisite intense thing" in which he had written that man had so darkened himself that "perhaps essentially now" it was the woman's turn to see what she could do, especially with her "peculiar strength of patience." Another poem he wrote was "Regents' Professor Berryman's Crack on Race," in which he confronted the militant black rhetoric of the moment with his own militant white rhetoric. What he hoped for was a standoff. Given charge and countercharge, what he asked was for the two sides to sit down and talk:

At least your camp & ours might camp together,
your wise ones brood by ours, and your fanatics
armed by the Pentagon with our fanatics
*have it out* & good riddance . . .

so that cooler heads, like Ralph Ellison, who had seriously considered the complexities of the race issue, might begin to be listened to. It was a poem, he confessed to Meredith, that would probably please no one. But what he hoped to gain with the new socially oriented poems was a more "wide-ranging" effect for his book. Then he went to work finishing up his new *Selected Poems: 1938–1968* for Faber & Faber, a volume he hoped would "stagger even my devotees."

At the end of August he and Kate flew to Mexico City for a week's vacation. It was a tense time, with Berryman's nerves screaming for a drink, and just before their return home, Berryman wrote some lines that indicated just how fed up he was with not drinking. He called his poem, "Man Building Up to a Slip":

> I haven't downed a whiskey for 4 months,
> a girl for years. Liebchen, I'm growing old,
> with seventeen thousand dollars in the bank
> & a restless restless.

Afraid of what might happen to him if he was away from home for a semester, he decided against the job in Montreal and taught instead at Minnesota. But even that did not stop him from drinking again. By the end of September, when he finished his elegy for Dylan Thomas, "In Memoriam (1914–1953)," he was up once more to a quart of whiskey a day, and the poem reflected how much now he wanted an end to his twenty-five-year struggle with alcohol. In the poem he recalled Dylan in St. Vincent's Hospital and then worked backward to their time in Cambridge and Seattle together. But it also recalled Dylan's thoughts on heaven and of his "radiant will to go there." Berryman ended the poem with a toast to his dead friend to join him and

> disarm a while
> and down a many few.
> O down a many few, old friend,
> and down a many few.

Knowing the stagefright Kate felt as she faced her first regular class of sixth-graders, he wrote a poem for her called "The Great Day":

> Thirty-one years to brief you for this morning
> & still you fear you'll find yr mind a blank
> facing their faces at nine.
> You won't, dear, and by three it will all be over.
>
> I recall my first day. I stood in the corridor
> looking down at the slant door of my classroom
> and I thought: *No. Impossible. I can't.*
> But I went closer—until I cd see
>
> a senior professor whom I'd met & liked
> sitting at the desk in the front of the room waiting
> to introduce me to the terrible youngsters—
> and I breathed again & went in.
>
> Then I adored that year, my kids in my pockets
> & coming out my ears, I taught like a madman
> no hour was long enough for everything,
> you'll have a high time, honey. Love & luck.

But he had gone a long way in those thirty-one years toward destroying his teaching effectiveness along with himself. He'd had to wait fifteen years to teach a course in the English department—his Hamlet seminar the previous winter—and had then proceeded to ruin it, forcing half his class by his ranting and bullying to leave and then meeting the rest each week at a bar in downtown Minneapolis. He would not be given another opportunity, Regents' Professor or no. If he was going to teach English, it would have to be his Humanities courses.

As his drinking intensified, so did his nightmares. He woke from one on the morning of October 3. Unable to fall back to sleep, he wrote a poem called "Ecce Homo," focusing on the crucified Christ he'd seen in a photograph: Burgundian, "painted & gilt wood,/ life-size almost," the beaten body

> attenuated, your dead head bent forward sideways,
> your long feet hanging, your thin long arms out
> in unconquerable beseeching. . . .

The following day he wrote Meredith. He had promised to read in Pittsburgh for Hazo's forum sometime "mid-week," then give a reading for Bill Heyen at the Brockport Forum Wednesday night and a television interview for him the following morning. He wondered if they might not have lunch together in Pittsburgh before he flew to New York to see Giroux. He would call Meredith from Hazo's.

But when he'd written Heyen on August 19 about reading at the Brockport (New York) Forum, he had confused it even then with the Pittsburgh Forum. So, while Meredith and Merwin waited for him at the airport in Pittsburgh one October afternoon, Berryman was in Brockport, extremely drunk. "I kept feeling," Heyen would write, "that Berryman was spending for vast returns, was driving himself toward the next poem in a necessary frenzy, and that he had been born to do this. He was always noting lines, sounding out lines, pulling one of his new short poems from one of his pockets." On the evening of Berryman's arrival in Brockport, Heyen stayed up all night with him, then tried to prepare him for his television interview the following morning. It was a bright autumn day, and Heyen thought he and Berryman could walk the short distance to the television studio. But after a few steps Berryman began complaining about his bad foot and about how Heyen was torturing him by making him walk.

The tape rolled. Berryman read "Song of the Tortured Girl," commented on it, and spoke of some of his influences. The artist was a sort of advance man for the culture, he noted, so that when Hart Crane had jumped from the stern of the S. S. *Orizaba* "he did not give a *shit* about the foundation of the country and so on." Art was "created out of ordeal and crisis," and it was the artist's job to record what he saw. But to do this, he had to prepare himself without any support from his society. Life itself amounted to little more than a series of ever sharper losses.

When Heyen asked him whether or not the artist had a responsibility to affirm something finally, Berryman answered no. How else, he added, could one explain someone like Beckett, who had a mind so dark it made one wonder "if the Renaissance ever really took place." Thinking of his own generation of poets, he could think of only two others like it: the English Romantics and the Soviet poets just after the Revolution. It was the price one paid for living in a bad time with an overdeveloped sensibility. Poets like him, he finished, wound up in hospitals, where they were judged "completely untreatable." In two days Heyen saw Berryman cry four times: when he called a young woman named Yvonne late at night and read her a new poem, which she apparently did not care for; then again, when he reminisced about Dylan and, later, Blackmur; and, finally, when he recalled the horrors of Belsen, Auschwitz, and Dachau.

On Friday morning, October 9, Berryman flew from Rochester to New York City to see Giroux before flying out to Minneapolis that night. When Berryman called Kate late that evening, he hung up without saying where he was. Kate waited up for him, but when he did not show up by Sunday morning, she called Heyen to ask if *he* knew where her husband was. Together they tried retracing Berryman's steps. Finally, Heyen called Kate Sunday night, only to learn that Berryman had in fact been in Minneapolis since Friday night. He had just shown up at home in very bad shape and was about to go back into the hospital.

Berryman never could remember all of what had happened to him after his plane landed in Minneapolis. He did remember calling Kate from the airport and then taking a taxi from the airport to get home and stopping at one of his old haunts for a nightcap. There had been a woman, "an Arab" graduate student, and he had wound up in her apartment. He remembered thinking at some point that this was it, that he'd had it, that he would wait till the stores opened Monday morning, buy himself a gun, and end the mess his life had become. But Sunday night he changed his mind and told the woman to drive him home. "Every light in the house seemed to be on," he would write later:

> He knew he was standing in his entry-hall. Wife facing him, cold eyes, her arm outstretched with a short glass—a little smaller than he liked—in her hand. Two cops to his left. His main Dean and wife off somewhere right. . . . The girl had gone. He was looking into his wife's eyes and he was hearing her say: "This is the last drink you will ever take." Even as somewhere up in

> his feathery mind he said "Screw that," somewhere he also had an unnerving and apocalyptic feeling that this might be true. . . .

"Six weird days & six nights" had come to their conclusion. Attended by two campus security guards, he was strapped down and taken by ambulance across the Washington Avenue Bridge to the locked ward at St. Mary's.

## chapter 31

# Thin Long Arms Out in Unconquerable Beseeching

## 1970–71

Sorry not to see you last Thurs here,'' Meredith wrote Berryman from Pittsburgh on October 14. ''Bill Merwin read real good'' and he and Merwin had waited at the airport to greet him. So it had not been a dream, Berryman realized, this having to be in two places at once. On the evening of the twenty-fourth, at the end of his second week at St. Mary's, he wrote to Paul, now thirteen, the age when, as a young Jewish male, he would enter manhood. No wonder people valued ''the chief writers of the world,'' he wrote his son. Who would not ''stand amazed at both the gifts of the Lord and the uses which certain miserable, ecstatic persons have been able to make of them''? The only thing harder than writing was to *try* ''to love and know the Lord, in impenetrable silence.'' In spite of his being an alcoholic, he pleaded with his son, he was not without value. He had worked very hard to make himself worthy of his art at great personal cost, and he was trying now—against mounting odds—to make himself worthy before God.

By the beginning of the third week of treatment, Berryman

was feeling strong enough to write poems again, and over the next three weeks managed seven. The first, composed on the twenty-seventh, stated the difficulty head on:

> Surely he has a recovery for me
> and that must be after all my complex struggles: *very* simple.
>
> I do, despite my self-doubts, day by day
> grow more & more but a little confident
> that I will never down a whiskey again
> or gin or rum or vodka, brandy or ale.
>
> It is, after all, very very difficult to despair
> while the wonder of the sun       this morning
> as yesterday & probably tomorrow.
> It all is, after all, very simple.
>
> You just never drink again all each damned day.

That same afternoon Peter Stitt had the first of his two interviews with Berryman, who sat on the edge of his hospital bed smoking Tareytons and drinking cup after cup of coffee. Stitt began by asking about Berryman's search for fame. He hadn't really been much of a poet as a young man, Berryman had to acknowledge, and he'd protected himself by refusing to read reviews of his work. But he hoped by now he'd *earned* his right to what fame he had.

He hated being lumped with the Confessional poets and despised the name. Besides, he added, he hadn't been to confession since he was twelve. He defended the unity of *The Dream Songs,* which had their own "personality" and a plan behind them, though in truth he hadn't known, any more than Henry, "what the bloody fucking hell was going to happen next. Whatever it was, Henry had had to confront it and get through."

His post-Henry poems, on the other hand, were based rather "on the historical personality of the poet": himself. For the first time in his life he'd managed to wipe out all his masks. The new poems had looked "so weird," so unlike anything he'd done before, that he'd needed "reassurance and confirmation" from his friends. But most of his pals had bombed the new poems, and Edmund Wilson had gone so far as to call *Love &*

*Fame* hopeless. Well, he had known the "Eleven Addresses" were "going to trouble a lot of people." After all, the country was "full of aetheists" who felt "threatened" by such poems.

But he also wanted it understood that the Addresses were *not* Christian poems. For while he was "deeply interested" in Christ, he never prayed to Christ. "I don't know whether he was in any special sense the son of God, and I think it is quite impossible to know," he explained, though Christ was surely "the most remarkable *man* who ever lived." He felt embarrassed now by his conversion experience, especially in light of the reversals that had come to him, so that he felt like a man too soon proclaiming his undying love and then becoming paralyzed when he saw what he'd committed himself to.

Since February he'd written over a hundred poems, and now he was "a complete wreck." All he actually wanted from the Lord was a mind fresh for writing and something worth writing about. "I hope to be nearly crucified," he added. "I'm scared, but I'm willing. I'm sure this is a preposterous attitude, but I'm not ashamed of it." Months later, chastened by new failures and reading what he'd told Stitt, he would scribble in the column next to these words the single word "Delusion."

The first notice of *Love & Fame* appeared in the November 2 issue of *The Nation*. It was by Hayden Carruth, who tore into the book as a "muddlement" of confessions, brags, and rants, "full of self-contradiction, special pleading, vagueness." What particularly irked Carruth was the sixth Address, in which Berryman had precisely dated his turning to God. What did this "boasting, equivocating secularist" take his readers for that he expected them to believe that Berryman—of all people—was capable of such a conversion? When he compared Berryman's poems with the work of his contemporaries, Carruth could see that all of them had produced poems while Berryman had only managed to make "language twisted and posed."

Berryman answered Carruth in the "Letters" section of *The Nation* four weeks later. As for the tone of that sixth Address, he insisted, Carruth had to have willfully misread it, for what he'd done there was localize his religious experience the way a lover "memorializes the date and place of his first kiss." If readers couldn't get at least the tone of *those* lines right, he was going to resign from poetry. As for the company Carruth had placed him in—Lowell, Bishop, Roethke—he found it "positively bracing! My pals!" He knew they'd written better short poems than any he had yet written. It was only with his long poem that he was "claiming parity."

Carruth had hated his work for fifteen years, he explained to Meredith six weeks later, and had probably thought he could nail Berryman with that review. Actually, Berryman believed he'd been gentle with Carruth in his response, even though he had felt it necessary to force Carruth "to bring the patibulum and the cross bar to the upright and put it up. Then, I nailed him on it, waited until he died, took him down, put him in the grave, filled the grave and placed a nosegay on it." *That,* he added, was how you crucified someone.

On November 5, Berryman wrote a poem from inside St. Mary's called "The Recognition." He thought of Kate, of all she'd had to put up with, and wondered if now he really had lost her. When he'd telephoned her, she'd been so short with him he was afraid it was so. But then she'd come to see him, concerned about one of her students and asking his advice. With relief, he read her coming as a sign that she still did love him.

"I am making myself into a new man here and sister, it hurts," he wrote Adrienne Rich on the eighth. That night he also wrote Meredith, delighted that Meredith had approved of the "Eleven Addresses," work—as Meredith had said—that had blessed Berryman's "high final transfigured working years." Berryman wondered if, after all, it was to this point that his life's work had always pointed. If God wanted him to fail, well, he would try to accept that as his fate. In any case, he was going to write now for one reason only: to make God happy. Such a notion, he realized, was "absurd," since God *was* happy. Nevertheless, he insisted, that seemed "to be the story!"

This third treatment for alcoholism differed, he believed, from his previous treatments, in that the experience this time round was "humbler but grander" than before. One morning during transactional analysis he had suddenly seen himself not as an actor in an amphitheater but as the amphitheater itself, watching the drama of life unfold before him. Desperate for a cure, he tried harder than ever to level with himself. He struggled to move outside himself and help the other patients on the ward. When one of them left, he applauded, wept, cheered. He listened to the suggestions made to him in therapy. But he also composed extraordinary poems that told him who he really was: a man who, for all his yesses, was still saying no:

> If after finite struggle, infinite aid,
> ever you come there, friend,
> remember backward me lost in defiance,
> as I remember those admitting & complying.

On the afternoon of November 13 he had a visit from a rabbi. He wondered if, in the wake of his conversion experience, he ought now to convert to Judaism. He pored over Milton Steinberg's *Basic Judaism,* underscoring passages and carrying on an extensive dialogue with the text. He thought of his many Jewish friends, of his love for the work of Babel and Buber and the Book of Job, of his struggle to learn Hebrew. Moreover, his only son was a Jew. "My uneasiness with Xt'y came to a head in Mass . . . this morning," he wrote that day. But for all his love and reverence of Judaism, he did not convert.

On the sixteenth, the beginning of his sixth—and last—week of treatment, he wrote to his mother. Had she saved the letters he had written her from South Kent? If she had, he wanted them as soon as possible, for they might hold the key to his present crisis. Then he gave her a list of questions to answer, pleading with her to be as candid as possible in her answers:

> 1) Did I *hear* Daddy threaten to swim out w me (or Bob?) or drown us both? or did you tell me later? *when?*
> 2) When did I first learn that he'd killed himself?
> 3) How did I *seem to take* his death when first told? Before the drive back to Tampa that morning? How did I *act* in the car? Back in Tampa? at the funeral parlour? At the graveyard in Holdenville? in Minn? Gloucester? thro' the 8th grade? (in Wash DC?—where I tho't I recognized him on the street one day—crushed? *During the summer before I went to SKS??* Please tell me everything you can remember abt me that summer.
> 4) I cannot recall *any* intellectual life in me during my 4 yrs at SKS. *Can you,* in me? What did I *read?* (I recall not *one bk*—tho' I read often, after lights out, w a flashlight under covers or in my closet.)
> 5) Can you pinpoint, or make any suggestions about, the begin-

ning of my return to *normalcy* and the busy effective life I led as a Freshman?

His mother began a letter on the eighteenth saying that the early letters had been stored in Anadarko and were lost, though, in fact, she was in possession of them. She tried reconstructing those early events twice, each time altering the story. Then, on the twenty-second, as he was about to leave St. Mary's, Berryman wrote to his mother again, apologizing for having laid such a burden on her. Perhaps it was better, as his AA counselors had advised him, to forget what had happened to his father. He had given up trying to recover the past first for a day, and then, feeling better, had decided to let it go for good. He considered that surrender "one of the major advances made in this treatment," for it did not seem to be "God's will that I shd at present—or possibly ever—find out any more abt those mysterious subjects."

That Thanksgiving he thanked the Lord for "warm walls all safe" and for Kate, who was pregnant again, as well as for the Thanksgiving dinner he would have, and asked simply that he might always do his family and his God

not sufficient honour
but such as we become able to devise
out of a decent or joyful *conscience* & thanksgiving.
Yippee!
Bless then, as Thou wilt, this wilderness board.

By December 1, he had been out ten days and congratulated himself that he felt fine. He would be in outpatient treatment for two years; his next drink would have to be on his deathbed. Earlier he had promised to give readings at ten colleges in Wisconsin before going off to New York to see plays and record his poetry. He invited Valerie Trueblood to come up from Washington to have dinner with him, if she was interested. Then he was going to fly to Haiti for ten days to read. He decided, however, to cut the ten Wisconsin readings to five and checked into the Chelsea on December 13. By then, having passed through several airports, he was once again drinking heavily. He began calling his New York friends and making long-distance calls at all hours of the night. He called Eileen, who was now remarried, and asked if he could talk with her in New York. She would see him, she told him, but not while he was drinking. He did not see her.

"We met one noon during the taxi strike at the Chelsea Hotel," Lowell would remember, the place

> dusty with donated, avant-garde constructs, and dismal with personal recollections, Bohemia, and the death of Thomas. There was no cheerful restaurant within walking distance, and the seven best bad ones were closed. We settled for the huge, varnished unwelcome of an empty cafeteria-bar. John addressed me with an awareness of his dignity, as if he were Ezra Pound at St. Elizabeth's, emphatic without pertinence. . . . I said, "When will I see you again?" meaning, in the next few days before I flew to England. John said, "Cal, I was thinking through lunch that I'll never see you again."

When Berryman got back home on December 23, however, he determined to resume his AA program, knowing too well what the grim alternative was. "O torso hurled high in great 'planes from town/ down on confulsing town," he wrote Christmas Day,

> brainsick applause
> thick to sick ear, through sixteen panicked nights
> a trail of tilted bottles. . . .

On the twenty-ninth he went to an AA meeting and spoke frankly about the pattern that had been his downfall: work till exhaustion set in, then reward oneself with a drink in an airport bar or from the hostess on the plane, and then another and another until once more one was a wreck. Work, that he had to do. He was driven to it. But he counseled himself to avoid "all avoidable nervous & mental effort for weeks to come."

Lowell wrote to say he had read the "Eleven Addresses" and could "hardly find words to praise it." And while it was "cunning in its scepticism," it really did feel "like a Catholic prayer to a personal God." He marveled at the "humorous, anguished admission of faults, somewhat like Corbière to whom your book is appealingly dedicated." The Addresses amounted to "one of the great poems of the age, a puzzle and triumph to anyone who wants to write a personal devotional poem." With the "Opus Posthumous" sequence, it formed the crown of Berryman's work. "You write close to death," Lowell ended, "I mean in your imagination. Don't take it from your heart into life." And, he pleaded, "don't say we won't meet again."

A week after Christmas, Berryman was interviewed at home by Martin Berg for the *Minnesota Daily*. There were books everywhere, filling the bookshelves and spilling over onto the coffee table and the floor. Berryman, smoking and drinking coffee and ginger ale nonstop, opened the interview by mentioning Lowell's praise for the Addresses. For the past ten months he'd been writing poems at the rate of two to three a week, so that his next book of poems was nearly finished. Sooner or later, he knew, the vein was going to dry up. "In the ordinary way, if there is any ordinary way," he explained, "maybe you write a poem a month. That's 12 poems a year, 25 poems in two years; publish a book." He had surpassed those numbers long ago.

While at St. Mary's he'd written "Another New Year's Eve," one of two poems he had printed as his Christmas card for the year. When it appeared in *The New York Times* on New Year's Day, he'd changed its title to "Year's End, 1970":

> The nation-wide spirit of Romp subtilized into
> the nation-wide spirit of Grump.
> Grump grump. Vietnam. Unemployment.
> The militants. Spiro malignant. *All* genuine causes!
>
> Warheads accumulating all over the place.
> Hi-jackings in midair.
> Greasy water. Another baby born blue. . . .

In such times how did one keep in touch with God? he wondered. He was not sure, but he was at least trying to use his talents and keep busy. And with a new year coming in, there was always the chance for a new beginning.

In mid-January he wrote a "Scholia" to the shortened second edition of *Love & Fame,* excising six of the book's more objectionable lyrics. "The initial American public reception of this book, whether hostile, cool, or hot, was so uncomprehending," he wrote, "that I wondered whether I had wasted my time.'' However uneven the book was, he insisted, it formed a whole, the later books ''criticizing backward the preceding, until Part IV wipes out altogether all earlier presentations of the 'love' and 'fame' of the ironic title.''

On the twenty-seventh he read as the year's William Vaughn Moody lecturer at the University of Chicago. The day before, he'd had a letter from Allen Tate, attacking him for the poems in the first three sections of *Love & Fame,* and he had become so upset he'd begun drinking again. By the time he flew into Chicago, he was roaring drunk. He had lunch with Saul Bellow and a young woman Berryman had invited to fly from the East Coast to see him, ostensibly to interview him. Later that afternoon Joseph Haas, a reporter for the *Chicago Daily News,* came by his room at the Quadrangle Club on campus and found him with the same young woman.

He also found a half-empty bottle on the table and a disheveled, chain-smoking Berryman nursing a waterglass filled with whiskey. Berryman mumbled, shouted, slurred unintelligibly, then turned off the tape recorder. *The Dream Songs* were about him and his friends and God. He had killed off Henry, then raised him from the dead to start over, putting him through test after test to see what he would do. America was a magnificent country with an ''atrocious government.'' He didn't much like the life-style of the young these days, and didn't like women dressing up like men. Yes, he was a male chauvinist. He was also a medium for the larger forces going on around him, a sort of national sounding board trying to be useful to the American effort. He was aware too that he sometimes shamed the notion of the American poet.

In the evening he read ''The Ball Poem,'' ''Song of the Tortured Girl,'' a selection of *The Dream Songs*, and some of his new lyrics. But he was too ill to read effectively anymore. ''He had arrived during a sub-zero wave,'' Bellow would remember. ''Thin coat and big Homburg, bearded, he coughed up phlegm. He looked decayed. He had been drinking and the reading was a disaster. His Princeton mutter, once an affectation, had become a vice. People strained to hear. We left a disappointed, bewildered, angry audience. Dignified, he entered a waiting car, sat down, and vomited. He passed out in his room . . . and slept through the faculty party given in his honor. But in the morning he was full of innocent cheer. He was chirping. It had been a great evening. He recalled an immense success. His cab came, we hugged each other, and he was off for the airport under a frozen sun."

When he got back to Minneapolis, he had himself admitted to the hospital for a nerve operation on his foot. After his "lost forty hours" of drinking, he righted himself, stopped drinking, and returned to his AA group. In mid-January he had begun an "Opus Dei" sequence that consisted of nine poems—the eight canonical hours, plus a new "Interstitial Office" for the 8:00 A.M. news hour. These lyrics were more complex, crabbed, harder and wittier than the Addresses, and they rubbed against the nerves in ways the earlier poems had not. In early February he wrote "Nones," a confession that he didn't think he had it in him to be counted among the saved. If only he could find some "middle ground," some "decent if minute salvation," he sighed, it would be enough.

He considered closing his next book of poems, *Delusions,* with this sequence, much as he had closed *Love & Fame* with the Addresses. On February 10, he wrote a draft of "Compline," the final poem of his new sequence. Was he like Josiah, who repented and went to his grave in peace? Or was he more like the king's son, "declared unfit by wise friends to inherit/ and nothing of me left but skull & feet/ & bloody among their dogs the palms of my hands"? Sin on, he wrote. Suffer now and suffer later, but not forever. Somewhere, dear God, it had to stop.

"I've got horribly behind w. letters, working at a poem on the Divine Office," he wrote his mother on February 28. He had also mislaid half his lecture notes, "so up to my neck in Dante, & three public lectures (last one next Wed, D[eo] G[ratias], and three readings (Chicago, Moorhead, Kansas City) etc etc." At last he had read her belated version of those final weeks in Florida before his father had killed himself and had been "amazed" by her vivid recounting. They would talk at length when she came out to Minneapolis that spring to live near them. He had bought Martha and Kate rings the day before: "Martha a little turquoise christened 'Patsy', & K a 5-ruby (v. small) gold one, handsome." He was treating himself to "Christian literature almost as fiercely as artbooks." Paul had been accepted at Andover for the fall. He had planned to go to Rotterdam in June for an International Poetry Festival, taking Martha and Paul with him, but he knew too well what long trips had cost him in the past.

As winter term ended, he wrote his chairman asking for a further reduction in his teaching assignments. He was at last becoming part of the canon of American literature and needed more time from his university duties for his own work. In March he and another member of his AA squad drove over to a bar on Nicollet Avenue to help an alcoholic who was having a bad time of it. Another time it was a trip to Stillwater Prison with another AA member to talk with the inmates there. It was not easy work for him, but reaching out to others helped keep him drinkless. He did it grimly, knowing what would happen if he ever went back to the bottle again.

On March 12 he read Frost's poem "The Draft Horse," the one poem he had found of use in all of Frost's last volume of poetry. He'd been lecturing on American power and was astonished to see that that was what Frost had been talking about in his poem as well. The problem with America, Berryman saw, was the same problem facing him: unwarranted arrogance based on the illusion of unlimited power. Such delusions would have to be surrendered if he and the country were ever going to heal themselves.

On the sixteenth he read a report on My Lai 4, commenting on the massacre three years after the event, and began a poem on the abuses of American military power. The unfinished draft read in places like an updated version of "The Waste Land":

> Rubble & jungle now, where Calley came,
> laced so with American booby traps & mines
> comes now from Tu Cung none, where joe sticks burn
> for the terrible non-survivors of his saving,
>
> Du Chuc scrutched a line of X's on the perimeter
> for rounds of artillery falling & falling & falling,
> then studied the dirt & drew an X: "This was
> my hut. My family was beginning breakfast.
>
> The white, the black, were shooting, and they killed
> 3 of my children and they wounded my wife."

Bells tinkle from the hut adjacent (this
is a 60-family ghetto . . .

for My Lai 4's) out of soft night
ghostly flares now on all the filthy cities of America
falling
falling falling burning out our ghettos & sin.

He finished the "Opus Dei" sequence on March 24 with "Vespers." He was still arguing with God, incredulous that man, this creature of vanities and ape-lusts, should be asked by God to love others. He considered Einstein and Anne Frank and puzzled over how such people had come to exist given the sorry condition of the human race. He ended the sequence exactly where he'd begun the "Eleven Addresses" ten months earlier, with the poet kneeling, awestruck, addressing the Unknowable.

A week later he wrote Sister Agnes Fleck of Duluth, Minnesota, who had written to thank him for writing the "Eleven Addresses." Her high school students had sent him a questionnaire that, had he answered, he twitted her, might have "been headlined in *The N.Y. Review*." He thanked her for tolerating the hellish poems of "vanity, greed, & lust" that had led up to the Addresses. True, he had taken an ironic stance toward those "despicable attributes," but those vices were still there. As for the religious poems, he could hardly take credit for those, since they had been, where they were any good, a gift from God. All he could hope for was to be God's instrument, "an attentive pen (highly trained, self-'sacrificing', in fair repair)." He asked Sister Agnes to pray for him, as he promised to pray for her. Then, at the top of the page, he noted that the Lord had been "very good to me yest'y afternoon on a crucial matter, twice, and late last night *I realized it*. I half-wept."

# chapter 32

# I Am Busy Tired Mad Lonely & Old

## 1971–1972

In the April 5 issue of *Time* magazine, Berryman read a piece on black holes that explained that "ninety percent of the mass of the Universe" had disappeared forever into pulseless, lightless collapsars. Was that 90 percent somewhere else, he asked himself in a poem he called "Certainty Before Lunch," or was it really gone forever? And had 90 percent of himself also disappeared forever? he wondered, walking with what was left of himself through Prospect Park with two friends on this particular morning with late snow still on the ground and Easter in the air. So it was not, then, a question of the disappearance of God after all, but rather a question of the disappearance of man, and of this man in particular. "My Lord," he ended.

> I'm glad we don't
> on x or y depend for Your being there.
> I know You are there. The sweat is, I am here.

He wished more and more now he could make Nixon and his "hatchet-boy," Spiro Agnew, and the Vietnam War disappear. By then he had renamed his American Dream course "The American Nightmare." He thought of the thousands of Vietnam vets wounded in body and soul, and was staggered by the news that "27 % of all returned veterans in hospitals are known to have actually tried to kill themselves—a phenomenon unique in history, so far as I know, & blood-curdling."

On April 10, he sent a letter to the editor of *The New York Times*. "With regard to the agony or outraged or complacent denial or apathy of millions of us over our share in the guilt of Lt Calley for what happened at My Lai 4, and over our share of responsibility for other things," he wrote, Americans might consider what the Roman Catholic theologian Monsignor Romano Guardini had said about "collective guilt." Actually there was no such thing as collective guilt, Guardini had argued, since the guilt resided in those individuals who had done the wrong. But there was such a thing as collective honor and therefore collective shame, both of which demanded that Americans rectify an evil situation for which they were collectively responsible. Looked at in this way, Berryman argued, Americans did seem "responsible . . . for a decade of Asiatic corpses and uninhabitable countryside and genocidal 'resettlement' of whole populations of Asiatic villagers." The *Times* did not print the letter.

Still troubled by Tate's response to *Love & Fame*, Berryman jotted down some notes, trying to understand Tate's charges: that he was vulgar and had patronized Tate and that *Love & Fame* was a bad book. All of these charges had *some* truth in them, Berryman was willing to admit. But he'd been "far too easily lured into joining the authoritative opinion" against himself. He had not only not patronized Tate, he had actually been "admiring & grateful" toward him. Tate's response, therefore, had been "unjust," inspired by his failure as a poet, as well as for "not figuring more prominently" in *Love & Fame* as one of his mentors.

So it was Tate's problem, after all, and not his. Having worked this through in the light of Guardini's essay and his AA book, he sent Tate a greeting card, addressed from Regents' Professor Berryman to Regents' Professor Emeritus Tate, age seventy-one, retired, and living in Sewanee. "YOU HURT ME," the print on the card read. There was no other message. When he received the card, Tate wrote beneath those words the simple, devastating rejoinder: "This was my intention." Then Tate put the card aside.

That Easter, Berryman reread Bishop Lancelot Andrewes's "great sermon on the Resurrection." Christ, he wrote his mother that day, "was always 'in medio,' " like himself, still looking for some middle way between extremes. Three days later he wrote "The Prayer of the Middle-aged Man," an address to Christ as mediator. Then he wrote another prayer, using the execration forms of the prophet Amos, which he directed against the Chinese for their covert support of the Vietnam War:

> For three insane things evil, and for four,
> will I vex Pekin in the latter days,
> their ancestors shall suffer for their children
> in turbid horror: so saith the Lord.
>
> For three insane things evil, and for four,
> baffle will I with victory Hanoi
> and gross pretenders, the black megaphone
> of doctrine over the tribes' hills saith the Lord.
>
> For three insane things evil, and for four . . .
> topple will I puny and greedy Thieu
> the potent client—harrowing that people on. . . .

On April 21 he wrote Bill Heyen, who had sent him a batch of Writers Forum programs to autograph. He had signed enough, he wrote in a friendly tone, and figured Heyen must be hoarding the damn things. But, he advised him, the bottom might drop out of the market at any minute. "2 or 3 yrs ago a friend of mine in Toronto [Deneen Peckinpah] got hard up & offered an old Xmas card of mine to a dealer who gave her $20 for it; that guy is going to get *stung* when instead of mounting to $45 (as he calculates) it plummets to $1.65 on alternate Thursdays."

In May, Drake University awarded Berryman his first honorary degree. He and Kate flew to Des Moines on the fifteenth so that he could give a reading. The following afternoon he attended commencement exercises, where he was capped, hooded, and honored. Then, on the twentieth, having successfully avoided the airport bars, he checked into the Shoreham Hotel in Hartford. Meredith was to come up from New London the following day and drive him to Goddard College in northern Vermont, where he would read.

But that night, alone in his room, drinkless and up late rereading Graham Greene's *The Power and the Glory,* Berryman sensed Someone in the room with him. Between 1:15 and 2:15 A.M. he wrote a religious poem that he called "The Facts & Issues" and that caught something of his fear and hysteria. If God wanted him to acknowledge His presence in that room, well, he was ready to, he shouted on the page. There were plenty of "smart cookies" out there who were ready to admit that God was in their midst too. But had Christ *really* died for the likes of *him*? Examining the evidence, it did seem that if God had suffered for humankind, then he too, with his "pathetic & disgusting vices," must be included. But why? So that John Berryman could be happy? Well, he was happy. In fact, he was "so happy" he could scream. "It's *enough!,*" he added. "I can't BEAR ANY MORE./ *Let this be it*. I've *had* it. I can't wait."

Later that morning, Meredith arrived in his old Mercedes and the two drove north. Berryman did not tell him that just hours earlier he had been contemplating suicide, but he did say that he'd called Kate at four in the morning to ask her to remind him "of any act of pure and costly giving" he'd ever done. He'd had enough of this either/or, this heaven and hell thing. He was willing to settle for some middle ground where he could get some sleep when the ordeal of living was finally over.

Late in the afternoon the car broke down and, instead of going to Bread Loaf as they'd planned, they decided to spend the night in Woodstock. Most of the trip that day had been taken up with Berryman's raving discourse on "the idiot temptation to try to live the Christian life," and by then both men were in need of sleep. Alcoholism was no longer the problem, he told Meredith, for, after struggling ineffectually with booze for the past quarter-century, he was wearing a tiny AA rosette in his lapel, the sign he'd stayed drinkless now for the past three months. That night, as he and Meredith walked the quiet treelined main street of the small Vermont town, Berryman began shouting out the dates for his tombstone. "John Berryman:

1914–19 . . ." But, he added, there was no particular hurry about filling in the blank.

After lunch the following day, two Goddard students, dressed in ragged jeans, loose blouses, and headbands, arrived to take Berryman and Meredith to Goddard. "You and I are the last of the unreconstructed snobs, Meredith!" Berryman shouted from the rear of the car, insisting on maintaining his decayed sense of courtliness at the same time that he distanced himself from the two hippies in the front seat. At the Goddard Poetry Festival, Berryman and Meredith were joined by Galway Kinnell, Marvin Bell, James Tate, Charles Simic, Louise Glück, Ellen Bryant Voigt, and others. At one point he made an awkward pass at Louise Glück, suggesting that the reason she'd been invited was because of her good looks. Glück chilled him quickly enough by telling him her looks were none of his business.

Nevertheless, that Saturday night he dedicated his reading to five of the "broads" sitting out in the audience, including Glück and his old flame Anita Philips. There was some lighthearted hissing from the women, and then he went on. It took him ninety minutes to get through five Dream Songs, Ellen Voigt would recall, with Berryman continually interrupting himself to veer off on some tangent.

Sunday morning the poets met at the guest house, with Berryman presiding over those who still remained. He was feeling very democratic just then, and began to expound on the idea that all this talk of major and minor poets was so much rot. Why, there were those who had been calling *him* a major poet for some time now, and surely—he waved his hand grandly toward Meredith—there were those who considered his friend there a minor poet. But, he beamed, even Meredith had written one great poem. Then he turned to the others and bade them magisterially to read out what each thought his or her best poem.

The following day Berryman, James Tate, and Simic flew to Boston for their connecting flights, Tate and Simic up front and Berryman in the back. Halfway through the flight, Berryman passed up a slip of paper with a poem on it. As Tate turned around, he saw Berryman beaming, waiting for the nod that would mean approval. It was a draft of "How Do You Do, Dr. Berryman, Sir?," and Dr. Berryman gave his answer:

Edgy, perhaps. *Not* on the point of bursting-forth,
but toward that latitude. . . .

Pickt up pre-dawn & tortured and detained,
Mr Tan Mam and many other students
sit tight but vocal in illegal cells
and as for Henry Pussycat he'd just as soon be dead

(on the Promise of—I know it sounds incredible—
if can he muster penitence enough—
he can't though—
glory)

From Boston, Berryman flew to Washington to see his mother and visit with some friends he'd made there seven years earlier: Keith and Debbie Fort. Through them he met a twenty-two-year-old student named Linda Lombardo, who showed him her sequence about a girl named "Sadeyes," whom Berryman praised as "Henry's twin sister." These were, he told them, the first poems that showed how others might use his idiosyncratic Dream Songs as a model. Later, while his hosts drank whiskey, he downed sodas. When Debbie Fort asked him how he felt watching others drink, he brushed the question aside. But after they'd gone to bed, he caught a full-breasted open bottle of Kentucky bourbon smiling at him from the kitchen counter. He let it go and went to bed.

Jill, now seventy-six, had clearly begun to fail, and Berryman was determined to move her to Minneapolis, where he and Kate could look after her. She lived like a recluse now and had been doing things like baking her letters and then putting gloves on to mail them so that her son's family wouldn't catch her cold. When Berryman came to the door, she screamed at him, accusing him of having abandoned her. Except for him, she shouted, she might have been a philologist. When Berryman spoke with her physician, he urged Berryman to get his mother out of Washington and closer to him. There were excellent medical facilities and physicians in Minneapolis, and Jill would have family to look after her. Finally Jill gave in. By the time Berryman flew back to Minneapolis, she had promised to follow as soon as possible.

* * *

Now Berryman retrieved one of his journals from Martha with her writing scrawled over its opening pages, and decided to use it to plot a novel called *Recovery*. He wrote out two pages, then showed them to Kate. Eventually he would show them to Bellow and perhaps to Mary Lou at the AA center, who'd helped him work his way through his third treatment. Everything seemed to be chiming with his new endeavor, he thought, as if God, though pulsing more dully now, still smiled on him. He continued his grim iron discipline over himself: dumbbell exercises (ten pounds), yoga, reading from the AA twenty-four-hour book, studying the Psalms and the lives of the saints, as well as Baudelaire and Pascal. He listened to Bach, Mozart, Beethoven. He revised the manuscript of *Delusions,* wrote letters, even tried, once more, driving a car, and put his office files in order. Each day he wrote a little on his *Life of Christ,* his primer for adolescents. He paid attention when he went to mass at St. Frances Cabrini's.

Having worked so hard, it was time, he felt, to reward himself. At the end of May he placed a personal ad in *The New York Review of Books*:

> POET-BIOGRAPHER-CRITIC-SCHOLAR, Pulitzer, NBA, etc., top tenure major university, paperback reprints selling briskly, readings & lectures country-wide, stonewalling seminar-leader, might be interested contributing radiance & the facts to an occasional change of scene. Next Jan–Febr bare possibility.

He took on yet another project. Just before the June 1 deadline, he applied to the National Endowment for the Humanities with a proposal to get on with his twenty-year-old Shakespeare project. "I'm in business at last. Hurrah," he cheered himself. He was sure he could handle his new freedom without wondering if he was going to steal a drink. Exploring every avenue of quick income to buy time for writing, he called an agent about reading fees. Split 70/30, the agent told him, he could get Berryman anywhere from $1,000–$1,500 a reading. So he was worth something after all.

As for the trouble he'd been having lately in his classes keeping his students interested, he would see what he could do about that. In the closing days of his seminar on The American

Nightmare, he had even come to agree with Agnew that "many students shd not be in college." He called his chairman and asked what could be done about the quality of students he was getting now, and was reminded that as things stood students could only get into his class with his express permission. He would have to remember that the next time he offered the course.

That week his picture appeared in *Time* magazine in the "Kudos" section receiving his degree from Drake. He dreamed of his upcoming trip to the Colorado mountains with Martha and Paul, and wondered what might be waiting for him out there. He celebrated the end of the term by working on his novel from half past five till half past eight that morning. He tried making up for lost time with his family. He taught Martha chess and helped her research a paper on black music by playing his Bessie Smith records for her. He tried getting back to his scholarship and began ordering books for himself by the gross. He fretted over the direction in which he saw his department heading, upset with the "inertness" of his chairman. He also worried that he might pick up the phone and call a cab to drive him to one of his old haunts in downtown Minneapolis.

"Dear old thing," he wrote Giroux on June 5, "All's well, better than well, everything plunging ahead, especially the novel. Last seminar yesterday, so now I'm four hours day [sic] on *Recovery* (besides most of the rest of the time too—it's hard to think of anything else in fact). That's probably 2 pp a day, a section (50 pages) a month, seven sections finished by Christmas. If not, no matter, but I think so." He'd already outlined the book for himself and shaped it around what he called its "16 High Points." The time covered would be the six weeks of his third treatment at St. Mary's, followed by his six months' outpatient treatment and the present with its "gradually undeluding experience." The book, he cheered himself, would *not* deal with Henry's solipsistic universe but with the "real world, people, events, [and] history."

On June 13, Jill Berryman arrived in Minneapolis. Berryman and Kate met her at the airport and took her to the new apartment they had found for her across the street from their home. But by the time Kate had driven them all back home, she was already in labor. She prepared dinner, ate, and was then admitted to the hospital. At 9:26 that evening she gave birth to a second daughter. "I just gave one mighty push," she told her husband, and there was Sarah Rebecca. For the next five days Berryman kept house indifferently, leaving dishes in the sink, Martha unwashed, and the air-conditioner running until it was caked with ice from overexertion, so preoccupied was he with his writing. Even Kate's homecoming became grist for his poetry. When he caught Martha peering through the car window at her baby sister, he decided he would end his next epic with that image.

On the twenty-fourth he wrote a draft of a poem for Sarah called "Hel*lo*." In it he remembered Kate nearly crushing his knuckles the night she had gone into labor. "Hel*lo* there, Biscuit!" he began:

> You're a better-looking broad
> by much than, and your sister's dancing up & down. . . .
> I can't wait seven weeks to see her grin
> I'm not myself, we are all changing here
> direction *and* velocity, to accommodate you, dear.

The Catholic Church Berryman had returned to that winter was not the Church he remembered from his youth in Oklahoma. Among other things were the reforms his beloved Pope John had instituted, and he did not find those changes to his liking. Since his devotion was more an interior affair, he did not take to the use of twangy guitars to replace the solemnity of the organ or to the use of the vernacular over the sonorities of the Latin. Nor did he like one iota shaking the hands of strangers at the Kiss of Peace.

On the Sunday after Kate's return from the hospital, the Berrymans listened to a newly ordained priest confess from the pulpit that he could identify with another priest who was leaving the priesthood after a twenty-year struggle. Christ's metaphor of the Good Shepherd caring for his sheep, the young priest had explained, was to be understood *only* as a metaphor. Up to that point Berryman had sat there fuming, but now he roared from his pew, "Only Christ's words." Then, having startled the entire congregation, he stormed out of the church.

At later masses, Berryman heard, the priest "was still inviting prayers for me," while Berryman walked "sadly up and down outside" praying for the priest "to come to his senses." He felt guilty about his uproar all that day, but next morning, reading the Twenty-sixth Psalm, he came across the passage "I have not sat with vain persons, neither will I go in with dissemblers, I have hated the congregation." Having received those words as another sign, Berryman was convinced he'd done the right thing.

Van Doren wrote to say that he'd sent the NEH a strong letter of recommendation and took the opportunity to tease his old student. They both knew Berryman was never going to finish any of his books on Shakespeare, for there would "always be metal more attractive: poems, novels, a memoir, a collection of pensées." It was an illusion—was it not?—that Berryman was still a scholar. Berryman disagreed with him, though he had to admit that instead of finishing his book of essays, *The Freedom of the Poet,* for which he'd signed a contract with Giroux two months earlier, he'd gone ahead and drafted an outline for a new book of essays instead.

To date he'd published thirteen books. He figured he had thirteen to go and maybe ten years left in which to write them, unless, of course, he went back to drinking, though that possibility, mercifully, seemed more and more remote. He had sixty to seventy letters to answer, many with manuscripts he'd been asked to read. But he meant to get to all of them. He also meant to finish his novel *and* his Shakespeare book.

That evening Giroux flew in to stand as godfather to Sarah. The christening, to which Berryman invited many of his friends in AA, took place at the Newman Center the following day. "Everybody & his brother dry thro' the afternoon, adoring Sarah & levelling," he noted. After the christening he showed Giroux the twenty-five pages of the new novel he'd written and was relieved to hear Giroux say he thought it marvelous and offering him what Berryman thought was a ten-thousand-dollar advance. Berryman was so keyed up with tension by then that, when Giroux left, he took a pain pill.

On July 1, he sent Bellow the news about Sarah. She was already twenty inches long, her hearing sharp as a lynx's, and she was "unusually beautiful . . . notwithstanding her evil parentage on one side." His son was due to arrive from New York that afternoon for two weeks to get to know Martha better and get some education from his father before beginning Andover. Berryman planned to have regular afternoon classes for Martha and Paul, and perhaps he would have Kate herself sit in on his lectures. Then he would take Paul and Martha up Pike's Peak before leaving Paul in Colorado with his mother on the sixteenth.

He spoke of his novel, adding that "bitter six-times-over experience" had taught him he could not write plays and might not be able to write a novel either, though he thought *Recovery* was coming along "hot as a pistol." Kate, naturally, still felt "too close" to the events leading up to his having had to be hospitalized for a third time to be able yet to judge the book, but he saw it as simply "a readable story abt a guy in real trouble." It would include "Encyclopedia data" on the AA "almost as heavy as Melville's abt whaling," and the "Outpatient section would include "a bloody philosophy of both History & *Existens,* almost as heavy as Tolstoy's" in *War and Peace* and would be "equally deluded and—alas—similarly tyrannical." There would be defeats and reversals, but in the end he envisioned "a sort of very provisional actual triumph." "Be on my side, Great Veteran!" he called now on Bellow. "Let's join forces, large & small, as in the winter beginning of 1953 in Princeton, with the Bradstreet blazing and Augie fleecing away. We're promising."

The day after Paul's arrival, however, Berryman realized that his educational plans for his children amounted to another of his grandiose delusions, and he abandoned his scheme. Instead, he wrote to the president of the university, asking for even more time off from teaching so that he could get on with his real work, since the university was getting "plus-strokes" out of him "every minute, no matter what" he did and he no longer wished to exploit himself. Someone had to protect him so that he could sustain his "not ordinary literary labours."

The more his poetic inspiration abandoned him, the more frenetic his schemes for publishing became. On July 3, he wrote a draft of a preface to yet another proposed book of essays, this one called, ominously, *Sacrifice*. The theme of exalted sacrifice, he noted, ran through a great deal of literature, from Henry James through Hemingway. It might well be that there was "an entirely new kind of freedom" for the poet in giving up all one's earlier freedoms as delusions. Might not the final change that death brought with it amount to nothing more than the last conversion, where one was changed, simply and irrevocably, into something else?

It was "a charming feature of the Amer[ican] intellectual scene at present," he went on, "that a halfwit like Miss Susan Sontag can flash from *P[artisan] R[eview]* & *The New York Review of Books* into *Time* mag & the academies and look like an original thinker and get $3000 for a lecture." He was incensed with the critical assumptions of her book *Against Interpretation,* which went against his own belief that the critical faculty was the hallmark of civilization itself. When Nixon, "the most powerful human being in the world" could loose "a half-paranoid half-hysterical hallucinating sentence on TV" and have it quoted "without insight by the nation's press for days & weeks afterward," where were the political analysts to point out his error? Or when "the outraged public of the world's supreme military-economic power" could flail over Lieutenant Calley's conduct "pro & con, why seek guidance from moral theology"?

Interpretation of events, of society, of the law, as of literature, was of supreme importance. "When six justices of the Supreme Court had turned out to be paranoid enough to vote for invasion of privacy," they too had engaged in an act of interpretation. Had not Daniel Ellsberg reinterpreted U.S. foreign policy "when he saw a human limb fly thro' the southeast Asian air"? The act of evaluating one's world responsibly was damned hard, no doubt about it, Berryman knew. But there was no way of avoiding that responsibility if civilization was to survive.

A few days later he wrote something on guilt and forgiveness for *Recovery* and was surprised to hear a "marvellous" talk at his AA meeting on the same subject. "Only somebody who has been forgiven knows what it is to forgive," he wrote, mulling over what Kate had just told him: that six months earlier she had slept with another man. Berryman had often placed her in dangerous situations, as if secretly hoping she too would be tempted and fall and so come to understand what he had had to go through over the years. Now, he learned, exactly that had happened.

The affair had begun while he'd been hospitalized for his third treatment. A man had shown up at 33 Arthur demanding to talk to Kate, purportedly about Berryman's advances toward his wife. Kate knew him as a recovering alcoholic, and he knew that Berryman was at St. Mary's undergoing treatment. He also guessed from his AA meetings with Berryman that Kate was lonely and beside herself with frustration and anger over her husband's repeated drinking. Now the man decided to act on Kate's vulnerability. The affair lasted a few weeks, and then Kate ended it. Learning of this now, Berryman understood that it was his turn to forgive.

He made the trip to Pike's Peak with Paul and Martha, saddened at what twelve years of separation had done to distance him from his son. Then, on the mountain, he had another premonition of impending death, a sense that the Douglas firs—"serried, noble beyond Beauty, attentive—above ten thousand feet"—were telling him something as he prepared his descent. At least, he understood, he had been very lucky in his life.

Back in Minneapolis, he wrote a belated letter to the *Times Literary Supplement* about an article in the April 4 issue that had dismissed Allen Tate's work. Upset as he still was with Tate, he was not willing to see him humiliated. In spite of their differences, he knew his generation of poets was indebted to Tate and that without Tate's assistance his own career might have turned out vastly different. Thirty-five years earlier he'd read Tate's work "to uncomprehending College societies" at Cambridge as well as to Dylan Thomas as an example of the best Tate's generation of American poets had had to offer. One simply did not patronize a man of Tate's accomplishments. The letter appeared in the August 7 issue of the *TLS,* and when Tate read it, he sent Berryman a postcard. He had "some good friends in England" who might have defended him, Tate wrote, but none had come forward. He thanked Berryman for writing on his behalf.

Berryman's private assessment of Tate, however, differed markedly from what he'd written the *TLS*. Writing to Eileen afterward, Berryman spoke of "Poor Allen, retired, neglected, grandiose in Tennessee, with half a dozen lyrics to his credit (not I'm afraid the famous Ode [to the Confederate Dead] which suffers from characteristic inflation, also what Randall hit in Washington as 'the lack of charm, feeling, tone of forbidding authority')—sweating with unacknowledged jealousy." Tate had hurt him by trying to read him "out of . . . the pantheon of art" as well as "the Book of Life" by accusing him "of every known immaturity," but Tate couldn't touch his poems. And that was all that mattered.

Thinking again of Jarrell, Berryman realized that 1972 would mark the tenth anniversary of the Library of Congress gathering. Now he wrote Roy Bassler at the Library of Congress that it was time to begin thinking about another gathering. True, the '62 affair had been "rather stuffy," but there was no need to repeat that. Why not haul Pound over from Italy, and Auden, and Lowell, "none of whom" had been there in 1962. Or, if not them, why not Allen Tate, Van Doren, or Ransom, or—among the British—Alvarez or Spender. "I myself despise Creeley, Bly & Miss Levertov," he added munificently, "and they shd be invited too." He was not interested in running things, but he did think such a gathering would be good for American culture, such as it existed under the Nixon administration. Only after he wrote a second time did Bassler respond. There would not be another festival, Bassler explained, especially since Lowell had taken the opportunity of a White House invitation to denounce President Johnson four years earlier. Since then, the Library of Congress's literary programs had "become increasingly hazardous."

On July 27, Berryman wrote Eileen again. He was still working on his novel, but death was mostly what he thought about these days. He'd lectured on Poetry and Death that spring in Minneapolis, and would lecture on it again come fall. At his AA meeting that evening he received his six-months' sobriety pin and then flew out to California and the Berkeley Faculty Club to try to get some serious work done on his novel. Suddenly his house had become too crowded, what with his mother and the baby added to the family. He had Kate's growing disaffection to think about, and he wanted to get away from the telephone and his mail and be alone. He could still swing at a moment's notice from tenderness to rage, depending on whether Kate or he was on top. He had never learned coexistence and shared responsibility, and he was too old now to start.

But now the novel too refused to budge. Frustrated, Berryman blamed the blockage on Kate. Eight days into his stay, he wrote her that he was still in a "very somber" mood and, "so far as getting on with *Recovery* goes, these last days," he might as well have been" in the Coloseum with the lionesses." By then the nightmares too had returned, until he'd been awakened by the force of two of them. The second, he noted, had ended with his "arriving home unexpectedly to find a decayed Russian aristocrat sleeping in front" of his fireplace and Kate in the background somewhere. The man "had been clipping holes" in his Shakespeare notes, and when Berryman had shown Kate the damage, she had seemed not to care.

As Kate had grown more independent of him, he realized, she had also become bolder, more willing to stare back at his anger, and that had led to his raging even more. To counteract his growing sense of impotence, he had his and Kate's joint checking and savings accounts converted to a single account in his name. When Kate was forced to take money from his wallet to pay the cleaning woman, he had raged at her in front of his mother and Martha until he could hardly breathe and Kate had broken down, sobbing that she knew he was never going to forgive her for her mistake.

"So you don't know whether you love me or not," he noted sarcastically now in his letter to Kate, "and expect me to sit here sucking my thumbs and working a novel while you brood out the Great Enquiry to its ultimate delusion." Well, he wasn't interested in waiting while she discovered, in the jargon of the day, who she was. "I don't believe we are going to make it." "Too late," he wrote afterward,

> Too late—too far distrust & guilt & pain
> too late for any return or any beginning
> of any nearness or hope again.
> All desire's blown out of me by loss,
> an aching backward only, dull, of our marvellous love.

He returned home from Berkeley, exhausted, defeated in spirit, picking at the bones of his novel and reworking the final drafts of *Delusions*. He took Kate and the girls to Bayfield, Wisconsin, and the Apostle Islands on a three-day vacation. He struggled to stay up with his AA group. He did what he could to help others, or pulled back where he felt he no longer had the strength. "I'm very sorry abt all your trouble," he wrote "Gene" on Monday, August 31, "and so will Mary-Lou be when

I tell her at AA tomorrow night (she is the nurse you talked to at Detox). She told me, and I felt sad that you'd slipped back. You didn't look too good but you sounded fine on the bus, so I was shocked."

Otherwise, the letters stopped almost altogether as fall came on. Ralph Ross saw Berryman late that summer and could not believe what had happened to him. "He was friendly & courteous," Ross would tell Allen Tate, "as to a new acquaintance, afraid to drink because, he said, it would kill him & he wanted to live. There was no real warmth shown us, or anyone, no excitement of mind, no ardor. I concluded that the only John one could love was a John with 2 or 3 drinks in him, no more & no less, & such a John could not exist."

In September, Berryman went back to teaching. He put *Delusions* into final shape, and asked his friends for their comments. On October 8, he wrote Wilbur that the book was "raging w. trash" and would need his keen ear. Wilbur read the manuscript carefully, offering suggestions, and once again asked Berryman to wait and make the book stronger. He would call Berryman and talk things over with him. But remembering what had happened to him when Tate had called him attacking *Love & Fame,* Berryman wrote Wilbur that he could not afford to have that sort of thing happen again. "Owing to a fantastic piece of treachery fr Allen late last January," he explained, "I'd rather have a written judgment."

He saw Richard Kelly, his former student, and they talked about Kelly's bibliography of Berryman's work. Unable to get on now with either his poems *or* his novel, Berryman worked on his anthology, *The Blue Book of Poetry*. What a "lucky fellow" his reader would be, he wrote in a preliminary preface to the book, "to have here within two covers what took me 37 years to locate & remain keen on." He had three biases as editor: toward contemporary poets, toward American poets, toward elegies, "esp. elegies for fellow-poets." He would include *only* "poets abt whom I care [or] have cared passionately."

He even considered cutting back on his smoking. He was up to four packs a day and Boyd Thomes had gone so far as to suggest hypnosis. Not only had his cough kept his family and himself up at night for years, but now Kate was furious with so much smoke around their daughters. But he was simply too weak to break a habit older even than his drinking.

Four days before his fifty-seventh birthday he wrote Robert Fitzgerald, thanking him for sending along his selected poems, *Spring Shade*. He still thought from time to time of getting on with his new long poem, *The Children,* "in 5 Books, maybe 200 pp.," but "time, money, pressures"—he was "down to 14 pounds less than I weighed at 16"—all conspired to make the new project's ever being completed seem "doubtful." As he wrote, he watched his Twiss, Fitzgerald's goddaughter, building a hut out of blankets and Kate's "great chair" across from him there in the living room. Martha was playing her violin under the blankets and, "beautiful" as she was, only managing to produce "horrid sounds." For weeks now, he quipped, his daughter had been reminding him that his birthday was coming. But could "57 be worse than 56?"

In early November he learned that he had the NEH for his Shakespeare book and would have the following year off to write. He made corrections on the galleys for his Faber & Faber *Selected Poems* and sent them off. He celebrated Thanksgiving with his family, then Martha's ninth birthday in early December. He visited his mother several times a week or had her over to his house. He even wrote the welfare offices in Minneapolis, demanding that they help his mother. On December 7, he taught his last class.

Six days later he recorded another nightmare. He was in a museum, standing in front of a "prehistoric statue" of a buffalo, when he saw a girl come over and touch it. As he went to touch the buffalo's hump, he noticed a couple in the next room watching him and found himself explaining that he'd already seen "a young artist" touching it. Then he put his hand out to touch the hump and suddenly it was shooting an "electric thrill" through his body. He stood amazed, as if "inspired by old magic." When he woke up, he knew that what he'd touched in his dream was something of the old power he was afraid now was gone forever.

He forced himself to work on his novel, upset to be working so hard for a mere one-thousand-dollar advance, and not the ten thousand dollars he thought Giroux had promised him. Then he checked himself, knowing how often resentment had led him to find solace in drink. But the depression that had been building all that summer and fall began to overwhelm him as winter came on. He thought constantly of suicide now, even as he told himself that that way out was "cowardly, cruel, wicked." It hurt him that he could no longer make Kate happy, and he caught Martha grinding her teeth at his deathlike smoker's cough. He was twenty pounds underweight, up every night with insomnia or nightmares, his "pathetic penis" shrunk into his groin. On his fifty-seventh birthday he'd written Eileen that he felt "grotesquely" old. Even with a good income (his salary alone beginning in 1972 would be twenty-six thousand dollars, with perhaps another twenty thousand dollars from royalties), he worried that it wasn't enough, even as he continued to buy by the carton expensive books that went unread.

He was terrified too that his religious faith might really be the final delusion after all, and found it increasingly harder to pray. He still wondered whether or not hell existed and thought constantly now of his father's grave. He found it more and more difficult even getting out of bed, though he knew if he stayed there, his mind would begin replaying the same old "boring" mysteries about life and death.

On the morning of the thirteenth, after Martha had gone to school and Kate had taken the baby and gone shopping, he thought of taking his Spanish knife and a gun and checking into a hotel in Minneapolis and just doing it. This time he even took his knife upstairs into his bedroom and then stared down at it until he realized what he was doing. Then he was on his knees, shaking and praying for help until the crisis passed.

Afterward he went downtown to do some Christmas shopping and clear his head. He would give up the novel after all, he decided, knowing he was never going to finish it to his satisfaction. When he told Kate, she merely shrugged. After all, what he did with his writing was his business. It was also time, he realized, to quit seeing his psychiatrist, since that route also seemed to be getting him nowhere. It was a delusion to think any of these things—his students, his books, his poems—could ever have fired him anyway. Strangely his depression lifted. It was, he thought, as if God were stroking him now for sacrificing everything. He would go back to work. He might still be able to write that *Life of Christ* for children.

* * *

On the sixteenth he wrote some lines he called "Dry Eleven Months," returning after two years to a five-line variation on the Dream Song stanzas. "O yes," he wrote,

> I've had to give up somewhat here,
> illusion on illusion, big books long laboured, a power
> of working wellness to some, of securing this house,
> the cocktail hour,—
> but I am not without a companion: there's left Fear.
>
> I've tried my self, found guilty on each charge
> my self diseased. That jury poll was easy;
> so was the recommendation, on solid showing
> the assassin had been crazy.
> But so too were judge & jurors. Now I see sitting large
>
> and sane and near an altogether new
> & well advised tribunal. When my ticker stops,
> as thrice this fitful year it has done, & restarts—
> each while poor spirit drops
> a notch—well, when it quits for good, I'm afraid of you.

"Bad poem," he noted the following day. He was getting nowhere and, what was worse, no longer had the energy to care. He thought he'd already *hit* bottom, that "*new* disappointments" would be "impossible" after what he'd already been through. But now he doubted that he really did have a book in "Shakespeare's Reality." He got up from bed to leaf through his notes and found his fears confirmed. In spite of the NEH, it didn't look as if he had a book there after all. "Tho'ts constantly of death," he wrote, before signing off in his journal. "Fear . . . of winter lectures."

Rummaging through his closet Christmas Eve, he found a poem he'd written earlier that fall called "Surveillance." "The only really comforting reflexion," he'd written there, was not

> 'we will all rest in Abraham's bosom' & rot of that purport
> but: after my death there will be *no more sin*.

Christmas Day he wrote Ted Hoagland a short note. Bellow was half-finished with another novel, this one "on our tragic beloved Delmore Schwartz" while he'd just "wasted" eight months on his own novel, "220 pp of it." He no longer had anything good to say for himself. On New Year's Eve the Berrymans went to a party at a neighbor's and a friend snapped several pictures of him. He is dressed in a suit jacket with a striped, broad-knotted silk tie and a handkerchief in his breast pocket. Between the third and fourth fingers of his right hand, he holds a Tareyton. In one photo, though he stares at the camera, his eyes seem far away. His beard is trim. The lenses of his horn-rimmed glasses catch the camera's flash.

Five days later, on Wednesday, January 5, Berryman bought himself a bottle of whiskey and drank half of it. This time Kate was too exhausted even to be disappointed; he was going to have to turn to his group to help him if that was what he still wanted. Before leaving the house that day, he left a note on the kitchen table that read, "I am a nuisance." With classes about to begin, he considered once more taking his life.

Now, at least, he knew how he would do it. He would climb over the railing of the upper walkway of the Washington Avenue Bridge, take his Spanish knife and slash his throat so that he would feel faint and have to pitch forward. He would not submit to another Iowa fiasco, with the cops locking him up and Professor Berryman losing his job. This time it would have to be for keeps. He may even have walked out on the bridge to dare himself. In any event, he found the strength to return home, where he wrote another poem. It was to be his last. "I didn't. And I didn't," he wrote, using Henry's Dream Song stanzas once again. He didn't, but he would, the way Hart Crane had prefigured for himself in the opening to "The Bridge": by simply tilting out from the railing and letting go:

Sharp the Spanish blade
to gash my throat after I'd climbed across
the high railing of the bridge
to tilt out, with the knife in my right hand
to slash me shocked or fainting till I'd fall
unable to keep my skull down but fearless

unless my wife wouldn't let me out of the house,
unless the cops noticed me crossing the campus
up to the bridge

> & clappt me in for observation, costing my job—
> I'd be now in a cell, costing my job—
> well, I missed that;
>
> but here's the terror of tomorrow's lectures
> bad in themselves, the students dropping the course,
> the Administration hearing
> & offering me either a medical leave of absence
> or resignation—Kitticat, they can't fire me—

Nothing fired him anymore. He put a slash through the poem and tossed it into the wastebasket. Then he put the bottle of whiskey away and called someone in his AA squad, asking him to take over for him at the next meeting, since he did not think he would be able to make it.

The following day—Thursday—he walked across the Washington Avenue Bridge again, this time on his way to the Wilson Library, where Richard Kelly spotted him. He was "deeply engrossed in some religious tome (a volume of James Hastings' *Encyclopedia of Religion and Ethics,* I think it was)," Kelly would remember. He and Berryman talked for a few minutes, mostly about the bibliography of Berryman's writings Kelly was completing, and then Berryman "went back to his earnest investigations," still looking for whatever it was he was hoping to find.

Friday morning, January 7, after another restless night, Berryman told Kate he was going to his office to put his things in order. Kate sent Martha to school, then bundled up Sarah to do the shopping. "You won't have to worry about me anymore," he told her as she went out. But she'd heard that one before too. At half past eight he put on his coat and scarf and walked down to University Avenue. There he caught the shuttle bus heading west toward campus. He passed the stores along the avenue, then got off with the morning crowd at Ford Hall. But instead of going to his office, he walked out onto the upper level of the Washington Avenue Bridge. It was bitterly cold, but, rather than use the glass-enclosed walkway, he began walking along the north side of the bridge toward the west-bank campus. Three quarters of the way across, he stopped and stared down.

A hundred feet below and to his right rode the river: narrow, gray, and half frozen. In front of him were the snow-covered coal-storage docks, and directly below the winter trees and a slight knoll rising like a grave. So it was still there, waiting. He climbed onto the chest-high metal railing and balanced himself. Several students inside the walkway stopped what they were doing when they saw him and stared in disbelief. He made a gesture as if waving, but he did not look back. From this height, he must have figured, the blade did seem redundant after all. Then he tilted out and let go.

Three seconds later his body exploded against the knoll, recoiled from the earth, then rolled gently down the incline. The campus police were the first to arrive and found a package of Tareytons, some change, and a blank check with the name Berryman on it. Inside the left temple of his shattered horn-rimmed glasses they found the name a second time. An ambulance took the body to the Hennepin County Morgue, where Berryman was officially pronounced dead.

About 10:00 A.M. Kate, carrying Sarah, returned from shopping to find Maris and Boyd Thomes, ex-mayor Art Naftalin, Bob Ames, chairman of the Humanities department, and the campus police, who had been first on the scene. Seeing them, she knew at once that her husband was dead.

The body was taken to the Hanson-Nugent Funeral Home on Nicollet Avenue, prepared for burial, and placed in a sealed casket. Father Robert Hazel arranged for burial at Resurrection Cemetery after services at St. Frances Cabrini. On Monday, January 10, at half past four in the afternoon, Berryman's wife, mother, brother, and friends gathered for the Mass of the Resurrection. The pallbearers included Ames, Giroux, Naftalin, and Thomes, the man who had tried to keep him alive as long as possible. There were readings from the Psalms, Lamentations, and Luke, a Beethoven Quartet, and a reading of the twenty-seventh and seventy-seventh Dream Songs. Finally there was a reading of the eighth of the "Eleven Addresses to the Lord," Berryman's prayer for himself, where he had asked the Lord to help him understand his terrible secrets and to "cushion/ the first the second shocks, will to a halt/ in mid-air there demons who would at me."

* * *

"Oh my dear," he had written Adrienne Rich fourteen months before to console her after the suicide of her husband. "I hope you are not feeling responsible, but I suppose . . . you probably are." She would have to fight that feeling, he explained, because suicide was a "purely personal, & aggressive" act, and in "our culture w. its taboo the actor is always deranged, out of control." For forty years his mother had blamed herself for his father's suicide, when in fact he had come to see that she'd probably done "everything in her power to prevent it." He would not pray for Adrienne's husband, he explained, because, frankly, he did not believe one survived one's death, but he would pray for her and her children.

Still, against the odds, he had managed to leave behind an extraordinary legacy raveled off his own skin. The thing that had fired him so long, whatever that might be, might lie somewhere up ahead, perhaps just around the next bend, like a shimmering dream. But for him, the desperate marathon, first from behind, then closing in, then running out ahead with only the roar of disembodied voices left to cheer him on, was at long last over.

# Index

## A

C



D

## E

## I



## J

Q



R



S

W



Y

Z